Between Sodom and Eden

Between Men ~ Between Women

Between Sodom
and Eden

A Gay Journey Through Today's
Changing Israel

Lee Walzer

Columbia University Press
New York

COLUMBIA UNIVERSITY PRESS

Publishers Since 1893
New York   Chichester, West Sussex
Copyright © 2000 Lee Walzer
All rights reserved

Grateful acknowledgment is made for permission to reprint the following copyrighted works:
Selections from *Gan ha-Etzim ha-Meitim* by Yossi Avni. Copyright © 1995 by Yossi Avni and Zmora-Bitan Publishers. Reprinted by permission of Yossi Avni and Zmora-Bitan Publishers.
Copyright acknowledgments continued following the index.

Library of Congress Cataloging-in-Publication Data
Walzer, Lee.
    Between Sodom and Eden : a gay journey through today's changing
Israel / Lee Walzer.
        p.   cm. — (Between men~between women)
    Includes bibliographical references (p.   ) and index.
    ISBN 0-231-11394-3 — ISBN 0-231-11395-1 (pbk.)
    1. Gays—Israel—Social conditions. 2. Lesbians—Israel—Social
conditions. 3. Homosexuality—Israel. I. Title. II. Series.
HQ76.2.I75W35   1999   99-42084
306.76'6'095694—dc21

Casebound editions of Columbia University Press books are printed on permanent and durable acid-free paper.

Designed by Benjamin Shin Farber

Printed in the United States of America
c 10 9 8 7 6 5 4 3 2 1
p 10 9 8 7 6 5 4 3 2 1

To Kevin
with all my love

Contents

Preface   ix

Acknowledgments   xv

Transliteration Guide   xix

Introduction
How a Nice Gay Jewish Boy Came to Write This Book   1

1. Together in Pride, Together in Hope:
   Lesbian and Gay Politics in Israel   13

2. *Yotzim m'ha-Aron*: Coming Out   58

3. The Personal Is the Political:
   Judaism and Gay People in Israel   82

4. Gays with Guns: Gays in the Military, Israeli Style`   114

5. Media, Culture, and Visibility   141

6. Hereinafter the Boyfriend: Same-Sex Families in Israel   178

7. Out on the Farm: Gay Life in the Kibbutzim   197

8. Twice Marginalized: To Be Gay and Palestinian in Israel   215

Conclusion   *Kadima*—Looking Ahead   248

Afterword   255

Glossary   261

Appendix   265

Notes   267

Bibliography   283

Index   291

Copyright Acknowledgments   301

Preface

Between Sodom and Eden is a nonfiction work aimed at presenting readers with an overview of Israel's lesbian and gay community, a community that in the past decade has moved from life at society's margins to substantial political and legal progress and social visibility. Previous works on the community have consisted of collections of personal histories, like Tracy Moore's *Lesbiot,* or an essay or two about gay and lesbian life in Israel, with nothing to date that delves into why Israeli society has become increasingly hospitable to its lesbian and gay citizens. This book focuses primarily on the period between 1988, when the Knesset repealed Israel's sodomy law, and April 1999. I have provided an afterword devoted to the 1999 Israeli elections, and a few other significant events, to bring readers as up to date as possible on a country and community undergoing dizzying changes.

As a nonfiction work, *Between Sodom and Eden* relies on a journalistic style of writing, researched through interviews and extensive source material. I am not the first person to use this style to write about lesbian and gay communities in other countries. David Tuller, author of *Cracks in the Iron Closet,* a look at gay and lesbian life in post-Soviet Russia, is a particularly skilled practitioner and I consider myself indebted to his pioneering work. While *Between Sodom and Eden* is not a historical, anthropological, or sociological work, neither a legal treatise nor political science, it ultimately borrows from some of these disciplines, reflecting my previous social science and legal studies. Arguably, each of the topics that I tackle in this book might constitute a book in its own right. I expect that, in time, most, in fact, will, particularly on issues like lesbian and gay culture and the status of gay and lesbian Palestinians.

This is also a very personal work, reflecting years of acquaintance with some of the Israeli gay and lesbian community's leading figures and a deep interest in Israeli society and politics. As such, I have not hesitated to present my own opinions about both gay issues and developments in Israeli politics. In admitting that this book takes a personal viewpoint at times, I do not believe that I am compromising necessary objectivity. Inquiry, however scholarly or detached, ultimately adopts a point of view. In the interest of objectivity I have disclosed my relationship in the appropriate places with individuals whose perspectives are presented, analyzed, and, at times, criticized. Furthermore, I have been involved as an activist in gay Jewish life, giving me additional familiarity with, and perspectives on, some of the issues presented in this book.

I see myself as both insider and outsider, in writing about Israel's lesbian and gay community, and Israeli society and politics generally. As a Jew and a Hebrew speaker, familiar with Israel through Jewish communal and gay activism over the years, I am able to claim some insider status. Yet, I am an American, not an Israeli, and can never be a true insider. This distance informs this work and has enabled me to look at the Israeli lesbian and gay community with a degree of intimacy coupled with sufficient detachment.

I journeyed to Israel for interviews in June 1997 and, again, in February and March 1998, traveling literally from one end of the country to the other. I interviewed roughly 110 people from all walks of life, gay/lesbian and heterosexual, Jewish and Palestinian, religious and secular, immigrant and native born. These interviews ran anywhere from ten minutes to two and a half hours, with most averaging forty-five to ninety minutes. I supplemented these interviews with several telephone interviews, both before and after my research trips. My interviewees encompassed activists, politicians, educators, and academics, military officials, journalists, cultural figures, and ordinary citizens. I deliberately sought out policy makers in various fields to see how they, as opposed to people in the lesbian and gay community, saw gays and lesbians, gay rights, and the place of these in Israeli society. Truth be told, the divide between these two groups proved not to be terribly large.

The lesbians and gay men with whom I spoke almost all had at least minimum identification with that amorphous entity known as the "lesbian and gay community." Although such an approach limits the range of homosexual experience expressed in this book, I think that the limitation is justified. The reasons that people with homosexual attractions fail to develop a lesbian/gay identity are fairly universal—and personal. For some, legal, political, religious, or social oppression prevents them from ever expressing their desire for emotional and physical intimacy with members of their own gender. For others, homosexual attraction is not as strong as heterosexual attraction. For still others, there might not exist a social construction in their society for gay identity as the term is understood today in most Western societies. These reasons apply in Israel, just as they do in many other societies.

In contrast, I was interested in how people successfully developed a lesbian or gay identity in a society that in many respects tries to limit that sense of identity, even while passing laws and issuing judicial decisions that make Israel, on paper at least, one of the most progressive countries in the world today on lesbian and gay rights. As shall be seen in the coming chapters, Israeli society has been slower to embrace gay and lesbian identity than legal and political equality for its gay citizens. This difficulty in seeing gays as a minority group has made the creation of a gay community more difficult but may ultimately provide more nuanced forms of identity and identity politics for Israeli lesbians and gay men.

I chose very deliberately to write a book about the gay *and* lesbian community. My two principal reasons for doing so were 1) personal experience with, and commitment to, the notion of a co-sexual, inclusive community; and 2) this book's focus on political and legal developments that impact gays and lesbians equally. I will admit, however, that being inclusive was not always easy. As a gay man, I had easier access to the gay male community. This is understandable, as women-only space is a necessary ingredient for lesbians trying to develop their community and culture. I have endeavored to be inclusive and write about some issues that impact lesbians alone, such as relations with the wider feminist community, internal ideological tensions, and the development of lesbian culture.

A note on language is in order as well. I typically have used *gay and lesbian* to refer to the Israeli gay and lesbian community. When addressing specifically lesbian issues, I, of course, have used *lesbian*. On some occasions, I have used *gay* as shorthand for *gay and lesbian* and have used *homosexual* more rarely, primarily when referring to sexual orientation rather than identity. And while it is common these days to refer to the "gay, lesbian, bisexual, and transgender community," I did not seek

out bisexual or transgendered perspectives, nor did any of my interviewees identify themselves as such. The decision not to seek out such perspectives was solely in the interest of keeping this work manageable, as
much as because in Israel these communities are still in their infancy. I
have, however, written about transsexual singer Dana International, who
identifies strongly with the *gay* community, and have included some discussion of transgender issues to the extent that they affect lesbian and
gay political strategy. I expect that future books about sexual minorities
in Israel will be able to explore more fully the experiences of bisexuals
and transgendered people.

How did I choose whom to interview? Because Israel is a small country, with an even smaller lesbian and gay community, this task was not
as hard as it might seem at first glance. I have followed developments in
the community for a number of years, through both activist work and
personal avocation. Thus I was able to generate a fairly substantial list
of individuals inside and outside the lesbian and gay community who
might have some insight as to how and why the community has progressed in recent years as well as what that progress says about Israeli society as a whole. In addition, I used contacts and friends within the community for suggestions about other individuals. Finally, in the course of
my stays in Israel I met people on my own or through the suggestions of
some of my interviewees. These unplanned contacts yielded fascinating
new insights in their own right.

While I interviewed several North American–born Israelis, particularly in Jerusalem where their presence is especially strong, as a rule I tried
to minimize such interviews, since 1) their perspectives have formed the
basis (or a substantial part thereof) of several past nonfiction books and
essays about lesbian and gay life in Israel, including Evelyn Torton Beck's
Nice Jewish Girls, Tracy Moore's *Lesbiot*, and Lev Raphael's *Journeys
and Arrivals*; and 2) the experiences of gay and lesbian North American
Israelis are substantially different from their Israeli-born counterparts,
both in terms of coming-out issues and how they see lesbian and gay
identity. Nonetheless, the North American–born/raised individuals I interviewed did provide me with invaluable perspectives.

I also tried to be geographically inclusive. It would be easy to write a
book such as this without ever leaving Tel Aviv, home to Israel's largest
concentration of lesbians and gay men and home to two of its principal
gay and lesbian organizations. But such an approach would not yield the
full diversity and complexity of Israeli lesbian and gay life today. Thus I

spent large chunks of time in both Haifa and Jerusalem and traveled to Beer Sheva, kibbutzim in the north, and several Palestinian towns in Israel. Gay and lesbian life in these three cities, let alone in outlying areas, raises different issues and challenges, and this work is richer for not being Tel Aviv–centric.

I conducted my interviews in Hebrew, except when interviewing native English speakers or, in a couple of instances, Palestinians. Some past works and essays about Israeli gay life have faced criticism that the authors interviewed only English speakers and/or that the authors did not know Hebrew themselves. Although most of my interviewees spoke English quite well, I wanted to ensure that they could express themselves freely and thus used Hebrew. With Palestinians I usually opened my interviews in Arabic, which I studied in college but do not speak fluently, to create a better comfort level in discussing sexual orientation and other personal issues with an outsider before switching to Hebrew (or English) for the interview itself. I found this effort appreciated and believe that it led to better interviews with the individuals concerned.

I did not interview people with a standard questionnaire. This book deals with a variety of issues, and a standard questionnaire would not have been practical. Through prior research I would arrive at interviews with a number of questions, both specific and open-ended, that I wanted to pursue. This format provided me with the flexibility to focus in advance on issues I hoped to pursue, while enabling me to pursue additional issues and perspectives that arose in the course of the interview.

In addition to interviews, I made ample use of books, scholarly articles, television programs, popular music, films, and newspapers, both before and after my research trips. I traveled twice to Harvard University to access such materials in its Judaica collection. Use of these materials has helped me present the dynamism and contradictions of today's Israeli society. The internet also proved to be a useful research tool. As my spouse will attest, I have spent the last two and a half years waking up and listening to the news on Israel Radio or Galei Tzahal, the Israeli army radio station, reading Israeli newspapers like *Ha'aretz*, coming home and watching Israel Television's *Mabat* newscast, and closing out the day with more radio programming—all online.

Finally, I was also a participant-observer. By attending various events and socializing in the gay community—whether a lesbian theater production, folk dancing with members of the Jerusalem Open House (an experience that shattered my previous loneliness as a gay man with two left feet), parties, or political/organizational meetings—I got to experience aspects of life as lived daily by gay and lesbian Israelis.

I have endeavored to present a full range of viewpoints in this book and it was not hard to find them, through both the interviews themselves and materials in print. Future works will undoubtedly offer new perspectives, as the Israeli lesbian and gay community develops in new directions.

Acknowledgments

The African parable popularized by American first lady Hillary Rodham Clinton, "It takes a village to raise a child," applies equally well to book writing. It truly does take a village to write a book. And there are a number of "villagers" who deserve my thanks and appreciation for helping me out with, and through, this process.

First thanks go to the countless Israelis who consented to interviews and shared with me aspects of their lives and perspectives on their society. Without them, this book would have remained just an idea. I am indebted to them for their openness and, often, for their hospitality and cups of Nescafé. A collective *toda raba* to all of you. A few merit special mention for the assistance they gave me: Dover Tzahal, the Israel Defense Forces spokesman's office; Tel Aviv City Council Member Michal Eden, for allowing me to observe one of her campaign strategy meetings; Chagai El-Ad and Dani Kaplan, for their help in deciphering Israeli military acronyms; Eyal Gross and Dori Spivak of the Tel Aviv University Law Faculty, for providing me with substantial amounts of legal materials; Alon Harel, Amit Kama, Yossi Even-Kama, Chana Safran, Daniel Weinshut, and Yuval Yonai, for providing copies of papers that they authored; and Shmuel Meiri of *Ha'aretz* for access to some of his reporter's materials. An additional thanks is in order to the Association of Gays, Lesbians, Bisexuals, and Transgenders in Israel (Aguda), for giving me access to its rich press archive.

In Israel Jewish mothers are known as "Polish mothers." There are a number of Polish mothers to whom I am forever grateful. These people housed me, fed me, and would even call me on my cell phone if I was out late to make sure that I was safe and sound. So, thanks and much love to Gil Nader and Motti Porat, Amnon and Limor Shilo, Eli, Ilan Vitemberg, Tal Weisberg-Bloch, and Yoel Bloch-Weisberg.

But the Polish mother of Polish mothers was certainly my friend Adib Jarrar, formerly of the New Israel Fund. Adib took my e-mailed lists of individuals I hoped to interview and set up exhausting itineraries for my two research trips to Israel. He opened doors for me that I never could have imagined. He was also a tough critic, and made me think through various thoughts and theories.

Once back from Israel I made two trips to Harvard University, the repository of a treasure trove of Israel-related research materials. Violet Gilboa, Littauer Hebraica Technical and Research Services Librarian at Harvard University's Judaica Collection, diligently obtained various newspapers, films, and television programs for me, and took a great interest in the book.

Deepest thanks and appreciation go to my agent, Robert E. Shepard, of the Robert E. Shepard Agency in San Francisco. Robert was my first affirmation that this project was feasible. He was a source of advice, encouragement, and friendship throughout.

At Columbia University Press I would like to thank Ann Miller, senior editor, and Larry Gross and Lillian Faderman, editors of the Between Men ~ Between Women series. They assisted me greatly in shaping this project as it grew from a proposal into this book. Alex Thorp, assistant editor, cheerfully kept things moving along. Susan Pensak, senior manuscript editor, helped refine and improve the manuscript, and Brady McNamara, senior designer, oversaw development of the cover.

On this side of the ocean there are a number of friends who provided moral support through this process: Susan Kirshner, Joel Miller, Liora Moriel, MaryAnn Nash, Neil Robinson, and Brad Wasserman. Joel, Liora, MaryAnn, and Brad deserve thanks for looking through various drafts, or parts thereof, and offering editing and content suggestions along the way from a variety of perspectives, as do Adib Jarrar and Dani Kaplan. Other friends and colleagues asked, "How's the book?" along the way, and their interest always made my day.

My parents, Jim and Maxine Walzer, proved exceedingly enthusiastic about this book and kept my spirits up from beginning to end. My father hopes that my next project will be a "steamy novel." We'll see.

Finally, last but certainly not least, supreme thanks and love go to my spouse, Kevin O'Keefe. Kevin, more than anyone else, had to live with this project from beginning to end, through its various ups and downs. He lived through prolonged absences, computer failures (some of my own making, but all of which he inevitably was called on to repair), high phone bills, ever mounting boxes of materials, and a book-obsessed spouse. Without his love and support, this book would not have seen print.

Transliteration Guide

Between Sodom and Eden contains a number of Hebrew and Arabic names and terms. While I generally separated out the definite article *ha* in Hebrew by means of hyphenation, I allowed some words and proper nouns that are often transliterated to appear in their common renderings. In the interest of simplicity, I have avoided attempting to render Arabic letters such as 'ayin into English, seeing that they represent sounds with no ready English counterpart, neither have I included the markings for Arabic's long versus short vowels.

Hebrew

Ai as in h*i*gh
Ch as in lo*ch* or the German a*ch*
E as in p*e*t
Ei as in l*a*te
I as in L*ee*
O as in t*o*ne
Tz as in Ri*tz*
U as in m*oo*

Arabic
A as in *a*h
Gh a guttural *r*, from the back of the throat

Ḥ an aspirated *h* sound, midway between *h* and *kh*

I as in L*ee*

Kh as in lo*ch* or the German a*ch*

Q a hard *k*, said with emphasis

U as in m*oo*

Between Sodom and Eden

Introduction: How a Nice, Gay Jewish Boy Came to Write This Book

In the fall of 1987 I was sitting in my dorm room at Northwestern University School of Law in Chicago reading the *Windy City Times*, one of Chicago's lesbian and gay newspapers. I had "officially" come out of the closet two years earlier when I started telling my straight friends from my undergraduate years at the University of Michigan and, eventually, other friends and family that I was gay. As a former political science major and then current law student (as well as someone who had always loved politics), I proceeded to embrace gay politics and current events, reading voraciously about my community's history and politics (to the detriment of my law school grades).

Flipping through the pages, I came across a picture of a magazine with Hebrew text. The caption announced the appearance of a gay monthly in Israel called *Maga'im* (Contacts) and stated that xeroxed copies were available from a member of Congregation Or Chadash, Chicago's gay and lesbian synagogue. I immediately called the individual in question and sent him a modest sum to cover copying and postage. Within the week I was gazing at the magazine's headline: *Yotzim m'ha-Aron: Ha-im Eimcha Yoda'at?* ("Coming Out of the Closet: Does Your Mother Know?").

If discovering *Maga'im* provided the spark for my interest in my fellow gay and lesbian Jews in Israel, my fascination with Israel goes back much further. I remember well my textbook on Israel, *Behold the Land,* from my fifth-grade Sunday school class at Temple Sholom in Chicago. Something in its depiction of life in Israel—from the idyllic kibbutzim to the status of Israel's Palestinian minority—grabbed my attention and grew into a lifelong interest. My later Hebrew and religious studies at North Shore Congregation Israel only strengthened that interest.

A year later, after my first summer at overnight camp, I was writing to one of my camp counselors, whom in retrospect I had a crush on, when my father said to me, "Why don't you get some pen pals in Israel?" Well, I did just that, thanks to an Israeli neighbor who gave me a copy of *Davar Liladim*, a children's magazine. I sent in my name and address and, before I knew it, I had eight pen pals, living everywhere from Kibbutz Manara on the Lebanese border, to Ashkelon on the Mediterranean coast, to Beer Sheva, planned by Israel's founders as the capital of the Negev desert.

At the time I had been studying Hebrew for two or three years in Sunday school. Those who know how American Jews learn Hebrew in Sunday school will recognize that this did not provide me with a great linguistic foundation. That didn't deter me. I bought a copy of the Ben Yehuda English-Hebrew/Hebrew-English dictionary, an absurdly antiquated work, and began looking up words, not knowing much or caring about the workings of grammar and the pitfalls of foreign language dictionaries.

Of course, as a twelve year old, I searched out "dirty words." I put this last phrase in quotes because most of the words I found had a completely different context from the one imagined in my obscenity-focused mind. For example, the Ben Yehuda dictionary said that "intercourse" (the closest I could get to the "f" word) was *masa u'matan*. It took several more years until I learned that *masa u'matan* really refers to negotiations!

I knew I had finally mastered Hebrew years later when, on visits, my pen pals began speaking back to me in that language rather than in English. Most of my correspondents have since dropped out, but I still write to and talk with my pen pal Amnon from Kibbutz Manara, who today is an ex-kibbutznik and, like me, a government lawyer.

As luck would have it, I was leaving two months after I discovered the existence of *Maga'im* on a law student trip to Israel sponsored by the National Jewish Law Students Network, in which I served as Midwestern regional director. Although the ten days of touring were pretty intense and didn't leave time for independent exploration, I stayed on three extra days to visit Amnon and arranged a day in Tel Aviv for myself at the end of the trip.

Although I wasn't ready to come out to my friend on this particular visit, I made a gaffe in Hebrew that should have led him to the appropriate conclusion. While I was getting ready to go to Tel Aviv, after two days of visiting him at Haifa University, Amnon was going off for a trip to Eilat, a resort town on the Gulf of Aqaba at the southern tip of Israel. Eilat is popular in the winter with Scandinavian tourists, so I attempted to make a wisecrack. "Kol ha-Skandinavim, eh, Amnon?" ("All the Scandinavians" [or, oops! all the Scandinavian men], "eh, Amnon?"), I grinned at him, thinking I was suggesting that he'd get lucky with some statuesque Swedish blonde. He looked up and corrected me instantly. "Lo, kol ha-Skandinaviot" ("No, all the Scandinavian girls"). Recalling that incident reminds me of lines from a poem by Israeli poet Yona Wallach: "Hebrew is a sex maniac . . . peeping at you through the keyhole."[1] I eventually did come out to my pen pal in a letter a few months after he married. His response was very supportive: "It takes a lot of guts to deal with those around you in as nice a manner as you do."

I made to the "Big Orange," as Tel Aviv is nicknamed, for my last day in Israel. That evening, I set off for Mo'adon ha-Tei'atron, the Theater Club, Tel Aviv's—and Israel's—gay club at that moment, on Mendele Street, just a block from the major tourist hotels on Ha-Yarkon Street.

In retrospect, I know I arrived too early. There was a fair amount of people dancing and socializing at the bar, but it was hard to tell in many instances who was gay and who was straight. The social cues I had absorbed in America were useless in Israel. There were male soldiers, with women friends in tow. Were they gay, or were they there "slumming" with their girlfriends? Too confusing! The only person I chatted with that evening was a young American Jewish guy from New York. We shouted at each other over the din of American disco music (where was the Israeli rock and pop that I expected to hear? Or maybe I was expecting everyone to be dancing the hora to the tune of *Hava Nagila*), and I subsequently went back to the youth hostel where I was staying—alone.

Although I didn't meet any gay Israelis on that trip, I did pick up another couple of issues of *Maga'im*, expanding my ability to discuss gay life and politics in Hebrew. I learned the words for "sodomy," "legislation," "support group," "bar," and, most important, the attempt to create an authentic Hebrew word for "gay": *aliz*. *Aliz*, like our *gay*, literally means "happy" or "merry," and the editors and writers of *Maga'im* were determined to try to spread its usage.[2]

A valiant effort on their part, but one that has not taken root. At the time, homosexuality, and gay people generally, were discussed only in euphemisms. The proper Hebrew word for "gay" was—and still is—*homosexual* (although today, the word *homo*,[3] once used as a curse, has achieved wider usage), a word that grated on my young PC ears. "Lesbian" was, and remains, *lesbit*. Other than that, there was *k'ze* ("like this"), as oblique a euphemism as I've ever heard, and *m'ha-chevre* ("from the gang"). These Israeli equivalents of "friend of Dorothy's" made sense in a society that still was intolerant of gays and lesbians, especially a communal society where everyone seemed to know everyone else—and everyone else's business. More recently, activists tried to encourage the use of the word *g'ei*, "proud," which has the advantage of sounding like the by now international word *gay*. During the 1994 Pride Month in Israel they sold bumper stickers that said, "Ani g'ei b'Yisrael," meaning both "I'm Proud of Israel" and "I'm Gay in Israel."

Immediately thereafter, I moved to Washington, D.C., to begin my law career in earnest. The summer of 1989 found me on a weekend trip to Rehoboth Beach, Delaware. I'd brought along a copy of the Israeli weekly *Ha-Olam ha-Ze* for beach reading. Imagine my surprise to find an article on Israel's first gay pride event in Tel Aviv. The article's headline: "Look Back in Pride." The article painted a picture of a community terrified of exposure, conflicted, and full of self-hatred ("What's There for Me to Be Proud Of?" read the headline of one section). Not terribly promising. One of the friends who'd gone with me to the beach was an Israeli who had immigrated to the United States with his American partner. I made some condescending remark about how backward gay Israelis were, and how they needed to learn more from the proud example of their American brothers and sisters. My friend was not amused, and we began heatedly arguing in Hebrew in the middle of Poodle Beach, as the gay stretch of beach in Rehoboth is called. He told me that life for gays in Israel was not so bad, that the people interviewed in the article were hardly representative of all Israeli gays and lesbians.

After working for three years I was ready for another visit and chose February 1991 as the ideal time of year—low airfare, decent weather, and Purim, the Jewish festival that commemorates the saving of the Jews of Persia from destruction, which is marked by great parties. Leave it to Iraqi president Saddam Hussein to throw a wrench into my plans.

There I was at my agency's law department annual meeting at an Embassy Suites in Northwest Washington in January 1991. Someone suddenly called out in the midst of a cocktail party, "The United States has begun bombing Baghdad!" Everyone gathered around a TV and turned on CNN to watch the high-tech bombing live. Two of my friends from work, Neil Robinson and MaryAnn Nash, raced with me to my apartment, and there we sat watching the beginning of the war, while munching on take-out pizza.

The next night I had an advanced Hebrew class at the District of Columbia Jewish Community Center. I walked into the center's townhouse and found a crowd of people standing silently watching the TV screen. "What's going on? Are we bombing Baghdad again?" I asked. Someone looked up at me and said, "The Iraqis have just fired Scud missiles on Tel Aviv!" Oh. So much for a trouble-free Gulf War. Needless to say, class was canceled that night.

As the Gulf War continued it began to occur to me that my vacation plans might change. Foreign airlines were canceling their flights into Tel Aviv, and Israelis were stuck in sealed rooms, with gas masks over their faces. For a while I was bravely determined to continue my trip, out of the sort of misplaced, over-the-top Zionist solidarity that only American Jews, gay or otherwise, are crazy enough to think about, but rarely carry out. Indeed, for most Israelis the delegations of American Jewish bigwigs who flew in for two days to visit sites where Iraqi Scuds had struck and then returned to the safety and comfort of America were nothing more than a joke.

My parents did not see it as a joke. They saw that I was seriously contemplating going to a war zone for my vacation and began to express more concern and, when the "concern" didn't do the trick, resorted to genuine hysteria. Even telling them that I would get a gas mask when I arrived at Ben-Gurion Airport didn't ease their worries. In the contest between Zionist commitment and parental concern, concern finally prevailed.

I reluctantly rebooked the ticket and took off for Israel in March 1991. From *Maga'im* I learned there was a new gay "hotel" in Tel Aviv, called the Motel Nativ Acher ("Other Path"). After flying for nearly twelve hours, traveling on two Israeli buses from the airport with bags in tow, and walking two blocks to Reiness Street, I reached my hotel, conveniently located a stone's throw from bustling Dizengoff Street, a café- and boutique-lined avenue. In its heyday Dizengoff Street even spawned a Hebrew verb, *l'hizdangef*, to stroll down Dizengoff.

The ground floor of the Motel Nativ Acher housed a bar and video room.

I went down to the bar and started talking with one of the bartenders. Somehow, we began talking about the gay and lesbian synagogue I belong to in Washington, Bet Mishpachah. He looked at me sardonically and asked how gay people can form synagogues when the Torah "clearly" forbids homosexual behavior. I wasn't prepared for this, nor was my Hebrew, especially after such a long trip. I could not begin to explain how the alleged prohibitions in Leviticus refer only to the cults of temple prostitution that flourished in the ancient Middle East. So I dropped that topic and asked him about Tel Aviv's new gay bar, Piccolo, on the rooftop of the exclusive Gan ha-Ir Shopping Mall in Tel Aviv.

Piccolo was one of the early gay rights cases for Israel's gay community. When the owners of Gan ha-Ir discovered that homosexuals would be congregating at Piccolo, they attempted to rescind the lease. The bar's owner sued—and won. A Tel Aviv district court actually held that Gan ha-Ir could not rescind the lease because of the sexual orientation of the bar's patrons and owners: a lease was a lease. But the judge didn't just look at the four corners of the contract. He instead recalled the trials and tribulations of the Jewish people in exile from their homeland, declaring, "When examining irrelevant considerations as in this case, the distance is very small to including considerations that can bring to memory very dark days in history."[4] Piccolo was a pioneer in other ways as well. The bar had big picture windows and was located in a very public place. Unfortunately, as I discovered at the Motel Nativ Acher, the bar was yet another casualty of Saddam Hussein's. During the Gulf War most Israeli places of entertainment shut down, first, on the orders of the government but also because most people were afraid to venture too far from home for fear of being caught in the middle of a Scud attack. Piccolo could not hold out and shut down for good just days after the war ended.

On that post–Gulf War trip I also met Israeli gay activists for the first time. On my last day in Israel, after spending two weeks traveling from Rosh ha-Nikra in the north to Eilat in the south, I ventured to the offices of the Society for the Protection of Personal Rights (Aguda), since renamed the Association of Gays, Lesbians, Bisexuals, and Transgenders in Israel. The group's offices were located in the basement of an apartment building on Nachmani Street in central Tel Aviv, just a few blocks from the Habimah Theater. A paper sign on the door was all that identified the office. Inside, a young North American Jew, Ron, who'd been living in Israel for the past seven years, chatted with me and brought me up to date on gay and lesbian activism in Israel. Notes from my journal on that trip indicate that, unlike in the United States, homophobic violence was largely unknown and press coverage was getting better by the week. The Israeli military did not kick out gay and lesbian soldiers, but getting a high-level security clearance was difficult. Changing this policy would require, Ron said, "lots of behind-the-scenes work, because the military is of racist hatred, nationalist hatred, chauvinistic hatred, and homophobic hatred, the hatred of homosexuals."[5] For her part, MK Yael Dayan called the "ugly violent outburst" against gays and lesbians at Yad Vashem the "tip of the iceberg."[6] They linked the abuse we had endured to the hatred and discrimination others, notably Palestinians, face in Israeli society.

The second experience occurred just three days later, when I was on my way to the World Congress board meeting at a hotel in Tel Aviv. I was coming that morning from Haifa, an hour to the north, where Kevin and I were staying with our friends Tal and Yoel. Due to the economic boom that Israel was undergoing, the Haifa–Tel Aviv highway was crammed with cars, and the bus inched along in a rush hour that would rival any in Los Angeles. I nervously began to conclude that I would be horribly late to the meeting. Once we reached the sparkling new Central Bus Station in south Tel Aviv, I hurried outside to catch a cab.

One driver ordered me out of his cab when I insisted that he turn on the meter (Israeli taxi drivers are required to use their meters but honor this requirement only in the breach). The next cab driver insisted his meter was broken and began bargaining with me over the fare. He wanted forty shekels (approximately thirteen dollars at the time) for a trip that was perhaps two miles. I began yelling at him that I was not a *fraier* (Hebrew slang for "sucker") and how dare he rip me off. He looked at me in all sincerity and said, "Chas v'chalila" (God forbid). As he inched through the Tel Aviv traffic, we settled on thirty shekels, and I resigned myself to being ripped off but at least making it to the board meeting on time.

Happy at having such an extravagant fare, the driver, a Jew of Middle Eastern origin, looked at my new 1994 Pride Month T-shirt and asked me what I was doing in Israel. I took a deep breath and told him that I was on my way to a board meeting for the World Congress of Gay, Lesbian, and Bisexual Jewish Organizations. He allowed that he had heard something about an incident at Yad Vashem (undoubtedly, since most Israelis, especially taxi drivers, are glued to the radio every hour on the hour for their news fix). He next asked me, in a tone filled more with curiosity than any hostility, "Why are you like that?" Meaning, "gay." I was intrigued by the question and replied, "Because that's the way I am."

After pausing for a second, my new conversation partner began talking about how we all needed to get along and people should be able to live as they please. We made it to the hotel, my taxi driver/con artist/conversation partner pocketing thirty shekels and, perhaps, a new perspective on gay people.

At the end of our trip Kevin and I decided to spoil ourselves with some five-star luxury in Tel Aviv. On the rooftop of the Carlton Hotel, on chaise lounges perched alongside the inviting swimming pool, we chatted with one of the British guys who'd attended the conference with us. Besides regaling us with his tales of after-hours adventures at the conference, he told us that when we left the country we should tell the security agents at the airport that we were a couple. Kevin, who'd been pulled away from me for separate questioning when we'd boarded our El Al flight to Israel in Prague, and had not appreciated the intensive grilling of the Israeli security guards, looked eager to try it out.

So there we were at 5:30 A.M. at Ben Gurion Airport, in an interminable line of travelers. A female soldier motioned me to come over. I motioned to Kevin to come with me and told the soldier in Hebrew that we were a couple. She didn't bat an eye and proceeded to ask us all the standard questions: Why did you come to Israel? Who did you meet? Did anyone give you anything to take on the plane? How do you know Hebrew? Gay couples obviously did not trouble Israeli security in 1994, yet another small sign of the progress that activists had made.

That trip to Israel, my first with Kevin, really cemented my love for the country and my interest in its lesbian and gay community. As my pride in the development of Israel's gay and lesbian community increased, I often found myself disappointed as an American gay man in the slowness of progress in the United States. I began asking myself why Israeli gays and lesbians had achieved so much political progress, especially as the country drifted rightward in many ways and religious politicians dictated more and more aspects of daily life (or tried to do so). As friends continued to supply me through phone conversations and the latest media, gay and nongay, with breaking developments, this curiosity only grew. My friend Tal Weisberg-Bloch would usually finish his letters to me detailing the latest gay progress with something along the lines of "We're now more advanced than even the United States."

My curiosity has led to this book. Its title, *Between Sodom and Eden*, points to where Israel's lesbian and gay community stands today. Israel has moved away from the condemnation of homosexuality popularly thought to be present (although I beg to differ) in the Biblical story of Sodom and Gomorrah. But life for Israeli lesbians and gay men is not yet Eden, either. The questions that Israel's lesbian and gay community raise are fascinating ones. How do gay rights progress in a country where the clout of religious parties grows year by year? How does lesbian and gay identity develop in a country whose own identity is unformed after fifty years, for which many competing visions exist? How does a sense of community develop in a country that lacks, and likely will continue to do so, "gay ghettos?" What does a rapid decade's worth of progress politically and culturally on sexual orientation issues say about Israel and the Zionist dream? *Between Sodom and Eden* will attempt to answer and analyze some of these questions and provide readers more generally with a sense of today's Israel as it heads into its second fifty years.

Between Sodom and Eden will raise questions for both Israelis and foreigners about lesbian and gay politics and community. In a period of ten years, lesbian and gay Israelis have attained rights that remain distant dreams for their counterparts in some western countries. They have done so by emphasizing rights for the individual rather than trying, initially, to create an identity separate from "the Israeli consensus." The issues that they selected—military service, employment discrimination, and even rights for same-sex couples—were issues that the wider public could relate to. While this is not a comparative work, the Israeli approach—gradual, sometimes even sub-rosa, and very mainstream—has yielded great success in the political and legal realms. Lest I seem too congratulatory, let me note here that gay rights has allowed Israeli elites to appear progressive, even as Israel ignores or struggles with other civil and human rights questions. Nor have Israeli activists' strategies been perfect. At times they have suppressed issues that might not be convenient for gay political strategy (such as AIDS), and building a community remains a challenge.

The mainstream approach has succeeded in creating the conditions for a community, in a very sudden fashion. It was only after I had completed research trips to Israel that evidence of the beginnings of a strong community—and perhaps more militant styles of politics—emerged in May and June 1998, when a series of political and cultural events brought out throngs of lesbians and gay men to celebrate and protest as such. The other evidence of this is the number of people I interviewed for this book who were ready to be identified by their full names. A decade ago some activists like Hadar Namir used pseudonyms in newspaper interviews. No longer.

Now that there are the beginnings of community, lesbian and gay Israelis will have to avoid mindlessly copying other, primarily American, models. Looking to other countries traditionally has helped the Israeli lesbian and gay community convince policy makers to end antigay discrimination. Today it involves comparing street riots over bureaucratic foul-ups to the great American Stonewall riots. Rather than develop their own traditions, lesbian and gay Israelis may be on the verge of slavishly imitating what they perceive as American lesbian and gay life. That would be unfortunate.

What made writing this book so exciting is that lesbian and gay politics and community are developing in a country that is undergoing constant dynamic change and is in the midst of major struggles over its identity, politics, and future. Because lesbian and gay community and politics are so new, and still fragile, they take place in the midst of these major battles rather than apart from them. The fact that the gay community has progressed so rapidly in one decade points to major changes in some of Israeli society's bedrock institutions and ideology. As such, *Between Sodom and Eden* is but a snapshot in time. The future of the Israeli lesbian and gay community will be a lot of different things, but boring will not be among them.

1

Together in Pride, Together in Hope: Lesbian and Gay Politics in Israel

A Knesset member who represents only accountants who come from Bukovina is a wasted Knesset member, just as is a Knesset member who represents only himself. Sexual preference similarly does not justify in and of itself representation in the Knesset.
—Israeli historian and journalist Tom Segev, *Ha'aretz*, 1995

This is another step toward gay or lesbian representation in the Knesset.
—Michal Eden, openly lesbian member of the Tel Aviv City Council, 1998

Israeli President Ezer Weizman was on one of his many visits around Israel, meeting the diverse citizens of his nation. A former fighter pilot with a roguish reputation and a blunt tongue, Weizman had transformed Israel's previously bland ceremonial presidency into a bully pulpit, serving as the "national seismograph" of Israel's divided citizenry. Not infrequently, his public musings have sent that seismograph off the charts. Chosen by Knesset vote under the government of the late Prime Minister Yitzhak Rabin (and reelected to a second term in 1998), Weizman managed to infuriate the late prime minister and his successor, Shimon Peres, with his calls on the Labor-led government to slow down, or even halt, the implementation of the Oslo Accords with the Palestinians.

He surely did not ingratiate himself with Peres's successor, the hardline Benjamin Netanyahu. First, he publicly issued what amounted to an ultimatum to the new Likud prime minister a few months after his election in 1996: meet with Palestinian Authority President Yasser Arafat or he, Weizman, would invite the Palestinian leader to his home in Caesarea, allowing Arafat to make his first official visit to the Jewish state (Arafat did, in fact, ultimately pay such a visit to Weizman's home). In June 1998 he went well beyond the bounds of his ceremonial position when he declared that Netanyahu was not "living in reality" and should call new elections. By the time that the 1999 Israeli elections rolled around, the Israeli president barely concealed his partisan preferences and disdain for Netanyahu.

Standing at a podium at the prestigious Reali High School in Haifa on the morning of December 20, 1996, Weizman fielded questions from the students: What were his views on the chances of peace with Syria? How could young people contribute to their nation in post-Zionist Israel? Was he interested in serving a second term as president? As the questions had been submitted to him in advance, he could not have been shocked by the one that followed: What did the Israeli president think about gay rights?

Never one to shrink from airing his personal views, Weizman fixed the student with his gaze and stated: "There are laws in the Bible against sodomy and bestiality. Are you for sodomy?" When the student ventured that he was not "for" sodomy, the president shot back, "Good. I'm glad." Weizman then expounded further on the gay issue: "To turn it into something where everyone comes out of the closet, this I can't accept. . . . I like a man who wants to be a man and a woman who wants to be a woman, not a man who wants to be a woman and a woman who wants to be a man."

The type of homophobia expressed by Weizman certainly is not unknown. The reaction, however, is indicative of the new consensus regarding gay rights among the predominantly Ashkenazi and secular Israeli elite in politics and the media. The Israeli media went into high gear, putting Weizman's remarks at the top of the hourly radio news within two hours of his speech.[1] That Friday evening Israel Television's *Yoman* newscast reported on the remarks with more than a hint of disapproval of the president, for good measure inviting Israel's best-known gay couple, Amit Kama and Uzi Even, into the studio to give their reaction to the president. They proceeded to use the airtime to call on supporters to demonstrate outside the President's Mansion in Jerusalem the following evening.

That Saturday night something unprecedented happened. The Aguda, the Lesbian-Feminist Community (KLAF), and Gei'ut, a new group of gays and lesbians working within the Meretz Party, got out three hundred people to demonstrate publicly against Weizman. To demonstrate against Israel's president, who wields no real power, was unheard of. Chagai El-Ad, the former chair of the Hebrew University gay and lesbian student group, Ha-Asiron ha-Acher (Asiron), noted to me that "in this country, the president is a national symbol and you don't demon-

strate against him." The demonstration constituted the biggest gay demonstration until then in Israel.

After a daylong hiatus for the Jewish Sabbath, Israel's Sunday newspapers prominently featured the story. *Yediot Achronot* headlined the
warning of Avi Sofer, then chair of the Aguda: "Weizman's Returning
Us to the Darkness of the Middle Ages."[2] The paper featured some of
Weizman's previous offensive remarks on other issues, most notably the
service of women in the Israeli military.

Two days later Weizman and his wife received a delegation of gay
and lesbian leaders at the President's Mansion. He admitted bad judgment, blamed his remarks on being of a certain age (seventy-two years
old) and his education as a youth, and hinted that his wife had chewed
him out over the remarks. But Weizman did not offer an unambiguous
apology either.[3]

Although no one noticed at the time, the Weizman affair marked a
turning point for Israeli lesbian and gay politics. No longer would the
community necessarily do things quietly. Rather, it would enter the fray
of Israeli politics on its own terms, unapologetic about itself and increasingly demanding of others. The new self-confidence became clear to
all eighteen months later when, in a demonstration combining equal
parts of *Fame* and Zo Artzeinu[4] (as one Israeli friend, Dani Kaplan, described it to me), lesbian, gay, and transgender activists blocked Tel
Aviv's busy Ha-Yarkon Street to protest the abrupt end of the annual
Wigstock Festival. Within four weeks of that catharsis they propelled
Michal Eden to second place in the Meretz primaries, leading to her election to the Tel Aviv City Council as Israel's first openly lesbian official in
November 1998. They then conducted what no one ever expected to see
anytime soon in Israel: the country's first Gay Pride Parade.

The Weizman affair shows why Israel's gay community has come such
a long way in such a short time. Israel is probably the first country to get
the gay-rights model in reverse. According to that model, outlined by gay
historians such as John D'Emilio, progress toward civic equality for gay
people comes years after lesbians and gay men have migrated to urban
centers and built their own community and culture.[5] Only after a certain
critical mass in community cohesion is reached can broader social and
political progress begin in earnest. D'Emilio also ascribes importance to
capitalism, suggesting that the industrialization and urbanization it engendered in the early part of the twentieth century contributed to the
growth of cities, with their anonymity, which in turn facilitated the development of gay communities. That is certainly a plausible explanation

for the way that gay politics and communities have developed in the United States.

Not in Israel. In a decade that saw Israel take steps toward peace with its Arab neighbors, the murder of a prime minister because of those steps toward peace, economic prosperity, and social transformation Israel's lesbian and gay community has achieved far-reaching political and legal victories under both Likud- and Labor-led governments. From repeal of sodomy laws to passage of a national law banning employment discrimination on the basis of sexual orientation, from gay speakers in the schools to court cases upholding spousal benefits for the same-sex partners of employees, Israel has joined the ranks of better-known gay rights trendsetters such as the Scandinavian countries and the Netherlands. Even the country's choice of a slogan for its jubilee celebration in 1998 inadvertently showed how far Israel has progressed on gay issues—"Together in Pride, Together in Hope" would be at home at any gay pride celebration. What is so fascinating about these victories is that so many of them came in the absence of a visible lesbian and gay community publicly mobilized to demand its rights. Instead, those few pioneering activists turned D'Emilio's model seemingly on its head, leveraging their political and legal progress into greater social visibility and community building.

"There Is No Homophobia in Israel, Only Heterosexism"

One of the reasons for the success in orchestrating progressive legislation and obtaining far-reaching judicial decisions is what I'll call The Mantra: there is no homophobia in Israel, only heterosexism. Most every lesbian and gay activist I interviewed for this book repeated this line to me at one time or another. Alon Harel of the Hebrew University School of Law, for example, told me that Israel has virtually no antigay violence. What it does have, he added, is a strong heterosexist outlook, in which one is presumed to be straight. Amalia Ziv, a doctoral candidate in comparative literature at Tel Aviv University (looking at pornography written by female authors), suggests that the absence of antigay violence might have a connection with the wider Arab-Israeli conflict: "Aggression against Arabs perhaps has something to do with the lack of gay bashing. The fact that we're (gays and lesbians) all Jews helps us be adopted into the national consensus." Other activists I spoke with note that there has never been systematic deliberate persecution of gay people in Israel.[6] But this official line is overly simple. In fact, gay bashings in public parks (and even pick-up murders) have at times constituted a serious problem, as has police harassment or indifference.

Others have a more basic explanation for some of the gay community's successes: the "fluky" nature of Israeli politics. Former Aguda chair Susan Kirshner, for one, points to the importance of connections and personal contacts. "If you know the right people and contacts, you can get things done. If people are open-minded, that's all you need." As an example, she points to Knesset member and former minister of labor Ora Namir, the aunt of lesbian activist Hadar Namir, who worked to amend the Equal Workplace Opportunities Law to include sexual orientation. While not pivotal to the amendment effort, Namir's aunt's role clearly did not hurt.

That approach—doing things quietly, even sub rosa—defined a period of Israeli lesbian and gay activism that dates from the 1980s through the early 1990s. During that period, fearful of the power of religious parties in the Knesset, gay rights supporters would call votes late at night, with only supporters present. That is how they ensured repeal of the country's sodomy law in 1988. Former Aguda chair Avi Sofer once remarked to me, "We live in a crazy system. We've never gotten a majority of 61 votes (out of 120) in the Knesset on any issue. Our victories are always 8–5, 16–9, 31–17. We sometimes hide Knesset members, or wait until it's a day of fasting. Then we rush our supporters into the room, call a vote, and disappear."

Kirshner's partner, former Aguda chair Liora Moriel, says that as a small and Jewish country, the Israeli government "wants to keep its [Jewish] citizens happy and content. So, people don't see the big deal in granting gays rights." She also believes that "there's a basic underlying sense of fairness and decency. When we show that there are some citizens who are not getting a fair shake, it helps." And that, she says, the Aguda was successful at doing: "The Aguda managed to get into the public's mind that we are citizens with needs not being met, and that should be met." As shall be seen, Moriel has a point. The way lesbian and gay activism in the 1990s appealed to public support has much to do with appealing to that sense of "We're One People."

The Knesset

The first stop on any tour of lesbian and gay political success in Israel is the modest office of Knesset member Yael Dayan. As someone accustomed to American politicians' imperial trappings of power, I come away from my interview with her convinced that less can be more. Dayan is in the midst of a busy day in June 1997 when I knock on the door of her office, the size perhaps of a large walk-in closet, which she shares with two legislative aides and which is located near the end of a corridor in the bowels of the Knesset. Crammed into the office are three desks and one computer.

While the offices of American politicians are covered with nicely framed photographs of the famous and powerful, Dayan makes do with a cork bulletin board on which are tacked snapshots of her with Palestinian Authority president Yasser Arafat, President Clinton, and Jordan's late King Hussein. There is one large photograph of her and her deceased father, Moshe Dayan, the one-eyed general who was a walking image of Israel to the rest of the world. On another wall hangs an Arab ceramic plate, inscribed by Mustafa Natshe, the Palestinian mayor of Hebron. As she turns toward me to begin the interview, I notice the white dove pin on her lapel, a symbol of her efforts at dialogue with the Palestinians.

Having heard Dayan speak before, I am not surprised by her initial bluntness.

There's been no change since Bibi[7] (Prime Minister Netanyahu) came to power. There've been no limitations on the [lesbian and gay] community. We've even amended the Libel Law this year to prevent defamation on the basis of a person's sexual orientation. Laws that didn't pass in the last Knesset won't pass now. I can't do anything right now.

In 1993 Dayan, a Labor Party member, called the first Knesset conference on gay and lesbian issues in her capacity as chair of the Knesset Committee on the Status of Women and proceeded to establish the Knesset Subcommittee for the Prevention of Sexual Orientation Discrimination. She has used her position to serve as a watchdog of sorts for the gay community, intervening with government bodies to rectify cases of discrimination.

She has championed the lesbian and gay community even since, sometimes flamboyantly. One week after her 1993 conference, she created pandemonium in the Knesset when, during a discussion about the Israeli military's treatment of gays, she declared, "Shmuel ha-Nagid was the chief of staff of the Army of Granada [in medieval Spain]. He was the first Jewish, gay chief of staff."[8] In response to heckling from National Religious Party MK Chanan Porat, she yelled back, "If you let me, I'll get to King David, or at least Saul."

PORAT: "Not everything's legitimate."
DAYAN (reading from the Book of Samuel): " 'I am distressed for thee, Jonathan. You have given me great pleasure.' "
PORAT: "Don't do it."
DAYAN: " 'Your love surpasses the love of women.' "
PORAT: "Don't do it."[9]

The gay community's most significant legislative successes—repeal of the country's sodomy law and passage of an amendment to the Equal Workplace Opportunities Law to include sexual orientation—took place, interestingly, under Likud governments, and before the establishment of her subcommittee. Dayan states that such changes could occur because "this is an equal society, with certain pockets. The changes came as part of our social-democratic awareness. What I did was bring the issue into broader public consciousness and give it legitimacy." This latter statement suggests a process of political elites working in top-down fashion to legitimize the gay community in the wider public, and even in the eyes of the community itself. Dayan herself estimates that the changes in the Knesset "gave the community self-confidence and enabled it to develop internally and to demand its rights publicly." And, in fact, without that societal stamp of approval, it would have been quite difficult for the lesbian and gay community to emerge.

Although Dayan is a committed left-winger, Israeli politics do not split so neatly between left and right, secular and religious, when it comes to gay rights. I spent two days in the Knesset in February 1998 going from one end of Israel's political spectrum to the other: from the offices of Tamar Gozhansky, a member of Chadash (basically, the Israeli Communist Party), to those of Beni Elon of Moledet, as far to the right in Israel as one can go without being banned from running for the Knesset on grounds of racism. The terms *left* and *right* become meaningful, however, only when discussing the Arab-Israeli conflict and the Palestinian problem. While the Israeli left—represented by Labor and Meretz—is more vocal in support of gay rights, one can find support—and homophobia—in unexpected places across Israel's political spectrum.

If Dayan's office displayed the accoutrements of hopes for peace, Beni Elon's displayed somewhat different yearnings—a poster calling for mass prayer at Rachel's Tomb outside of Bethlehem. While waiting for him to arrive, his parliamentary aides, both Orthodox and both immigrants (from the U.S. and France respectively) engaged me in conversation about gay issues as well as idle chitchat. The French-born aide, a woman dressed in a fashionable head covering and long skirt, suddenly brought up the Monica Lewinsky affair and opined that "the difference between Clinton and Bibi (who admitted to an affair while married to his third and present wife) is that women don't complain about Bibi."

In person, Elon, a big bear of a man, turned out to be charming rather than the ranting extremist I half-expected to encounter. Before we began, he, an ordained Orthodox rabbi, asked me where my Hebrew was from. I replied, "You might be surprised but I'm the product of a good Reform Jewish education." Elon smiled and said that he was not surprised at all. He had recently returned from speaking at a Reform Jewish day school in Miami and said that Israel and Hebrew are what keep Reform Jews Jewish these days.

In the first issue of the Israeli lesbian and gay newspaper, *Ha-Zman ha-Varod*, Elon declared that "there's a feeling that the left is for the advancement of the status of gays and the right is against. That's incorrect and I hope that this feeling will pass in the present Knesset."[10] This seeming openness intrigued me at the time, as Elon belongs to a party that, among other things, advocates the "transfer" of Arabs from the West Bank. Elon's fellow Moledet MK in the Fourteenth Knesset, Rechavam Ze'evi (perversely nicknamed "Gandhi"), is not pro-gay at all.

I asked Elon how he, as an Orthodox rabbi, could take a seemingly positive approach to gay rights in view of Orthodoxy's condemnation of homosexuality. In reply, he asked me, "Where's it written in the Torah that one should discriminate against gays?" True, but the Torah does seem to condemn same-sex relations, I replied. "That's *dinei shamayim* (laws of heaven)," rather than a law that is rigorously enforced practically or relevant to day-to-day life, Elon told me. The law should protect the civil rights of all people, he continued, as everyone is created in God's image.

Elon takes a sometimes contradictory approach to gay rights. On the one hand, he said he was against discrimination against gays and claimed he was supportive of laws to protect lesbians and gay men from discrimination in employment, which he defined as a matter of privacy rights. He struck me as quite sincere about that. When it comes to equality for same-sex couples, however, Elon is far more cautious, to be charitable about it. "I don't want the Jewish state to undermine the value of the [traditional] family," he declared to me. Yet he claimed that he wasn't opposed, say, to Adir Steiner's efforts to win a pension as the surviving partner of the late gay IDF colonel Doron Maisel, just to efforts to uniformly amend all Israeli laws to formally enshrine same-sex couples as equal to heterosexual ones.

Not surprisingly, Elon did not see lesbians and gay men as a community. "To focus on just this one issue is sick. It's like an addiction to drugs," he opined, his rhetoric edging up a notch. In his view, most lesbian and gay Israelis—"the silent majority," as he put it—don't want to change the cultural makeup of society. "They just want to live without being persecuted." As an Orthodox rabbi, Elon also could not abide a gay synagogue, as such a synagogue, being organized around a sin, would be akin to organizing a "synagogue of Sabbath violators." He similarly took a diffident approach to the controversy over the screening of a segment about gay youth on the *Open Cards* program (which he had not personally seen), a battle ultimately resolved by the Israeli Supreme Court. "It's legitimate to oppose a program that can confuse the development of young peoples' personalities," he patiently explained, "but if it is supposed to help kids who are suffering, and thinking of suicide, I would favor the program."

An interview the next day with Eliezer "Modi" Zandberg of the right-wing Tzomet Party (which ceased to exist after the 1999 elections) underlined how the Arab-Israeli conflict imposes an artificial dynamic on Israeli politics that would collapse the moment Arabs and Israelis reached a resolution of their conflict. For now, says Zandberg, the issue of the territories is what drives the Israeli political debate, creating odd constellations in the process. Looking at his left-wing rival, Meretz, Zandberg saw a political party that, yes, takes a liberal stance on the Palestinian issue but, when it comes to economics, is made up of a "weird combination" of capitalists from its Shinui faction and dyed-in-the-wool socialists from its Mapam wing. Zandberg, too, is forced into some strange contortions. His party takes a hard line against any concessions to the Arabs ("There won't be peace. The Arabs want to destroy us, eliminate us, in all sorts of ways") yet sits uneasily in a government coalition with the ultra-Orthodox whose religious coercion it opposes.

As for gay rights, Zandberg says that he supports it as a "liberal," but that it was not a major issue for him. He did everything possible to downplay his involvement in the issue, although I found his reticence puzzling. In fact, he spoke at the festival following Tel Aviv's Gay Pride Parade in 1998, the only figure from the Israeli right to do so that year, and often offers his views on the issue in the Israeli press.

Politicians, Politics, and Pride

Former Aguda chair Itzik Yosha summed up for me the politics of gay rights thus: "There's no great hatred of gays and lesbians in Israel. No huge persecutions. The government didn't arrest us. People consequently didn't come out. Thus, things came from the top. Yael Dayan turned this into a big campaign, a big political issue." And, he notes, as with any big issue, it has attracted a variety of politicians eager to ride the wave.

Watching Tel Aviv Pride unfold in Gan Meir over the weekend in June 1997, I cannot help thinking that Yosha may be correct in believing that gay rights has become almost chic in certain political circles. Labor Party MK Eitan Kabel takes the stage in front of a throng of perhaps three thousand gays, lesbians, and friends, and declares,

> I think that this "happening" is good and reflects something in Israeli society. This is only a beginning. In Israeli society, there still exists much ignorance—some of it comes from education, whether religious or secular. I come here as a Knesset member to identify with you, to raise your spirits, and to reach out.

He spends a quarter-hour offstage, his attractive wife in tow, easily chatting away with gay political leaders.

An hour later, Tel Aviv mayor Roni Milo, a then-prominent Likud politician, takes the stage. Milo at the time was gearing up for reelection (he ultimately decided not to stand for mayor and went on to help form the new Center Party that ran in the 1999 Israeli elections) and was very much the ward politician that day. Judging from his remarks and their tone, he was in a rather expansive mood: "I want to congratulate this gathering and say to those here that only here in Tel Aviv can such a gathering take place so openly. We're a free city, tolerant, where people can live as they want." Then, he talks *tachlis*, practicality. "We're among the few municipalities that help the Aguda with funding. More funding will certainly come."[11] The crowd erupts in cheers. He concludes with a rousing "Have fun with your festival. We'll continue to provide funding, and we'll keep Tel Aviv a free and tolerant city." This latter remark has great resonance for his audience beyond the issue of gay rights, for Milo has been at the forefront of efforts to fight the growing power of the ultra-Orthodox.

Menachem Sheizaf himself seemed as expansive as Mayor Milo that day. Sheizaf, a consultant to a variety of Israeli politicians and concerns, has since become chair of the Aguda as well. A round-faced man in his early forties, he rides into Gan Meir on a motorcycle, a red helmet on his head. We retreat to a far end of the park, to get away from the loud disco music that disk jockey Ofer Nissim is blaring from the stage between speeches.

Sheizaf himself saw little impact from Netanyahu's victory on the direction of lesbian and gay politics in Israel. "Experience has taught us that the community got big changes under Likud governments." He sees the Israeli situation as unique, telling me that "there aren't such laws in most countries." He sees two remaining political challenges for the gay community—inheritance and pension rights and second-parent adoptions. Perhaps because of the celebratory mood of the day, he puts a positive gloss on the wider social situation for the gay community, insisting that "tolerance is big here. We don't have a big problem with coming out. I'm very out and work with some of the biggest concerns here."[12]

He takes pains to point out to me the importance of Milo's and Kabel's appearances. "Roni Milo, when I was his adviser, was very liberal and enlightened. No politician [in Tel Aviv] can minimize the importance of the gay vote. Tel Aviv has a higher percentage of gays, because of the anonymity and support that a big city can provide." He sees a recognition of the importance of the gay vote on the national level too. Eitan Kabel, he points out, comes from Rosh ha-Ayin, a poverty-stricken town populated mainly by Yemenite immigrants and their progeny northeast of Tel Aviv. Although he does not say so, the future Labor Party primaries, which will determine a candidate's place on Labor's Knesset list in any election campaign, probably were the impetus behind Kabel's visit to Tel Aviv Pride Day and his congratulatory, supportive remarks.

Ten months later I had the chance to talk with Menachem Sheizaf again, this time in his new capacity as chair of the Aguda, a position he had occupied for little more than half a year, following the resignation of Itzik Yosha. His election to this position marks another turning point in Israeli gay politics and suggests how gay rights have become a relatively safe political issue among the secular public, very much part of the "Consensus."

As a lobbyist, Sheizaf counts among his friends a rather unlikely collection of Israeli politicians, ranging from Tel Aviv mayor Milo, to ultra-Orthodox deputy minister of health Shlomo Benizri, to Arab Democratic Party–United Arab List MK Tawfiq Khatib, a religious Muslim. He has lobbied for clients on a variety of issues that, in an Israeli context, would seem quite distant from the interests of the chair of one of Israel's principal lesbian and gay rights organizations: for a jubilee pardon of prisoners (which would benefit Shas leader Arye Deri, convicted on assorted corruption charges in 1999) and for moving Saturday soccer games to a weekday, so that religious Israelis could attend such matches (he counts the Israeli Soccer Association among his roster of clients). The Aguda has never had such a high-profile chair, one with such ready access to the Israeli political elite.

Sheizaf's status is a mixed blessing, however. While he told me that he would not work for legislation that would hurt the interests of lesbians and gay men, the potential conflict between his career and his chairmanship of the Aguda is always present. In many ways the Aguda is but another "client" of Sheizaf's, albeit one that he is "representing" on a pro bono basis and not without possible damage to his own career interests.

A small example of the potential conflict lies in a radio interview that Sheizaf gave in which he said that "gays have forgiven Ezer Weizman" for his homophobic remarks. He did not state in the interview that he was speaking as a citizen and lobbyist rather than as the chair of the Aguda.

At the Aguda's general meeting in March 1998 Sa'ar Natanel of the Hebrew University gay and lesbian student group, the Asiron, raises the issue of Sheizaf's remark and states quite bluntly that not all gays had forgiven the Israeli president his homophobia. At this the meeting begins to dissolve into an approximation of the Knesset, with people screaming over each other and waving their hands. Although the atmosphere is heated, I get the impression that everyone knows they are just acting out a bit, as indicated by the half-smiles on everyone's faces, even as the shouting grows louder.

Sheizaf tried to minimize the damage by admitting that "I shouldn't have suggested that 'as a gay man I support Weizman.' " At the same time, he recounted working for Weizman's candidacy's during the Israeli president's efforts to secure the support of the Knesset the first time around and admitted, "There are many things I like about him," such as the way he pays condolence calls to any family whose sons are killed in combat.

Someone else yells out that "Sheizaf's remarks increase the alienation of gays from the Aguda" and that the Aguda has to figure out a way to deal with the "conflict" between Sheizaf's lobbying work and his work as chair of the Aguda. At this, Avi Sofer, the Aguda's former chair, yells back that "we should be thanking him (Sheizaf), that he is able to work with Shas."

A lawyer present at the meeting sums up the issue best: "Menachem Sheizaf is a package deal. People know he's gay, that he's chair of the

Aguda, yet he can work with Shas and with Weizman. That you can be a lobbyist and an out gay man is important. It can also be difficult."

The nature of lesbian and gay progress has varied in recent years, depending on the composition of the government. During Yitzhak Rabin's premiership the gay community got practical recognition in the form of budgets and publication of National Sex Education adviser Chava Barnea's booklet *Same-Sex Orientation (Homosexuality and Lesbianism)*, courtesy of the Ministry of Education. Yet, under right-wing governments, substantial pro-gay legislation has made its way through the Knesset into the law books with their tacit acquiescence and even outright support. In the first quarter of 1998 alone, the Knesset passed a strong sexual harassment law that includes a provision barring sexual harassment on the basis of a person's sexual orientation. Section 3(a)(5) of the law as adopted by the Knesset defined sexual harassment to include "scornful or humiliating responses directed at a person concerning his gender or his sexuality, including his sexual orientation."[13]

During debate on the law MK Beni Elon raised a reservation about including sexual orientation, since the term *sexuality* would presumably encompass it. Likud MK Reuven "Rubi" Rivlin stated in response that "if there's harassment concerning a person's sexual orientation, we'll do good if we come and say, Stop it."[14] MK Rivlin then added that,

> with all modesty, I've studied and researched, and sexual orientation is something you're born with. We've already been through this issue many times, the question has been asked and it's entered into Basic Law too. If we've asked to let every person, according to his sexual orientation, to live his life, the committee has done good.[15]

Elon ultimately dropped this particular reservation.

The reason for the greater legislative success under right-wing governments lies in the peculiarities of the Israeli system of government, where no party has ever been able to govern alone, dependent instead on shifting, often unstable, coalitions. Left-wing governments typically must obtain the support of at least one of the country's religious parties to maintain a viable government coalition. Because of their more progressive stances, they also must take greater pains to prove their bona fides with the religious parties. As a result, the left is paradoxically less able to push legislative changes on gay rights when in control of the government than when sitting in the opposition.

Gay Rights and the Ballot Box

Whether gay rights are an electoral plus is a difficult issue to analyze in the context of Israeli politics. Compared to Americans, who elect candidates to local, state, and federal office on a district basis, giving them a person to turn to for solutions to political problems, Israelis traditionally have not had much direct influence on the day-to-day governance of the country. There is no "personal" representative in the Knesset, or even on city councils. Rather, Israelis vote for a party slate. Susan Kirshner, for one, thinks that this makes it easier to advance gay rights: "MK's don't have to worry if their decisions are popular—citizens don't have a direct voice." Thus, Knesset members are not subject to the direct citizen lobbying pressures that legislative representatives can face in a direct representational system. The contrast with the American system is obvious. As Canadian professor David Rayside could note in his look at gay participation in mainstream politics in Britain, Canada, and the United States,

> The United States system multiplies the sites from which progressive and regressive initiatives can emerge. Even though many favorable openings are thereby provided, the work required to ensure success is monumental and the outcomes unpredictable. Initiatives to block or undermine progress are given just as many opportunities, and often emerge without warning. Proponents of progressive change thus confront a task more daunting than that faced by activists in virtually any other political system."[16]

It is not clear yet, however, whether support for gay rights can advance a candidate's chances of electoral success. MK Dayan made a point of telling me of the "high price" that she had paid personally and politically for her support of gay issues. Dayan's contention is a bit disingenuous, however. It is more likely that she has paid a political price for her unstinting support of the Palestinian cause and her outspokenness on issues of religion and state.

Another factor perversely benefiting Israeli lesbians and gay men is the marginality of gay issues to Israeli political discourse. Gay issues are simply not central defining ones for the Israeli political system. The marginality has more to do with the sheer weight of issues on the Israeli national agenda, rather than any deliberate view of gay politics as somehow not counting, although that is also a factor. Even for someone as committed to the issue as Yael Dayan, gay rights is only one of many issues on which she concentrates.

The Politics of Israeli Identity Politics

As Israel has become more powerful economically and militarily, and the chances of a peaceful settlement with the Arab world have increased, Israel has had the luxury of beginning to define just what type of society it wishes to be. While Israel's more secure regional position has opened the door to discussion of women's rights, the environment, and lesbian and gay rights, the most salient issue on the national agenda after peace and security concerns is the identity of the state. The state's identity boils down, in turn, to the question of what kind of "Jewish" state Israel is to be, or whether it should be a "state of all its citizens," as the country's Palestinian minority and portions of the Israeli Jewish left would prefer.

That identity today is up for grabs. There are no more eternal truths in Israeli society. The socialist, secular certainties of the Founders have given way to a cacophony of clashing visions—religious nationalism, Palestinian irredentism, secular liberalism. But the growing divide in sociopolitical identity among Israelis impacts lesbians and gay men in another way: the almost desperate desire to create the semblance of unity in Israeli society. Where once Zionism provided a common vision, many Israelis today feel that their society is coming apart at the seams. Thus Matan Vilnai, abruptly passed over for the position of IDF chief of staff in 1998, could decry the changes in values in Israeli society in recent years in an interview with *Ha'aretz*:

> The society into which I was born was a mobilized society. Spartan. A society in which people were ready to sacrifice. A society in which the interests of the whole were everyone's interests. . . . Thus, when I look at today's Israel I see on the one hand an extraordinary start-up country, but on the other hand a country whose social bonds have frayed. And these bonds are what held us together. . . we knew we had no choice but to be united.[17]

In 1998 Israelis were treated to a billboard campaign called "Different Views, One People" (more accurately, one *Jewish* people). Leading antagonists from the Israeli left and right—from its most vociferous secular spokespeople to some of its leading religious politicians—posed together with smiling faces under this slogan, attempting to create the facade of national unity as the country's jubilee, the subject in its own right of a national quarrel, approached. While the campaign sought to encourage different views within the Israeli family, it had a more sinister side—to tranquilize the public into believing that such radically different viewpoints could happily coexist.

The country's jubilee encapsulated the tension between the desperate desire for national unity and growing estrangement between different segments of the Israeli public. Israel Television broadcasted a series on Israel's history called *Tekuma* ("Rebirth"). Yet the telling of the national narrative did not lend itself to celebration. Instead, because the series gave voice to points of view long suppressed (Israeli Arabs, the Mizrachim, and even Palestinian terrorists), the Israeli right denounced the series in increasingly vitriolic terms as calling into question the country's—and Zionism's—very legitimacy. The series narrator, singer and actor Yehoram Ga'on, himself a potent symbol of the Consensus, resigned in protest over one segment dealing with the Palestine Liberation Organization's terror campaign against Israel in the 1960s and 1970s.

The retelling was long overdue. The certitudes of the founding parents no longer hold up under scrutiny, nor does the history they constructed. Groups long marginalized by the state's Ashkenazi secular founders—be they Palestinian citizens of Israel, Mizrachim, feminists, the ultra-Orthodox, or gays and lesbians—are clamoring to tell their version of the Israeli story.

It is the growing fragmentation of Israeli society that in turn has created the beginnings of a gay voting bloc. Marc Tennenbaum, an immigrant from France, is among the founders of Gei'ut. Gei'ut represents a new innovation in Israeli gay political strategy—trying to bring about political change by organizing a gay and lesbian presence within Israeli political parties. In the early 1990s he, along with Hadar Namir, founded Otzma as the Aguda's political lobbying arm, which played an important role in passage of the 1991 amendment to the Equal Workplace Opportunities Law that banned discrimination in employment on the basis of sexual orientation. In perhaps the first visible gay political activity in Israel, Otzma started a petition campaign on the streets of major cities to gain support for that measure.

Gei'ut was not the first effort in Israeli politics to try to turn gays and lesbians into a political bloc, although it represents the first gay effort at doing so. But these early efforts were premature, coming before a visible gay community had taken root. In August 1991 the Labor Party's Young Guard published an advertisement in the gay magazine *Maga'im* asking,

"What have you done for yourself today? And what are you doing for the community?"[18]

The advertisement, the first of its kind in Israeli politics, created a minor storm at the time. Within the Labor Party itself opinions were split. MK Chaim Bar-Lev called the advertisement "tasteless" and added that he wouldn't run an electoral appeal in a newspaper for nudists either. But both MK Shlomo Hillel and MK Michael Bar-Zohar failed to see what all the fuss was about, although they, too, in an era in which narrow appeals to an ethnic or other social group were suspect, questioned the need for advertising directed at the gay community.[19]

Activists laid the groundwork for Gei'ut after the last national election in 1996, following Professor Uzi Even's campaign as an openly gay man in the Meretz primaries (he failed to place high enough for a realistic chance at a Knesset seat). What is murky is whether clear alignment with one political party, particularly one that raises the hackles of the Israeli right like Meretz does, ultimately benefits gay interests.

The Meretz leadership has been supportive of this intraparty gay organizing. MK Yossi Sarid, one of the leading figures of the Israeli left, told me in an interview that the establishment of Gei'ut is a positive development, because "we respect [the gay community] and want to help it—culturally, politically, and civilly." In Gei'ut's first newsletter Sarid wrote that "the public activism of the community itself is critical today more than ever. At any time and at every opportunity, it's appropriate to rouse public opinion in support of the repair of Israeli society and its attitude toward those who are different within it."[20] The party provides Gei'ut with support, with MK Sarid admitting that the support may be "more than the numbers might warrant."

Gays and lesbians have had to fight the perception of some elites that there is no need for gays and lesbians to have one (or more) of their own in public office. What clearly irked MK Dayan during my interview with her is the possibility of having an openly gay or lesbian Knesset member, a development that is most likely to occur because of Gei'ut's work within Meretz. When I raised the issue of openly gay representation in the Knesset, Dayan was dismissive: "The meaning of a gay Knesset member is useless." She pointedly added that "a gay Knesset member would end up doing less for the community" than she had been able to accomplish. Moreover, she contended that sexual orientation is not a sufficiently unifying basis to qualify for Knesset representation, stating that "gays are quite varied [politically]." MK Sarid, in contrast, told me that he welcomed a gay representative in the Knesset.

Dayan's views are not unique. In December 1995, when Professor Even announced that he was running in the Meretz primaries, Israeli historian and journalist Tom Segev wrote an opinion piece about Even's candidacy titled "One-Issue Politics" in *Ha'aretz*. Segev stated that "a Knesset member who represents only accountants who come from Bukovina is a wasted Knesset member, just as is a Knesset member who represents only himself. Sexual preference similarly does not justify in and of itself representation in the Knesset."[21] While most lesbian and gay activists disagree with Segev's analysis as patronizing, it was unclear until very recently whether there was a sufficient mass of lesbian and gay voters who could be persuaded to vote primarily on the basis of a candidate's sexual orientation. This task is that much harder when the political system has been responsive to many of the demands of the lesbian and gay community.

Those questions ended in June 1998 when Michal Eden, a twenty-nine-year-old lesbian and Meretz activist, came in second in the Meretz primaries for the Tel Aviv City Council elections and then won a seat in the November municipal elections. I first read of Eden in the July 1997 issue of *Ha-Zman ha-Varod*. She brings an interesting background to the electoral field: lesbian, feminist, and Mizrachit, the latter notable only because most Mizrachim, alienated by their treatment at the hands of the Ashkenazi establishment in the early years of the state, tend not to vote for Meretz or other left-wing parties. She comes to politics with years of activism in KLAF and two years as a member of the Tel Aviv Meretz leadership. In her personal life she did not have a rosy coming out: Her parents threw her out of their home when they learned of her lesbianism and, six years later, still do not speak with her.

I got to observe some of her campaign up close and initially was uncertain whether she would place high enough in the primaries. I first met Eden in March 1998 at the festive opening of Pet Café, billed as "a café for pets and other people," which became a popular gay gathering place (a rainbow flag hangs from the building). She had set up a booth outside the café encouraging residents of Tel Aviv to join the Meretz Party and vote for her in the June 23, 1998, Meretz primaries. With some of her campaign volunteers, she was working on a draft manifesto of gay-related demands that she would raise if elected. The twelve-point manifesto tackled the full range of lesbian and gay needs, including demands for an office of multiculturalism, establishment of an emergency shelter for gay youth, and promotion of gay and lesbian culture.[22]

Apart from her specific policy goals, her aim is to create greater visibility for gays and lesbians both broadly in government and also by serving, in her own words, as a "role model" for the Israeli lesbian and gay community. As she complained to me when we met a few days later at Tel Aviv's Café Nordau, "There are no role models, and so people don't come out. We have nothing authentic. We imitate culture from abroad."

In line with the general approach of Israeli lesbian and gay politics, Eden takes a very practical approach to gay representation in the Tel Aviv City Council: she wants to see gays and lesbians get their fair share of the city's fiscal resources. The community's organizations only recently began receiving 100,000 shekels per year (roughly $25,000) from the municipality and Eden deems this a drop in the bucket. She throws out a figure of 2 million shekels per year as what the community deserves based on its putative size. Such a sum would be comparable to what religious institutions receive from the city government.

Eden was not a one-issue candidate by any means. Her general publicity materials stated her goals as equal opportunity in education—in all parts of the city and in all population sectors, battling religious coercion, equitable distribution of resources—to women, pensioners, the disabled, Arabs, lesbians, and gays, and environmental protection.[23] It is her ability to appear multifaceted that may explain her success, even as Uzi Even in 1999 placed thirteenth on the Meretz Knesset list, not high enough for a realistic shot at election. One difference between the two of them may lie in Israeli society's unease with the notion of distinct gay identity. The public, and even some in Meretz, tend to see Even first as a gay activist, despite his many accomplishments and talents. In his 1999 effort he claimed that he could bring Meretz three Knesset seats worth of votes from the lesbian and gay community. Eden, in contrast, while very active in KLAF, worked within Meretz as a party activist rather than as a lesbian. Moreover, as a Mizrachi woman, she also could put a more diverse face on the party's public image. Yet it is unfair to label Even any more one-dimensional on the issues than Eden. His military background and work in higher education would bring important contributions to the Knesset.

Despite Eden's multiissue candidacy, it is clearly the lesbian and gay issue that propelled her race and it is on the community that she was pinning her hopes for election, strategizing how to get out a large gay vote on her behalf. As she put it to me, "I have an advantage over other Meretz contenders—I have a community to turn to."

Whether Eden in fact had a community behind her was the Million Shekel Question. Her strategy depended on convincing sufficient numbers of gay and lesbian residents of Tel Aviv to join Meretz, and then turn out to vote on Primary Day. At a Saturday night meeting with gay male volunteers at Pet Café, Eden asked them to gather names and addresses of gay friends so that her campaign could contact gay voters more easily. She also hoped that these gay volunteers, several of them board members of the Aguda or otherwise active in gay community affairs, would gather their friends at parlor meetings and sell them on her candidacy. She pursued a similar strategy in the lesbian community. As she told me some months after her victory, "I did a lot of work, going house to house. I showed that my candidacy was realistic and that it could benefit gays and lesbians." In addition, she had her own monthly column in *Ha-Zman ha-Varod*, which gave her added community visibility, even if the column contained little more than platitudes about the necessity of coming out.

On June 23, 1998, she scored a stunning second-place finish, placing only twelve votes behind veteran Meretz Tel Aviv City Council member Michael Ro'e.[24] If the Israeli political class had doubted that a gay voting bloc existed, Eden's primary victory provided a clear answer.

That Eden was able to do so well in her first shot at elective office points out how Segev's and MK Dayan's views suddenly no longer reflect the reality of Israeli politics. In an Israel where the Knesset is increasingly a collection of special interest parties—be they Russian, religious, or Arab—there is no great ideological justification for denying gays and lesbians their own elected voice.

Journalist Daniel Ben-Simon, in his 1997 book *A New Israel*, noted that "until not so long ago, an ethnic party was considered a negative phenomenon, an existential undermining of the unity of the people, a danger to the Zionist enterprise. No longer."[25] The 1999 Israeli elections took this new factionalization to new, even absurd levels. Two Russian parties, a "men's rights" party, a party representing Israel's south, and one advocating for marijuana legalization were slated to compete at the ballot box.

Had Eden tried to run even two years earlier, it is not certain she would have done as well as she did in the Meretz primaries. The 1996 general election in Israel symbolized a revolt of the marginalized against the Ashkenazi, secular sabra elites of Israeli society. That climate helped her two years later, the barriers against sectoral interest parties having tumbled down.

Although gays and lesbians themselves once were marginalized, Eden, and the lesbian and gay community, are allying themselves with the traditional pillars of Israeliness rather than the ethnic/religious rebellion against the Old Order. The traditional elites in Labor and Meretz today embrace gay rights and other progressive causes, their previous collectivist impulses having mellowed. Yet, it is the revolt of other once marginalized groups, like the Mizrachim or the religious, who have created the climate in which lesbians and gay men could coalesce as an identifiable political bloc and have this seen as increasingly legitimate.

Eden's victory also shows how fast-paced Israeli political life is. A year before her victory Amalia Ziv presented me with an analysis that would have seemed to doom Eden's chances. She noted to me that nongay Israelis often ask, "Why do you need to separate yourselves? Why do you need a ghetto?" Identity politics is not viewed positively in Israel, she told me. Although individualism is growing, she continued, the prevailing ideology still works against difference and says, "We're all Jews." Moreover, Ziv added, "at the ideological level, there's still the fiction of collective identity."

The emergence of a distinct gay identity became clear with the 1998 Pride Day. In 1998 the community was no longer content to have its nice fair in a park. It decided to take to the streets in a parade under the slogan "Together in Pride, Together in Love," a takeoff on the already pro-gay sounding jubilee celebration slogan "Together in Pride, Together in Hope." This was an unheard-of step. Many activists had previously told me that Israelis do not "do" parades. Clearly, times had changed. Just as previously marginalized groups were redefining what it meant to be Israeli, so, too, was the lesbian and gay community. Part of the decision reflected a desire to be part of the worldwide gay phenomenon of Pride parades. Radio Tel Aviv, one of the sponsors of the 1998 Pride Festival, broadcasted ads declaring, "This year, Tel Aviv joins New York and Amsterdam." Menachem Sheizaf echoed that sentiment by phone a few weeks after the parade, saying, "We want to be like the entire world." While the 1997 Pride events I attended were different from what I, as an American, was used to (relatively few organizational and business booths, lots of heterosexuals in attendance), the 1998 parade would have been at home anywhere. Leading off the parade were lesbian-feminist motorcyclists, followed by activists and politicians carrying a giant Rainbow Flag the width of a city street. The parade featured an eclectic mix of youth groups, parents, children of gay or lesbian parents, and, of course, drag queens—all the requisite ingredients for a "real" Gay Pride Parade, be it in San Francisco, New York, Paris, or, now, Tel Aviv.

The Shift to Activist Tactics

What else might help build a community? After years of doing things quietly and behind the scenes, some suggest greater public activism in the form of more Weizman-like demonstrations. As Asiron chair Sa'ar Natanel commented to me, "People make noise in this country—that's how you win." Avital Yarus-Chakak from KLAF similarly posits that "demonstrations could help us build a community. The Weizman demonstration was the first time so many people were ready to come out." Because large gay communities overseas all seemed to use public demonstrations as a political tool, the Israeli lesbian and gay community, despite its impressive political and legal victories, must be lacking something, many activists seemed to feel.

Natanel got his wish for greater militancy in 1998. On May 22, 1998, a huge crowd gathered in Tel Aviv's Independence Park for the Wigstock Festival, an annual drag extravaganza to raise money for AIDS services. The Aguda had a police permit allowing the event to continue until 7 P.M., but City Hall had issued another permit good until 8 P.M.

At 6:45 P.M., the emcee came on stage and announced that the police had ordered the event to end, as the Jewish Sabbath was about to begin. Some in the audience were outraged and began voicing their protest. Veteran community activist Hadar Namir was in the first row, and she was angry. As she told me by telephone, "I went backstage and began arguing with the organizers. The drag queens had spent hours putting on makeup and were ready to perform." She took to the stage and declared that "we haven't struggled for fifteen years for the police to stop our event." A tense standoff ensued. Michal Eden strode onto the stage and declared that if the music did not resume, the crowd should block the adjacent Ha-Yarkon Street, a major seaside thoroughfare. Behind the scenes Menachem Sheizaf was arguing that the Aguda had gotten caught up in a bureaucratic snafu and Wigstock organizers should ask the crowd to behave responsibly and disperse peacefully.

That is not what happened. The crowd, spontaneously angry and egged on by some activists, did indeed block Ha-Yarkon Street for two hours. Several people were arrested, including Natanel, who whiled away several hours in a Tel Aviv jail. Eventually, the crowd did disperse, and a group of participants marched to Rabin Square and hoisted a Rainbow flag up the City Hall flagpole.

There were a variety of explanations for the events, which *Ha-Zman ha-Varod* melodramatically labeled the "Israeli Stonewall." If it was a

Stonewall, it was the first one to take place because of an ordinary bu-reaucratic gaffe. Natanel, along with several others, told me that Dana International's victory in the Eurovision Song Contest two weeks earli-er had filled Israeli gays with pride and that the riots constituted a "re-lease" of pent-up energy. Hadar Namir, along with former Aguda ex-ecutive director Gil Nader, said that those present were fed up with religious coercion. Why should such an event have to end because of the Jewish Sabbath, she asked me, when the park was in a relatively isolated part of the city and the event would not disturb the religious? Namir was hoping that activists might engage in more direct action in the future. She added that "people are tired of always playing good boys and girls."

The Aguda, which put on the festival, had a mixed reaction to the events. While Sheizaf called it "a mistake" when we spoke by telephone, even he conceded that some good might come from it—here at last was proof that gays and lesbians would take to the streets. Nader similarly felt that the stormy demonstration proved there was now a community coming into existence.

Echoes of the new self-confidence have continued through the end stages of writing this book. In September 1998 singer Meir Ariel gave a wide-ranging interview in which he proclaimed his frank homophobia. In response, both the Aguda and KLAF organized demonstrations out-side Ariel's concerts, leading the singer in late September 1998 to cancel the remaining performances of his concert tour.

The Aguda's Sheizaf, in a demonstration of the new gay assertiveness, declared, "I'm sorry about the depths to which Meir Ariel has sunk. He's playing the role of the robbed cossack, but no such game will cover up the fact that he's a sick person, who sank out of an urge for publicity and other reasons into the abyss of dark racism."[26] Activists similarly dis-rupted an Education Ministry–sponsored fair on tolerance in December 1998 after KLAF was excluded on the grounds that religious attendees might take offense!

It is clear that some elements in the community, led by *Ha-Zman ha-Varod*, wish to canonize the Wigstock riots as some magical turning point. Academics Dori Spivak and Yuval Yonai captured the dynamic of minor-ity struggle well in a recent article about Israeli legal discourse on gays, noting that "organization of a social struggle and recruitment of members and supporters requires the creation of 'an imagined community' of gays and lesbians with a shared mythical past of oppression and struggle with heroic heroes with whom they can identify."[27] But in a country where it took top-down messages of acceptance and legitimization to create a more open gay population, the Wigstock riots could only occur in a climate of growing public acceptance rather than public repression.

The Wigstock riots marked the first time that Israeli activists did not care about presenting a nice image to the wider public. The type of people who have come out in Israel is an interesting topic in its own right, one that had positive repercussions for the community at the political and legal levels. Although no one suggests it was deliberate, most of those who have waged public battles and noted their homosexuality or lesbianism seem to be very "straight-looking, straight acting."

Chagai El-Ad noted to me that "in Israel, it was the very 'straightest' gays, like [Professor] Uzi Even, who came out and fought for their rights." Whenever I raised the issue of community image in interviews, Even's name usually surfaced quickly. Many activists pointed to his masculine demeanor and his respected position in the Tel Aviv University Chemistry Department as pluses for the community. Others, less enamored with some of his political stances and tactics, were less complimentary, with one activist snidely labeling Even's image as that of a "gay *shabaknik* (internal security officer)." This strategy made sense at the time that the community was trying to change stereotypes about gays. As veteran activist Dani Lachman could write in the July 1998 issue of *Ha-Zman ha-Varod*, "I'm not sorry that that's the line I put in place. It was right for its time. It was important first of all to bring the community closer to the world and the world [closer] to the community."[28]

Dan Yakir, counsel for the Association for Civil Rights in Israel (ACRI), also noted this phenomenon. Choosing his words carefully, Yakir admitted that, in gay-related court cases, "It probably was important that the couples in those cases were living according to a certain model." While he admits that he would like to see other models of family recognized by the Israeli court system, he says that he recognizes, as someone who must select winning test cases, the importance of presenting sympathetic plaintiffs to the courts. Tal Yarus-Chakak similarly admitted that "when you come out, you want to show the similarity. You need role models. We need to show in the long-term the diversity [of the community]."

Limitations to the Mainstream Approach

While the mainstream approach brought great success in a short time in the political and legal worlds, it has had its costs. In looking at gay political strategy, two disconnects—the relative status of gay versus AIDS issues and the progress of gay rights versus feminism—quickly emerge. Moreover, some would argue that there is an unseen ethnic divide—between Mizrachim and Ashkenazim—afflicting the community.

AIDS

The problem of AIDS in Israeli society, and how the country's establishments—gay and straight—have dealt with it, suggests some of the limits of the gay community's mainstream political strategy. That the AIDS arm of the Aguda, Bela Do'eget, felt it necessary in 1997 to print up stickers and posters with a young man proclaiming, "I didn't think there was any AIDS problem in Israel" suggests how activists for many years neglected AIDS issues.

Yet AIDS is a sort of Rorschach test in which two people can draw completely different pictures. The vague status of AIDS as a "gay issue" in Israel led me personally to debate long and hard with myself whether to even write about it in a book dealing with the Israeli lesbian and gay community. What finally persuaded me was the growing discussion of the issue within the gay community and what AIDS activism (or the lack thereof) says more broadly about the tactics of Israeli gay activism.

There is agreement between AIDS activists and the government and medical establishments about the number of *known* HIV-positive Israelis—approximately two thousand—but there agreement ends. The Israel AIDS Task Force's former executive director, Patrick Levy, a genial French-born man, contends that the actual number of HIV-positive Israelis is three to four times the actual known number. The medical establishment, personified by Dr. Tzvi Ben-Yishai of Haifa's Rambam Hospital and head of the government's National Steering Committee on AIDS,[29] insistently disagrees, stating that the actual multiplier is only a factor of two. Each presents a distinct analysis of why *his* figures are correct. Levy points to the lack of anonymous testing sites in Israel (there currently is only one, operating in Tel Aviv) and cites a World Health Organization study suggesting that in countries lacking anonymous testing the true number of HIV-positive individuals is four to five times the actual known number. Dr. Ben-Yishai disagrees with the study and with the Israel AIDS Task Force,[30] stating that it is only correct with respect to countries where there is no registry of HIV-positive individuals. And in Israel confidential testing centers report a person's HIV-positive status and name to the medical authorities.

Somewhat sinisterly, Ben-Yishai insists that "there's no way not to know ultimately who's HIV-positive. You can't hide the development of AIDS. Those who develop the disease will come in contact with the health system." Because there is universal health coverage, there is no chance, he claims, that a person will opt not to seek medical treatment at some point for the various symptoms of HIV and AIDS.[31] Of those who seek treatment, he claims, 80 percent were already known to the health authorities as HIV-positive. The small size of Israel makes it easy to discover new AIDS cases, contends Ben-Yishai. Here again, the small size of Israel, and the lack of anonymity, would seem to retard progress on AIDS issues and discourage people from getting tested. The official response offered by Ben-Yishai is that such fears are nonsense, that there is no great stigma anymore against persons with HIV and AIDS in Israeli society.

While the early cases of AIDS were overwhelmingly among gay men, both Levy and Ben-Yishai agree that the statistics today are quite different. Roughly one-third of the cases currently are among gay men, one-third among Ethiopian Jews,[32] and the remaining one-third among heterosexuals.

As in many other countries, AIDS caused an initial wave of hysteria when the disease emerged in Israel in the early 1980s. A particularly homophobic example from 1987 was an ad put out by Kupat Cholim, the country's major health insurance cooperative, supposedly to increase AIDS awareness. The ad text read, *Al Tilech Ito la-Mita*—Don't Go to Death with Him—a play on words with the word *mita* (death) which, when written with the letter *tet* rather than a *tav*, means "bed."[33]

The government budget for AIDS-related matters totals only $2 million per year, of which perhaps only 10 percent is for HIV and AIDS-related education among the population. The Israel AIDS Task Force does publish its own more explicit materials and information, including a book titled *Life With AIDS*, discussing treatment and financial issues associated with HIV infection.[34] The heterogeneity of Israeli society, and the taboos that Orthodox Judaism has toward sex outside marriage, also may make the government unwilling to undertake sexually explicit education campaigns. And the potential for misunderstanding campaign messages is great. Levy recalled for me a government campaign two years previous that featured a condom and a *chamsa*, a hand-shaped amulet popular among Mizrachim that is supposed to ward off the evil eye. The message that some people took away, however, is that putting a condom in your pocket along with a *chamsa* would protect you against HIV.

The secular high schools do feature AIDS education and the level of awareness about how AIDS is spread is high, both Levy and Ben-Yishai agree. The problem is in internalizing those messages and changing one's own personal behavior. Israelis like to talk a lot about sex, says Levy, but are quite shy one-on-one on sexual matters. In fact, a well-known joke is that the best part of sex for Israeli men is running and telling their friends about it. Many Israelis take the attitude that AIDS won't happen to them—that it's a problem, but someone else's problem.

Israelis can take that attitude because of a widespread belief that AIDS does not happen in Israel, a concern of countries and groups distant from the Israeli consensus. This belief has nothing to do with homophobia. It has more to do with the way Israeli Jews view themselves and the uniqueness of the Zionist experiment. Since the establishment of the state there have been two competing strands of thought in each Israeli, and in the country's vision of itself: one holds that Israel should be a country like any other country, while the other, based on the notion of the Jews as the Chosen People, argues that Israel must be "a light unto the nations." Obviously, a country that believes it's like any other nation will have less difficulty accepting the existence of various social problems as an ingredient of being a normal people. More often, however, the Chosen People strand takes the upper hand initially in dealing with any social problem. Thus, while Prime Minister Netanyahu could lend his support to the growing national campaign against family violence, there was a time only twenty years ago when feminist attempts to bring the plight of battered women to the national agenda were met with the belief that "Jewish men don't beat their wives."

While the press does cover AIDS and HIV issues, it has not done so with the same intensity, or sympathy, that it devotes to wider gay and lesbian concerns. Avner Bernheimer, a well-known gay editor and cultural journalist for *Yediot Achronot*'s *Seven Days* weekend section, gave me a sketch of how the Israeli media has covered AIDS. As noted above, when AIDS first appeared in Israel there was an initial wave of hysteria, which newspaper coverage reflected and even fanned. After the initial hysteria, he notes, "It became forbidden to link gays and AIDS," a state of affairs that is no longer accurate in his view. If there is less coverage of HIV and AIDS, and less sympathy generated, he said, it's because of "the unwillingness of persons with AIDS to come out and show that they're just like everyone else." Shmuel Meiri, an *Ha'aretz* journalist currently based in Haifa who has written on gay community issues, put a harsher spin on the Israeli media's coverage of AIDS: the Israeli public doesn't like stories about *miskenim* (unfortunates). As Meiri summarized the Israeli attitude to me, "If someone falls, he steps aside, and everyone continues onward."

The feeling that AIDS isn't "our problem" makes providing social services to persons with HIV and AIDS a difficult proposition. While the Israel AIDS Task Force has a Buddy Program and support groups in place, recruiting volunteers is problematic. Here, too, the nature of Israeli society is more to blame than homophobia or plain indifference. Activists of all kinds—AIDS, lesbian, and gay—all pointed out to the lack of volunteerism in Israeli society, although there are a variety of explanations offered. No'am, a young straight woman who is an AIDS volunteer with the Jerusalem AIDS Project, told me of her friends's reactions to her volunteerism: "What do you get from it?" Her volunteer work even created strains with her former boyfriend. She attributed the reaction to the growing materialism of Israeli society, a byproduct of Israeli society's growing acceptance of individualism. Even as rising living standards enable Israelis to see more of the world and absorb more ideas—including lesbian and gay rights—from overseas, the increased standard of living leaves people less likely to work for social change, particularly for free. It lets Israelis act as passive observers and supporters of social change and encourages a knee-jerk political correctism in which Israelis of a certain social and political milieu "know" what they're supposed to say about various issues, even as they fail to internalize such beliefs.

The other major explanation for the lack of volunteer spirit is the pervasiveness of military service. The vast majority of Israeli youth still enlist at age eighteen and give two to three years of their lives to the military. Men continue to serve as reservists until their early forties, with annual reserve duty that can run for up to thirty days. In essence, Israelis already give time—and their lives—to the nation, and there is little time left over for causes.

Politically, AIDS offered the gay community two distinct choices: it could use AIDS as a means of educating the wider heterosexual public about the gay community, or it could try to disconnect AIDS from discussions of homosexuality. Until two years ago the community's leadership chose the latter path. It is easy to understand. When AIDS emerged in Israel in the 1980s there was comparatively no awareness of gay issues among the public. The existence of the sodomy law in the criminal code made homosexuality "illegal" in the eyes of the public, and any link between AIDS and the gay community would not contribute to the latter's image.

The 1988 repeal of the country's sodomy law and the concurrent explosion of coverage of the gay community in the Israeli media at that time and beyond should have lessened the fears of the country's gay leadership regarding more vocal activism on AIDS-related questions. It did not, however, as the Aguda was pursuing a very mainstream strategy and image at that time—demonstrating that gays and lesbians are "just like everyone else," serving in the military, and living in committed long-term relationships. But the image of gays as "just like everyone else" did not extend to gays developing HIV infection "just like everyone else."

The Aguda's AIDS strategy may have changed because of a realization: the view that AIDS did not impinge on the gay community was having a possibly adverse impact on safe-sex practices among gay men. *Ha-Zman ha-Varod* ran a cover story in March 1997 blaring the alarming headline "2,800 Gays in Israel Don't Know They're Infected."[35] The article went on to trumpet an alarming statistic, namely, that there was a 100 percent rise in the number of gays infected in the previous year when compared to the year prior to that.

What is needed more within the gay community is support for those who are infected or ill. Although the Aguda and the Israel AIDS Task Force both offer support groups and even a café for people with HIV and their families, more such services are needed; there currently are not services such as meal delivery for those too ill to care for themselves. Moreover, the level of social awareness, of the need *not* to isolate persons with HIV and AIDS, needs to grow significantly. Bela Do'eget has produced a series of comic books to spread that message. Bela's message at the end of one is that "the fear of gossip, isolation, and rejection from the gay-lesbian community itself forces carriers to hide this fact from their friends and those with whom they maintain sexual and romantic relations. No, they're not irresponsible spreaders of infection but people who engage in safe sex because they don't want to hurt others."[36] Another pamphlet, *Sex Between Men*, recently produced by Bela Do'eget states that "although the virus can infect anyone, regardless of sexual orientation, gays are still at much greater risk than the rest of the population."[37]

Feminism

The other notable disconnect in Israel is the one between the progress of feminism and the progress of the lesbian and gay rights movement. While the women's movement has been in existence since the early 1970s, preceding the Israeli gay rights movement by a few years, by many measurements the gay and lesbian rights movement has advanced farther, in a shorter period, than broader women's issues. Part of the gap between the two movements in their relative political progress stems from the different time periods in which each coalesced. Feminism arrived in Israel in the early 1970s, a few years after it burst on the scene in the United States. Not surprisingly, awareness of women's issues was a significant cultural contribution of North American immigrants to Israel, which also brought benefits to the lesbian and gay community, since many of these immigrants have devoted themselves to lesbian and gay causes as well.

The society to which American-accented feminism arrived, however, was a much less pluralistic one than exists today in Israel. Former MK Marcia Freedman, one of the founders of Israeli feminism and, later, an out lesbian, recounted to me by telephone from Berkeley, California, that "the American immigration of the late 1960s had a huge influence on civil rights, feminism, and environmental issues in Israel." The society to which these immigrants arrived was still in thrall to great ideological certainties, to collectivism. The feminist message also collided with the myths of early Zionist pioneer women and equality for women within the kibbutzim. Individual rights were not yet a rallying cry for the Israeli elite or society in general. In the early 1970s there was not a single lesbian or gay organization operating in Israel, although there were, of course, informal meeting places and friendship networks.

Terry Greenblad, today director of Kol ha-Isha (Woman's Voice) in Jerusalem and active since the late seventies in women's and lesbian-feminist issues, looks back on the early period and acknowledges that North American immigrant women "tried to transplant an alien model of feminism" and brought with them lingering racist and classist baggage, along with the "cult of American celebrity leadership." In her view, the failure to tailor feminism to local conditions alienated native-born Israeli women unnecessarily. Not only was the essence of feminism—that women are equal to men—a new, even jarring message for Israeli society at the time (and still, to an extent, even today), but the early feminist movement, like its counterparts in the West, took on some of society's sacred cows, including racism, classism, and various national conflicts.

In Israel that translated into taking on the Palestinian cause as a feminist issue as well as discrimination against Mizrachiot and Palestinian women in Israeli society. The latter issue in particular served to divide the feminist movement and alienate it from wider support among the Israeli public. Greenblad recalls a 1982 feminist conference that, in her words, "blew up" over proposed support for Israeli Arab women. As for a true sacred cow like Israel's Law of Return, which grants automatic citizenship to any Jew seeking to immigrate to Israel, that was simply beyond the pale, too much to bear for the many American Jewish feminist women who made Israel their home. Former MK Freedman sees the development of Israeli feminism in a more optimistic light. While admitting that the initial wave of feminism came from educated, middle-class Western women, "it wasn't wrong that it happened that way. It had to begin that way and then broaden." She sees a flourishing feminist movement in Israel today, where she spends half the year, and "if [the initial approach] was wrong, the movement would not be where it is today."

The gay rights movement, in contrast, while formally in existence since 1975, benefited from entering the public consciousness in the late 1980s and early 1990s, when Israel had already begun the transition from a mobilized collective society to one that could allow individuals greater freedom. The social oppression and invisibility that homosexuals and lesbians faced earlier did not allow much of a public movement to emerge, unlike the case of women, who could not be invisible and could find support networks for speaking out and challenging society.

A concrete example of this state of affairs is a booklet that the Aguda issued in the early 1980s to Knesset members. Titled *About Homosexuals in Israel: Background and Facts*, the booklet opened with an apologia under the heading "Gays Should Be Able to Live in Self-Respect Too":

> Not a few of them (gays) feel deep guilt over their orientation and lifestyle, and see themselves as "abnormal." Others, who after years of suffering and doubt came to terms with their orientation, are forced to cope with a hostile atmosphere, or to hide their sexual preference from the eyes of others lest they, God forbid, be subject to social isolation or even fired from their jobs.[38]

Israeli feminism did not take such an apologetic approach.

Feminism challenged prevailing attitudes, while the gay rights movement has largely focused on solving specific problems of discrimination against lesbians and gay men in Israeli society rather than on posing a challenge to social norms about masculinity/femininity or family. As Marcia Freedman put it to me, "Israel is not up to confronting lifestyle issues. So long as rights are around domestic partnership, that is less threatening than the feminist vision of changing the family structure."

The lesbian movement lies somewhere between these two poles. A common refrain I heard from KLAF activists and other lesbian feminists in Jerusalem, Haifa, and Tel Aviv was about KLAF's image, that of a bunch of white, middle-class, Ashkenazi elitist lesbians. These activists certainly were not afraid to be self-critical. Avital Yarus-Chakak, in a *Klaf Chazak* cover story on "KLAF and Mizrachi Lesbians" reinforced this perception (without meaning to) when asked why KLAF doesn't organize parties in cooperation with lesbian party promoter Ilana Shirazi (whose parties a lot of Mizrachiot attend): "I'd like to, but our women don't want to be linked to Shirazi's parties, and the women who go to Shirazi's parties don't come to KLAF's parties."[39] Matzada, a young Mizrachi Jerusalem lesbian, complained to me that "KLAF is not accepting of differences. Mizrachiot are not made to feel welcome." She added an additional criticism: "Even in the 1990s people who are right wing can't be open in KLAF."

The other problem in combating various "isms" in an Israeli context is the sheer pull of the Arab-Israeli conflict on people's lives. KLAF founder Chaya Shalom, an admirably strong woman in fighting for her worldview, says that lesbian feminists have to constantly struggle against two isms in particular—the machoism of Israeli society, which educates women to view themselves as the helpmates of men, particularly in light of the role that the military continues to play in Israeli society, and the related issue of what she calls *bitchonism*, "securityism." As she told me, "Radical feminism can reject all of this, and we do have this approach. Or, alternatively, it can seek to connect [to the wider society], because it's so internalized. Women internalize the need to serve in the military." Israeli feminist scholar Simona Sharoni similarly has noted the pull of the military:

> From 1948 onward, women had no space to assert themselves outside the confines of their role as male-supporters or to protest the erosion in their status. . . . With the militarization of motherhood and the additional national glory attached to the production of sons—that is, future soldiers—and given their limited access to decision-making levels of social and political institutions, women had few options other than the socially-accepted roles of wife and mother. They did not mobilize to protest their collective social and political predicament nor did they take explicit political positions as *women*, especially not on questions of war, peace, and security.[40]

Yet, Israeli lesbians have contributed greatly, although not necessarily openly, to the Israeli peace movement. Chana Safran, a Haifa activist, has written a paper titled "Alliance and Denial: Feminist Lesbian Protest Within Women in Black." The Women in Black were a group of women who began a weekly vigil in 1988 against the Israeli occupation of the West Bank. They would stand in silent vigil every Friday afternoon with banners in Hebrew, English, and Arabic demanding, "End the Occupation."

Safran notes that participation in the vigils was open to any woman, regardless of political, social, or personal background. She points out that "political differences, differences of class, culture or life style were seldom raised or discussed in the groups. . . . This ideological inclusion created an alliance between Zionists, anti-Zionists, old, young, Jews, Palestinians, poor, wealthy, lesbians and straight women."[41] The problem with such diversity was that these differences were ignored because of the fear that they would harm the group's unity and goal of ending the occupation. Reactions to a *women's* demonstration against the occupation were fierce, with many vigils absorbing a great deal of sexual verbal abuse from male passers-by, yet participants resented the efforts by those with greater feminist consciousness to draw the connections between the oppression of Palestinians and the oppression of women. And, as Safran concludes, the inclusion of the Women in Black "was a form of denial because there was no in-depth dialogue between different women which ultimately would allow them to develop a reading of the vigils that would include lesbians."[42]

The ethnic and political divides are not the only internal fissures facing the Israeli lesbian movement. The younger generation of lesbians arriving to KLAF events is not as interested as its elders in political activism and ideology. A 1998 article titled "Straight Women and Lesbians in the Feminist Struggle in Israel" led off with the following anecdote:

At the first lesbian conference, at the plenum discussion, one of those present stood up—among the founding mothers of the feminist movement in Israel, a proud lesbian for many years—and came out against the desirable woman contest that stood at the center of the [tenth anniversary] issue of *Klaf Chazak*. . . . A young woman, with a youthful appearance, came out shooting against the remarks and claimed heatedly that it's necessary to remove the *f* from KLAF because there's no connection between lesbianism and feminism.[43]

This struggle between older, ideologically committed lesbians and younger, more apolitical ones was particularly acute in Jerusalem, a city where one might expect a more ideological approach to prevail, in light of the city's religious and national pressures. Gali (a pseudonym), one of the members of KLAF's Jerusalem steering committee, sees the different interests of the young as positive because they help break down the stereotypes about KLAF participants (elitist, left-wing) and make the organization more dynamic. In fact, she would like to see a less ideological lesbian community, claiming that "practical things move people to get involved. After we solve the practical problems, we can turn to ideology." Matzada similarly complained that "the young who come to KLAF are made to feel unwelcome. The younger women who come want to be around other lesbians and discuss issues like coming out to one's parents." She defined herself as a feminist, which for her meant "believing in equal rights," but not the type of feminism espoused in her view by the "older" women in KLAF.

As in other countries, relations between the wider women's movement and the lesbian community have not always been smooth and here lesbian feminists faced the same marginalization and homophobia that their gay male counterparts faced. As the anonymous author wrote in her 1998 article about straight feminists and lesbians in Israel, "The lesbians were present-absentees:[44] Their presence in different struggles was impressive and their contribution central. . . . But, for the most part, they couldn't and dared not give expression to their identity and needs as lesbians."[45] In fact, lesbian feminists were (and are) subject to triple oppression in their work: as women in a sexist society, as lesbians in the women's community, and as lesbians in the "lesbian and gay community."

Activist Chaya Shalom established KLAF in 1987, following a feminist conference abroad the previous year where she saw lesbians from Asia and Africa organizing in their countries. As she mused to herself at the time, "How can this not be happening in Israel?" KLAF filled both a social and political need for many Israeli lesbians. The women's movement was quite homophobic at the time, fearful of being identified with lesbians because of concerns about hurting further its not very positive image among the Israeli public.

Yet, the Aguda, notes Avital Yarus-Chakak, was "very male-identified" and did not make room for women. Another long-time activist, Chana Klein, joined the Aguda soon after its founding in 1975. By 1978 most of the women then active in the Aguda broke away because of both personal and political disputes. As Klein put it, "The Aguda had rules that we did not agree to. We wanted a 50–50 split in power within the organization. Most of the people who kept the Aguda going were women, but there was only one woman on the board."

Despite the early emphasis on ideology, KLAF was not publicly very active on gay rights concerns, leaving women interested in advancing these issues with a dilemma: should they cast their lot with KLAF, which was working at internal community building through cultural events and women's discussion groups, as well as feminist politics, or should they work for political change for lesbians and gay men by joining the male-dominated Aguda? Susan Kirshner and Liora Moriel joined the Aguda— and led it to many successes—because KLAF at the time (the early 1990s) was not doing extensive political work and they wanted to contribute to political progress. As women, however, they did not always have an easy time, they say.

Kirshner recalls little understanding of women's issues within the Aguda and even derision toward them. As an example, she points to the issue of ticket pricing for various events. When she suggested that the prices might be beyond the reach of many Israeli lesbians, the response was that women earn as much as men, even though in Israel, as in many other countries, this is objectively not true. There was insensitivity toward other issues, as well, ones that women's organizations are often more aware of. Like wine sales. Kirshner recalls how, at one Aguda annual meeting, there was a vendor selling wine. When she raised the issue with some of the Aguda's gay male activists, the response, she claims, was 1) why should we care? and 2) any recovering alcoholics present need not drink.

Moriel remembers how, in 1994, the Aguda extended more support and enthusiasm to No'am Meiri's *He Has Words of His Own*, a critically acclaimed play portraying the life experiences of gay men, than to an evening of women's culture called *Hot Night* in whose organization Moriel played a critical role. Looking back, she comments that "there is no vision of encouraging women within the Aguda." Current Aguda activists claim that they want more women involved, and in the summer of 1998 the organization hired its first female executive director, Luba Fein.

Amalia Ziv suggests that feminism remains comparatively unpopular in Israel, with an unwillingness by many women to identify as *feminists*, even if, in fact, they hold to feminist positions on various political and social issues. She attributes the relatively more advanced state of gay rights to percentages. "Fifty percent of society is female. Thus, feminism can be seen as threatening because of the numbers involved. Gays and lesbians constitute a smaller percentage of the population and thus appear less threatening." Perhaps the challenge posed by the Israeli gay and lesbian rights movement is more theoretical to the average Israeli, in the absence (until recently) of a visible and organized community.

Thoughts on "The Second Israel"

The ethnic divide is the most complex one to analyze. While KLAF activists are self-conscious about the lack of Mizrachiot in their ranks, the reaction I received most often when I raised the issue of relations between Mizrachim and Ashkenazim within the community was denial: denial that there ever was a problem and denial that such a problem exists today. The denials that I heard were more striking because many of them came from Mizrachim themselves.

Most of Israel's Mizrachim arrived in the 1950s and 1960s, following the birth of Israel, the hostility of the Arab and Muslim world to the new Jewish state and the problem that posed for the Jews in their midst, and the collapse of French colonialism in North Africa. They came, in the main, from tradition-minded backgrounds to a revolutionary society that was full of the certitudes of socialism and disdainful of religion.

Like other immigrants, the Mizrachim were housed in spartan conditions in their new homeland, often sent to development towns on the edge of nowhere to build up the new state's periphery. Some of them arrived illiterate in any language. The children of the Mizrachim, educated in Israel in the ways of the secular Zionist movement, often rebelled against the traditional ways of their parents, creating great familial and social dislocation in their communities. In the case of the North African immigration, the difficulties they had in adjusting to their new homeland were aggravated by the fact that those communities' educated classes immigrated, in the main, to France or Canada rather than Zion. Their culture, based of course on the Arab and Islamic cultures of which they were a part, was derided in an Israel at war with the Arab world. Even into the 1980s their music was derided by the predominantly Ashkenazi cultural establishment as "bus station music," a reference to the stands around the old Tel Aviv Central Bus Station that sold such cassettes. These cultural differences and educational disadvantages turned the Mizrachim into the "Second Israel," an Israel with values different from those of secular Ashkenazi Zionism, an Israel whose homecoming to Zion proved marginalizing.

In the early 1970s a group of young Moroccan Jews formed the Black Panthers, a short-lived protest movement against the deprivation many

Mizrachim experienced. In a still-remembered incident, then-prime minister Golda Meir dismissed them as "not nice." Such rejection from the Labor Party establishment brought the Mizrachim into the Likud Party, bringing the election of Israel's first Likud government in 1977. The Likud-Mizrachi alliance remained a force in Israeli politics until 1999, when growing numbers of Mizrachim turned to Shas as their protest vehicle.

The problems between Ashkenazim and Mizrachim are not primarily race- or color-motivated, although such prejudice also exists. Rather, economics and the rejection of their culture and adherence to tradition in the state's early years shaped these tensions. And, in recent years, some of the previous inequities have ameliorated. Gaps in education and income levels between Mizrachim and Ashkenazim have narrowed, although they are still too wide. Today there exists significant levels of intermarriage between the two groups. Finally, the Mizrachim have become a force in Israeli politics and culture, whether former president Yitzhak Navon, former Likud defense minister and Center Party leader Yitzhak Mordechai, or the many performers who have turned so-called bus station music into a hugely popular genre.

With these types of still unsolved social tensions in Israeli society, I began this book expecting to find similar tensions within the gay community. I found little evidence of such tensions, however. If anything, Mizrachim play a significant role in Israeli gay politics. Aguda chairs Avi Sofer and Itzik Yosha are both of Mizrachi descent, as is Asiron chair Sa'ar Natanel and lesbian activists Chaya Shalom, Avital Yarus-Chakak, and Tel Aviv City Council member Michal Eden. And although the stereotype is that Mizrachim are more conservative about homosexuality, I quickly saw that it was difficult to make that generalization, whether with regard to coming out to Mizrachi parents or in politics.

The reason the Mizrachi issue might be on the surface a nonissue lies in three factors, I believe: 1) the basic issues of discrimination that the gay community needed to rectify before it could begin to coalesce; 2) the socioeconomic background of many, if not most, of the interviewees for this book—middle-class and/or well-educated, and possessing a strong lesbian/gay identity, which supplants other identifications; and 3) the lessening (although not disappearance) of such ethnic tensions within the wider Israeli society. At the same time, the perception that gay and lesbian organizations are elitist and unattractive to Mizrachim of working-class backgrounds remains. And there may be a wish to deny the existence of such problems, based on the "We're All Jews" ethos that still prevails in parts of Israeli society. As the community becomes more rooted, it will be interesting to see whether the ethnic tensions of the wider society penetrate the community as well. Michal Eden, for one, postulated to me that the issue hadn't arisen because the community itself is so young. Those who identify with the community, she added, tend to place sexual orientation at the top of their list of identifications.

Gay Rights Go Local

The Yarus-Chakaks both pointed out to me that the feminist and gay/lesbian movements share one common problem: while legislation on women's and gay issues is, on paper, among the most progressive in the world, both groups must deal with societies that are still quite conservative. MK Yael Dayan tried to minimize this gap. She seemed to feel that Israel's progressive legislative agenda on both sets of issues was the real story and that translating legislation into social change and acceptance in society at large was an issue hardly unique to Israel.

Dayan is largely correct in her analysis. The changes wrought so far in the Knesset and the courts are slowly are working their way down and leading to broader social changes. Although Hadar Namir complained to me that the changes at the top have yet to penetrate downward, one noticeable change has been the spread of lesbian and gay activism from Tel Aviv to other cities "in the periphery," as anywhere outside of the greater Tel Aviv metropolitan area is labeled. The growth of such activism has the potential to create a more diverse and rooted lesbian and gay community.

Haifa, the birthplace of Israel's women's movement, nurtured an active, albeit small, lesbian community from the 1970s onward. Organized activity for gay men was slower in coming. In November 1991 a group called New Line sprang up and met weekly, under professional guidance, serving as a discussion group for gay men. From that beginning New Line expanded its activities to organizing parties and bringing in new people. The group had ties with the Aguda but was not a formal arm of the Tel Aviv–centered organization.

Soon, the group invested in a phone line that gave out information on gay-related activities in the Haifa area. At this point New Line formally approached the Aguda and asked for help in renting a place of its own. The Aguda agreed, and the Haifa group became a formal arm of the Aguda. The Aguda covered the group's rent and, in return, the group turned over all moneys raised from its activities to Tel Aviv.

As is the case in Tel Aviv, the Haifa branch of the Aguda enjoys good relations with the Haifa municipality. The current mayor, Amram Mitzna, was elected three years ago following his retirement from the military, where, as head of the army's Central Command (which has responsibility for the West Bank), he earned a liberal reputation as a result of his dovish views about the Palestinian issue. Tal Weisberg-Bloch, the chair of the Aguda's Haifa branch, says that Mitzna agreed to meet with representatives of Haifa's gays and lesbians and the group received city funding for its help line. When the Aguda inaugurated its new community center in Haifa in 1996, the deputy mayor was on hand to offer the city's congratulations. Today, the Aguda's Haifa branch receives 15,000 shekels (roughly $3,700) annually from the city government.

I myself met with Mitzna, whose office happens to look out on one of the city's cruising parks, in March 1998. The mayor reflects the reality of the Israeli elite's dealings with gay issues: he knows he is supposed to be liberal and open-minded on the subject, but, at an emotional level, His Honor admitted to me that "I won't say I understand [homosexuality] or that I'd be happy if my son were gay." At the same time, however, Mitzna is adamant that "no one has the right to 'distribute' rights. The right of a person to be equal is a given." For the mayor it was natural that he would support gay rights—he asserted that Haifa is a center of tolerance, where Jews and Arabs, secular and religious, live together in relative harmony. Adding gays and lesbians to this mix was no problem for the mayor.

A contrast to liberal, tolerant Haifa is Beer Sheva, a city of over one hundred thousand people in Israel's Negev desert. To borrow from Gertrude Stein, "There's no 'there' there." When they were involved in the Aguda, Liora Moriel and Susan Kirshner, who lived in the town of Meitar outside the city, founded the Negev Group to bring together gays and lesbians in Israel's southern periphery. For years I corresponded with a pen pal who lived in Beer Sheva, and I had visited the city several times. In the seven years that had elapsed since my last visit the city had metamorphosed into a boom town, thanks to immigration from the former Soviet Union. Today, Beer Sheva boasts a Hilton and a gleaming mall across the street from the Central Bus Station, both signs of the economic revolution Israel has undergone.

I met Shimon Zisk, a thirty-five-year-old building planning engineer, at the mall's Kapulsky's (a chain of cafés). He began talking at a rapid clip and my note-taking hand struggled to keep up. He had kept the Negev Group propped up for a couple of years after Liora Moriel and Susan Kirshner left for America, but the gay citizens of Beer Sheva were deep in the closet and the group did not last.

In its place Sagol, a student group at Ben Gurion University, formed. Zisk said, however, that gay life in Beer Sheva continued to be very closeted and revolved mostly around cruising the city's public parks. It was not easy to meet anyone, he complained, but work kept him in the city. Shmulik Ben-Menachem (a pseudonym), a journalist who had lived in the city, told me that gay life in Beer Sheva was sorely lacking. Sagol, said this journalist, drew the same ten to fifteen people to its meetings. Moreover, it was acceptable to be gay and married in the city, and people were "afraid to be seen in daylight." He painted an even more grim picture in an article he wrote for *Chad Pa'ami* in 1998. One line from his piece summed up well the suffocating atmosphere of the city for its gay residents: "In a city like Beer Sheva, you can tell me that I'm black or white, you can even call me affectionately or dismissively *ars*[46] or Ashkenazi hunk of soap,[47] but never, ever call me gay."[48]

The problem with Beer Sheva is that it has the worst of both worlds. Dominated by more conservative Russians and Mizrachim, it lacks the liberal attitudes associated with cities like Tel Aviv or Haifa. And while Jerusalem, too, is a conservative city increasingly dominated by the ultra-Orthodox, it benefits from a steady trickle of progressive immigrants who have left their marks on the gay and lesbian communities.

In Jerusalem, the Asiron provided one base for an expanding community, although in Israel's capital there has long been lesbian-feminist activity. The Asiron has chosen a different path for organizing. The group has no formal membership because, says El-Ad, "It's simply too bureaucratic." Most weekly meetings draw sixty to seventy participants. The group, as a student organization, can use university facilities but does not receive funding from the student government or other university sources. El-Ad explains that, while American college campuses provide fertile ground for all types of student social and political organizations, Israeli campuses boast little in the way of extracurricular student activities, perhaps because most students can begin their studies only after having completed their mandatory two or three years of basic military service and are subsequently older. He also points out that the largest organizations on campus are affiliated with Israeli political parties, which provide funding and support for their campus affiliates. At weekly meetings featuring lectures, films, or discussions the group asks attendees for a five-shekel contribution. In 1997, when the group organized the first-ever Jerusalem Pride, it found outside support from the New Israel Fund and received a free full-page advertisement courtesy of the Jerusalem weekly *Kol ha-Ir*.

A gay and lesbian community center opened in March 1999. That such an idea has taken root in the Holy City owes much to the wider political changes in Israeli society. On a June evening in Jerusalem a group of twenty people sit in the spacious stone home of Eli, a Jerusalem architect, accessible by climbing up a wrought iron staircase and walking across a footpath. Four of those present are lesbians. The purpose of the meeting: to strategize how best to establish a gay and lesbian community center in the Holy City, alongside those already in existence in the coastal and more liberal cities of Tel Aviv and Haifa. The organizers, including American-born psychologist Jerry Levinson, hoped that the center would provide a home for the gay, lesbian, and bisexual community and also serve as a center for tolerance and pluralism in Jerusalem.

The idea for the center is still young that night, and those present are earnestly debating the best structure for turning the idea into reality. Some want to establish an independent nonprofit, while others believe that the fledgling group should affiliate with the Tel Aviv–based Aguda and work within its more established framework. The group ultimately votes to set up an independent nonprofit. Considering the volume at which Israelis usually debate ideas, I am impressed by the soothing tones and carefully reasoned arguments. A farther cry from Israel's Knesset you'd be hard-pressed to find.

When we first met, Levinson estimated that the group would need $500,000 to buy a place of its own and maintain it. In 1998 the group received a $15,000 grant from the New Israel Fund and found a very visible central location on the Ben-Yehuda Pedestrian Mall. The center, he says optimistically, could provide space for lesbian and gay religious Jews and for gay and lesbian Palestinians in the city. And in the months since our first conversation there is some evidence for Levinson's optimism. The Jerusalem Open House hosted a group of gays from Jordan who sought out the center on their own. Some of the city's Palestinians also have come to the group, but the Open House is only beginning to deal seriously with diversity issues. Although the welcome mat is out and intentions are good, coping practically with different national and religious issues may be more complicated than the group's activists acknowledge.

Nevertheless, the Jerusalem Open House is off to a strong start. Unlike most organizations in the gay and lesbian community in Israel, the Jerusalem Open House has worked hard at bringing in women, and they occupy leadership roles in the organization. The group has established strong ties with the Jerusalem chapter of KLAF, and lesbian activists in the city like Avivit and Gali themselves expressed enthusiasm for the Jerusalem Open House's work.

Organizers hope to raise some of the funds among gay and lesbian Jews overseas but also from Israelis, straight and gay. Levinson says that "we're a sexy issue right now for liberal secular Israelis concerned about pluralism. I am optimistic that we can work for pluralism and tolerance toward minorities in Jerusalem."

Looking over these assorted pieces, what likely accounts for some of the success of Israeli activists is not simply The Mantra, but their pragmatism and their pursuit of a mainstream approach—a strategy that some might condemn as "assimilationist." A 1997 article in *Ha'aretz* summarizing the types of music played on the country's radio stations until recently could summarize equally well Israel's gay politics: "Whoever doesn't stand in the middle of the road doesn't go anywhere."[49] But, rather than assimilationist, the strategy that gay and lesbian Israelis have pursued is a realistic one. They have taken the measure of their society and political system and know that their society is conservative in many ways. Gay and lesbian activists also know how to use the political process and exploit its quirks, even if it means quiet backroom dealings and understandings and working closely with heterosexual members of Knesset.

The mainstream approach is due partially, as well, to the weak underpinnings of individualism in Israeli society. Individualism as a value is of recent vintage for most Israelis, as Amalia Ziv notes. Most of them were educated in schools, youth movements, and the military to think of the common good rather than their own self-actualization.

There are a variety of explanations for the growth of individualism. Many point to the Yom Kippur War in October 1973—a war that Israel failed to anticipate—as a turning point. The war caused great disillusionment in the country's leaders and ideals and led many to begin questioning the sociopolitical consensus that had existed until then. I actually would point to an equally provocative economic factor. One of the legacies of the late Likud prime minister Menachem Begin was economic populism. In the months leading up to the country's 1981 elections, Begin's finance minister, Yoram Aridor, slashed taxes on televisions, electronics goods, and airline tickets. The sudden discount in products that had been economically out of reach for many Israelis led to a mass buying and travel frenzy (which cost the country dearly after the election). The long-term consequences were more subtle but no less important: the opening up of Israel to outside influences, including social influences like lesbian and gay rights.

Not surprisingly, Israel's activists, even those with a self-proclaimed "radical" bent like Hadar Namir and KLAF as a whole, do not try to pursue utopia. Gay and lesbian Israelis, activists and ordinary citizens alike, until recently tended to want to blend into Israeli society rather than emphasize their distinctiveness and difference. They wanted to be Israelis who happen to love members of their own gender.

Israeli activists, even those imbued with a more radical vision, conscientiously chose until recently to present the "nice face" of the community to the Israeli public. As Hadar Namir put it to me, "On an intellectual level, I'm a radical, but I'm also practical. I went with the liberal approach of 'salami tactics.' " Similarly, Tal Yarus-Chakak, despite her activism in an organization that takes a very expansive ideological approach to social change, acknowledges the importance of first showing a group's similarity before focusing on some of the differences.

In showing how much gays and lesbians are "just like everyone else," Israeli gays and lesbians have won some significant victories for the community as a whole, setting the stage perhaps for one that is more diverse to ultimately emerge and benefit from rights won by the community's nice face.

In the Israeli context, considering the extent that lesbians and gay men experienced marginalization until recently, the go-for-broke, top-down politics approach might have been the only realistic option. Amit Kama, the Aguda's former executive director, set out his view of the options to me in calculated terms: "I'd rather be working for a law that potentially down the road will benefit three hundred thousand people than establishing a support group that might help forty or fifty people right now." Although such an analysis might sound harsh at first glance, Kama's strategy was unassailably smart for the time. Because Israel is a small country, where the ability to maintain one's anonymity is limited, it was never realistic to expect a critical mass of people to come out and establish a separate community with its own culture in the absence of political and legal change.

The proof that this approach has merit comes in the issues that the Aguda currently includes in its agenda. Gil Nader, Amit Kama's successor, worked to establish a transgender support group in the Aguda. A few years ago the Aguda would not have touched the issue, out of fear of what it might do to its image. But in a country whose state-operated broadcasting authority voted to send transsexual singer Dana International to represent Israel in the 1998 Eurovision Song Contest it is now is perfectly legitimate for the Aguda to concern itself with such problems.

The Aguda even led a demonstration in front of a Tel Aviv beauty salon that refused to cut transsexuals' hair in the summer of 1998. When I spoke again with Sheizaf in September 1998, just prior to the Jewish new year, he mentioned a real change in attitude: "While I feared on the one hand some negative response from the public and politicians at large [to being inclusive of transsexuals], I had to weigh it against the notion of gays pushing part of the community into the closet." He attributed the Aguda's willingness to include transsexual issues to the growing strength of the community, giving Aguda the confidence, in turn, to push such issues to the fore.

Similarly, in March 1998 Yael Dayan's Knesset committee convened to discuss, with the Aguda's active participation, the problem of minors engaging in homosexual prostitution. A few years ago, when the Aguda and other groups were struggling to change society's perceptions of gay men and lesbians, few would have worried about such an unseemly problem, particularly one that exposed a less than wholesome segment of the gay community. Today one primary goal of the Aguda is to establish a hostel for homeless gay youth, in hopes of lessening the need for such youth, often kicked out of their homes by their parents, to support themselves through prostitution. The recent burst of AIDS activism from within the gay community similarly demonstrates how the community can now concern itself with issues it once shunted aside as it struggled over some that were more basic.

The other proof of this approach's success is the expansion of lesbian and gay organization to cities outside Tel Aviv. The legitimacy bestowed by the Knesset, the courts, and the media on the lesbian and gay community has encouraged at least grudging social tolerance of gays and lesbians, enabling lesbian and gay groups to develop even in small towns like Hadera or in more conservative cities such as Beer Sheva.

A final and interesting ingredient of gay activism in Israel is the active support of straight people. Long before the Aguda emerged from the shadows in 1988,[50] following repeal of the country's sodomy law and before Yael Dayan's election to the Knesset in 1992, politicians from the Citizens Rights Movement Party (now part of the Meretz Party) lobbied for sodomy law repeal and equal rights for the country's gay citizens. In fact, as academic Yuval Yonai notes in an article exploring the repeal of that sodomy law, "Despite the wish to bring repeal of the [sodomy] law, the community was almost completely uninvolved in attempts to achieve this change."[51]

This involvement stems from a strong streak of support for "individual rights" among the Israeli political and social elite, which stands out because of the lack of a clear consensus in support of equality for other groups in Israeli society. The Israeli establishment in both politics and the media, characterized by its strong Western outlook, pushes for gay rights out of all proportion to the relatively small size of the active, self-identified gay community. While the record on gay rights is impressive, it is a low-cost issue for the Israeli political system, as the gay community does not challenge the consensus and because of the community's small size. The push for gay rights masks more difficult social issues, like the status of Palestinian citizens of Israel.

Now that it has achieved basic discrimination protections, the lesbian and gay community, benefiting from the fragmenting of Israeli society into tribes and the growing legitimacy of identity politics, can push for its own vision without the risk of great social or political backlash. The only thing unusual about this is that the lesbian and gay community, unlike other newly empowered groups, enjoys close ties with, and the support of, the traditional Israeli elites.

But developments over the past decade have left activists free to push in new directions. There is little danger that the victories they've won could be suddenly overturned by Knesset vote or government action. The achievement of basic civil rights protections has left Israeli activists free to turn to the struggle to create a more developed community.

2

Yotzim m'ha-Aron: Coming Out

In a world progressing toward the 2000s . . . homosexuality and lesbianism . . . no longer represent a perversion that needs to be denounced, condemned and fought.
—Israeli Supreme Court in *Society for the Protection of Personal Rights v. Minister of Education, Culture, and Sport*, 1997

Blonds among Jews aren't normal either.
—Devora Luz, coordinator of Tehila, Israeli Parents and Friends of Lesbians and Gays, on the program *Open Cards*, 1997

Hadar, an eleventh grader from the Tel Aviv area, and her girlfriend of three months, a twelfth grader from Jerusalem who prefers to remain nameless, met through Hamon Aliza,[1] a group for young lesbians organized under the auspices of the Aguda. They're waiting that Wednesday evening in June for Hamon Aliza's meeting to begin in the Aguda's spacious community center.

Both young women have come out to their parents. Hadar's have been the more supportive, with her mother encouraging her to attend the group's activities. She has also told some of her friends in her high school about her identity. Her girlfriend has had less support from her family, and she hesitates to tell friends at her more conservative Jerusalem high school. They both worry about their upcoming military service, less because of their sexual orientation and more because of the separation it will impose on them as well as the relative lack of interesting jobs for women soldiers in the military. Even with their difficulties, the two young women are part of a growing phenomenon of young Israelis discovering their sexual orientation at an earlier age, looking for and finding support, and helping influence society's perceptions of what it means to be lesbian or gay in Israel.

At the same time, Israeli society, through its educators and the media, is hardly indifferent to the issues surrounding coming out and, to the extent that it deals with these issues at all, is working to channel the way young people come out and develop their sense of lesbian or gay identity. It seeks to contain the seeds of lesbian/gay separatism by inculcating the notion that gays and lesbians are "just like everyone else" and that sexual orientation is an individual trait, not the basis for a separate community. This approach seems to encourage at least superficial notions of "tolerance" while at the same time reducing social alienation, more of which Israel cannot afford. This approach, as seen in chapter 1, has contributed to lesbian and gay political success while slowing the internal development of a rooted gay community.

To come out in Israel means coming out—period. If Americans view the closet as a cramped uncomfortable space, the living room in Israel isn't much more spacious. It is only in the past two or three years that a broad-based lesbian and gay community has emerged. The farthest gays and lesbians in Israel can move is from Metulla to Eilat, roughly from one end of New Jersey to the other. Not that such moves are common. Israel, because of both social conditioning and the country's small geographic space, is not a highly mobile society. Not only is physical distance small but so is psychic distance. The Jewish community in Palestine prior to the birth of Israel was known as the *yishuv* (settlement, community). The name hints at the closeness of Israel's Jewish inhabitants. Israeli sociologist Oz Almog, in his 1997 work, *The Sabra—A Portrait*, could point out that "Jewish identity, with its historical baggage, cultural and economic isolation in a hostile expanse, the shared traumas and uniting mourning rituals of the entire people—all these strengthened the intimate character of life in Israel."[2]

The extent of Israeli society's intimacy became apparent for Ilan Vitemberg, the former chair of the Aguda's Haifa branch. Vitemberg, a former kibbutznik, returned to Israel in September 1996 with his American partner after several years of study in the United States. One night the two of them happened upon the gay and lesbian community center in Haifa. Upon entering the center, Vitemberg came face-to-face in short order with one former boyfriend, a high school classmate, and *five* soldiers from the building where he worked while in the military. I experienced something of the same sense of intimacy many times in the course of this research. Attending a lesbian theater production in Jerusalem one evening, I easily knew about 20 percent of the audience after only one week in the city.

While the enforced intimacy of Israeli society impacts coming out, so does the importance of family. Gay Israelis are divided about what that impact is, however. Those with supportive families, not surprisingly, tend to take a positive view. On the other hand, Chagai El-Ad and David Meiri, a couple, and both graduate students at the Hebrew University in Jerusalem who enjoy the support of their families, speculate that the emphasis on family in Israeli society can delay coming out of the closet, because of the fear of losing the support of one's family. This is no small matter in a country where parents often buy their child his or her first apartment and even college students typically return home to their families on the weekend. Tal and Avital Yarus-Chakak, longtime activists in KLAF, Israel's major lesbian organization, and the parents of three young sons, also point to the possibly negative impact that family ties have on coming out. Tal: "Family is the big limiting factor for people. Even as acceptance grows, [being lesbian or gay] is still not a big source of pride. It stands out."

Coming out in such a society has implications beyond the individual involved, of course. As Yuval Yonai, a Haifa University sociologist, could note, "Many activists explain that, as opposed to many Americans who can move to big cities where no one knows them, the Israeli lesbian or gay man who moves to Tel Aviv certainly may meet the neighbor's son from the small town when they go to the gay bar, or the aunt doing her shopping when they sign a petition on the street."[3] Some argue that the close-knit ties of Israeli society create a special Israeli coming out dynamic whose overall effect is positive. Amir Somkai-Fink, writing in the May 1997 edition of *Ha-Zman ha-Varod*, Israel's self-styled queer monthly, states:

> In Israeli society, in which there never were true community ghettos, it's impossible to create a phenomenon of coming out on the basis of a supportive gay community. Israeli coming out is not involved in moving to San Francisco or New York. Often not even to Tel Aviv. We as Israelis are forced to come out of the closet in our natural environment and thus, it's a quieter coming out in its character, but penetrates more deeply into hearts. There's nowhere to run away to in this country, and whoever stays lives his life and learns in a short time that it's not possible to hide. From the moment he starts to come out, he becomes an agent of all gays.[4]

The Nesher High School, outside of Haifa, is a laboratory of sorts for Somkai-Fink's theory. It's Sunday morning, and a noisy stream of students is making its way into the building, dressed collectively in torn jeans, Chicago Bulls T-shirts, and Fila sneakers. On the way up the hill to the school, Tal Weisberg-Bloch stops to give a lift to a gay student in the eleventh grade, Chaim (a pseudonym), a tall, shaggy-haired young man, who comes to various social events in Haifa such as the annual Pride Cruise.

The halls of the school are decorated with student artwork, posters warning against motorbike accidents and drug use ("Drugs Throw You Out of Society and Endanger Your Freedom"), and posters decorated with pictures of Arabs and Jews calling for tolerance, a societal buzz-word since the murder of Prime Minister Yitzhak Rabin in November 1995.

Weisberg-Bloch and Tami, a twenty-seven-year-old Haifa lesbian, are at Nesher High to speak to the eleventh-grade class about being gay and lesbian in Israel. While coming out is rarely easy, what seems to distinguish the Israeli experience in the past few years is the growing availability of school discussion of homosexuality as well as independent youth groups for gay and lesbian adolescents. The school principal has invited the pair through the Aguda's and KLAF's lecture services. Invitations to lesbians and gays to address the country's high school students often come in the context of high school civics curricula rather than through sex education classes. The idea is to instill tolerance for difference in Israeli high school students, as part of a broader effort to ensure the health of the country's still-young democratic institutions. A by-product of the lectures is to encourage straight students to accept their gay and lesbian counterparts.

Haifa, a northern port city that some label "Israel's San Francisco" because of its hills and bay, always has had a liberal reputation. In the past it was known as "Red Haifa" because of its socialist ethos. Weisberg-Bloch and lesbian activist Yael Zaks had met several months earlier through the Aguda's lecture service with Devora Ezra, director of the Education Department in Haifa's municipal government, and with Dr. Dalia Lorentz, an Education Ministry official in Haifa and coauthor of a ministry booklet for educators on gay issues.[5] The two activists received their blessing to go into the area's schools, provided that the Aguda initiated the contacts and confined their outreach to the secular school system.[6]

As suits a civics class, Weisberg-Bloch and Tami first set out ground rules for the day's discussion: "I'm gay and Tami's lesbian. That's why we're here. You can ask any question, give any view, whatever comes into your head. I ask for your respect—between us, and between each of you and the rest of your classmates. We'll keep things on a civilized level that way." They also write the telephone numbers of hotlines run by the Aguda and KLAF.

After some preliminaries about the Aguda and KLAF, including the existence of the Aguda's youth groups for lesbian and gay teens in Haifa, Weisberg-Bloch and Tami then proceed to present their life stories. I've heard the thirty-eight-year-old Weisberg-Bloch's before. Previously married to a woman, father of two boys aged fourteen and eleven, employed by a high-tech firm, and currently married to his partner of seven years, Yoel. He inserts a bit of humor, noting that he and his partner are trying to get pregnant but haven't been successful yet. The quip draws laughter, some of it nervous. He sums up their relationship as "we have a house, joint overdraft and mortgage, joint quarrels, and lots of love."

Tami says that she's an engineer, has never been married heterosexually, and has a girlfriend. The two of them have a joint mortgage.

I came out earlier, at the age of twenty-one, before getting involved with guys and marrying. I can go back to five or six years old and see glimmers of my future lesbianism. I couldn't deal with it until I was twenty, though. In high school, I had a boyfriend and was satisfied. But something didn't add up inside of me. I felt a lot of confusion and had to stew in my juices until I could admit that I was attracted to girls. I thought that perhaps I'm bi. At one point I made a deal with myself: "Whoever wins my heart first, that'll be that." That lasted two weeks. I finally cracked and told a close friend. I thought that it would be an earthquake, that she'd freak. But she just said, "OK."

The introductions completed, they open the floor to the thirty-five to forty students crowded into the classroom. The students appear to be a fairly broad cross-section of Israeli Jewish society. Native-born and immigrants, Ashkenazim and Mizrachim, even one student wearing the knitted yarmulke of the modern Orthodox (most religious students study in the parallel state-religious school system). The students are in a vocational high school track rather than one for the university bound.

The first question, directed at Weisberg-Bloch, comes from one of the young men: How do you deal with your children? He explains that he has been coming out gradually to them over the years, in terms that they can understand. They've always come to visit him and Yoel and see them go to sleep in the same bedroom—he's even translated the American book

Daddy's Roommate into Hebrew for them. When they were younger, he used to tell them that he and Yoel were "men who love men." Gradually, he introduced them to the term *gay.*

The follow-up question, from the same student, is predictable: If one of your boys is gay, will you feel guilty about it? Weisberg-Bloch goes into civics mode: "As a society, we need to accept differences—red-haired persons, Ethiopians, Russian immigrants, gays. There's the basic right of everyone to happiness." He then turns more personal. "My life as a gay man isn't easy. It's become a lot easier. What I do choose is to live as a gay man, to come out, to give and get love as a gay man. I hope that if one of my sons is gay, he'll be able to come to me and discuss it earlier than I was able to."

Yishai, the yarmulke-wearing student who is carrying a cellular telephone attached to a rabbit's foot key chain, raises the religious issue: "God created you to be with a woman and then you toss it all aside to be with a man. You had two kids. Couldn't you restrain yourself? Isn't this sort of [expletive] up?" After assuring the students that they can use any words they want to express themselves, including expletives, Weisberg-Bloch turns to the issue at hand.

> God created me as a gay man. My decision is to accept myself. It may not be normative to be gay but it is normal. I'm not going to debate religion, because I can't. My debate is more principled. I don't accept the Bible like you do. The prohibition [on homosexuality in Leviticus] stems from the homosexuality-based idol worship among other peoples at the time that the Bible was written.

Tami offers a more pointed retort: "What's natural? It would be natural for us to live naked in the jungle. I don't think that sex is always designed to lead to procreation."

A young woman with a pierced nose asks the two lecturers how their parents deal with their sexual orientation. Tami, who is lecturing only for her second time, is less loquacious than Weisberg-Bloch. She says that "my family is OK. My partner's family isn't. They can't deal with the issue at all. She told them when she was sixteen. I can't ever go to their house. It's very unpleasant." Weisberg-Bloch, whose own family is very supportive, waxes a bit philosophical. "This is the hardest part. It doesn't matter what age you are. We all need family. There's a basic need to know that there's always a place to go where we can feel secure and loved."

The discussion between the two activists and the students finishes with another civic-minded appeal from Weisberg-Bloch: "Tolerance, talking, and accepting differences are what you should take out of here. Let's help each other out. For gay youth your age, there are a lot of problems. In addition to all the problems of adolescence, they have the additional problem of coping with their surroundings. Think about how you can be tolerant and help. Accept." He then asks them whether they know any lesbian or gay people. I hold my breath for a minute, because Chaim, the gay student whom we gave a lift to earlier, is sitting right in the classroom. He has not come out yet to any of his classmates. Two people raise their hands slightly. Chaim is not among them.

Nine months later I was back at Nesher High. The school was preparing for Israel's fiftieth anniversary celebrations, and I couldn't help but notice the rainbow-colored jubilee poster with a Magen David. Other posters extolled "My Beautiful Land of Israel" and the country's waves of immigration, in which some groups suffered greatly as they tried to assimilate into their new country ("We're All Children of the Tents").

I head first to the office of Ilana Flinker, a twelfth-grade guidance counselor. The Israeli educational system provides advisers for each grade to whom students can turn for counseling or informal advice. The presence of these advisers is ubiquitous and there were a number of students who came in and out of Flinker's office during our interview.

She noted that Nesher is a conservative working-class town, with many students coming from a traditional religious background, 90 percent of whom, in her estimation, identify with the ruling Likud Party. She personally has a long acquaintance with gay people, having been active in the Israeli feminist movement all the way back to the movement's beginnings in the 1970s and counting gay people among her friends. Practical considerations—a gay student who came out at Nesher the previous year—led her to begin raising lesbian and gay issues with students. The first student who came out, she recalled, felt a need to be very public and, in her view, rather in your face about his sexual orientation, putting up announcements about gay events without permission and dressing provocatively. Perhaps because he was the "first," that particular student experienced quite a bit of harassment from his classmates.

The lessons she seeks to impart to her students: tolerance, "acceptance of 'the Other.' " For her, tolerance is part of her Judaism and constitutes a means of reaching those who come from more traditional religious backgrounds. I pressed her on the issue of tolerance, seeking its sources in light of the generally intolerant attitudes (toward Arabs) of many of her students. Flinker attributes the growing tolerance of gays and lesbians to attitudes conveyed by the media, both in its reporting on the subject and through the number of gay-themed entertainment programs on Israeli television such as the acclaimed series *Florentin* (a view that other Israelis, gay and straight, echoed).

Interestingly, Flinker claims that she's received no negative feedback from Nesher parents on discussions of gay issues at the school. Not because parents are necessarily thrilled by such discussions, but because second-guessing educators is not typical. Whereas Limor, a high school teacher and the wife of my longtime pen pal Amnon, recounted to me that she had given students the choice to write a paper about homosexuality in the Middle Ages and had received a complaint from one parent, there has never been in Nesher, or anywhere else in Israel, a movement or parents group formed to stop discussion of homosexuality—or sex education in general—in the schools.

Flinker had a surprise for me at the end of our interview: one of her gay students wanted to sit and talk with me about his experiences as a gay teenager at Nesher. The student turned out to be Chaim, the student to whom Tal Weisberg-Bloch and I had given a lift the previous June and who had since come out to most of his classmates.

While waiting for Chaim, I sat in the hall at Nesher High reading a book and immediately attracted attention. "What are you here at Nesher for?" a group of guys asked me. After some hesitation, I told them I was in Israel researching a book about the gay community and had met with Ilana Flinker. "Oh, we have a gay student in our class. Everyone knows about him," one of them volunteered. I asked them what they thought about gays. "I don't have a problem with it. They don't bother me at all," piped up one young man, with the others nodding in assent. The only negative response came from a young woman with them, who, when I mentioned that I had a partner, asked me, "What do you do in bed?" and then erupted in giggles.

Chaim eventually came along and we went off to talk. I was curious to see just how tolerant he found his high school, whether his views were in accord with the optimistic ones Flinker had fed me. To my surprise, he had a positive take on his school: "The school's liberal. The principal believes in equality, in live and let live." He gave me a copy of the school yearbook, which had an article on gays, an article on AIDS, and one about Israel's 1998 entry for the Eurovision Song Contest, Dana International. In his twelfth-grade class he knew of three other boys and five girls who were gay or lesbian. In fact, his best friend at school, another young man, is also gay (a fact he was surprised to discover at the time). He'd attended the gay youth group in Haifa once, but, as he put it, "I ran out of there. It was so serious."

He was also quite optimistic about his future. He would be enlisting soon in the IDF and hoped that the army would place him in a special academic program from which he'd obtain the rank of officer. He planned to stay in Haifa after completing his army service, telling me that there were plenty of gays in the city and, in any event, he saw no need "to segregate" himself. As for a relationship, he said he didn't feel ready for one, that he was too young to settle down.

Chaim's wish not to segregate himself is the type of view that pleases Israeli educators. Many Israelis, liberal educators included, have a difficult time with the notion of a distinct gay community. Their goal is to integrate gays and lesbians into the fabric of the wider society, not set them apart. One educator with whom I met once piped up, "Why do you talk about 'community?' What do you need a 'community' for? We accept you. You can live with your boyfriend right alongside us."

Educators at a high school in Israel I visited[7] provided me with the results of an exercise that they had done with their students, asking them to write out what came to mind when they heard the word *homosexual,* at the start of a school discussion on gay issues. The responses were quite varied, ranging from "deviant," "abnormal," and "disgust," to "make-up," "anal sex," "special clubs," "hard to think about the subject in a nonsexual way," to "blue and white" (slang for Israeli), "10 percent of the population," and "the religious hate and fear them."

Yet surface (and sometimes contradictory) tolerance reigns. A nineteen-year-old soldier, Yossi Even-Kama (the foster child of gay activists Uzi Even and Amit Kama), gave me a copy of a research survey he'd conducted for a high school project.[8] He distributed questionnaires at four Israeli high schools to twelfth-grade classes: City High School D, in North Tel Aviv, City High School G, a mixed Jewish-Arab school in Jaffa, Denzinger High, in Kiryat Shemona, near the Lebanese border, and the Arab Comprehensive High School in Jaffa. The results, out of a survey of 130 students, were illuminating. Grouped together, 50 percent of the students surveyed agreed that "attraction to one's own sex isn't natural" and a plurality of 40 percent agreed that "a homosexual chooses to be that way." Yet, at the same time, 53 percent felt that gays should be able to adopt and 60 percent agreed that "a gay couple, and the child they adopt, are a family like any other family."[9] The positive attitudes toward gay couples and their offspring existed in the three high schools with Jewish students, with only students in the Arab Comprehensive High School expressing highly negative attitudes toward gays and lesbians.[10] The seeming dichotomy in attitudes between believing that gays and lesbians are not normal and a readiness to permit gays to adopt might stem from the importance Israeli society places on having children. It also likely stems from a view, inculcated increasingly by the schools, that sexual orientation is an individual trait that one should respect even if one doesn't accept it as normal.

The results of Even-Kama's survey for a high school project seem to dovetail with a poll conducted for *Yediot Achronot* in September 1998. The poll, part of an article on today's Israeli youth, showed that 51 percent had a "negative" view of gays and lesbians. Twenty-five percent said they had neither a positive nor negative view, and 23 percent characterized their views as "positive."[11] The poll did not ask questions about discrimination against gays or lesbians or views toward same-sex couples and families.

Another recent study on the attitudes of Israeli youth toward "The Other" by Dr. Devora Karmil, a sociologist, revealed some surprising findings, most notably that 55 percent of the eight hundred teenagers surveyed believe that "the country should recognize gay couples."[12] Such tolerance was the exception, however. Her study, as reported in *Yediot Achronot*, revealed that more than 60 percent of the youth believed that Palestinian citizens of Israel did not deserve equal rights and 73 percent believed that Arab representation in the Knesset endangers Israel's security. More than 68 percent stated that they could never befriend an immigrant from the former Soviet Union. The possible reason for the discrepancy between the seemingly pro-gay and anti-Arab/anti-immigrant beliefs is the positive messages being conveyed about gay people through lectures like Weisberg-Bloch's and Tami's, as well as in the media, as compared to the complicated reality of the Arab-Israeli conflict and the sensationalized portrayal of the immigration from the former Soviet Union. Young Israelis view the Arabs as "competing" for their land and immigrants as competing for their jobs.

I met Karmil over coffee at Arcaffe, one of the many businesses catering to Israel's new moneyed classes in the Ramat Aviv Shopping Mall, to discuss her research, which she conducted as a cross-cultural study with some German researchers. She said that one part of her survey asked students to write down which groups they hate. The answers included Arabs, the religious, tourists, foreign workers, and those with different political views. No one, she told me, included gays and lesbians in their response.

There are several ways of looking at the relatively positive response toward gay couples. First, Karmil's survey did not ask personal questions about attitudes toward gays, such as, "Could you be friends with a gay person?" Rather, the question, which she admitted was a spontaneous addition, dealt with whether "the state"—a more distant entity—should recognize such couples. A second possibility is that the lack of gay social segregation, in the form of separate neighborhoods or political parties, discourages the type of hatred of gays that young Israelis are directing at Arabs or immigrants. She noted that Israeli society is developing more fissures, and Israelis are increasingly alarmed by the trend. The notion of segregating oneself is seen to be very threatening to an already frayed national unity, and the group most successful at creating social segregation for itself, the ultra-Orthodox, is strongly resented. A third and related factor is that Israeli society does not see gays as demanding too much. The demand for equal treatment and equal duties—like the right to serve in the military like everyone else—strikes a chord among Israelis and stands in contrast to the demands of religious and ethnic parties, who demand more and more for their communities' particularistic needs rather than for the benefit of society as a whole.

The efforts at the secondary school level are important, in view of a recently conducted survey of Hebrew University students. The study, conducted by psychologist Daniel Weishut, revealed that most students did not personally know gays and lesbians, while 36 percent of them had ridiculed someone because of his or her perceived sexual orientation. Weishut did find that religiosity correlated with stronger antigay prejudices and that personal acquaintance with gay people led to more favorable attitudes toward lesbians and gay men.[13] By exposing high school students to the issue in high school, educators might be able to reduce the manifestation of such prejudice later on in life. Weishut, it should be noted, did not survey attitudes concerning political issues affecting gays and lesbians, like support for laws prohibiting discrimination on the basis of sexual orientation or recognition of same-sex families. The cumulative results of Even-Kama's, Karmil's and Weishut's surveys suggest a disconnect between personal attitudes toward gays and lesbians and views about discrimination against them. This gap in attitudes may stem from the relative marginality of gay political issues in Israeli political discourse and/or the perceived lack of demands that gays and lesbians make on the state.

The approach of the sex education experts in Israel's Ministry of Education is to teach that homosexuality is normal, even if not the norm.

Chava Barnea, National Sex Education supervisor, and one of the authors of *Same-Sex Orientation (Homosexuality and Lesbianism)*, says that the idea for the booklet, distributed in 1995 to advisers in the country's secular high schools,[14] stemmed from the increased prominence of gay issues in the media and the movies (she cited as examples *The Bird Cage*, screened in 1998 on Israel Television, and *As Good as It Gets*) as well as the lack of material in Hebrew on the subject. In the introduction, Barnea writes that

> Western society, including Israel, has grown more tolerant of behaviors that differ from the norm—we see more movies dealing with the subject, the press reports on events in which gays are involved, the movement for personal rights has fought for equal rights for gays and has won achievements. . . . But, at the interpersonal level, the issue isn't discussed. Adults have a hard time touching the subject, as they fear it and don't know how to deal with it. Students, exposed to the issue, are fed by hearsay, from the press and movies. Thus, they not only don't get reliable answers to their questions but often their feelings of fear, confusion, and stereotypes are strengthened.[15]

The booklet goes on to present an overview of research on same-sex orientation and homophobia, myths about homosexuality, and the coming-out process. There is a chapter dealing with the legal system's approach to homosexuality in Israel, another containing the personal perspectives of the mother of a gay child. Finally, there are group exercises for classes, dealing with the development of internalized messages.

The back of the book contains a series of questions and suggested answers on gay issues. Regarding the question "Are homosexuals normal?" Barnea's booklet counsels:

> If "normal" means "belonging to the majority," then homosexuals are not normal. But if we accept this point, we will be forced to say that those who are left-handed aren't normal, whereas today we accept the physical difference of being a "lefty," as a completely normal phenomenon. Similar to left-handedness, a person's being homosexual does not reduce his humanity, his (or her) normal desire to love, to be loved, to contribute to society, and to succeed in life.[16]

And in response to the question "What can a person who feels he's homosexual do?" Barnea advises:

There's nothing bad in homosexuality, but it's difficult to be gay in our society. If you feel OK about your homosexuality, the only problem you may have is how to "come out of the closet" or to reveal it to others—like to parents. . . . Sometimes, you may want to wait until you're eighteen, or until you're finished with your army service. Even then, it's not easy. If you're having a hard time accepting the fact that you're gay, I recommend going for psychological treatment with a psychologist who accepts homosexuals as they are. Only from such a person can you get the help and encouragement that a young person needs.[17]

The booklet, while an important step forward, has its shortcomings. Most important, it lacks the first-person voice of young gays and lesbians. This reduces gays and lesbians to specimens being studied under a microscope. Instead, Barnea's booklet brings stories of the suffering of parents when they first discovered their children's homosexuality; one mother's story was entitled "I Was Born to Suffer to Death."

All this talk of tolerance and enlightened education never reached the Likud government's now deceased Minister of Education, Zevulun Hammer, however. Hammer, a longtime stalwart of the National Religious Party, tried to ban a program on Educational Television about lesbian and gay youth. This saga began back in November 1996, when the minister took the highly unusual step of overruling the professional advice of Educational Television, which he oversaw, and halted the planned screening of an episode of the *Open Cards* television series. The series features a handsome young emcee named Nativ Robinson, a panel of youth, and a high school–aged audience that asks the panel questions. Each weekly episode features a different topic, ranging from drugs, to cults, to lesbian and gay youth.

Apparently, this last topic was too much for the Orthodox Jewish minister. In January 1997 the Aguda and KLAF, together with ACRI, brought suit against Hammer in the Israeli Supreme Court,[18] claiming that he had exceeded his authority in banning the broadcast of the *Open Cards* episode. A June 24, 1997, hearing at the Israeli Supreme Court demonstrated in which direction the court was heading: the justices gave Hammer fourteen days to consider a compromise proposal that he permit the program to run on television, with a separate program of experts to run afterward, and only then continue legal proceedings; Hammer rejected the proffered compromise in August 1997.[19]

Most remarkable about the hearing was the pro-gay stance of Justice Ya'akov Kedmi, who had issued a minority opinion in 1994 opposing a Supreme Court decision ordering El Al Israel Airlines to grant free plane tickets to the same-sex partners of its gay employees, as it did to hetero-sexual partners.[20] At one point Kedmi interrupted the remarks of State Attorney Yehuda Shefer and demanded, "You are constantly talking about 'problematic,' about a problematic issue. What's the problem?" According to *Ha-Zman ha-Varod*, Justice Kedmi noted the difficulty in coming out of the closet and defined the case as "a matter of youth who dared to come out, to appear on a television program, and only seek to say, 'We're not monsters.' "[21]

In an affidavit replying to the suit, portions of which were reprinted in *Ha-Zman ha-Varod* in May 1997, Hammer stated that the *Open Cards* episode "deals with a subject that is an object of debate among the public, is not balanced from a values and pedagogical standpoint, and does not present the issue to youth watching the program as an educa-tional program." From his preliminary allegations Hammer went on to weightier issues:

> The program ignores a normative values approach that rejects homo-sexual behavior and sees it as a moral flaw. The program ignores col-lective values, such as family and continuity, which are entitled to men-tion in the framework of an educational program. . . . Among the professionals who reviewed the program . . . were those who felt that included in it were direct and indirect messages of encouragement to experiment with homosexual behavior. This opinion is the object of public and scientific dispute and is not suitable for inclusion in a pop-ular educational program broadcast during afternoon hours to many homes in Israel.[22]

Three days before the June 24, 1997, Supreme Court hearing, I found myself seated in the comfortable Tel Aviv apartment of Golan and Dani, together with Aguda executive director Gil Nader and ACRI attorney Dan Yakir, eating Golan's homemade pie and drinking Sprite and Nescafé (seemingly the Israeli national beverage) while watching a tape of the much disputed episode. The episode opened with the black-vested Robin-son introducing the four panelists: Yossi Even-Kama, Shachar Lubin, a gay youth with a Mohawk haircut, Chai Arma, a model and self-pro-claimed bisexual, who proclaimed himself open to most any sexual experience ("I go with whatever's good for me"), and Tami, a twenty-one-year-old lesbian.

Each panelist shared his or her coming-out story, with Yossi Even-Kama being the most articulate of the four participants. He told the audience that he had come out to his mother about his sexual orientation after she had asked him, and how she had cried. Smiling a bit wanly, he added, "All mothers cry." His father had a much more severe reaction to news of his son's sexual orientation. He refused to speak to his son, forced him to get an AIDS test, and refused to be in the same room with him. Soon after, his parents made an agreement with Professor Even and Mr. Kama that their son would live with them.

In addition to the participants, in the audience was Devora Luz, the mother of a gay son and the founder of a group for parents of gay and lesbian children. She recounted how she had learned sixteen years ago that her son was gay. She said that she went through the usual stages that parents go through upon learning of their children's lesbian or gay identity: "How I am guilty. I took the role of God, that I made him like this. I was too controlling. I was afraid that he'd be lonely. I wanted him to go to a psychologist, since I thought it was a phase and his sexuality might not yet be completely developed."

The second half of the program consisted of questions from the audience, ranging from "Is it a problem for you to shower with guys in the army?" to "Are same-sex relationships the same as relationships between men and women?" In a concluding comment Devora Luz made a statement that could only occur in Israel. Discussing the issue of what's "normal," she declared that "blonds among Jews aren't 'normal' either."

Golan, my host and fellow viewer that Saturday afternoon, made an astute observation: "Had Hammer not refused to show this program, everyone would have forgotten about it the following week." I would have to agree. The program was valuable, in that it allowed viewers to see a cross-section of sexual minority youth, but it was not brilliant television.

As the hearing suggested, the Israeli Supreme Court did not find Hammer's arguments convincing. In a September 1997 decision the three-justice panel ordered Hammer and the Ministry of Education to broadcast the program.[23] Justice Kedmi wrote that "the [physical] appearance of the four interviewees was pleasant, their remarks fluent and characterized by a heartwarming honesty, and their positions clear. . . . The general picture drawn from the meeting with them was that gays and lesbians are like all other youth, that nature gave them characteristics that do not put them 'outside the encampment.' "[24] He then proceeded to declare that

in a world progressing toward the 2000s...homosexuality and lesbianism...no longer represent a perversion that needs to be denounced, condemned, and fought....The era in which we live engenders individual
rights and carries the flag of understanding and tolerance toward minorities and those who are different....Like others who are different, [gays
and lesbians] constitute an integral part of our societal framework.[25]

The Israeli youth press also has brought a message of tolerance to its
readership. Shai Kerem, the editor of one of the major youth magazines,
Rosh Echad, views his colorful magazine's main goal as "creating some
fun" for young people who, he says, have to deal with so many difficult
issues growing up in Israel, such as terrorist attacks and the ongoing state
of war with some of Israel's Arab neighbors. At the same time, a review
of some issues of his magazine reveals an ongoing message of tolerance
peeping out from its pages. As he told me one evening in Tel Aviv, "Everyone's a human being and can live as he or she sees fit." One way that
Kerem and his main competitor, *Ma'ariv Lano'ar*, have brought attention
to the gay issue is via the hugely popular transsexual singer, Dana International. Thus, in one issue, Kerem, who has become one of International's managers, wrote a long article about International and her struggle
for acceptance. He wrote that "Dana's victory is a victory for all of us, for
Israeli society. It's the victory of anyone who thinks that people are equal,
that there aren't those who are more equal and those who are less. It's the
victory of anyone who relates to people as human beings."[26]

Kerem's message of individualism couldn't have worked twenty years
ago, he admits. Until the 1970s individualism was frowned upon. "You
couldn't be different," he shrugs, "because you'd be detracting from the
war for survival."

The message of tolerance isn't limited to gays. A review of only a couple of issues of *Rosh Echad* uncovers articles about a Jewish boy living
in a settlement in the Gaza Strip who was rescued by Palestinians after
falling off his horse (the implicit message, without getting into detailed
discussions of the Palestinian-Israeli conflict, is that not all Arabs want
to murder Israelis). Another article dealt with Reform Jews (a soft way
of encouraging religious pluralism by writing about the lives of young Israeli Reform and Conservative Jews, showing that they're not different
from their "secular" counterparts, without getting into the wider incen-
diary issues of religion and state in Israel).[27]

Gay and lesbian youth also can find visibility on the pages of the youth
magazines' advice columnists, although the advice dispensed sometimes

seems a bit befuddled. A sixteen-year-old gay Orthodox youth who wrote to *Ma'ariv Lano'ar* about the pressure he felt he was receiving from his mother and sisters to date girls received the following advice:

> It's clear to me that you have a problem. A youth's coping with a ho-mosexual orientation isn't easy in our society, which remains conser-vative. So much more so in a religious setting, where homosexuality is officially defined as an unacceptable deviancy. . . . I don't know how religious your family is, but I get the impression from your letter that you're free to inform them of your sexual orientation. If so, the only way you have in such circumstances is to play a "neutral game," in other words, make clear to your mother and sisters that you're not in-terested for the time being in a relationship with a girl. . . . In the mean-time, you'll be able to decide how you want to cope with the issue.[28]

The advice column also provided the number of the Aguda's White Line, in case the youth wanted further advice. Kerem indicated to me that *Rosh Echad* takes a similar approach with advice to gay youth, with an emphasis on accepting one's sexual orientation and providing re-sources in the gay community that can help lesbian and gay young peo-ple come to terms with their sexual orientation.

Against the backdrop of media visibility and Education Ministry book-lets dealing with homosexuality, lesbian and gay youth are increasingly establishing their own support and social structures. One afternoon I sit with Jerry Levinson, an American-born psychologist and chair of the Jerusalem Open House, and talk about coming out and the role of youth groups for lesbian and gay teens in that process. For over four years there have been gay and lesbian youth groups operating in Israel, and Levinson played an active role in their early activities. "The first groups," he recalls, "came ready-made. At one of the Aguda's conferences at the B'nei Dan Community Center in Tel Aviv, a group of teenagers were in attendance, made contact, and spontaneously began a group of their own." This early group had no age restrictions, met every week or two, and was having trouble finding a permanent home of its own.

The Aguda offered to help but stipulated several conditions, including separation by age categories and professional supervision. Susan Kirshn-er, a former Aguda chair who worked intensively with Levinson to set up the structure for the youth groups, recalls that the youth "were irate. They didn't understand the potential problems with having twenty-two and fourteen year olds together. We felt that high school students and young people in the military were very different groups, and we established separate groups."

Some 150 teens went through the youth group in its two and a half years. Today, the Aguda operates Hamon Aliza, the group for young lesbians, Tzahal Bet, a Hebrew acronym meaning "Gay, Lesbian, and Bi Young People," for eighteen to twenty-two year olds (and also a play on words with the Hebrew name of the IDF), and a youth group in Haifa. Groups have also sprung up in Kfar Saba, Rishon l'Tziyon, the Upper Galilee, Ashdod, and Afula. Efforts have also been made to establish groups in Karmiel and Beer Sheva. The Aguda employs a part-time social worker, Iris Sheinfeld, to oversee the groups.

Kirshner also recalls the efforts to convince the Aguda to permit the youth to use the Aguda's facilities: "There was a division within the Aguda. Older members feared that we would face a backlash, that irate parents would be calling us, that we would be accused of recruiting." None of these fears, she relates, came to pass. Several years after their establishment, Kirshner still looks back on the youth groups with wonderment. "The gay youth in Israel are amazing," she tells me. "They have a sense of themselves. I still don't know where the ones who got involved got their awareness from."

The Haifa youth group is finishing its meeting on Saturday night in the Aguda's Haifa community center, a two-room apartment located off a downtown pedestrian mall. In the main room hangs a Hebrew poster for the movie *Beautiful Thing* along with flyers announcing future events in the lesbian and gay community. The other room serves as the center's library, with shelves of lesbian and gay books and magazines, almost all in English, donated by gay and lesbian Jews overseas. Plastic chairs are scattered about and people are rushing out the door to attend parties and movies.

Perhaps fifteen people were at tonight's meeting, five of whom were young women. Anna (a pseudonym), a twenty-seven-year-old lesbian who serves as one of the group's facilitators, agrees to speak with me. The group operates under strict privacy, and the participants were not ready to have me, an outsider, attend the meeting without greater advance planning.

Anna has been facilitating for the past year, following a request from a gay friend of hers. Today the two of them serve as a team. The Haifa group has three rotating teams of facilitators, usually consisting of both a man and a woman. She says that the group provides social interaction in an atmosphere that allows for the expression of individuals' thoughts with minimal pressure: "We try to give legitimacy to all points of view and promote tolerance within the group of all types of differences."

The average age of participants in this group is seventeen, with the youngest being a fifteen-year old woman, Anna tells me. "In recent years there's been a growing awareness of lesbian and gay issues in the wider public, and this filters down to young people, as well." The Aguda spreads word of the existence of the Haifa young people's group through the gay press as well as some of the local weeklies. Word of mouth also helps, with friends often bringing friends. Despite the Aguda's forays into local schools, it is still rare for school counselors to refer gay and lesbian youth to the group's activities. Some reach the group through either the Aguda's White Line or KLAF's Purple Line, both of which offer the referrals.

The relative lack of lesbians in the group is a problem, admits Anna. "The Aguda is identified with the gay male community. Women don't want to feel like a minority within a minority. There are weeks when a teenage girl might find herself the only young women in the youth group." Yet, she says, KLAF has not yet attempted to start its own youth groups for lesbian teenagers. From my own observation, the lack of participation by young lesbians across all the groups is considered a given. Neither the Jerusalem nor Afula group meetings I attended had any young women present. Hamon Aliza addresses some of the needs of young women, but the Aguda has not yet developed effective outreach in outlying areas that might give greater access to a wider variety of young women, not only those who either live in the Tel Aviv area or who have the means to pay for transportation.

Iris Sheinfeld, the Aguda's part-time social worker, contended that the close-knit nature of Israeli society has a good impact on the various gay and lesbian youth groups. Her role is to work with the counselors for the various gay and lesbian youth groups throughout Israel. She defines it as "to give tools for the instructors, and ideas for activities, as well as to enable the counselors to share what they're experiencing as they work with the different groups." The youth themselves provide each other substantial peer support. As Sheinfeld put it, "There's a common struggle and needs in Israel. Kids want their rights, want to support each other, so that other kids won't have to go through what they experienced." At the same time, Sheinfeld counsels gay teens through her private practice and sees more problems, particularly self-esteem issues. This suggests either that the "It's OK" attitudes demonstrated in the youth groups are false bravado or that the kids, outside the framework of a supportive group, actually feel freer to share some of their deeper needs and concerns. And, not surprisingly, those who come to the groups from the "periphery" feel greater isolation and know less about gay community life than those who come from Tel Aviv or other big urban areas.

These issues of self-esteem show up elsewhere too. At an Aguda rap group I attended, I heard a number of individuals in their twenties, and even early thirties, express real conflict about their sexual orientation. Several of them, although living a gay life for several years and even out of the closet to family, said that they still hoped to marry a woman one day. That lack of self-esteem shows how important growing gay awareness in some high schools may be and how difficult it has been in Israel until recently to be openly, comfortably gay. Some activists even labeled such people the "desert generation," a reference to God's forcing the Israelites to wander in the Sinai for forty years until the generation that had experienced slavery in Egypt died out.

Israeli society might have more success trying to direct the development of lesbian and gay identity among young people, as most gays and lesbians do not grow up with gay and lesbian parents. Thus, gay and lesbian Israelis, growing up in a society that is only beginning to form a rooted, distinct gay community, may be easier for society to shape and guide, particularly those who are just beginning to actualize their identity during their formative high school years. When asked, the educators with whom I spoke were emphatic that they view sexual orientation as an individual trait. Even Ilana Flinker, who encourages those lesbian and gay students who come to her to get involved in the Haifa gay community as a way of developing social contacts and self-acceptance, does so in the hope that her students will seek to fit in. The response of educators at Nesher High to the first gay student to come out, with his penchant for "provocative dress," suggests societal alarm at students who seek to overly emphasize their same-sex identity and distinctiveness. That may explain why Chaim, who has come out more quietly and gradually and does not see a need to separate himself from the wider society, has experienced fewer difficulties at Nesher.

Devora Ezra, director of the Secondary Education Department in the Haifa municipal government, opined that being gay is "a personal matter. . . . We want to see the person as an individual." Ezra sees gay issues as easier to bring up in the Haifa schools because "it's not as political. Subjects that have a political aspect to them are more difficult to deal with."[29] As for the notion of "gay community," Ezra takes the view that "any public that wants a culture or community of its own, that's fine, so long as it doesn't hurt the security of the state and so long as it's not anti-Zionist."

But Ezra's views demonstrate how superficial even some educators' notions of tolerance, diversity, and democracy are. Ezra views gays and lesbians as individuals, not necessarily part of something larger. For her they do not make waves, let alone call into question the fundamental tenets of Israel's Jewish and Zionist underpinnings. So long as they do not do so, it's easy to preach tolerance.

The effort to integrate gay and lesbian students works, as long as those students do not deviate too far from the Israeli consensus. The Nesher High student yearbook, in an article on gay issues, states: "Gays, lesbians, or those of a different sexual orientation are part of us and equal to everyone. Thus, there's no need to single them out and throw them out of society."[30] But another article, dealing with the Druze (an Arab minority group), shows that true acceptance extends only so far: "The Druze aren't Arabs like we think. It's true that their culture is different from ours, but they're just like us: they serve in the IDF, have a social life just like ours, study in schools like ours, and even go out to clubs like us. . . . So, let's act with tolerance toward them."[31] These articles suggest just how fragile notions of tolerance are among Israeli young people. As long as their peers do not call into question fundamental issues of identity or lifestyle, they can accept their fellow gay/lesbian or Druze students. But if those students should set themselves apart from consensus views, then it is likely that the tolerance shown will be more fleeting. The views expressed in high school yearbook suggest that students have not completely internalized the notion of honoring and respecting differences.

The Israeli educational system's approach, while well-meaning, can also be seen as condescending and limiting: We'll accept you so long as you conform to our expectations. The norm in this approach is heterosexual, and gays and lesbians are automatically turned into a group that is foreign and must be tolerated. The Israeli educational model for dealing with gays and lesbians as one of several Others that young people need to respect might work better if educators, as well as the Aguda's lecturers, conveyed that gays and lesbians are different on various levels, in that they have a distinct culture and need for community. But Israeli society is just beginning to deal with such questions, and educators, shaped by a previously collective society, ironically may be the last to absorb the new message.

The beginnings of openness benefiting young people are similarly beginning to help their parents. In Tel Aviv, Haifa, and Jerusalem there are now groups for the parents of gay men and lesbians, informally affiliated with the U.S.-based group P-FLAG. Ruth Moriel, mother of former Aguda chair Liora Moriel, helped break the silence that kept many parents in the closet when she appeared with her daughter and her daughter's partner, Susan, on Israel Television in the early 1990s. In a society that places such a high value on getting married and having children, it can be exceedingly painful for parents to learn of their child's homosexuality.

Early Thursday evening at the Aguda's community center in Tel Aviv finds a disparate group of nineteen individuals, most mothers, along with two fathers and a couple of siblings. Almost all the parents present are parents of gay men rather than lesbians. Devora Luz, who appeared on the *Open Cards* program, along with one of the founders of the group, Yonatan Danilovitz, the gay flight attendant who successfully sued El Al Israel Airlines for a free flight ticket for his partner. The parents groups have been in existence for several years, but their audience is limited. As was plainly evident during the meeting, most of the participants are middle class and Ashkenazi. A couple of those present were Russian immigrants, a couple more were American, but most were middle-class, educated, native-born Ashkenazim, there to cope with their children's, or sibling's, homosexuality. Although some Mizrachim have attended the group, few stay for any long period of time. Whether a matter of education or cultural differences, Tehila is not an environment in which they feel comfortable.

The topic for the evening was daring, in a way. Danilovitz was to lead a discussion about "Why Gay Pride?" The topic immediately created intense discussion, first and foremost over the goals of the group. Some of the parents present were there for the first time and were clearly uncomfortable.

But, in the main, Danilovitz's question du jour created spirited debate. Some of the comments took the same form as those posed to me by Israeli educators—Why a separate community? Why segregate yourselves? Even as they struggled to accept their gay children, they could not see the legitimacy of gay space, where their children could be themselves and live their lives as they see fit. Danilovitz even tried to steer the discussion to issues that should have struck a chord—the struggle of Jews to preserve their identity throughout the ages, the Maccabiah Games for Jewish athletes from throughout the world (with obvious parallels to the Gay Games). Yet the efforts to create a commonality between straight Israeli Jewish parents and a gay Israeli Jew in this regard did not bear fruit. Apart from the fact that many of the parents were at the start of a long journey that might lead to easier acceptance of their children's homosexuality, their conditioning as Israelis made it difficult to see homosexuality as something other than an individual trait. A few parents did understand the need for Pride, with one parent plaintively asking, "Why do you think so many of our children go to Holland, Canada, or the U.S.?"

After the meeting I asked Luz if she felt there were any difficulties unique to Israel that made parents' acceptance of their children's homosexuality more problematic. I was surprised when she said that she didn't see issues unique to Israeli society in the way parents do or don't come to terms with their children's sexual orientation. The importance of family, and of getting married, are two factors that do make the initial decision of a lesbian or gay man to come out more daunting. While these factors may exist elsewhere, they have a particular centrality in Israeli Jewish society. Luz herself described the importance of children's weddings in Israeli society, noting that a small wedding, at least in her circles, is 250 people. For her, and for many other Israeli parents, having to give up this ritual is particularly difficult. These societal expectations are quite strong and do, I believe, constitute a special difficulty that Israeli society poses to parents' acceptance of their children's sexual orientation.

So where does Israeli society go from here? As recognition of gay issues, and the needs of gay young people, has grown among educators and in the media, it may have dawned on some that the country can channel the development of its gay and lesbian youngsters in more positive directions, by exposing them to role models in the classroom through lecturers like Weisberg-Bloch and Tami and by exposing both them and their straight classmates to the notion that gays are "just like everyone else," which is certainly the message that the two Haifa activists imparted at Nesher High. Exposure to clean-cut gay and lesbian professionals like Weisberg-Bloch and Tami, both in long-term relationships, may strengthen kids' belief in their own futures and make them feel connected to their surroundings, thus preserving Israel's close-knit social structure.

Obviously, the mere existence of these resources does not ensure that gay and lesbian youth will partake of them. And they do not guarantee a problem-free coming out. Surveys of Israeli adolescents and university students show high levels of prejudice against gays, which makes coming out of the closet that much more difficult. And the Jerusalem Open House is trying to start up a project to examine whether Israeli gay and lesbian youth are at a greater risk for suicide than their heterosexual counterparts. Not only does coming out remain difficult for many, but the existing resources for gay youth are not evenly distributed through-out the country or to all segments of the population. In fact, the Aguda has had no success in its efforts to send lecturers to schools in Tel Aviv, a city that has the largest gay population in the country. But in a small country like Israel such services, along with TV programs like *Open Cards*, ensure that lesbian and gay youth will at least not face complete societal silence as they struggle with issues of sexual identity.

The existence of these groups for young people, and the relative lack of controversy organizers claim they create in the wider public, is prob-ably invaluable for the future development of the lesbian and gay com-munity. The Pride Boat that set sail in Haifa Bay in June 1997 looked like a school outing. Gathered on the dock prior to departure were probably forty to fifty lesbian and gay youth (some two hundred people in total went on the cruise), many of them to all appearances still in high school. Some of them were there with their girlfriends/boyfriends, holding hands or kissing. Weisberg-Bloch, for one, sees in these young people the future leadership of Haifa's gay community. Some of them, he says, are already involved in wider community activities.

Israeli gays and lesbians do not yet have the luxury of well-established communities, with a wide variety of organizations and activities, that gay people in other countries have. Israeli activists have, however, devoted time, energy, and monetary resources to reaching young people, both gay and straight, in hopes of ensuring well-adjusted individuals, comfortable with their sexual orientation and their surroundings. Such work benefits not only the community but the country as a whole, as Amir Somkai-Fink, with his talk of coming out in one's natural surroundings—and re-maining there—would probably agree. It is hard to think of a better use of any gay community's resources. Seeing what is going on in high schools like Nesher High and the various youth groups, I can't but come away believing that the "Israeli paradox" likely will diminish in the com-ing years, as younger people come out with less anxiety than the "desert generation" knew.

3

The Personal Is the Political:
Judaism and Gay People in Israel

Jews do not engage in sodomy.
    —Babylonian Talmud, Tractate Kiddushin 82A

If a man sees that his urge overcomes him, he should go to a
place where no one knows him, dress and wrap himself in black
and thus he shall not desecrate the name of Heaven.
    —Babylonian Talmud, Tractate Chagiga 16A

The rain was beating down in torrents on Friday afternoon in Jerusalem in March 1991, barely two weeks after the end of the Gulf War. Israelis were rushing about, getting ready for the arrival of the Jewish Sabbath. I was among them, dashing from the Machane Yehuda market, where I'd bought a bag of fresh pita, some fruit, and some cookies to tide me over between the meals I planned to take at Beit Shmuel, a gem of a youth hostel run by Reform Judaism's Hebrew Union College.

On a busy street stood a group of some thirty women, all dressed in black, all carrying signs expressing their opposition to Israel's occupation of the West Bank and Gaza Strip. These women, the Women in Black, had been holding this vigil for years, often braving verbal abuse at best, assaults and spittle at worst, from right-wing Israeli passersby.

I began talking with some of them. One of them, a native-born Israeli, asked me if I was a member of any synagogue in Washington. I told her that I was a member of Bet Mishpachah, the gay and lesbian synagogue of Washington, D.C. She smiled at me and said, "You should come to my synagogue tomorrow morning. You'll feel right at home."

So I set off the next morning for Kol ha-Neshama, one of Jerusalem's fledgling Reform synagogues. Kol ha-Neshama was unlike any Reform temple I had attended growing up—no imposing edifice, no organs blaring doleful Germanic music, no hidden choir, and no English, although most of the attendees seemed to speak Hebrew with a distinctly American accent.

Kol ha-Neshama was no ordinary Reform synagogue, in fact, but a *notorious* Reform synagogue. In 1986 it made headlines in Israel and the United States when, in the course of a Simchat Torah celebration, an Orthodox rabbi arrived with some followers. Appalled at the sight of men and women dancing together with the Torah scrolls, he began screaming, "Whorehouse, whorehouse!" The rabbi and his followers attempted to make off with the Torah rather than see such "desecration" go on unchecked.

Inside Kol ha-Neshama I found a service pretty much like any I'd experienced at Bet Mishpachah or at an intimate religious retreat—much singing, innovative and inclusive liturgy, and a female service leader. Looking around as more people arrived, I could tell that I'd come to the right place. My "gaydar" was working in high drive.

After services I began talking to some of the members. One woman, Deborah, was an American-born lesbian who invited me to go with her to another synagogue, where her brother Yehuda (both of the names are pseudonyms) was worshipping that morning. It turned out that he, too, was gay. The two of them invited me back to Deborah's for Shabbat lunch.

Yehuda was immersed in Orthodox life, trying to find a way to fuse his religious beliefs, homosexuality, marriage, and children. Deborah too was observant and involved in a fledgling Jerusalem-based group called Orthodykes–a group of Orthodox Jewish lesbians. Over a lunch of salad, bread, and stuffed cabbage we discussed Judaism and homosexuality in Israel.

Of the two of them, Deborah seemed to have the easier time, surrounded by a community of religious lesbians. She saw less of a conflict in need of resolution between her Judaism and her lesbianism than did her brother—perhaps because she had found a community of like-minded people (although some of the women in Orthodykes, she told me, did experience conflict between their lesbianism and commitment to Orthodoxy).

That Shabbat lunch in Jerusalem is atypical of the social realities in which Israel's gays and lesbians live. Most Israeli Jews don't go to synagogue on Shabbat. Nor do most lesbian and gay Israelis struggle with religious issues in coming to terms with their sexual orientation. For that matter, Jews outside of Israel do not live in societies where Judaism as a religion is political, and where the (Jewish) personal is very much the (Jewish) political.

From the outside the progress of Israel's gay community is remarkable, when one considers the role that religion plays in Israeli society and civic life. American gays and lesbians who worry, with good reason, about the role played by the religious right in American politics would be shocked by the power that Israeli religious parties wield, by the pervasiveness of religion in Israeli society, and by the way that Israeli gay and lesbian activists have progressed nevertheless.

But those who would look to Israel for models of how to integrate religious and gay ways of life would do well to look elsewhere. While it is certainly possible to be lesbian or gay and religious in Israel, it is almost never easy, particularly for sabras.

This chapter will discuss the tension and fusion between homosexuality and Judaism in Israel, in both the political and spiritual realms. Thus far Orthodoxy has grudgingly coexisted with Israel's organized gay and lesbian community while continuing to denounce homosexuality as *to'eva* (a word most commonly translated as "abomination") and occasionally foiling some gay-related legislation. This coexistence, though not especially warm, is instructive as to how Judaism's outlook toward homosexuality, when fused to a political system in which religion today wields more and more clout, can produce unexpected results.

Orthodox Jewish Approaches to Sexuality . . . and Homosexuality

To understand the relationship between religion and homosexuality in Israel requires an understanding of Judaism's approach to sexuality and sin in general and homosexuality in particular. Unlike many Christian denominations, Judaism views sexual relations, albeit within certain prescribed parameters, as good in their own right, even when divorced in individual instances from procreation. As the eighteenth-century German rabbi Jacob Emden put it: "There is nothing better than sexual relations in the proper framework: in the wrong framework, there is nothing worse."[1] Judaism views sexuality as an experience that can create an atmosphere of holiness. At the same time, while potentially holy, sexuality outside of the "taming" framework of marriage is deemed *ha-yetzer hara*, the evil impulse, and can debase human beings.

Thus, sexual relations have their time and place in Judaism—like most everything else in a religion that regulates conduct not only in a religious setting but in everyday life as well. In Orthodoxy's world view heterosexual marriage provides the only proper outlet for physically intimate relationships. Premarital sex, not to mention extramarital liaisons, is not deemed acceptable.

Because sexuality can be expressed only within the context of marriage, the Orthodox and ultra-Orthodox go to some lengths to minimize social interaction between men and women in order to prevent *ha-yetzer ha-ra* from gaining the upper hand. Any physical contact between the sexes—*n'giya*—be it hand-holding, embracing, or kissing, is barred, although the so-called Modern Orthodox are more lax in this regard.

Within marriage, Judaism deems sexual relations between husband and wife as a mitzvah, a good act. And, as Judaism is not only a religion but a way of life, with rules of conduct that govern one's every moment, from birth to death, from the time that one wakes up to the time that one goes to sleep, it offers a series of ideals and parameters for sexual relations within marriage.

As part of a Jewish marriage ceremony, the bride and the groom sign a ketubah, a marriage contract. While the ketubot that Reform and Conservative Jewish couples sign often contain highly individualized vows and goals for a life together, the ketubah in Orthodox Judaism is simply a contract by which the groom acquires his wife. Although such a concept seems archaic, if not downright offensive, in the modern era, the ketubah centuries ago marked a real advance in the status of women, giving them rights, material and otherwise, within the marital relationship.

Among these rights is the right to sexual fulfillment. In the Orthodox ketubah the groom undertakes to provide his wife with *ona*, marital relations. According to Michael Kaufman's *Love, Marriage, and Family in Jewish Law and Tradition*, a husband's duty to provide *ona* is separate from his obligation to engage in sexual relations for the purpose of procreation. The Talmud states quite bluntly that "he who neglects his marital duties to his wife is a sinner."[2] Or, as one thirteenth-century codifier of Jewish law quoted in Kaufman's work put it: "As it is written, "And he shall cause his wife to rejoice. . . . And behold how important is this positive mitzvah . . . for even when his wife is pregnant it is a mitzvah to cause her to rejoice when she is desirous."[3]

Kaufman notes that the Sages prescribed in great detail a husband's obligation to provide his wife with physical fulfillment, including minimum frequencies for sexual relations based on a husband's occupation, the physical labor involved in his work, and the amount of time his occupation requires him to be away from home. In addition, Jewish law gives the wife a say in determining the frequency of the couple's sexual relations. The Jewish philosopher Maimonides noted that the failure to provide a wife with physical fulfillment constitutes valid grounds for a divorce under Jewish law.[4]

Homosexuality, because it takes place outside the framework of marriage, is one of many prohibited forms of sexuality, quite apart from any disapproval of it per se. Traditional Jewish attitudes toward homosexuality stem from a variety of factors, most notably verses in the Torah that are interpreted as prohibiting same-sex intimacy.

The Book of Leviticus states that "you shall not lie with mankind as with womankind; it is an abomination."[5] In Leviticus 20:13, in a discussion of various sexual offenses, the Torah states, "If a man lies with a male as one lies with a woman, the two of them have done an abhorrent thing; they shall be put to death—their bloodguilt is upon them." There is no specific mention of lesbianism in the Torah, but later commentators agreed that the prohibitions in Leviticus subsumed female homosexuality as well (although the penalty for lesbianism is less severe than for male same-sex relations).[6]

There is another verse in the Torah that might shed some light on the social context in which the prohibition on same-sex relations arose. Deuteronomy 23:18 states, "No Israelite woman shall be a cult prostitute, nor shall any Israelite man be a cult prostitute." Gunther Plaut's *The Torah: A Modern Commentary* notes that "sexual orgies were a well-known part of many peoples' fertility rites and took place even in Jerusalem, until King Josiah put an end to them."[7] In short, the ancient Israelites may well have seen homosexual relations in the context of pagan rituals and idol worship, which they, believers in one God, sought to combat.

Orthodox Judaism views these verses as an absolute prohibition on all forms of same-gender sexual intimacy and, thus far, has not sought to examine them in light of the social and religious realities of the ancient Middle East. Although halacha, Jewish law, interprets and explains various biblical commandments and obligations, there is little in traditional Jewish commentary that attempts to soften this prohibition.

In fact, Orthodox Judaism deems the prohibition on same-sex relations to apply not just to Jews but to non-Jews as well. The Talmud's Tractate Sanhedrin imposes seven commandments on non-Jews (as opposed to the 613 that Jews are supposed to observe). These so-called Seven Laws of Noah include a prohibition on forbidden sexual activities, including homosexual relations.[8]

For all the Torah verses prohibiting homosexual activity, in Orthodox Judaism homosexuals as persons do not exist. Rather, persons who engage in homosexual acts exist. Not only do "homosexuals" not exist, but a leitmotif of some ancient Jewish commentary is that that Jews were less likely to engage in homosexual relations than other peoples. The Talmud, in Tractate Kiddushin, states, "Jews are not suspected of sodomy."[9] The subtext of such commentary, of course, is that homosexuality is a non-Jewish practice or way of life. One commentary on the Book of Leviticus warns, "'You shall not copy the practices of the land of Egypt where you dwelt, or of the land of Canaan to which I am taking you. . . . What did they do? A man would marry a man and a woman would marry a woman."[10]

The Mishna (a collection of medieval commentaries on the Torah) teaches that Rabbi Judah forbade two bachelors from sleeping under the same blanket, for fear that this would lead them to sexual temptation. Other commentators at the time disagreed with this ruling because of the belief that Jews were not homosexually inclined. But by the sixteenth century Rabbi Joseph Caro in his *Shulchan Aruch*, one of the most noteworthy codifications of Jewish law ever produced, declared: "In our generation, lewdness is rampant, and it is best for a man to avoid being alone with another male."[11] As in almost any rabbinical debate on Jewish law and practice, there were disputes concerning Caro's warnings about men in the company of men, with some arguing that it applied only to Jews from certain geographic regions.

Although many commentators went to some lengths to suggest that Jews indeed were not suspected of sodomy, the phenomenon obviously was not unknown among Jews. There would be no need for centuries of Talmudic discussions about the issue if that were the case. At the same time, it is possible that homosexual relations might have been less frequent among Jews than among other peoples because of the high level of social control in Jewish communities and the difficulty of living outside of that society in countries where anti-Semitism thrived.

The rabbinical literature also contains discussion of the penalties for those who engaged in same-sex sexual relations. The Torah, of course, imposed a penalty of death by stoning for such "offenses." In practice, however, Jewish law was surprisingly lenient. Maimonides noted that, to impose the penalty of stoning, two witnesses were required.

The Gemara (an exposition on the Mishna), in Tractate Sanhedrin of the Talmud, further discusses whether the passive partner in a homosexual act can bear witness in a proceeding to impose the penalty of stoning for the "offense" of homosexual relations. The Gemara discussion concludes that the passive partner cannot bear witness once he enjoys the sexual act.[12]

There is little discussion in the rabbinical literature about the penalty for lesbian relations. While lesbianism was forbidden, such acts were not judged in a rabbinical court. Nor were the social sanctions identical to those for male homosexual acts. Rabbi Shmuel wrote that he had forbidden his virgin daughters from sleeping together in the same bed. Rabbi Huna subsequently wrote that "licentious women" (the talmudic term used for lesbians) are barred from marrying men of the priestly class, the *kohanim*.[13] Rashi (Rabbi Solomon ben Isaac of Troyes, one of the earlier Ashkenazi Jewish commentators on the Bible and the Talmud) disagreed, however, writing that such women were only forbidden to marry high priests.[14] The lesser sanctions for lesbianism might stem from patriarchal attitudes that sex between women does not *really* constitute sex. In addition, lesbian sex does not entail the "spilling of seed" for nonreproductive purposes, as would be the case with sexual relations between two men.

The Talmud contains several possible reasons for Orthodox Judaism's prohibition on same-sex intimacy. One commentary notes that the word *to'eva* could be viewed through a play on words as *to'e ata ba*: "You go astray because of it."[15] Thus, another commentary suggests, because the major purpose of sexuality is procreation, Judaism cannot accept same-sex relations because they supposedly defeat that purpose (adoption and artificial insemination obviously did not come into play in this analysis). Another commentary proposes, however, that "going astray" meant that a man might hurt his marriage by seeking same-sex intimacy.[16] Such a construction of sexuality suggests that sexual orientation categories were not always as rigid as they are popularly perceived today.

A review of the above rabbinical literature suggests, unsurprisingly, that Orthodox Judaism has been fairly consistent in its view of homosexuality. The only significant difference that has arisen between Orthodox rabbis in modern times is whether homosexuality is the product of *ones*—a lack of free choice—or constitutes a freely chosen behavior.

Nevertheless, even on as charged a topic as homosexuality new Orthodox viewpoints are emerging. In 1995 the Israeli newsmagazine *Jerusalem Report* published a Torah commentary by Rabbi Tzvi Marx, an

Orthodox rabbi and, at the time, director of applied education at the Shalom Hartman Institute in Jerusalem. Rabbi Marx tackles seemingly ironclad Jewish truths and arrives at some interesting conclusions. First, no matter how clear the Torah appears to be on an issue, "One never assume[s] that a subject is closed."[17] In fact, Rabbi Marx finds evidence for this proposition in several discussions of sexuality in the Torah and various Jewish commentaries. For example, he writes, the Torah prohibits eunuchs from marrying.[18] The Talmud, however, explains that this seemingly absolute prohibition applies only to those turned into eunuchs by another human being and not to those born with such a condition.

Although Rabbi Marx concedes that the sages did not deal with how to regard "a child who is conventionally male or female in some ways but not others—that is, a homosexual," he posits a possible answer, derived from Tractate Brachot in the Talmud. This tractate teaches that one who sees a "physically unusual person" (Rabbi Marx's terminology) should recite: "Blessed are You, Lord, who makes creatures differently."[19] In the thirteenth century, notes Rabbi Marx, the Meiri (Rabbi Menachem Meiri of Perpignan) interpreted the blessing as a response to the "experiencing of new things, without necessarily enjoying or being troubled by them."[20] Rabbi Marx concludes his Torah commentary by inviting reinterpretation of traditional texts in light of new insights.

In thinking through Judaism's approach to sexuality and homosexuality, I had a long telephone conversation with Rabbi Marx while he was on a research sabbatical in the Netherlands. Our talk took us far beyond the limited approach first outlined in his *Jerusalem Report* commentary. Despite his unorthodox (and perhaps un-Orthodox) treatment of same-sex love, he said that he had received not one negative response to his article and quite a few positive ones.

Rabbi Marx suggested several new ways of relating to homosexuality in Jewish law and practice. First, he told me, one must ask whether God would create "abominations." There are a number of commentaries, he related, stating that all of God's creations are good. Second, he added, "You can't 'textualize' people. You're talking about human beings. I believe that the Torah is compassionate."

I asked Rabbi Marx whether his outlook was really consistent with the way that Orthodox Judaism approaches analysis and interpretation of the Torah, since devout Jews hold that the Torah is God's direct word. His response: "It's Orthodoxy's way to be interpretive. When someone says that you're stuck with the literal language of the text, that's just rhetoric." Rabbi Marx's views at this point are decidedly not in the Orthodox mainstream but merit discussion because they suggest possible future paths for Orthodox Judaism to take on the issues of homosexuality and gay rights.

The Stressed-out Status Quo

To understand the interplay between Judaism and homosexuality in Israel also requires an understanding of Jewish religious politics and the role that religion plays in national and personal life. In Israel one cannot marry in a civil ceremony. Jews can only marry Jews in Israel, Muslims can only marry Muslims, and Christians can only marry Christians, although civil marriages contracted abroad are recognized. Marriage and divorce, one's religious status, and burial all fall under the rubric of "personal status" over which religious authorities enjoy an absolute monopoly. For Jews this is especially problematic because the only stream of Judaism recognized in Israel is Orthodoxy. Although the Reform and Conservative branches of Judaism that are familiar to most Diaspora Jews have adherents and synagogues in Israel, the rabbis from these two branches cannot perform legally valid weddings or conversions.

After the birth of Israel then Prime Minister David Ben-Gurion made a deal with the religious parties to entice them into joining his government and giving him the governing majority that he needed. This deal came to be known as the "Status Quo." In return for their participation in his coalition, Ben-Gurion ceded to the religious parties and the Orthodox rabbinate control over personal status questions and agreed to shut down public transportation and entertainment on the Jewish Sabbath. Ben-Gurion and Israel's other founding parents made these concessions to the religious because they sincerely believed that Orthodoxy had no future and would die out within a generation in Israel; the Holocaust had decimated Europe's centers of Jewish learning and the Zionist pioneers viewed the remnants that survived as a quaint relic whom the New Jews that Zionism sought to create would supplant.

But the Status Quo is increasingly under siege. Today, one can find restaurants and nightclubs open on the Sabbath, even in Jerusalem. Conversely, the Orthodox have successfully shut down El Al Israel Airlines on the Sabbath and have currently succeeded in shutting down one of Jerusalem's major arteries, Bar Ilan Street, during prayer hours on the Sabbath. They continue to try to redefine "Who is a Jew?" and fine the growing number of businesses that have begun to open during the Sabbath. The Israeli Supreme Court in turn has begun confronting these issues head-on, creating a collision of world views. Rabbi Moshe Gafni of the ultra-Orthodox Degel ha-Torah party labeled Israeli Supreme Court president Aharon Barak an "oppressor of Jews" in 1999 because of such Supreme Court rulings, and two hundred thousand ultra-Orthodox gathered in Jerusalem in February 1999 to protest what some viewed as "anti-Semitic" court decisions.

The religious parties are the kingmakers of Israeli politics, because neither of the two major political parties, Labor or Likud, has ever been able to obtain a parliamentary majority in its own right. This situation only worsened in the May 1996 elections, when both Labor and Likud saw their share of the popular vote—and numbers of Knesset seats—decline significantly. The religious parties, some of which barely recognize the existence of the State of Israel, have not hesitated to use their clout to bring down governments over "Sabbath desecration," archaeological excavations, or other religious issues. Thus, back in 1976, they caused the collapse of Yitzhak Rabin's first government because American fighter planes being delivered to Israel had landed after the Sabbath had begun.

Although the Orthodox retain control over personal status questions, conversely, and perhaps perversely, the overwhelming majority of Israeli Jews are secular. They drive on the Sabbath and even eat pork and other foods forbidden by Judaism's dietary laws. But this state of affairs is not as simple as it seems at first glance. The September 22, 1996, weekend section of *Yediot Achronot* ran a long piece titled "Secular, But." A survey revealed that 52 percent of Israeli Jews define themselves as secular, while 31 percent call themselves "traditional" (meaning, in Israeli terms, that they might go to synagogue on the Sabbath but won't think twice about driving to a soccer game immediately afterward). Only 10 percent called themselves religious, and 7 percent said they were ultra-Orthodox.[21]

As an American Jew who believes in God and practices his religion, I have been alternately amused and horrified by Israeli friends who eat bread during Passover (25 percent of Israelis, according to the *Yediot Achronot* poll) and do not fast (27 percent), let alone attend synagogue (31 percent) on Yom Kippur.[22] The bottom line is that Israelis, while overwhelmingly not religious, do incorporate some religious traditions into their lives, just as many Jews in the Diaspora are "twice-a-year Jews" or light the Hanukkah candles.

Because of the security threat that Israel traditionally has faced from the Arab world, secular-religious tensions traditionally were manageable, subordinated to the "We're all Jews" ethos in the face of the struggle with Israel's Arab neighbors. Thus, the secular majority did not attempt to challenge religious hegemony, even though segments of it despise the religious and even, in some extreme cases, Judaism itself. When *Ha-Zman ha-Varod* asked a series of artists and journalists for Jewish new year greetings in 5759/1998, artist Yigal Tomerkin replied, "I wish a Happy New Year only on December 31. I'm not a religious person. The sounds of the Shofar (a ram's horn) and children with side curls don't move me. Rosh ha-Shana is an unhappy and gloomy holiday because everything's closed."[23]

While external conflict with the Arabs has lessened, internal secular-religious tensions have heated up. As religious parties have made more demands on the state and secular connections to Jewish texts and traditions have frayed, the gulf has only widened. Both sides in this struggle over the state's character increasingly look to provoke the other. The Israeli media and the political discourse of certain political parties regularly portray religious Jews as corrupt, unscrupulous, and plain hateful. If a North American or European television network or politician aired similar programming or painted similar portrayals, there would be prompt accusations of anti-Semitism.

Or consider how the ultra-Orthodox tried to tamper with Israel's Jubilee celebrations in 1998. Organizers, after a series of fiascoes, planned to put on a gala show in Jerusalem, including a piece by the Batsheva Dance Troupe called "Echad Mi Yodei'a" ("Who Knows One?" based on the Passover song of the same name), in which dancers clad in ultra-Orthodox garb would proceed to strip down to their undergarments. Ultra-Orthodox politicians, representing communities that barely recognize the state's existence and who, in any event, would not attend a secular entertainment extravaganza, demanded cancellation of the piece as blasphemous. The organizers yielded, prompting secular protestors to greet National Religious Party politicians (who championed the ultra-Orthodox demand) the next day with cries of "Good Morning, Iran." This event has given new impetus to a view of the religious as a spreading cancer that must be stopped before it consumes Israel's secular body politic.

The cries of "Good Morning, Iran" came from a 1998 song by the same name, written and sung by Israeli rock's enfant terrible, Aviv Geffen. Geffen's song, clearly directed at rabbis in Israel rather than ayatollahs in Teheran, expresses well the angst among secular Jews in late 1990s Israel:

Good morning, Iran
The broadcaster announces

How we feared this day would come
Everyone began to sweat
When they suddenly saw freedom fly away
Good Morning, Iran
Here we live
Good morning, Iran
It looks like we were silent
Good morning, Iran
Here we'll live in fear
Good morning, Iran
Here we'll die together[24]

The negative imagery of the religious shows up in recent Hebrew literature as well. Consider how appealing this description from Dov Elbaum's novel *Elul Time* is: "Reb Hirsch's belly scattered out sideways, shaking and widening, its flesh quivering like a hunk of fresh kugel."[25] Elbaum's novel about a fourteen-year old yeshiva student opens with a scene in the mikve, the Jewish ritual bath, which comes across for secular readers as a dirty ugly place.

A commentary by journalist Arye Kaspi in the September 13, 1996, issue of *Ha'aretz* shows how deep the antipathy of many Israelis toward religious Jews runs: "The religious are Other. . . . They speak with us in the same tongue, but in a different language."[26] And that was before recent clashes over Independence Day celebrations and Supreme Court decisions.

The Orthodox and ultra-Orthodox return Kaspi's favor with increased vehemence. Brigadier-General Ya'akov Amidror, an Orthodox Jewish aide to former defense minister Yitzhak Mordechai and an ultimately unsuccessful candidate for the head of Israeli military intelligence, for one, dismissed secular Israelis in a 1998 newspaper interview as "no more than Hebrew-speaking goyim [gentiles]."[27] In 1999 Rabbi Yisrael Eichler could write in the ultra-Orthodox *Ha-Machane ha-Charedi* that "if they weren't engaged in war with the Arabs, the secular would kill our children like Pharaoh and Hitler."[28]

The Religious Politics of Gay Rights

Although they have torched "immodest" advertisements at bus stops, stoned cars passing near their neighborhoods on the Sabbath, and demanded a halt to the sale of pork, religious Israelis and their political parties have not yet made gay rights issues a rallying cry. Their verbal opposition to gay advances is quite blunt, however, as if they seek to reassure themselves that the alleged Biblical prohibitions on homosexual relations still apply.

When MK Yael Dayan convened the first Knesset conference on gay rights in 1993, *Ha-Tzofe*, the organ of the National Religious Party, editorialized:

> MK Yael Dayan still hadn't rested from the disturbance she created with her trip to Tunis and her meeting with the murderer [Palestinian leader] Yasser Arafat, and she's created noise again in the Knesset. . . . She invited representatives of homosexuals and lesbians, who have various complaints of deprivation and discrimination due to their deviancy.[29]

A guest editorial in the same newspaper the following day was even more strident:

> The sect of deviants that gathered this week in the Knesset came to demonstrate not only its lack of shame over its deviance but also demanded for itself status and recognition from Israeli society. . . . It was a shameful show, one that caused deep disgust, even if the hosts— Knesset members—expressed sympathy for the deviants and promised to fight for their recognition and rights.[30]

Similarly, when the Israeli Supreme Court ordered El Al Israel Airlines to provide gay flight attendant Yonatan Danilovitz with an annual free plane ticket for his partner, religious rhetoric became quite shrill. MK Moshe Gafni declared that "the Supreme Court has given legal legitimacy to the animalization of society—and will bear responsibility for young people, who will understand henceforth that this phenomenon—which every human being should despise—is legitimate."[31] For his part, MK Avraham Ravitz stated that "we henceforth will not be able to state that 'from Zion goes forth Torah,' but rather that 'from Zion goes forth *tum'a* [ritual impurity, pollution].' "[32] And Yitzhak Levy of the National Religious Party, presaging U.S. Senate majority leader Trent Lott by a few years, declared that "it's like approving a law allowing kleptomaniacs to steal because it's considered a mental problem."[33]

Yet, until recently, despite such tirades, the Orthodox battle against gay rights in Israel has been waged solely on the verbal battlefield, in the

Knesset. The religious parties, even under the Netanyahu government, have not made gay issues their primary rallying cry, nor have they succeeded in stopping gay advances. In fact, there are divisions among them on how to deal with gay issues, with some Knesset members and religious public figures taking a *very* tolerant attitude toward Israel's gay and lesbian minority. Just contrast Moledet MK (and Orthodox rabbi) Beni Elon with the utterances of his ultra-Orthodox colleagues.

I myself sought the views of Israel's Chief Rabbinate on gay issues and finally received a reply from Rabbi Raphael Frank, from the office of Ashkenazi Chief Rabbi Yisrael Lau. The letter was opaque, demonstrating that homosexuality is not a question that Israel's religious establishment wishes to deal with in any detail. Rabbi Frank wrote, "In response to your questions, the Chief Rabbinate is a halachic body that acts according to the laws of the Jewish religion, based on accepted tradition over generations. The issue with which you are dealing is discussed in the Torah and in books of halacha. The position of the Rabbinate is in accord with this position."[34]

Rabbi Frank's letter leaves many questions unanswered. As shown above, the issue of homosexuality certainly is discussed in halacha, but various views about punishment and the origins of homosexuality exist side by side. Moreover, what would the Chief Rabbinate say about more recent Orthodox discussions of the issue such as that by Rabbi Marx? This appears to be an issue the Chief Rabbinate would like to avoid. When the Chief Rabbinate has discussed the issue, it has occasionally staked out a moderate position. Thus, when President Weizman made his homophobic remarks in 1996, Rabbi Lau first attacked the public hostility that greeted the president's comments, but then added that one should deal with the issue of gays sensitively and quietly and not turn it into an issue for public discord.[35]

The reasons for these varied views are complex, and perhaps inexplicable, considering the importance that Judaism traditionally has placed on heterosexual marriage and reproduction. I will posit several possibilities: 1) Judaism's relatively sex-positive nature—and *tzniyut* (modesty) about sexual matters; 2) the belief that few Jews are gay or lesbian; 3) the emphasis in Judaism on deeds (good or otherwise) rather than sin as a basis for judging human beings; 4) the "usefulness" of the lesbian and gay community from a religious perspective; 5) other, more pressing religious political priorities; 6) the common outlook between Israel's "gayocracy" and the wider secular elite; and 7) the tribal bonds of Judaism that, though frayed these days, ultimately can trump the other (and many) divisions among Israeli Jews—including differences based on sexual orientation.

The first explanation—that Judaism is relatively sex-positive—does not explain the religious political response to the Israeli gay and lesbian community. As detailed above, Judaism is sex-positive, but only within the context of marriage. Among the Orthodox and the ultra-Orthodox contact between unmarried men and women is sharply restricted and/or supervised, to prevent any intimacy between the sexes, let alone premarital sex. And although Rabbi Tzvi Marx, for one, has proposed a halachic basis for accepting gay people, his view is clearly that of a minority among observant Jews, who continue to see homosexuality as an abomination and thus far refuse to wrestle with the meaning of Leviticus.

While Judaism has a positive outlook on sexual relations within the confines of marriage, it is considered improper to discuss sexual matters openly. The issue of modesty—*tzniyut*—among religious Jews on sexual matters probably does affect the willingness of the Orthodox, and even the politicians who represent their interests in the Knesset, to take up a battle cry against gay rights. Rabbi Marx told me during our telephone interview that the Orthodox are "embarrassed to deal with sexual issues. Even talking about it [homosexuality] is uncomfortable." They can threaten to bring down an Israeli government over issues like Sabbath desecration, he said, because the Jewish Sabbath "has no shame connected to it." An opinion piece in *Ha-Tzofe* attacking the Supreme Court for its decision in the *Open Cards* case did not once use the words *homosexual* or *lesbian*. Rather, the author talked of "abominations" or "sex against the way of nature."[36]

The belief that Jews simply aren't homosexuals, or that Jewish homosexuals are very rare (in Orthodox communities), likely is one of the reasons that Israel's gay rights movement has not faced a strong Orthodox backlash. This attitude finds ample support in rabbinical literature, notably with regard to the disagreement with Rabbi Judah's ruling centuries ago that two bachelors should not share a blanket.

One can find additional support for this theory when one examines a recent gay rights debate in Israel. In December 1995 the ultra-Orthodox Shas party threatened a vote of no confidence in the government if the Labor Party did not table a bill that would have granted pension rights to the surviving partners of gay and lesbian government employees. The Knesset debate produced some of the greatest verbal pyrotechnics ever seen on a gay rights issue, with one member, Rabbi Moshe Maya, calling for the death penalty for gay people. While the mainstream Israeli press

devoted substantial coverage to the debate and subsequent political maneuvering, two newspapers, *Ha-Tzofe* and *Yated Ne'eman* (an ultra-Orthodox newspaper), remained strangely silent, even though Knesset members from both groups led the battle against the legislation. This silence
arguably stems from a belief that homosexuality is a marginal issue as
well as the desire to avoid even mentioning the subject among deeply religious Jews.

That is not to say that they are unaware of the issue. But when homosexuality surfaces in ultra-Orthodox confines, the ultra-Orthodox
take action to stamp out its manifestations. Journalist Amnon Levy recounted in his book *The Ultra-Orthodox* how one Tel Aviv yeshiva expelled half the students in one class because of suspicion of homosexual
relations. Other yeshivot, he writes, have eliminated communal showers
or bar their students from locking doors, or even sitting on another
pupil's bed, lest such actions lead inexorably to forbidden homosexual
contact.[37] Because of the strict rules governing sexual relations of any
sort in ultra-Orthodox society, it is not surprising to see on occasion
many ultra-Orthodox men cruising Israel's urban parks. There's even justification for it in the Gemara, notes Levy. The Gemara teaches that "if
a man sees that his urge overcomes him, he should go to a place where
no one knows him, dress and wrap himself in black and thus he shall not
desecrate the name of Heaven."[38]

Dov Elbaum's novel, *Elul Time*, too, portrays a yeshiva world in
which homosexuality is both rampant and ruthlessly suppressed. Some
students furtively engage in such activity, even as the rabbis rail against
it, and against the spilling of seed. The struggle among these young students against evil impulses of all kinds is a theme of the book; the central protagonist, Nachman, even takes a vow of silence in the two weeks
leading up to the High Holy Days in an attempt to purify his body and
soul. But the struggle against temptation never ends, as the following
passage illustrates:

> Striechman agreed to go to his room, because Sheinin promised to help
> him with the big end-of-year exam, but went first to Schwartz, one of
> the righteous [students]. Schwartz told it immediately to Drucker the
> Guard, and the two of them laid an ambush for Sheinin, hiding in the
> closet by the door. When Streichman entered and Sheinin had already
> approached him and began to touch him in the darkness, they burst
> out of the closet, turned on the light, and caught him in the act. The
> story they told to Rabbi Hirsh, and Schwartz also spread it afterward

throughout the entire yeshiva, was that Sheinin had tried to pick figs and had been caught by the orchard guard. Drucker this time said more than that, that Sheinin had become worse than ordinary fruit pickers, that he had sought real male-knowledge with Streichman, which could have led God forbid to penetrator-penetratee, as with a rabbit and a hare.[39]

But, the religious can remain relatively inactive on this issue politically because the "sin" of homosexuality is one sin of many, albeit one deemed an "abomination." Judaism is very much a deeds-based religion in which one remains Jewish even if one violates certain commandments. The Talmud notes that "even though he sins, he is a Jew."[40] In Judaism, unlike some conservative sects of Christianity, committing a "sin" does not call into question one's status as a Jew. If a Jew keeps kosher and observes the Sabbath, these acts are good in their own right—one is always supposed to strive to be a better person. In an interview with the Israeli gay and lesbian journal *Tat-Tarbut*, then political consultant Menachem Sheizaf could state that "in my conversations with religious people, they explained to me that there are so many prohibitions that if a person violates a few, but makes sure not to violate many others, he's still considered a good person."[41]

This outlook reminds me of an experience I had while still in law school. A Lubavitch classmate of mine invited me to his home for the weekend to experience Shabbat in a religious setting (the Lubavitch are an ultra-Orthodox sect that engages in extensive outreach to the wider Jewish community). At the time I was very busy with classes, job searches, and extracurricular activities and did not particularly want to give up a weekend. So he invited me to come just for Friday night dinner and then return home. In accepting his invitation and carrying out this plan, I desecrated the holiness of the Sabbath by traveling on a bus and carrying money. Yet my classmate was willing to overlook these violations because I would be observing mitzvot associated with a Friday evening Shabbat meal. He hoped, of course, that experiencing an Orthodox Sabbath would eventually lead me to embrace Orthodoxy.

What my Lubavitch classmate applied to me personally, the religious have applied to many of their interactions with Israeli society and participation in Israeli politics. In December 1995 openly gay Tel Aviv University professor Uzi Even announced that he intended to run for the Knesset under the auspices of Meretz. This set off a debate among religious politicians over whether they could join a government coalition that included an openly gay person. Shas MK Shlomo Benizri told *Ha'aretz* that Shas's response to Even "would be like its response to Sabbath violators and eaters of unclean creatures, with many of whom Shas has sat in a government coalition."[42] Thus, the religious, and even (or especially) their politicians, view homosexuality as only one facet of a person and do not turn it into a strict litmus test about a person's Jewishness.

Moreover, the emergence of an Israeli gay and lesbian community serves the goals of the ultra-Orthodox in a broader context. While the Orthodox view the rebirth of Israel as a sign from God, the ultra-Orthodox view the State of Israel with mixed feelings, since their belief holds that only the Messiah can bring about the rebirth of a Jewish nation in Israel. Some of them actively refuse to recognize the existence of the state, while others view it as a fact, albeit an unpleasant fact. Ultra-Orthodox Israelis probably view the emergence of Israel's gay minority as proof of the corruption of the "Zionist enterprise," which they continue to despise as religious heresy and as further evidence that only their reclusive way of life will preserve Judaism in the face of Westernization and growing secularism. Their views about the corruption of Israeli society have increasingly influenced segments of the Orthodox as well. An article in the February 1995 edition of *Nekuda*, the journal of the West Bank settlers (whose most committed members are religious), attacked "the moral failure of the Supreme Court" following the court's ruling in favor of gay El Al flight attendant Jonathan Danilovitz. The writer asked, "Isn't there in the Supreme Court's ruling an irresponsible ignoring of phenomena dangerous to society, physically and mentally?"[43]

The struggle over Jewish society's character in the Land of Israel is a long-standing one. In ancient Palestine there was a fierce struggle between those who sought to embrace Greek culture—its art, literature, and science—and create a synergy between that culture and Judaism, and those who resisted cultural assimilation and fusion. For Israeli religious Jews the emergence of a gay community in Zion is the ultimate example of *hityavanut*, Hellenism, and a prime example of "moral decay" among Jews who have strayed from a religious lifestyle.

It may be that the Orthodox religious parties view equality for a sexual minority as less of a threat to their way of life than relaxed public observance of the Jewish Sabbath, decreased funding for their religious institutions, or the end of their monopoly over marriage, divorce, and conversion. Rabbi Marx contends that the Orthodox community in Israel has not turned gay rights into a cause célèbre in part because it does not impinge on their daily life. There is a lot of support for that contention. As Menachem Sheizaf put it in 1995: "[The religious] are too busy forcing things on us that hurt them greatly. Take for example widespread Sabbath desecration. The emphasis is on widespread. They're ready to ignore and agree by silence to things that are not widespread."[44]

Ultra-Orthodox Jews live their lives largely apart from the rest of Israeli society, in their own neighborhoods and schools.[45] The ultra-Orthodox are not supposed to read secular newspapers, watch television, or attend movies. Gay images, or even debates about gay rights, are not likely to sully their eyes and ears. Within their own communities overt expressions of homosexuality are suppressed, along with other conduct deemed immodest or immoral. Cars passing through their neighborhoods on the Sabbath are much more disturbing and threatening than gay lecturers in the secular school system (which their children do not attend) or a gay film festival at the Tel Aviv Cinematheque (which they similarly would not attend). That might explain National Religious Party MK Chanan Porat's professed willingness in August 1998 to grant economic benefits to same-sex couples.[46] His proposal came in response to other, more far-reaching proposals for civil marriage, and Porat, head of the Knesset Constitution and Law Committee, might have been willing to concede a few points on rights for gay couples, which the courts have been granting anyway, rather than risk the erosion of the Rabbinate's monopoly over marriage for Jews in Israel (the legislation ultimately failed, in any event).

Another factor that likely has helped preserve gay rights gains has been the common outlook between gay activists and the secular establishment. The disinterest of Israeli activists in religion dovetails with the perspective of the wider societal elite, who similarly aspire to an open pluralistic society and to limit the power of the Orthodox over public and private religious observance. Gay rights are just another piece of that puzzle. As previously shown, gay rights today are an integral part of the secular Israeli consensus and have become one of the fronts, albeit minor, in the struggle with the Orthodox and the ultra-Orthodox.

Finally, the tribal bonds of Judaism have moderated, until now at any rate, what should be a fierce religious reaction to gay life and politics in Israel. There's a Hebrew saying that "every Jew is responsible for his/her fellow." This sense of communal bond and responsibility, even in the face of growing individualism in Israeli society, helps keep Israeli society from completely fragmenting and alleviates even the harshest disagreements (although those bonds are under severe strain today and could well fray further).

Including disagreements on gay rights. An ultra-Orthodox government minister allegedly has said that he would rather his son be gay than a Sabbath breaker. If asked by the media, of course, the minister would deny such a statement and issue a denunciation of homosexuality. That an ultra-Orthodox rabbi could feel a sense of kinship with gay and lesbian Israelis underscores that Judaism is more than just a religion—it is also a people and culture.

Gays and Lesbians as Secular Vanguard

Israel's gay community is very much a part of the country's secular landscape. If a picture is worth a thousand words, one published in *Ha'aretz* in October 1998 speaks volumes. Taken by Alex Libak for his weekly "Our Land" photo, the picture, titled "Tel Aviv, Yom Kippur, 5759," showed two nicely muscled gay men, one on rollerblades, one seated on his mountain bike, kissing on the empty Yom Kippur streets. A third friend, also admirably built, pirouettes in the background on his rollerblades.[47] The picture paints Israeli gays as the ultimate secular vanguard. This connection probably has strengthened following the 1999 secular demonstration in defense of the Supreme Court's independence. Prominent at the rally, called in response to the much larger ultra-Orthodox one, was the gay rainbow flag.

Many in the Israeli gay and lesbian leadership, like most of its heterosexual counterparts, look at the Jewish innovations created in America over the past three decades with a mixture of amusement, disdain, and at times, incomprehension. Former Aguda executive director Amit Kama came to the United States on a fund-raising tour in 1994. To the surprise of his hosts (yours truly and my partner), he had to be virtually dragged into attending Friday evening services at Bet Mishpachah, the gay and lesbian synagogue of Washington, D.C. On the ride to the synagogue he boasted that he had not set foot in a synagogue since his early teenage years and had grown up in a militantly secular household. His successor, Gil Nader, who came to Washington in late December 1996, was much more willing to go and, in fact, enjoyed the experience, but approached the service almost as an anthropologist studying an exotic culture.

Similarly, at the board meeting of the World Congress of Gay, Lesbian, and Bisexual Jewish Organizations prior to a conference, Avi Sofer stated that gay and lesbian Israelis do not attend such conferences in greater numbers because "Israeli lesbians won't go to conferences where

Jewish lesbians are involved with lighting Sabbath candles." What he meant was that Israelis have little interest in conferences predominantly devoted, in their view, to workshops on developing gay and lesbian Jewish rituals and explorations of Jewish spirituality.

The detachment of much of Israel's lesbian and gay leadership from Judaism stems from the culture and educational system developed by the early Zionist pioneers and the socialist ethos of the State of Israel's founding parents rather than from any alienation due to their sexual orientation and Orthodoxy's response to it. Early Zionists rebelled against the Orthodox Judaism that their parents practiced in the shtetls of Poland and czarist Russia. They were out to create a New Jew who would transcend the religious beliefs and Diaspora mentality of their forebears. Sociologist Oz Almog's study of the sabra details how thoroughly Zionism sought to reject the Diaspora: "Negation of the Diaspora and the Diaspora way of life, and especially the stereotyping of the Diaspora Jew, served as a hidden means of sharpening the boundaries of the religion of Zionist nationhood and its superiority over the traditional Jewish religion that gave birth to it."[48]

The early educational system and youth movements instilled in young Israelis an almost visceral dislike of the Diaspora and the Jews who remained there. Almog quotes one sabra girl describing the new immigrants who had arrived in her kibbutz: "The odor of the Diaspora wafts from them. I doubt whether the kibbutz will know how to educate them and instill in them the smell of the Land of Israel."[49]

As many Israelis will tell a visitor, living in Israel is Judaism enough. There is no need, in their view, to attend synagogue because, as Theo Mainz, the coordinator of the Aguda's support group for gay religious Jews, HOD, put it: "Jews in the Diaspora attend synagogue to be with other Jews. Here, almost everyone is Jewish."

All this is true, but the secular today are at a disadvantage in the struggle with the Orthodox and the ultra-Orthodox because they concede that the Judaism practiced by the religious is the only "authentic" Judaism. But much of what they consider "authentic" and eternal developed only in the past few centuries in the shtetls of Eastern Europe. Such beliefs only underscore their ignorance of their own religion and its historic evolution. The antireligious attitudes of the founding parents, together with the coercive behavior of the religious, have combined to render all too many Israeli Jews—including lesbian and gay ones—intellectually lazy when it comes to understanding their faith.

Jewish Explorations in the Lesbian and Gay Community

Although the Israeli gay rights movement is largely secular, some within the community are exploring how to fully express both their sexual orientation and their commitment to Judaism and Jewish religious practices. In 1994 a gay and lesbian synagogue, Kehilat Ga'avat Yisrael (Congregation Pride of Israel), formed under the auspices of the Aguda. The Aguda's Hebrew magazine, *Nativ Nosaf*, announcing the creation of the synagogue, began its story with the following lead: "A surprising idea has conquered the community recently: Judaism."[50]

Unfortunately, Kehilat Ga'avat Yisrael was not long for this world. Theo Mainz noted that the founders of the synagogue were largely Americans and that people stopped attending after the novelty—and the potential social benefit—wore off. In fact, other attempts to create religious outlets for lesbian and gay Jews in Israel (such as the Orthodykes), as well as Reform congregations, are often American Jewish efforts. This is not surprising considering that most American Jewish immigrants to Israel are used to Jewish life centering around a synagogue.

In Jerusalem a group called Mo'ach Gavra has sprung up. Put together by a gay American Orthodox rabbi, Steve Greenberg, the group meets regularly to read and discuss Jewish texts pertaining to homosexuality. I was able to attend a session of the group, fortuitously the night it was beginning to discuss the verses in Leviticus that allegedly prohibit all same-sex sexual behavior. Most interesting was the mix of the participants—nearly equally divided between men and women and religious and secular lesbians and gay men—a state of affairs that is pretty rare at any Israeli gay or lesbian event or group.

The rabbi handed us all the relevant verses and asked us to discuss them preliminarily with a study partner, a *chevruta*. I actually had two partners, one a man, the other a woman, both Israelis, and we conducted the discussion of the text in Hebrew, itself a new experience for me when analyzing Jewish texts. At my synagogue in Washington, we'd had classes on what Jewish texts say about homosexuality, but the texts and the discussions were always in English. The language made all the difference, making the texts more immediate and powerful. We dissected practically every Hebrew word in the relevant verse, focusing in particular on the term *mishkavei isha*, usually translated into English "as lying with a woman." We argued over whether it prohibited all contact between men that mimicked the way a man might make love to a woman, or whether it merely applied to the act of intercourse itself. Another interesting point that arose was whether the Leviticus prohibitions might only apply to men whose sexual orientation was heterosexual.

Although the group was a study group, there was clearly an element of support group to it for the religious participants. For the religious men in particular, coping with their homosexuality was a difficult task because of the way religious Israelis interpreted Leviticus, along with the social pressure that they faced to marry. Some of the men talked openly about trying to find a religious lesbian to marry, so that they could form a family and fulfill the commandment to be fruitful and multiply. In fact, the bigger issue for most of those present was not their homosexuality per se but how to have children. The women, although subject to social pressure, felt less conflict because Jewish law, as outlined above, takes a more tolerant attitude toward lesbianism. As a result, they don't tend to feel to the same extent that they're living in opposition to Jewish law.

One American-born religious lesbian and Orthodykes member, Sarah (a pseudonym), shared some of her perspectives with me one afternoon in her Jerusalem home. She had been living in Israel eight years and had moved out of ideology, because "I'm a Jew, and Israel is the Jewish homeland." At the same time, the State of Israel was not exactly her ideal; she admitted to no respect for the government and administration, saying that Israel was not exactly what she'd been taught in Hebrew School in America.

Sarah had moved in part because she felt it would be easier to be both Jewish and lesbian in Israel. Like other religious lesbians I'd met, Sarah did not feel a terrible conflict about her lesbianism. She saw a halachic distinction between male homosexuality and lesbianism. She viewed lesbianism as no more serious than for "two unmarried heterosexuals to hold hands" (which would violate the prohibition against intimate contact between anyone other than husband and wife). Leviticus itself spoke very specifically to men. The Torah, she noted, did not mention lesbianism at all, and there were only a couple of discussions of the topic among the Sages. In any case, she explained to me, "a person's religious life involves more than one issue. I experience more conflict about the quality of my prayer. Homosexuals didn't suddenly just appear. We were there at Mount Sinai and we received the Torah."

Sarah's experiences, and those of the participants in the Mo'ach Gavra study group, are not typical of the reality most gay and lesbian Israelis experience. Most of them grow up secular or come to reject religious tradition as they grow older.

Israeli lesbians and gay men do gather to mark such festivals as Hanukkah, Purim (commemorating the saving of the Jews of Persia from destruction), and Passover, although the reason for gathering is usually social rather than religious. In fact, some of these celebrations are unlike any ever seen in the Diaspora. In 1998 gay Tel Aviv could mark Rosh ha-Shana at a club called Freedom, where a Madonna impersonator was scheduled to perform. If that seems strange to Diaspora Jews, it isn't for Israelis. Certainly no stranger than the lavish meals some of my best Israeli friends gather for with their families during the day on Yom Kippur, when Jews are supposed to fast. On Purim clubs, restaurants and hotels compete to offer the most lavish/garish Purim parties. Tel Aviv in 1996 boasted nightclubs offering a "Kinky Purim Party," gay Purim bashes, and even one for bisexuals (at a club called "Du Mi Ni"—a play on the Hebrew word for "bisexual" and the more vulgar English slang expression, "Do me").

The March 1998 issue of *Ha-Zman ha-Varod* even featured a gay reinterpretation of the Purim story, written in a gay argot—a mix of Hebrew, Iraqi Arabic, English, and made-up expressions—that originated among clubgoers and which the newspaper popularized. The story developed in decidedly un-Orthodox ways. In this gay midrash Esther, Mordechai's sister, was once a man who had since undergone a sex-change operation. Haman, still the Purim villain, intended to kill the gays of Persia rather than the Jews.[51] But, I would contend, the adaptation of the story is in the best tradition of the Jewish people. Jews have always sought to make the stories of their people relevant to the times in which they live—turning Purim into a parable of early gay struggle is just the latest example of a Jewish community continuing that tradition. Even the use of gay argot to tell the story is very Jewish. During their exile Jews developed vernacular languages like Yiddish, Ladino, and Judeo-Arabic, based on, but not exclusively, Hebrew.

My own Israeli Purim in the year 5758 began and ended like no other Purim I'd previously experienced. On a sunny Tel Aviv morning I headed off to the corner grocery store to buy my daily dose of Israeli news in *Yediot Achronot*—the Nation's Newspaper, as its advertising slogan proclaimed. The radio behind the counter was tuned to Reshet Gimel, Israel Radio's all-Israeli music station. As I handed the cashier my 3.20 shekels for the paper, the DJ proclaimed, "Purim with Dana International," and began playing a song by Israel's famous transsexual singer in which she sang about Mordechai and the Purim holiday. Quite an unexpected juxtaposition, I mused to myself. I walked out of the store, only to see two guys ride by on motorbikes, in drag.

Between interviews that day I made my way to Ben Yehuda Street, where Tel Aviv's Purim parade, the Adloyada,[52] was getting underway. Vendors were selling Barney balloons and people were dressed up in all manner of costumes. Children as fairy princesses and policemen, and adults in . . . well, most anything. In contrast to my American Jewish childhood, there were few Queen Esthers or Mordechais in view. One guy with a rainbow armband, lipstick, and a feather boa sauntered past. My gaydar began beeping and I approached him. He was, in fact, gay. I asked him what the holiday meant for him. "It's a chance to get dressed up and have fun!" he replied, heading over to meet friends. The parade looked like the Israeli version of Macy's Thanksgiving Day Parade. Tel Aviv mayor Roni Milo, dressed up as Tel Aviv's first mayor, Meir Dizengoff, led the parade dressed in a frock coat and riding a horse. Next came a group of dancing girls, dressed in Israeli flag costumes, followed by a police band. Then came the floats, many commemorating Israel's jubilee. Even the *chartzu-fim*, puppets from a satirical Israeli television show who depict leading political figures, paraded through Tel Aviv to the crowd's delight.

Walking down Tel Aviv's Sheinkin Street later that day, past the Häagen-Dazs store, the chic clothing and optical shops, and the multitudes of revelers of all ages and sexual orientations, I came upon a park that borders a yeshiva (Sheinkin boasts large numbers of both Israel's trendy Ashkenazi cultural elite and ultra-Orthodox residents). A group of teenagers with multiple earrings and piercings were dancing in a circle, while a few feet away, Lubavitch representatives were handing out treats to passers-by.

The next evening I got dressed up for Ofer Nissim's Purim Party, at Freedom, one of Tel Aviv's gay clubs of the moment. My friends, Gil Nader and Motti Porat, made up my face in patriotic Israeli blue and white and gave me a lovely turquoise Japanese robe for the evening. Their costumes were more garish, believe it or not, with Motti dressed up as a three-breasted something and Gil looking like a cross between a witch and a gypsy woman. For most of the people lined up in the middle of the night at the club (at 1 A.M., the club was just opening), it was just another club night, even though the advertisements posted on Sheinkin Street called it "Diva Purim," and promised the screening of Dana International's Eurovision entry, "Diva," on a giant screen, along with drag queens from Amsterdam. The party promoters certainly were not serving hamantaschen, a traditional holiday pastry. Rather, most clubgoers (few of whom were in costume) seemed to be clutching a Maccabee beer.

More intriguingly, even the Aguda, never a place particularly interested in Judaism in my personal experience, may be getting a dose of old-time religion. In asking Aguda chair Menachem Sheizaf about the relationship of lesbian and gay Jews in the Diaspora to Israel, he volunteered to me that he hoped to organize a Pride Service in 1998 at Beit Daniel, Tel Aviv's Reform synagogue, to open up Pride Week events. "I know gay Jews abroad are connected to Judaism on a religious basis. I'd like to see gay congregations here as well," he added. I chalked up the comments to good PR until I attended the Aguda's general meeting a couple of nights later and heard Sheizaf raise the idea publicly. As he quipped to those assembled, "We're two persecuted minorities. They (the Reform) are even the more persecuted one lately." The service ultimately did take place, but with mixed results. The rabbi declined to devote his sermon to a gay-related topic and only mentioned in passing that there were gays and lesbians present that night at synagogue.[53]

To Be Gay and Orthodox in Israel

For many of those who are religious and gay/lesbian, life is not easy in Israel. As noted earlier in this chapter, open discussion of sexuality is deemed "immodest" in religious circles, and open homosexuality within religious neighborhoods does not exist. HOD until recently ran a hotline called *Ha-Kav ha-Sarug*, the Knitted Yarmulke Hotline, a telephone hotline for observant gay Jews.

Because an Orthodox way of life is all-encompassing, just as life within a gay or lesbian community can be, coming to terms with a homosexual sexual orientation can be painful, indeed impossible, for gay Jews who grew up Orthodox in Israel. The headline for an article on gay religious Israelis in *Yediot Achronot* for April 1996 summed up the beliefs that such individuals have to overcome: "God Created Me a Sinner." Boaz, one of the gay Orthodox Jews interviewed for the article said, "I don't belong to anyone. Not to religion, because from a spiritual standpoint, I've gone down, and not to homosexuals. I have only one hope, that God will make a bit of effort for me and help me marry quickly. My judgment I'll accept in the afterlife."[54] As Boaz put it, "I know what punishments await me: death by stoning, immersion in boiling water. . . . For those engaged in sodomy, it is written, there will be no awakening when the dead are resurrected. . . . . Eternal loss."[55]

I spoke with another man in the dead of night in Jerusalem's Independence Park. Of Mizrachi background, he told me that he was married and the father of six children. Straining a bit to understand him through his Hebrew's Arabic-style cadences, I asked him what he was doing in the park at such an hour. He looked at the friend I was with and said, "I'm looking for someone nice." He said that his name was Moshe and he was from Ramot, a Jerusalem neighborhood with a large religious population. I asked him why he was not wearing a kippa. "I take it off when I come to the park. I keep things separate. God over there, this stuff over here." He claimed that he had been coming to the park since he was thirteen but insisted that he was not "gay." In fact, he said he did not like "gays." Why, I asked. "Because there is no need to go make a big deal over this." "This," I understood, referred to his nocturnal wanderings in the park. I asked him whether his wife ever asked him where he was going in the middle of the night. Moshe looked at me and replied, "No, it's none of her business."

Another religious Israeli I met in that park expressed fatalistic sentiments. Udi, a twenty-eight year old of Moroccan descent, told me that he walks around "with a lot of guilt" about his homosexuality, but it wasn't something that he could suppress. "It's like the need for air or food," he explained, philosophizing that "you can be rich, have money and a nice car, but if you had no sex, you wouldn't be able to be happy." Sin or not, that's the way it was for him with his homosexuality.

Because Orthodox, and especially ultra-Orthodox Jews, live apart from Israeli society, it is difficult for gay and lesbian Orthodox Jews to get basic information about sexual orientation issues let alone learn of the existence of the Aguda. Theo Mainz, who revived HOD this year by putting ads in weeklies in Jerusalem and Tel Aviv, told me that those who come to the group learned of it by reading forbidden secular newspapers in secret. The lack of information creates an image of gays among the religious as "Friends from Another Planet," to borrow from a headline in *Yediot Achronot* describing a rare encounter between gay activists and Orthodox youth in 1997 in Hod ha-Sharon, northeast of Tel Aviv.[56]

Along with a lack of basic information about homosexuality, Mainz notes that young Orthodox men and women face tremendous pressure to marry. Many yeshiva students who become aware of their sexual orientation are afraid, he told me, that they will not be able to perform sexually on their wedding night. Moreover, until they are married, Orthodox Jews usually live with their families. This adds to their difficulty in coping with their sexual orientation. Some gay and lesbian Orthodox Jews go on to marry, many live a double life, and a few *chozrim b'sh'eila*, question their religious faith and take the path toward a secular life.

Although HOD exists to help observant Jews manage the seeming contradictions between their religious beliefs and sexual orientation, there are other groups such as Orthodykes that take a more proactive approach. As Sarah demonstrated to me, along with a briefer conversation I had with a religious lesbian who was living with her partner and partner's children in one of the West Bank settlements located near Jerusalem, religious lesbians had relatively fewer theological issues to sort through since Jewish law took a more lenient approach toward lesbian sexuality. Moreover, lesbians did not have to wrestle with the prohibition against spilling seed and could comply with the commandment to be fruitful and multiply with greater ease than their gay male counterparts could. And as mentioned earlier, less traditional gay and lesbian Jews have also congregated at Kol ha-Neshama and other Reform synagogues in Israel that offer a more welcoming environment for gay people.

Nasty Brew: Gay Rights, Religious Politics, and Reform/Conservative Judaism in Israel

But both the Israeli Reform and Conservative movements have their own difficulties with gay issues. Most disturbing, from my own perspective, was the extent to which those difficulties stem from the movements' political calculations rather than any particular problems with interpreting halacha or the personal beliefs of some of their leaders. The positions of the Israeli Reform (Progressive) and Conservative (Masorti, or Traditional) movements on homosexuality and the role of lesbians and gay men in their communities are a consequence, in my view, of what happens when a country lacks separation of religion and state. In seeking to become part of Israel's recognized religious establishment, Israeli Reform and Conservative rabbis are getting involved in some of the dirty politics that they decry among their Orthodox and ultra-Orthodox counterparts—and engage in some of the same self-serving political calculations.

In early 1997 the Council of Progressive Rabbis in Israel (known by its Hebrew acronym as MARAM) met to discuss what the movement's position should be with regard to religious ceremonies for same-sex couples, echoing a similar debate in the Reform movement in the United States. MARAM proceeded to adopt several resolutions, with varying degrees of unanimity. The first resolution, accepted unanimously, stated that "MARAM is aware of the basic human need of every person for love, warmth, couplehood, family, spirituality, and holiness." The second resolution, also adopted without opposition, stated that "MARAM views the holiness of the marriage covenant between a man and a woman as the Jewish ideal for the establishment of a family and the continuity of the Jewish people." Resolution 3, adopted by a vote of 11–4, declared that "because at the present time it's reasonable to believe that homosexuality is not the result of free choice but rather the result of heredity and possible additional environmental factors, MARAM does not accept the definition of [homosexuality] as a to'eva (abomination)." Resolution 4, also unanimous, then proceeded to state that "despite the above, MARAM does not view as possible marriage ceremonies according to the Law of Moses and Israel for partners of the same sex." The final resolution, adopted by a narrow 10–8 vote, states that "MARAM allows its rabbis, according to their conscience and their Jewish responsibility to decide how to respond to the request of a same-sex couple to conduct commitment ceremonies *that are not* marriage ceremonies."[57]

A reasonable reading of the resolutions would lead one to believe that MARAM had decided to allow individual rabbis to conduct commitment ceremonies for same-sex couples, so long as those ceremonies were not "weddings" and did not use the linguistic formulas used in such ceremonies to wed heterosexual couples—namely, that they took each other as spouses "according to the Law of Moses and Israel." That certainly is what Rabbi David Ariel-Yoel of Jerusalem's Reform Har-El synagogue thought.

So, it was quite interesting to be in Israel in June 1997 as a contretemps broke out when Rabbi Ariel-Yoel conducted a religious ceremony for two lesbians. The ceremony, featured on the front page of *Ha'aretz*, created a lot of unhappiness in Israeli Reform circles, coming as it did right in the midst of debate on the so-called Conversion Law, which sought to ban recognition of Reform and Conservative conversions conducted in Israel and, possibly, outside the Jewish state as well. The president of MARAM, Rabbi Michael Boidan, proposed removing Rabbi Ariel-Yoel from the council if it became evident that the rabbi's ceremony had included elements of a Jewish wedding ceremony (nothing ever came of that threat).

I met Rabbi Ariel-Yoel one evening in his office at the synagogue to discuss both the ceremony and how the Israeli Reform movement deals (and should deal) with lesbians and gay men. When asked about the traditional interpretation of homosexuality as to'evea, he looked at me and said "a to'eva is a society that goes into people's bedrooms. That's not the type of society I want to live in. The tragedy is that the religious establishment has persecuted gays for thousands of years. We need to be bringing people closer to Judaism." His forthright positions on gay-related issues place him quite a distance from his more politically concerned colleagues.

While he views the prohibition in Leviticus as a very direct ban on homosexual relations, he did not feel that the ban could be relevant, as Judaism itself had evolved, as he put it "from a biblical Judaism to a Judaism of the sages." The sages, he noted, had found ways to bring innovations into Judaism or interpret ancient prohibitions out of existence.

Concerning the specific ceremony he conducted, he said that, notwithstanding the charges by some in the Israeli Reform movement, he had not conducted a wedding ceremony for the two women. In fact, he felt the need for unique ceremonies for same-sex couples, as such couples are not in his opinion the same in their nature as heterosexual couples. "Different, but equal" was the way he said he wanted to design such ceremonies. He expected that the battle over the place of gay people in the Reform movement in Israel would follow the same path as the debate over ordaining women as rabbis. The role of women in Reform Judaism was once the subject of vociferous debate. In the Reform movement that debate is long settled, with women rabbis now an accepted part of the religious life of the denomination.

Rabbi Uri Regev, the head of the Center for Religious Pluralism, is one of the leaders of the Israeli Reform movement, and one of the principals in the struggle against the Israeli religious establishment for recognition of the Reform movement. He paraphrased the founder of Reconstructionist Judaism, Mordechai Kaplan, to summarize the role of halacha in Israeli Reform Judaism: "Halacha has a vote, not a veto." Ever cautious, Rabbi Regev counseled that gay issues are not something that a group of rabbis should decide without a process of discussion within their synagogues, although he personally presented a pro-gay front on most issues.

If Regev was cautious about same-sex ceremonies and even gay issues generally, his Conservative counterpart, Rabbi Ehud Bendel, was that much more so. The Conservative Movement in Israel starts from the premise that halacha is binding but must cope with the times Jews live in and the problems of a modern society. Conservative Judaism in Israel, he said, starts off from a more conservative place than its American counterpart (the same is true, actually, of Israeli Reform Judaism). Thus, while Conservative Judaism in America allows its members to drive to synagogue on the Sabbath, its Israeli counterpart does not.

On homosexuality Rabbi Bendel drew the analogy of Conservative Judaism's approach to the role of women, specifically, ordination of women rabbis. For a long time, he said, the issue of ordination of women was not thought to be an "Israeli issue." When Israeli women began to raise the issue, the Conservative movement in Israel began to struggle with the question and debate it internally. At the same time, when the women's issue came up in Israel in 1984, Rabbi Bendel said that he told the movement that it couldn't reach a resolution all at once, even though the issue was causing a lot of anguished debate.

Although the Conservatives are more traditional in their approach to halacha, Bendel, rather surprisingly, admitted that halacha is not the only consideration. Speaking of women's ordination, he admitted that the movement looks to image questions as well. He explicitly said that "I have to consider the social reality. I have a much greater responsibility to the Masorti movement and its image." Thus, he implicitly suggested that enough pressure could force a change in Conservative Judaism's approach to a particular problem.

Bendel admitted to problems with the traditional halachic approach to homosexuality as well. "I respect an openly gay Jew as a Jew. He can be part of a minyan,[58] have an aliyah, be a member of a Conservative synagogue." At the same time, he wants to win state recognition of the Masorti movement that consideration of gay issues could only delay and complicate. *Tikkun ha-prat* (repair of the individual) must come before *tikkun olam* (repair of the world) was his realpolitik view of the gay issue. In other words, move cautiously. As for same-sex couples, Rabbi Bendel can "respect" same-sex couples, and count them among his friends, but does not want to give them a religious stamp of approval. Yet, he said, "I support economic rights for [same-sex] couples, as a citizen, not as a rabbi." Rabbi Bendel also supports, "as a citizen," civil marriage, but "as soon as a rabbinical body says we support [same-sex marriage], it causes problems from religious Jews." The Reform movement, he says, can move ahead on an issue like same-sex marriage, because "it doesn't have standards. We do." The citizen's rights approach to homosexuality certainly isn't unique to the Israeli Reform and Conservative rabbinates. Their American counterparts took their first steps on gay issues by proclaiming themselves against antigay discrimination in employment, and the like, long before they began wrestling with theology and homosexuality.

The Reform movement's, and most definitely the Conservative movement's, position on homosexuality in Jewish religious law, and ritual commitments for same-sex couples, stem as much from politics as they do from each movement's approach to Jewish tradition. The recent but by no means finished struggle between the two movements and the Israeli Orthodox religious establishment presented ample proof of how politicized the subject of homosexuality in Israeli Judaism can become. As *Ha'aretz*'s religious affairs correspondent, Shachar Ilan, put it, in an article on Rabbi Yoel-Ariel's ceremony for the lesbian couple:

> The first same-sex marriage ceremony conducted by a rabbi from the Reform movement couldn't have taken place at a worse time. On the day the ceremony took place, the representatives of the Reform and Conservative movements reached a compromise with the [government] coalition on the Conversion Law. In the days following publication of the news of the ceremony in *Ha'aretz*, the Reform feared that the event not only would blow up the agreement but also destroy their cooperation with the Conservatives.[59]

And Rabbi Ariel-Yoel's ceremony did not pass unnoticed in Orthodox circles. In an article about elections to the Chief Rabbinical Council, a writer for the National Religious Party–affiliated newspaper, *Ha-Tzofe*, could not resist writing about Rabbi Ariel-Yoel (with "rabbi" in quotation marks in the article) and blasting the proposed Conversion Law compromise establishing a conversion institute run by the three denominations. Commenting on the rabbi's ceremony, the writer wrote that "it's clear to all what wind is blowing from 'the Hebrew Union College.'"[60]

Despite the one-time-only popularity of Kehilat Ga'avat Yisrael and study groups for gay men and lesbians, most Israeli lesbians and gay men, unlike their Diaspora counterparts, are ultimately not all that interested in "reconciling" their sexual orientation with their religion. In this respect they are not different from their heterosexual secular counterparts who see in Israeli identity the expression of their Judaism, or even a substitute for it. The failure of non-Orthodox streams of Judaism to take root in Israel ultimately points to the success of both Zionism and Orthodox religious coercion. Both have conspired to keep too many Israelis, including lesbian and gay ones, in the dark about their religion.

4

Gays with Guns:
Gays in the Military, Israeli Style

*Recognizing that homosexuals are entitled to serve in the military
as are others, the IDF drafts those of this orientation for service.*
        —K-31-11-01 Service of Homosexuals in the IDF, 1993

*The fact is that the number of homosexuals in the population
constitutes a small minority, and the situation is no different in
the military. Thus, the chance that one will find by chance a partner for homosexual sexual contact is not great.*
        —*Eliezer v. Chief Military Prosecutor,*
    Military Appeals Court 1995, the case establishing consent
            rules for same-sex relations in a military setting

Amid the throngs at Tel Aviv Pride in June 1997 I saw a lone soldier in
uniform wandering about taking in the sights and talking with friends.
Lior, a twenty year old from Tel Aviv doing his stint of mandatory military service as a medic, agreed to talk to me for a couple of minutes. I
asked him whether appearing in his uniform at a gay pride event might
cause him problems. "No, not at all. I can come here in uniform. The
military command is accepting of it (gay and lesbian soldiers)." Although
not concerned about being seen, Lior was not out in the military. "It's
tough. . . . If I'm asked, I'll tell. I was supposed to be sent to a certain
military base and they asked whether I'm gay. I didn't say I was. But the
more I've developed, the more ready I feel to tell [them]." And how did
he feel on this day, Pride Day, as a gay Israeli soldier? "I'm feeling very
proud. I contribute to the country."

To understand why this is the case, and why the military environment
is not necessarily a hostile place for lesbian and gay Israelis, some background on the Israel Defense Forces' (IDF) mission is necessary. Simply
put, the IDF plays a formative, unifying role in Israeli society. Almost all
men, and most women, undergo a period of mandatory military service
at the age of eighteen for two or three years. Men are subject to annual
reserve duty until well into their forties. In a nation populated with Jews
from around the world, the IDF has traditionally been the great unifier.

If public schools in the United States taught successive waves of immigrants in the 1800s and early 1900s what it means to be an American, the IDF has played that role in Israel since the establishment of the state in 1948. It throws together Jews (and some Arabs) from different social classes, educational levels, and life experiences to create the closest thing to a shared Israeli identity that the State of Israel today possesses.[1] It provides at least the theoretical possibility of social advancement to Israelis and new immigrants from disadvantaged backgrounds. Until recent years those who did not go through the collective experience of military service faced widespread social stigma and limited job advancement opportunities. For those who do serve, the friendships—and connections—they make in the IDF often are lifelong.

In an article about today's Israeli youth in the Independence Day section of *Ha'aretz*, the newspaper could report, despite all the changes in Israeli society, that "they all believe in the IDF, in the importance of serving in it, in its centrality in Israeli society. . . . It's a framework with Israeli coloring. Not Jewish, not religious, not ethnic, nothing—Israeli."[2] In a country where little agreement today exists on fundamental questions of peace or on the country's identity as it heads into its second fifty years, the IDF, despite a tarnishing of its reputation in recent years, still stands as a shared experience for most Israeli youth.

The young lesbian and gay Israelis I met certainly did not seem to differ from their heterosexual peers in their view of the IDF. Chaim, the gay student from Nesher High, hoped to join the IDF's academic track and earn officer rank in the process; he acknowledged that he might get combat unit duty instead, but said that would be fine with him. Educational advisers at the Israeli high schools that I visited claimed that none of the gay and lesbian students they had counseled raised concerns about their upcoming military service based on their sexual orientation. The likely reason for the apparent lack of hesitation is that the requirement to serve is so entrenched as part of Israeli life. Former IDF chief military psychologist Reuven Gal could report that "service in the IDF usually receives unequivocal support from society. Parents in Israel discuss with their adolescents their prospective military service the way American or European parents discuss college studies with their teenagers."[3] Thus military service is seen as a natural part of one's life progression.

Perhaps because the military understood how great the stigma was against those who did not perform military service, Israeli gays and lesbians never have been barred officially from serving in the IDF because of their sexual orientation. Until 1993, however, there was a policy in place, haphazardly applied, that barred them from serving in sensitive positions, such as in the Intelligence Corps, that required high-level security clearances. Manpower Division Standing Orders from 1986 decreed as follows:

K31–11–01 Service of Homosexuals in the IDF

1. The placement of homosexual soldiers (in the standing military, mandatory service, and the reserves) and military employees and any limitation due to their orientation, is due to the fact that the above-mentioned orientation may constitute a security risk.
2. Nevertheless, because the above-mentioned orientation does not constitute a mental illness or deviance, such a soldier will not be rejected or restricted a priori. Rather, each case will be dealt with on an individual basis.
3. If information reaches a unit commander, mental health officer, or security officer that a soldier is homosexual, he shall refer the soldier, through the unit physician, to the mental health center.
4. The examination shall be conducted by the mental health center and by field security staff.
5. The mental health center's examination shall deal with two issues:
    A. Is the above-mentioned orientation accompanied by additional signs indicating a security risk.
    B. The level of the examinee's mental strength and maturity (the ability to withstand "pressures").
6. In light of the results of the mental health center's examination, which shall be forwarded to him, the head of the Field Security Department will decide:
    A. To recommend the termination of the soldier's or employee's service or employment.
    B. To recommend limitations on his deployment.
    C. To order the conduct of a comprehensive security investigation as appropriate to the soldier's or employee's position.
7. In every case, the security investigation shall be conducted by a senior sergeant or officer authorized to conduct a security review, during which no actions shall be taken that may humiliate or constitute harassment, blackmail, or a threat against the soldier, due to the suspicion that he may be homosexual.
8. The recommendation of the head of the Field Security Department to terminate service or employment in the IDF will be transmitted by

the Chief Adjutancy Officer or his deputy, to the Head of Command Administration, or to the head of the Center for Military Industry and they will initiate the termination of the soldier from mandatory service or reserve duty, allowing standing army service according to High Command Order 3.0501 or termination of the employee.

9. In no case shall homosexual soldiers or employees serve in top secret positions, in the intelligence community, or in encryption positions.

10. A soldier or military employee against whom there is a suspicion of homosexual orientation shall be under security supervision during his service or employment in the IDF.[4]

Such policies, reinforced by the conservative social climate, did not encourage gay visibility in the ranks. Gal Ochovsky, today *Ma'ariv*'s cultural editor, wrote a column in the late 1980s called *Boys/Moshe* for the Tel Aviv weekly, *Ha-Ir*. In one of his columns he described a three-week stint of reserve duty: "In Company C there are no gays. There are bachelors, marrieds, divorcés, and prudes, those who screw a lot, those who talk a lot, those who remember, and those who still have not understood. Gays—there aren't any."[5]

The military's restrictive policy soon came under public fire when, in 1993, MK Yael Dayan held the first ever hearings on gay issues and concerns. Themselves precedent setting, the hearings created a public sensation when Professor Uzi Even, then chairman of Tel Aviv University's Chemistry Department, told the committee how, in the 1980s, he had been stripped of his officer rank and barred from further sensitive research, solely because of his sexual orientation. Even was no ordinary IDF reservist. Although he would not disclose the exact nature of his military work, his background as a chemist led many to speculate that he had contributed to the development of Israel's nuclear program. Sitting in his Ramat Aviv home, Even recounted for me some of the events and considerations that led him to tell his story. What finally pushed Even to appear at the Knesset, despite much initial trepidation, was that "I knew that my story would arouse intense curiosity and that I could point out the consequences of army policy."

The revelation created a public storm—against the military and for Even, who comes across in person as very much the army officer, no-nonsense and masculine. Within two days of his testimony he received a call from Eitan Haber, the director of the Prime Minister's Office, saying that the military was prepared to restore Even's rank and security clearance. Even recalled to me that he retorted he had not just come out to the entire country only to fix a personal problem—he wanted to see the entire policy changed. Late Prime Minister Yitzhak Rabin stated at a cabinet meeting the week after the Knesset hearing that he saw no reason to discriminate against gay and lesbian soldiers. Although Rabin's government was prepared to address the issue, there were still prejudices to overcome. For example, in a Knesset debate called to discuss the military's policies toward gay troops, Minister of Health Chaim Ramon, speaking for the government, stated that "it's known in scientific and medical literature—and now I'm responding as minister of health—that a higher percentage of [gays and lesbians] have problems, we check the matter. It's necessary to check."[6]

Haber consulted with then chief of staff Ehud Barak (today the chair of the Labor Party) and said that it would be necessary to establish a military committee to deal with the issue. The committee consisted of Field Security, the Military Advocate General, the Mental Health Department, and Eitan Haber. Although not a part of the committee, the military consulted regularly with Even and other activists. The initial military proposals, said Even, did not please him or other activists. He told me he insisted there be a statement in the policy that the military does not discriminate against lesbian and gay soldiers and that Field Security, rather than the Mental Health Center, conduct any necessary follow-up investigations. After two months of drafts Chief of Staff Barak signed off on the new policy, as did the Knesset's influential Security and Foreign Affairs Committee.

The 1993 amendments to K-31–11–01 did constitute substantial progress:

Definitions

1. In this order *soldier* includes a female soldier and a male or female IDF employee.
2. Recognizing that homosexuals are entitled to serve in the military as are others, the IDF drafts those of this orientation for service on condition that they are fit for security service according to the criteria in force for all candidates for security service.
3. As a rule, the hiring of IDF employees or the placement of homosexual soldiers in basic service or reserve duty or their advancement shall not be restricted. Nevertheless, in certain cases there's a possibility of creating a security risk, and in those cases the placement and hiring of such individuals will be examined on an individual basis.

Report to Field Security Department

4. A unit commander who becomes aware that a soldier has the afore-mentioned orientation shall report the fact to the Field Security Department's Intelligence Branch—the head of the Manpower Review Wing, directly or via the unit's security officer. Transfer of the report shall be timely and to the addressee alone.

5. The head of the Field Security Department shall decide, on the basis of the report received from the soldier's unit, additional material on the soldier, and additional investigations if there's a need, and consultation with additional officials (including in the investigatee's unit) if his homosexual orientation, in light of his position, requires special treatment and security consideration.

6. At the end of the investigation and considerations the head of the Field Security Department shall recommend, based on his authority, taking one or more of the following possibilities:

    A. Not to undertake any step regarding placement, promotion, or service.

    B. Order the conduct of a comprehensive security investigation in accordance with the soldier's position.

    C. Place limits on his placement.

    D. Recommend early release, termination of service, or termination of employment.

7. If the head of the Field Security Department decides that the orientation presents no security risk, no limitations shall be placed on the soldier's placement or advancement.

8. In every case where it's decided to conduct a security investigation, it shall be conducted by a senior sergeant or officer, authorized by the head of the Field Security Department to conduct security reviews, and no actions shall be undertaken during it that might hurt the soldier, harass him, or humiliate him due to the possibility that he's homosexual.

    The soldier shall not be asked to divulge information about other soldiers if such information is not relevant to his security classification.[7]

The military did not try to hide or minimize the changes it was implementing in the treatment of lesbian and gay soldiers. Its news-magazine, *Bamachane*, triumphantly headlined the policy change in an article titled "Discrimination Has Ended." The article featured a sidebar with reactions to the policy change. While Max Fishbaum, a master sergeant in the Field Corps Command, stated that "service in the IDF demands being in Lebanon, on the front lines, and they [homosexuals] can't be everywhere," Obi Sabak, a master sergeant in the elite paratrooper unit, was more enthusiastic: "If they contribute to the IDF, great. I don't think there'll be any problem with them in the military. Why not? Now we've got more fighters."[8]

The difference between the 1986 and 1993 policies is substantial upon analysis. The 1986 Manpower Division Standing Orders start with the presumption that gays and lesbians in the military constitute a security risk that must be contained. The 1993 orders, in contrast, declare the IDF's "recognition that homosexuals are entitled to serve in the military like anyone else." Second, although the 1986 orders declared that the military did not consider homosexuality to be a mental illness or deviancy, the orders did implicitly accept stereotypes about gay men and lesbians, namely, that they are somehow weaker and less able to withstand "pressure" as compared to heterosexuals. Those regulations specifically ordered an investigation by military mental health authorities to evaluate a gay soldier's ability to cope with mental pressures and stress. Whether intentional or not, the use of such a framework implicitly stigmatized lesbians and gay men, suggesting that the mental health of gay and lesbian soldiers—and gays and lesbians generally—was somehow suspect.

The 1993 orders changed—on paper at least—this balance. Henceforth, the IDF's rule would be that there should be no limits set on the placement or employment of gay and lesbian soldiers or employees unless there existed an identifiable security risk.

But even the 1986 policy still stands out positively, considering that the public widely viewed homosexuality as "illegal," since the country's criminal code still prohibited sodomy, a behavior associated in the public mind with gay men. The 1986 rules still allowed gays to serve, keeping them in the Israeli family.

Today, says *Ha'aretz* journalist Shmuel Meiri, "young people can say they're gay and see themselves as part of normal society and the state. Israeli society has undergone a change from a mobilized society to a normal society where there's room for the individual. I have a friend who's in the military police and he goes to parties in uniform. The army obviously doesn't have a problem."

One factor that might make it easier for the military to adopt an open approach toward gay and lesbian soldiers is the fact that Israeli soldiers are not cut off from civil society for extensive lengths of time, even during their two or three years of mandatory military service. Former Chief

Military Psychologist Gal noted in an article about IDF policy toward gays that Israeli soldiers often return home at the end of each day or, at worst, receive weekend passes.[9] Every Thursday and Friday afternoon, and then again on Sunday mornings, I would see soldiers disembarking at the central bus stations of Israel's major cities, on their way to and from their homes. Fathers would take their sons and daughters to the bus station, help them unload their duffel bags, and give them a kiss good-bye as they met up with their fellow unit members, bought drinks and newspapers, and settled in for the long ride back to their bases. The integration of the military with civilian life is far-reaching in Israel, extending from these bus station scenes to citizens' ongoing connection to the military, and vice versa through reserve duty, to the role that retired military figures play in the nation's civic and political life.[10]

I contacted Dover Tzahal, the IDF Spokesman's Office, two months before leaving for Israel in February 1998 with a request to interview several military officials, including the chief manpower division officer, the chief women's corps officer, and the military advocate general. Dover Tzahal ultimately agreed to make the military advocate general available for an interview. That is how I found myself waiting for my Dover Tzahal escort in a sandstorm at the corner of Kaplan and Elazar Streets in Tel Aviv one March morning. The offices of Israel's military and Ministry of Defense reflect the informal, somewhat haphazard nature of the Israeli military. The warren of buildings, in all sorts of architectural styles ranging from a high rise with space needle at its top to less majestic barracks, occupies a few square blocks in central Tel Aviv. Despite its prowess in battle, the IDF is not a spit-and-polish operation. During my travels in Israel I ceased being surprised at seeing uniformed soldiers in track shoes. The Israeli military is probably the only military whose soldiers all seem to carry cellular telephones as part of their equipment (a phenomenon that the military has tried to combat without much success, even when members of one unit serving in Lebanon used their phones to have a pizza delivered to the border). One of Israel's cellular telephone companies even markets a package called *PAKAL*—an Israeli military acronym for "standing battle orders"—to the young men and women in uniform.

The military advocate general, Brigadier-General Uri Shoham, works out of a low-rise house a few steps from the appointed intersection. An extroverted, mustachioed man, he proved rather eager to paint a positive picture of the IDF's own gays-in-the-military experience. As we engaged in small talk, he first brought up his own experiences with the American military, in which he had spent some time through an exchange program. A diploma from the Judge Advocate General's School in Charlottesville, Virginia, hung on his wall. He admitted an inability to understand the American gays-in-the-military debate, but reflected that the feeling was mutual: the Americans with whom he worked and studied could not grasp that Israel could let avowed homosexuals serve in its armed forces.

Shoham contended that the IDF was already considering changing the 1986 Standing Orders on homosexuals' service in the IDF when Uzi Even made his appearance before Yael Dayan's subcommittee in February 1993. The Rabin government had begun passing a series of Basic Laws that were to serve as the precursors to an Israeli constitution. These laws, building on those passed by previous Knessets, included such far-reaching Basic Laws as the Law on the Dignity of Man and His Freedom. The army, claimed Shoham, aware of the greater respect for individuals and individual rights accorded by the Basic Laws, decided that there was a basis for further refining military policy toward lesbian and gay soldiers. Even accepting Shoham's version of events, there should be little doubt that Even's public *J'accuse* against the military's practices was the push that the military needed to institute its reforms. His public coming out forced an issue that may have been discussed in internal military forums into the open. While Shoham contended that there were very few investigations launched under the 1986 Standing Orders, the fact that Even lost his security clearance because of such policy some years earlier suggests that the military did try to weed out known gays and lesbians from "sensitive positions." Shoham himself told me that "the Command accepted the idea that gays were not suitable for some tasks—out of security considerations." He further analogized to me the security risk behind being gay to a heterosexual soldier having a mistress.

After reciting some of the considerations behind the 1993 amendments to the Standing Orders, the military advocate general surprised me by stating flat out that the General Staff was currently examining whether the IDF even needed the existing policy. In other words, the IDF was reconsidering whether gays could ever constitute a security risk because of their sexual orientation. The developing view was that the IDF had focused on the wrong area—it was not open gays and lesbians who might be a problem but those who were trying to hide their sexual orientation.

So, how does the IDF currently see lesbian and gay soldiers, I asked. The brigadier-general's response: soldiers with equal rights and duties. As shall be seen forthwith, that response is largely, but not completely, correct. For example, the IDF currently does not take measures to educate its troops about homophobia. Although officially the military might not see gay soldiers as different from their heterosexual counterparts, it does not want to be a "melting pot" on this issue. The failure to undertake such education is significant, because the IDF, as pointed out earlier in this chapter, plays an important role in Israel by bringing different sectors of Israeli society together and providing a means of social advancement. Brigadier-General Shoham himself said that it is important for the IDF to serve as a bridge between immigrants and sabras, between the "Second Israel" (the Mizrachim) and the Israeli Ashkenazi elite.

In contrast, he told me, "sexual orientation doesn't interest the military, except regarding security issues." Despite the IDF's efforts to reduce social gaps and prejudice, it is reluctant to take the issue of sexual orientation on because it is the subject of some public controversy. That suggests a failure of nerve on the military's part. Although the Israeli political, media, and judicial elites have done much to educate the public on gay issues through laws, positive press coverage, and legal precedents, the military, because of the universality of military service among Israeli Jews, could further reduce homophobia and homo-ignorance were it to undertake the kind of education that might truly break down the remaining barriers facing lesbians and gay men. Moreover, it is precisely because the subject is controversial that the IDF should confront the issue head-on. The IDF tries to break down stereotypes about new immigrants or Mizrachim because these groups do face stereotyping and discrimination in Israeli society.

So, how does the military deal with harassment of openly lesbian and gay troops? Shoham contended that harassment of lesbian and gay military personnel is very rare and that he could recall few if any cases he had had to deal with. That answer is a bit disingenuous though, as it assumes the harassment will reach criminal proportions and the harassed soldier will bring a case. Some Israeli lesbians and gay men told me that commanders would take care of most harassment cases and that it was unlikely to reach the military advocate general. The reality is that there is no way to completely prevent harassment. As Shoham put it, "I can't promise that in Golani (an elite combat unit) everything will be OK, but I would deal with [harassment] accordingly."

The success of Israeli activists in winning such a rapid change in military policy owes much to the central role of the military in Israeli society and the ongoing security threats with which all Israelis must cope. It also owes much to the commitment of activists themselves to obtaining equality in all aspects of military service, to a sense of patriotism that sexual orientation and historic marginalization have not dimmed.

Ironically, Israel conducted its gays-in-the-military debate at the same time a similar debate raged in the United States. A General Accounting Office committee even journeyed to Israel to learn how the vaunted Israeli military could allow homosexuals into its ranks and survive. The Israeli military found the whole American debate rather strange, as a report in *Bamachane* suggests:

> American military rules dictate to soldiers how to conduct their sex lives. For example, officers are barred from having sexual contact with women soldiers serving under them. It's forbidden to have sexual relations on military bases, except for married couples—but only when they are in their home. American soldiers cannot engage in oral or anal sex, even off base. But it's necessary to note that while heterosexuals may collide with military rules because of certain sexual behavior, a homosexual collides with the law not only because of acts but because of his "orientation." And that, of course, is serious discrimination.[11]

The end results of these two debates, of course, differ markedly. The failure of gay and lesbian activists in the United States to attain similar policy outcomes probably stems from four factors: 1) the greater military threat faced by Israel, which causes the military to pause before deeming individuals, let alone groups, unfit for military service; 2) the lack of enthusiasm among many American activists for the military debate, stemming from their own decidedly mixed attitudes toward this institution and their more radical sociopolitical outlook; 3) the peculiar sexual overtones of the debate over gays in the military in the United States, which Israelis, as evidenced by the above article in *Bamachane*, had a difficult time comprehending; and 4) the strong link in the United States between support for the military and conservative political and social stances.

In fact, the IDF's new openness toward gays works too well for some. Prior to the issuance of the 1993 Standing Orders, activists told me, there were some gays who used their homosexuality to avoid military service or reserve duty. Today, homosexuality will not give you a pass on doing your national duty. *Yediot Achronot* journalist and editor Avner Bernheimer told me of a friend in a combat unit who wanted to get out of reserve duty because he was going to be sent to the Gaza Strip and tried to use his homosexuality as a reason. The military refused to exempt the reservist from his tour of duty. Bernheimer himself, who works in air traf-

fic control while on reserve duty, had to undergo a special military investigation because of his sexual orientation. His description of the investigation: "apologetic and short" (a view seconded by my friend, Ilan
Vitemberg, who also recently underwent such an investigation). As he
mused, "The army's paranoid. It doesn't want to make mistakes."

The IDF's official openness shows up in surprising places—like sexual conduct rules. Perhaps trying to shock me with the military's liberal
official attitudes, Brigadier-General Shoham recalled a case he had decided as a military judge—one, he said, that established whether same-
sex relations would be deemed consensual rather than coerced.

The case, *Eliezer v. Chief Military Prosecutor*, grew out of an appeal
from a reservist's conviction for forced sexual acts and sodomy with a
nineteen-year-old soldier performing his basic military service at a base
in the south of Israel. The reservist, Private Eliezer, a thirty-two-year-old
married father of five, approached Private Yaniv one night as the latter
was awaiting the arrival of a group of soldiers to go on base patrol. According to Private Yaniv's testimony:

> He asked me when was the last time I had "come"—look, I've had a
> girlfriend for two years and I slept with her on Sunday. We started to
> talk about sex. He began to tell me that he's got girls from Beer Sheva
> and proposed that I leave the base with him the next day at 5:30 P.M.
> and he'll arrange for a nice girl from Ofakim, and he said that she likes
> men with a big penis. . . . Then he said to me, "How many centimeters
> do you have?" I said to him, "About 20,"[12] and he said, "Show me,"
> and stuck his hands in my pants.[13]

Private Eliezer then proceeded to try to force both oral and anal sex
on Private Yaniv, until the latter was able to push the reservist off of him
and flee the room.

The military appeals court did not accept Private Eliezer's contention
that he sincerely believed that Private Yaniv was interested in sexual relations with him. In examining whether Private Yaniv could have consented,
the IDF court proceeded to establish criteria for consensual homosexual
relations between soldiers. The court first noted that Private Yaniv's exposure of his penis "can be explained in its entirety by his desire to stand up
to the challenge that the appellant posed and one cannot conclude from
that that he asked for or was ready to try a homosexual experience."[14]

The court's criteria for homosexual relations in the military boil down
to three points: 1) the initiator must "cautiously" check the readiness of

his partner to engage in homosexual activity; 2) the initiator must reach an unambiguous conclusion that his prospective partner is gay and interested in sexual contact; and 3) the sexual activity must be private. With regard to the first condition, the court noted that "the number of homosexuals constitutes a small minority, and the situation is no different in the military. Thus, the chance that one will find by chance a partner for homosexual sexual contact is not great."[15] Concerning the second condition, the court stated that "the demand that we have set forth takes on additional force in a chance meeting, in a place that does not serve as a known meeting place for homosexuals, especially when there was no prior acquaintance between the two."[16] The court effectively established a certain equivalence between heterosexual and homosexual relations in noting that "while, in a heterosexual relationship, it is necessary to clarify if the female partner consents to sexual relations one way or another—in this case it is necessary to predetermine the sexual orientation and preferences of the other party."[17]

The privacy requirement should come as no surprise, especially considering the circumstances of the *Eliezer* case. The military appeals panel declared that "it is unthinkable that the complainant would agree to a homosexual sexual relationship in an unlocked room that his comrades might enter at any moment and call him up for patrol."[18] Taken as a whole, the *Eliezer* case suggests a tolerant yet practical attitude in the Israeli military toward sexual relations between soldiers. Brigadier-General Shoham reiterated the points of the case to me and added that relationships within the chain of command similarly are forbidden. It's not that the IDF *encourages* sexual relations in a military setting among soldiers; it doesn't. But it has established commonsense guidelines to minimize the likelihood of collateral complications from such relationships, including homosexual relationships. Like so much else concerning IDF policy toward lesbians and gay men, it is unclear just how much the official (and very enlightened) policies filter down into the day-to-day life of soldiers. While the IDF does conduct training to combat the problem of sexual harassment of female soldiers, it does not discuss homosexuality as part of its educational efforts—thus it is unlikely that the average soldier is aware of the case and the guidelines that the military appeals panel effectively set out.

To learn more about gays in the military, Israeli style, I spoke with Dani Kaplan, a graduate student in psychology at the Hebrew University in Jerusalem, who had just completed his master's thesis and presented a lecture at Jerusalem's Van Leer Institute titled "Coping Strategies of Homosexuals in Combat Units—Construction of Walls and Their Breach in the Stronghold of Masculinity."[19] Kaplan, a compactly built, sandy-haired man, who turned his thesis into a book, titled *David, Jonathan, and Other Soldiers*, tells me of his research over dinner in rapid-fire Hebrew.

Kaplan spoke with fourteen soldiers who had served in the IDF's elite combat units in a period extending from 1980 through 1996.[20] He found his research subjects through acquaintances and through an advertisement placed in a newspaper. He says that the purpose of the research was not to address military policy per se but rather to test how gay soldiers in such a hypermasculine environment coped during their service and how they viewed their military service retrospectively.

Kaplan found that the soldiers he interviewed viewed military service as a social norm, as a natural part of life in Israeli society. He himself pointed out to me that "the army is a part of growing up. For boys there are three milestones in Israel: *brit* (ritual circumcision), bar mitzvah,[21] and IDF enlistment." One of his interviewees, Rami, told him, "I think that service in the IDF is a very important part of how society sees you and how you see yourself as part of society, I don't think I'd give it up. . . . I feel I contributed, and that I was a part of those same people who go do the work. This is something very important in Israeliness, in the Israeli experience."[22]

Among those gay interviewees who served in combat units, Kaplan found no significant difference between them and a control group of Israeli soldiers studied by another Israeli researcher in their coping with the rigors of combat unit service. Looking at the issue of how gay soldiers fit into combat units, Kaplan found that some of his interviewees viewed combat service as a way to strengthen their masculine self-image. He posited two models for how gay troops relate to the hypermasculine culture of IDF combat units: compartmentalization and engagement.

In the case of compartmentalization, says Kaplan, a soldier views his service as he would a job. Those who fall into this model, he says, draw a line between their professional duties and their social life. Those who choose this option, he says, tend to express greater dissatisfaction with their military experience, are more likely to be platonic friends with women soldiers during their service, and tend to retain fewer friends from the military. Kaplan compared this coping strategy with that employed by some women soldiers in Western militaries, who similarly must try to fit into a hypermasculine culture.

In the case of engagement soldiers lean on social success as a coping strategy. They are gung ho about the entire military experience, viewing it as successful test after successful test of their masculinity. Unlike compartmentalizing soldiers, who tend to be indifferent or cynical about military symbols, engagement soldiers identify with military training as a set of hurdles for masculinity and take part in heterosexual discourse, including talk about women. Perhaps most important, they are very social, developing close ties with their fellow unit mates.[23]

Significantly, most of Kaplan's interviewees did not fully know of their homosexuality when they enlisted. Instead, their awareness of their homosexuality grew during their military service—twenty was a common age, according to Kaplan. Kaplan told me that soldiers' gayness, to the extent that they were aware of it during their military service, did not affect their identification with the image of the combat unit. That is not surprising, considering that those just coming to terms with their sexual identity are usually dealing with immediate issues rather than philosophical insights.

In rating his interviewees' comfort with their sexual orientation, Kaplan found data that have a potential wider impact on the development of Israel's gay community. Kaplan told me that his research suggests that combat unit experience may strengthen a tendency toward integration rather than gay pride. Although combat troops are a minority in the IDF, this tendency toward integration finds expression outside military life, in the lack of the types of visible indicia of gayness common in many Western countries and perhaps in the strategies used by Israeli gay activists in the political arena.

The military, as very much a part of Israeli society, presents the same paradox for gay people Israeli society does in general: the gap between progressive laws and practices versus a social climate that makes gay people cautious about coming out exists in the IDF as well. Just as the intimacy of Israeli society works as a barrier to coming out of the closet to friends and family, so can the constant influence of the IDF on one's life have a similar limiting effect. Former chief military psychologist Reuven Gal compared a soldier's reserve unit to an "extended family," noting that "the Israeli [reservist] may sometimes spend two or more decades of his life in the same reserve unit, basically in the same company, and with the same core of peers and leaders. Only the wars change."[24] In essence, if gay Israelis have a difficult time coming out in a country with such strong family ties, it stands to reason that coming out in one's reserve unit, which functions like a family, would be similarly difficult.

Sexual tensions are not completely absent in the Israeli military. A few of those who follow the engagement model take the intensity of combat unit service, and the closeness it engenders, a step beyond and do develop intimate relationships with some of their fellows. Although most of Kaplan's interviewees did not have gay sexual experiences during their military service, a few did, even while having girlfriends at the same time. As Menashe, one of Kaplan's subjects told him, "As I told you, I also at the time I was with her (his girlfriend), if I had the chance to be with a man, I would try. . . . So I had a girlfriend and everything was good and the gang knew her and there were parties and everything was okay . . . so I defined myself as perhaps bisexual."[25]

Those few who did have same-sex experiences tended to have adopted the model of engagement outlined by Kaplan. Menashe described to Kaplan one such experience:

> He began to say, "If my girlfriend were here, the things I would do now," and I begin to tell him, "If my girlfriend were here, the things I would do now." Ah . . . talk, talk, talk about girlfriends and what you like . . . and if my girlfriend were here, what a blowjob she'd give me . . . and then, I don't remember who said it first, "You know what? Instead of breaking our heads . . . come on, man, blowjob for blowjob?" You know such a guy'll say, "What, I don't have any balls? I'll do it." So that's how it happened. And that's how it continued. Thanks to the IDF [laughs].[26]

As Kaplan notes, "When the entire military is a chain of tests of masculinity, homosexual sex can turn into part of the matter, if you know how to present things 'right.' "[27]

Those lesbian and gay Israelis performing their basic military service usually prefer not to come out. As one young man put it to me, "I want to avoid any hassles [while doing mandatory service]. Once I begin doing reserve duty, I'll worry less about coming out." And, as Kaplan posited, another factor is that many young gays and lesbians begin to deal with their homosexuality only at some stage during their military service. Under those circumstances, one cannot expect that large numbers of gays and lesbians would make their identities known.

Those who told me of their coming out experiences in the military generally reported positive responses, which makes sense. If you are comfortable with who you are, others will be too. Yossi Even-Kama serves in one of the Women's Corps' training bases in the south of the country, where he works as a clerk to the base commander.[28] Everyone on his base knows of his sexual orientation, and when Educational Television finally broadcast the *Open Cards* program, a group of people gathered in the base commander's office to watch. But he knew of other gays and lesbians on nearby bases who were afraid of the consequences of coming out.

Lots of people on base asked him questions about being gay, he reported, especially some of the master sergeants. Many of them came from the same macho-guy environment he grew up with in Jaffa, and the fact that he could relate well to them, he recalled, enabled him to establish a common language. Serving his country, he added, gave him legitimacy in the battle for gay rights, since he was making his contribution to Israeli society.

One young gay Israeli, Udi, from Nesher, even took issue with those who think that their homosexuality will make it difficult for them to serve in the IDF. He wrote a letter titled "Green? It Suits Me" to *Ha-Zman ha-Varod*. Printed in April 1998, the letter constituted a paean to the IDF that Dover Tzahal could not have written any better:

> More than once has the fear been expressed concerning how gays, especially effeminate ones, will integrate into the army. I have a suggestion: integrate into the IDF with the help of the IDF! I'm a very active and open gay in Haifa (establishment of the youth group, coming out of the closet, interviews in the media). I'm also effeminate, and drag shows are among my hobbies. Two weeks ago I finished basic training at Camp 80, where by the end of training half the class knew about me personally, and the rest from rumors, that I'm gay.
>
> The responses? Some were surprised, some were interested, and there were even those who said that gays are better people. There was even an effort at matchmaking. I heard no negative response, even though most of them were religious or traditional. Most of them pray every day, keep kosher, wear yarmulkes, etc. Those from all ranks of the corps helped me and took an interest in how I was doing. Even when I couldn't take it any more and cried, they encouraged me and supported me. So, there's hope that after the makeup, the wig, and the high heels, we all can also be soldiers, because the IDF wants us and is ready to help us.
>
> Just as it's important to fight homophobia, it's also important to fight Judeophobia and protect our country. So, boys, girls, and all the rest, green's not such an ugly color.[29]

And if a self-described effeminate man who likes drag can embrace military service as part of his national duty, so can more mainstream types. Near the end of one research trip I journeyed to Beer Sheva, to meet a young gay Mizrachi officer, Oren, building a career in the standing army. All the typical adjectives I could bandy about would actually apply in his case: tall, dark, and handsome as hell. If they put a picture of this officer on posters and sent them to gay synagogues overseas, the rate of aliyah probably would increase substantially!

Oren came to our interview out of uniform but still carrying his army-issued pistol, which he showed me. As a Jew in the Diaspora (and a gay one on top of that), no one had ever encouraged me to perform military service. Thus, I will confess here to a certain fascination as he took out the gun. Oren was the personification of the Zionist dream—that Jews would no longer be powerless, that they would know how to fight and defend themselves and their people, unlike their weak Diaspora counterparts.

One year in the standing army, Oren had undertaken a series of operational tasks and undergone officer training. From the time he enlisted, he had excelled, finishing first out of 160 men in his unit's basic training course and going from one success to another in the military. He had served in a number of sensitive positions, including in the Gaza Strip. Oren has chosen not to be officially openly gay—at least at this point in his career. If asked, he would tell and estimates that in reality he would have no problems with the military. As he put it, "I don't deny it. I don't say I have a girlfriend. I do my work and I'm successful." So successful that he was under consideration for a prestigious officer's award when we met.

When I pressed him further on the atmosphere for gays in the IDF, he shot back, "There's no problem. You might run into a homophobe, but that's his problem, not mine." He felt no need to be more open, saying, "To go with a flag and say 'I'm gay, I'm gay,' what's the point?" When I asked him why such a macho institution as the military did not cause greater problems for gay men in particular, he looked at me like I had taken leave of my senses: "There's no contradiction between 'macho' and gay," Oren declared with finality. He was, I suppose, living proof of that sentiment. Oren's attitudes again demonstrate how gay or lesbian identity is still in its infancy in Israel, where sexual orientation is still considered an individual matter. His service in the great Israeli melting pot called the IDF merely strengthened, as Kaplan's study postulated, that tendency.

Oren felt free to have boyfriends. He had had one-year-long relationship when he was nineteen, which, he admitted with evident regret, he had "thrown away." As an officer, he just had to make sure not to become involved with anyone in his chain of command. He had just met an eighteen-year-old young man doing his basic military service a week before we sat down to talk, and he was off to meet him after our interview. Although he was not sure whether he would make the IDF a lifelong career, he said he liked military life a lot. He was more certain that he would meet Mr. Right and settle down into a permanent relationship, preferably monogamous, and have children as well.

Oren's story points out how, for many in Israel, discovery of their sexual orientation does not axiomatically lead to feelings of difference or alienation from society's defining institutions. His discovery of his sexual orientation at the age of fifteen did not lead him to doubt his masculinity. Like some of Kaplan's research subjects, the army gave him the basis to demonstrate the lack of contradiction between his sexual orientation and the military's macho environment.

Unlike most countries, Israel also has a draft for women. The prevailing myth abroad is that Israeli women train for combat and play a vital role in the IDF. In reality, however, Israeli women served in combat roles only during the country's War of Independence in 1948 and today serve mostly in support roles. Reuven Gal cites a 1980 pamphlet issued by the IDF Spokesman's Office to illustrate how distant the myth about women's military service is from the reality:

> Sorry to disappoint you if you have been influenced by the Hollywood image of Israeli girl soldiers being amazon-type warriors accoutered in ill-fitting male combat fatigues and toting sub-machine guns. Today's Israeli female soldiers are trim girls, clothed in uniforms which bring out their youthful femininity. They play a wide variety of non-combatant, though thoroughly essential, roles within the IDF framework and within certain sectors of the civilian community.[30]

In recent years a greater range of jobs has opened up for female IDF conscripts, and women have successfully sued the IDF for the right to join the elite fighter pilot course.[31]

In that context, how do lesbians view IDF service? Hadar and her girlfriend, whom I met at the Aguda's Tel Aviv Community Center, were not looking forward to their military service—not because of concerns about disclosing their sexual orientation, but because women typically do not receive interesting jobs. As Tal Yarus-Chakak noted to me, "Women have no real role [in the IDF]. Women don't do reserve duty. . . . It's more important for us to fight the army as feminists rather than as lesbians."

Hadar Namir voiced a more principled complaint about the military—that anything connected to it moves to the center of the national agenda, including the gay community's agenda. She told me that Yael Dayan's 1993 conference on gay issues in the Knesset was supposed to be about general education of the public on gay issues. "Then Uzi Even came out. The focus turned to the military and changed our agenda. It's an important issue here, but [the military] also is antifeminist." Yet even committed feminists can only challenge the military so much. Nurit Barkai, a lesbian and former secretary of Kibbutz Rosh ha-Nikra, admitted to me that "I'm antimilitary, but you have to be balanced about it. Katyushas fly over my head here. I have to defend myself."

A *Klaf Chazak* issue published in honor of KLAF's tenth anniversary contained an article titled "Lesbians in the Military." Michal B., the article's author, wrote that there are no statistics about the number of lesbians in the IDF and, when information about a soldier leaks out, "the commanders tend to ignore it and not pass it forward." But she adds that "it depends on the direct commander's worldview, the contribution of the [lesbian] soldier, and in accordance with matters that have nothing to do with her sexual preference but rather with human relations."[32] And, as is the case with men, many women soldiers do not realize or come to terms with their sexual orientation during the two to three years of basic military service.

Michal served at first close to home, which enabled her, she writes, to relate to the IDF as an employer—Kaplan's compartmentalization model comes to mind. Her concerns only grew when she was transferred to a military base in the south of Israel. Living on a base twenty-four hours a day made hiding an elementary part of her identity increasingly difficult, yet she feared social isolation if she shared the truth about herself. The pressures finally convinced Michal to tell close friends of hers on base, and "I was never disappointed with the responses."

She even chose to bring her partner to one of the base's social events. She writes that "the decision was preceded by consultations with my professional commander. . . . He recommended to me quite warmly not to hide my orientation and promised to support me professionally if there were any problems following my revelation." Her commander even approved leave for her so that she could attend Pride Week events. As her commander put it, "My Druze soldiers get leave for their holidays, so there's no reason you should return to base during such an important week."[33]

Michal writes that, while her story might not be typical, it was also not unique. She did, however, profile another soldier, Rinat, who chose to hide her sexual orientation during her military service for fear of the

consequences. Rinat recounted how she served in a base where the officers tried to sleep with female soldiers. "The thing," she told Michal B.,
"was that any girl who refused got a reputation as a lesbian. And the
way it was portrayed was very dirty. It's true that none of them were lesbians, but the response to them was so harsh that I didn't dare say anything."[34] Even though Rinat's commander eventually took care of this
problem, her recollection of these soldiers' humiliating treatment stayed
with her and kept her closeted.

Other women I interviewed have fond memories of their military service. Debbie, a young American-born lesbian, told me that she remembers
the army as a place where close ties between women can develop. Avivit,
another Jerusalem lesbian, went through a platoon commander's course
in which half the participants were lesbians, but, as she recalled to me,
"you don't think about it a lot. The hardest part of army service for me
was because I had a girlfriend." Her current girlfriend, Ronit, remains in
touch with lesbians she served with during her army days. The banality
of these statements suggests a different dynamic at work. Most young lesbian and gay Israelis, many just coming to terms with their sexual orientation, don't think of the difficulties of military service in terms of their
sexual orientation: they recall the hard work, the physical and mental
challenges, being separated from loved ones, or, in the case of women, the
menial work they often have to perform as part of their service, which is
geared toward "supporting the men."

Although many of the above stories appear quite positive, the new policy on gays' military service in the IDF is not flawless in practice. Nor can
it be said that harassment of lesbian and gay soldiers has disappeared, as
Rinat's example of lesbian-baiting suggests or as even Brigadier-General
Shoham admitted.

In 1993 the Aguda held its Gay Pride celebration in a park on Sheinkin
Street in Tel Aviv. Among those attending was a young soldier in the prestigious Nachal unit named Yossi Macaiton. He spoke to a newspaper reporter while in uniform, standing next to the symbolic closet that the
Aguda erected at one end of the park. The unit's commander, Brigadier-
General Menachem Zotorsky, removed Macaiton from the unit, allegedly
for violating military regulations barring unsupervised interviews with soldiers in uniform. The harshness of the sentence surprised many, because,
in practice, many soldiers give interviews while in uniform on nonmilitary
matters without advance coordination or approval from Dover Tzahal.

More recently, *Yediot Achronot* trumpeted the story of a nineteen-
year-old gay private who went AWOL rather than face continued ha-

rassment on the military base where he was serving. The story's headline says it all: "The Commanders Called Me Homo Over the Loudspeaker—And My Life Became Hell." The soldier, who was serving in the army's Northern Command, told of how he was forced to eat at a separate table, how no one would bunk with him, and how he was able to shower only twice a week, because he was barred from showering with the other troops. The private received a military discharge, and his parents still do not know the real reason: "Once they know about [my being gay], for them it will be as if they no longer have a son."[35] The newspaper story did not detail whether the army was taking action against his tormentors.

I asked Dani Kaplan about these stories and whether they suggest that IDF policy toward gays really is not as enlightened as it appears at first glance. He felt that such cases were an exception and pointed out to me the absence of homophobia as a motivator in basic training. Commanders, he said, do not challenge their troops as "faggots" if they are not performing at peak. Although "homo" is often thrown about, it is used more between soldiers kidding each other.

When I raised these cases with the military advocate general, his response was that if those were the only cases I could point to, the military's policy in fact was quite successful. He reiterated that he had never had to deal with harassment against gay troops in his career as a military lawyer. Considering that the Aguda, too, has little criticism of the military's policies suggests that they are working about as well as can be expected.

Uzi Even, in many ways the parent of the 1993 policy, was even more adamant than Brigadier-General Shoham. Some of the early cases of alleged harassment that hit the media after the IDF issued the 1993 Standing Orders came to the attention of Yael Dayan's Knesset committee, which launched investigations of any complaints that arose. Even was involved with that process and insisted that none of the cases had their roots in antigay bias. In one case two (heterosexual) soldiers made a one hundred-shekel bet to see who would perform oral sex on whom, and did this in the midst of a military dining hall. Both Even and Brigadier-General Shoham said to me that the incident appalled gay soldiers present at the time. Even was similarly dismissive of the substance of other complaints that arose.

If anything, certain IDF units have developed a reputation as quite gay friendly. Kaplan specifically mentions the Intelligence Corps, the Nachal (a paramilitary brigade), and medics units, as well as the military entertainment corps, as those that have developed a gay reputation and even a "gay culture." My own observation during my research trips to Israel bears out Kaplan's analysis. Ilan Vitemberg, Chagai El-Ad, and David Meiri all served in the Intelligence Corps, and I lost count of others whom I met who had served in that unit as well. Meiri quipped to me that it is no wonder that the Intelligence Corps has large numbers of gays, since "it draws educated and intelligent people."

I ask El-Ad and Meiri whether they still do reserve duty. Both do. In that they are increasingly an exception. The IDF has become concerned with the high numbers of reservists trying to shirk their annual stint and the Israeli press, in typical sensationalist fashion, has been full of dire predictions on the subject. Typical of such articles is one in *Yediot Achronot* from October 1997 headlined "Out of Eleven Reservists, Nine Evade." The article warned that, in Israel's next war, the Israeli army might find itself strapped for troops.[36] When I originally interviewed him, Dani Kaplan disagreed about that issue, saying that the phenomenon is not as widespread as reported, and in fact is an issue only for "secular, Ashkenazi Tel Avivians." In a subsequent communication to me he indicated that he had changed his mind; he knew more and more people, gays among them, who were trying to get out of reserve duty. The evasion of reserve duty reflects the decline in collectivist values in Israeli society and the growth of a more individual-focused ethic.

El-Ad and Meiri told me about what happened to them when their reserve tours came up. Reservists fill out a form listing whom to contact in the event of an emergency. El-Ad wrote down Meiri's name. He soon received a form in the mail for his partner, requesting updated security clearance information for the "partners" of reservists. Meiri duly completed the form and soon it was El-Ad's turn to go through the same process, similarly without incident.

How far the military has come, and how much Israeli society has evolved, is reflected in the story of the late colonel Dr. Doron Maisel and his partner, Adir Steiner. Their story also reflects the distance the army still must cross. Maisel, who by the time of his death from skin cancer in 1991 had become the head of the IDF's Medical Corps training program, rose through the ranks over the years and was rumored to be the leading candidate to become head of the IDF Medical Corps. He had started his military career married to a woman and fathered two daughters. In his thirties he grew aware of his long-suppressed homosexuality and began the long process of coming out of the closet. Once he came out, his climb up the military command was not an easy one. If Uzi Even put a public face on gays in the military, Maisel was that face within the IDF command. A few senior officers tried to block his rise, because of his declared homosexuality, but his own talents, and the support of other senior officers, prevailed over such opposition.

After coming out, Maisel met the love of his life, Adir Steiner, then barely eighteen years old, at a party in Tel Aviv. The two fell in love, despite the difference in age and Steiner's own impending military stint, and remained together until Maisel's death.

As Maisel continued to rise through the ranks, the military began to treat Steiner very much as Maisel's spouse. Like the family members of any top military brass, Steiner had to undergo a thorough security clearance because of his relationship with Maisel. Israel's highest political and military echelons, including the late Prime Minister Yitzhak Rabin, were all quite aware of the colonel's long-term relationship. Maisel was a frequent visitor in the Rabins' North Tel Aviv home and his death reportedly affected Rabin strongly.[37] Former Likud defense minister, Yitzhak Mordechai, was one of Maisel's biggest boosters among the IDF brass. As Maisel neared death, Israel's top military officials came to say farewell to the colonel. Former chief of staff and current One Israel Party leader Ehud Barak took Steiner aside and told him to be strong. When Maisel passed away, Steiner was very much front and center at the colonel's funeral.

Because of the IDF's importance in Israeli society, IDF Widows and Widowers are entitled to a variety of rights that symbolize, says Steiner, "the relations between the state and the bereaved family. The state says that 'you have given us everything most dear to you, and we want to try to make your burden a little easier.'" These rights include invitations to state memorial ceremonies, the right to include an entry in memory of the deceased in the IDF's Memorial Album, letters from the Defense Ministry each year on Memorial Day, and the right to receive the deceased's military pension.

In view of the recognition that Maisel's and Steiner's relationship had received from the military while Maisel was still alive (apart from treating him as a spouse for security clearance purposes, the IDF paid for Steiner to accompany Maisel as his partner for medical treatment in the United States), Steiner applied to the IDF for the status of IDF Widower, confident that the military would do right by him and help him rebuild his life after his loss. To his surprise, the IDF rejected his request.

Steiner then took the very bold and public step of suing the army. A military panel under the Law for Families of Soldiers Who Perish in Battle (Compensation and Rehabilitation) rejected Steiner's suit on a variety of grounds, some of them quite homophobic. First, the panel parsed the title of the relevant statute and the language of the law in question, concluding that Steiner was not a "family member" for purposes of the law. It interpreted "family" to mean a man and a woman (whether married or not) who, at least theoretically, can bring children into the world.[38] Partners in a same-sex relationship cannot give birth to children from their union and thus cannot establish a family, held the panel.[39] The panel's strict constructionism led it to declare that "if society in the State of Israel wishes to see a male homosexual couple as married and grant them the rights of husband and wife under law, the way to do this is an amendment of the law by the legislative branch."[40]

Steiner took his case to the civil courts and, on January 10, 1997, a Tel Aviv District Court Appeals Panel ruled that the IDF must recognize Steiner as an IDF Widower and grant him the benefits that go along with that status. The court stated that the purpose of Israel's Military Service Pensions Law was to protect the kin of deceased soldiers and that such protection was both for a partner who underwent a legal marriage and a partner who was not considered married. It added that it agreed with Steiner's analysis that the law applies equally to same-sex relationships.

Most striking was the broad language used in the two-page decision, which was in complete disagreement with the decision of the previous military panel. The special panel, consisting of Judge Shaul Aloni, Military Judge Colonel Shlain, and Military Judge (Res.) Yitzhak Brenner, wrote that "the principle of sexual equality has found a permanent place in our constitutional law and outlook."[41] The judges pointedly added that "there is no disagreement that if Steiner were a woman, he would be entitled to all the rights of a common-law spouse" and that, quoting the *Danilovitz* decision, "it is clear that the refusal of a benefit to a same-sex partner constitutes discrimination and an attack on equality. Indeed, the sole reason for refusing the benefit to a same-sex life partner is sexual orientation, this and nothing more. This difference is not relevant at all."[42] While the court in this case used sweeping rhetoric in favor of the rights of same-sex couples, it was short on analysis. The two-page decision failed to analyze the law in question or establish a detailed constitutional framework to guarantee the rights of same-sex couples.

By the time I met Steiner, in March 1998, his struggle was coming to a positive end. In 1995 he had initiated a new strategy after receiving a letter by mistake from the Ministry of Defense, inviting him to submit a biography of Maisel for a military memorial album. It made him realize that he should separate his suit for the material benefits that come with IDF Widower status from his demand for the right to participate in memorial events. After reviewing the relevant statutes, the military's legal officers advised the Ministry of Defense that the IDF could not prevail against Steiner on his right to symbolic benefits, like attendance at memorial events. Steiner had to submit all sorts of material to a public committee that advises the Ministry of Defense on memorial matters. The vote on whether to recognize Steiner for memorial purposes ended in a tie, requiring the minister of defense, Maisel's longtime friend Yitzhak Mordechai, to rule on the request. Mordechai acceded to Steiner's request in 1996. The military recognized him for these purposes, not as a "partner," but "as if he were an heir." As a result, the Medical Corps invited Steiner to its memorial ceremony in 1997 and, henceforth, he will be receiving a regular invitation to the event.

The military's decision regarding symbolic benefits put it into a rather absurd situation. In granting Steiner symbolic recognition while denying him more concrete benefits, it looked truly small-minded. It had decreed that Steiner can be an IDF Widower in some circumstances but not in others.

Not surprisingly, both sides ultimately reached a settlement. I met with Steiner, his present attorney, Dori Spivak, and the military advocate general over two days in Tel Aviv and received similar stories from each side. For his part, Steiner would like to get on with his life. The battle, thrusting him into public view, had taken its toll and he was eager to see things to an honorable conclusion. The military also had strong reasons to settle. While the two sides disagree on whom the law favors more, their efforts to convince me of the merits of their respective arguments occurred before the Israeli Civil Service Commission agreed in principle in late March 1998 (roughly ten days after I met with Steiner) that it might be willing to provide pensions to the surviving same-sex partners of state employees. While based on a different statute than the military's, the civil service's readiness to grant pensions removed one of the military's principle arguments—that it doesn't want to be out there ahead of the rest of society or the government itself.

Brigadier-General Shoham claimed that the IDF was interested in reaching a settlement with Steiner only for public relations reasons and not due to the legal merits of the case. Even that admission is telling, however. The IDF used to be above public criticism, certainly on a matter of relatively marginal importance to its role like the *Steiner* case. Looking at the facts in this case, it seems that the IDF's "public relations" concerns were a cover for greater concern about the strength of its legal case. Steiner received his share of sympathetic press coverage, but there had not been a sustained public outcry over the IDF's refusal to recognize him as an IDF Widower.

The final settlement in June 1998 conformed to the general outlines painted by Steiner, his attorney, Dori Spivak, and the military advocate general. Steiner got most but not all of the monetary benefits to which IDF Widowers are entitled. He received a large (and thus far publicly unspecified) one-time payment and will get monthly payments once he turns thirty-five. The settlement further specifies that, should the law be changed to expressly recognize the rights of same-sex couples, Steiner will get all the rights to which he would be entitled were he an opposite-sex spouse. One of the sections of the settlement specifies that it will not constitute a binding legal precedent. I spoke with Steiner in September 1998 and he pronounced himself very pleased with the outcome. He told me that the decision in his case will in fact be seen as precedential in future cases, even if not formally so. The settlement, he said, represented the first time that the State of Israel had actually made a monetary payment to the surviving partner of a same-sex couple.

I asked him whether he felt any bitterness toward the IDF. Not at all, he replied. The military, in his view, had not acted out of homophobia. The IDF was stuck with a particular law and, while it could have stretched it to apply to his case, was in a difficult position. If the IDF were confronted with a case similar to his in the future, Steiner believed it would probably push to reach a compromise along the lines of the settlement that he, Steiner, had reached.[43]

The *Steiner* case, and the lack of education on gay issues in the military, are issues that the IDF likely will cope with in the future. As younger people come to terms with their sexual orientation at an earlier age, the IDF is likely to see more openly gay and lesbian recruits showing up at BAKUM, the IDF induction center. Such a development likely will force the IDF to confront more concretely the openness of its official policies toward gays and lesbians. It may have to educate its forces about gays and lesbians in ways it has thus far resisted. Like the rest of Israel's policy elites, the top echelons of the IDF have made the decision to adopt a tolerant approach toward gays and lesbians, although they have not yet completely internalized the practical meaning of their decision. As a more assertive community emerges, that is likely to change.

5

Media, Culture, and Visibility

If there's only one type of gay presented today, it's because of years of miserable gays, of quotes that all gays want to be women. We're not a country that's so enlightened that you can allow a freak show.
—Avner Bernheimer, *Yediot Achronot* journalist and editor, 1998

The lesbian experience deviates from the limits of the Zionist ethos that controlled Israeli literature for many years.
—Amalia Ziv, *Tat-Tarbut*, 1995

On November 9, 1997, barely two years after the assassination of Prime Minister Yitzhak Rabin by a Jewish fanatic, viewers of the TV series *Florentin* were treated to an extraordinary event in the annals of Israeli television: the prime-time coming out of the series' central character, Tomer, to his parents against the backdrop of Rabin's murder.

Florentin is a tale of postarmy Israeli twenty-somethings getting on with their lives in the south Tel Aviv neighborhood of Florentin, Israel's version of SoHo or Tribeca. Tomer, fresh from a postmilitary service trip to India (a favored destination of young Israelis seeking some postarmy breathing space) discovers his homosexuality and falls in love with Iggi, a young man he meets one day out on the street. Series promos showed their lovemaking interspersed with the heterosexual couplings of some of the show's other characters, rendering the two symbolically equal. As they make love, the "Song for Peace" that Rabin sang at a peace rally in Tel Aviv just minutes before his untimely death, is playing.

The November 9 episode opens with the characters' reactions to Rabin's murder. Tomer's boyfriend, Iggi, dressed in an "I Can't Even Think Straight" T-shirt, lies on his bed glued to the television coverage of the murder and its aftermath. Shira, an actress on a hit children's TV show, locks herself in her room for a week, not uttering a word to anyone. As for Tomer, he's going to his parents' home the day of the Rabin funeral, ostensibly for a film project for school featuring his family.

The scene shifts to Tomer's parents' home, where his mother is busy preparing snacks for her husband and two sons as funeral coverage blares in the living room. The family watches as Rabin's son, Yuval, says Kaddish, the Jewish prayer for the dead, for his murdered father and then Noa Ben-Artzi gives her tearful personal eulogy for her beloved grandfather.[1] Tomer suddenly but quietly says to his parents and brother, "I have to tell you something." As they look at him distractedly and ask what's the matter, he stammers, "I don't know if it will be a surprise" and "I think you should know that I won't be getting married," and then finally, "Ani homo"—I'm gay. His father, in shock, asks, "In the middle of the funeral, this is what you have to say?" His mother cuts in, "You're my son; don't worry. But is it so urgent that we have to talk about it right now?" When the father accuses Tomer of being confused, the enlightened brother launches into a diatribe, "You should do what parents should do, you accept, you . . . " and then storms out of the living room. In the kitchen, Tomer embraces his sniffling brother, and then the cameras cut to scenes of Tomer's neighborhood—laundry hanging out to dry, posters of the assassinated prime minister, and Israeli flags hanging limply from buildings.

The first time I watched the famous episode, I was entranced by the quick-paced plot and the catchy soundtrack but also wondered whether Eitan Fox, the producer of the series, had perhaps taken things too far— that staging a coming out against such a traumatic societal event was at best in bad taste, if not outright cynical manipulation. But the more often I watched the it the more my understanding of the episode changed, and the more I saw how this seminal gay cultural event was also an all-Israeli event that said a lot about gay culture in Israel.

Fox used Tomer's coming out to explore how the trauma of Rabin's murder affected Israelis in a variety of ways, big and small, leading them to do things that they would not otherwise do. In parallel to Tomer's coming out was Shira's decision to radically change her life. She ended a taping of her children's program with an announcement that she was leaving the show. She then returned home to her boyfriend, Ma'or Noiman, and announced that she was ending their relationship and that she needed to get away.

The acclaimed episode ends on an all-Israeli note: film clips of the public mourning for Rabin followed by Tomer's visit to a military cemetery to visit the grave of his high school friend, Erez Blum, killed in the line of duty in Lebanon. Tomer tells him about the memorial assembly held in Tel Aviv a week after Rabin's assassination, "where they played all your favorite music." He also recounts how the emotion of the memorial assembly, mingled with his memories of Erez, led him to embrace his boyfriend in the midst of the throng and break down and cry. Thus the series deftly merged the personal grief of a gay man with the national mourning that gripped Israel during that awful November. The episode ends with Tomer telling his deceased friend that he thinks that Erez would like his boyfriend, "maybe not at first, but after that you two actually would get along well. That's what I think." He half-smiles and the camera cuts away slowly as Tomer quietly sits by Erez's grave, with singer Shlomo Artzi's "Uf Gozal" (Fly, little bird), played at Blum's funeral, ushering out the episode.

Lesbian and gay culture has existed, of course, in Israel for many years, if one defines "culture" by workshops and community events rather than the more narrow definition of publicly published, produced, or exhibited works. But the past several years have seen the first rumblings of a cultural revolution, following the political and legal successes of activists.

What is interesting about this revolution is not merely its occurrence but what it symbolizes: rather than the flowering of alternative and alienated voices, much of the new gay culture is taking its place safely within the Israeli consensus. The early voices of homosexual cultural expression, like author Yotam Reuveni and the late filmmaker Amos Gotman, whose works documented their social alienation, and that of Israeli gays generally, in a less pluralistic and tolerant Israel, have given way to the likes of producer Eitan Fox, lesbian author Noga Eshed, gay author Yossi Waxman, and Eurovision Song Contest winner Dana International, whose works and lives reflect, albeit to varying degrees, the integration that Israeli sexual minorities have achieved in recent years. What makes lesbian and gay culture in Israel that much more intriguing than its counterparts in other countries are the links to wider Israeli political events, as the episode of *Florentin* demonstrates. Lesbian and gay culture, both because of the small size of Israel and the immediacy of broader political events, cannot develop in a vacuum.

While the new tolerance in politics has benefited gay and lesbian culture, that culture also benefits paradoxically from the growing factionalization of Israeli society described in earlier chapters. While giving rise to such disquieting phenomena as the growing strength of the ultra-Orthodox and developing of Russian ghettoes, the splintering of Israeli identity and resurgence of long suppressed voices have also led to a flowering of new literary perspectives—those of women writers, Mizrachim, and Palestinian citizens of Israel. The decline in collectivist values in recent years is also a factor in the birth of such personal literature. As Israeli political scientist Yaron Ezrachi has written:

> I was growing up in a country obsessed with collective liberation and cultural revival. The Zionist leaders and educators of the time, focused so intently on the monumental implications of the ancient tribe's return to its land, were not concerned with cultivating the solitary self, the lyrical personal voice of the individual. The modern Hebrew prose and poetry we read in our elementary and high schools were immersed, in both style and content, in the collective political and cultural agenda of the Zionist revolution; they offered few examples of personal expression.[2]

Writing about lesbian Israeli literature in *Tat-Tarbut* in 1995, Amalia Ziv similarly notes the impact of this phenomenon on lesbian cultural expression:

> The lesbian experience deviates from the limits of the Zionist ethos that controlled Israeli literature for many years. By its very nature the lesbian experience is placed in the private telling (what belongs more to private telling than sexuality?) and presents women disconnected from their national role as companion and mother. In a literary framework, where the personal story has meaning only to the extent it encompasses the national story, the lesbian story is meaningless from any point of view, and lesbian existence itself can be understood only as a decadent phenomenon, which does not go together with the Zionist ethos.[3]

Much the same might be said of gay literature—and lesbian and gay culture generally—in an Israel where the personal was suppressed and where the New Jew (read masculine Ashkenazi heterosexual male) was the cultural ideal of the reborn state.

Lesbian and gay culture also is influenced by the lack of a "gay ghetto." In immediate terms, that means there is little physical gay community on which to base one's art, music, or writing—no gay territory. This leads some works to feel almost claustrophobic, while others focus not just on lesbian or gay identity but on the relation of that identity to the broader Israeli identity. The relative lack of physical lesbian and gay space may not ultimately be a handicap to gay cultural expression, however. Just as the Jewish people had to adapt Judaism and make it relevant after the destruction of the Temple and the exile of the Jews from Israel, so too can lesbian and gay Israeli artists create meaningful art in the absence of the physical "homeland" that gay ghettoes represent for many.

The other question that intrigued me as I began this book is the extent to which Israeli lesbian and gay culture is "Jewish" and struggles with the sometimes troubled relationship between Judaism and same-sex identity. To my surprise, against the backdrop of Israel's secular culture, I discovered cultural figures struggling with these questions, whether in Ilan Sheinfeld's poetry, the formerly religious rebbetzin portrayed in Yossi Waxman's *My Darling Alexandria*, the short stories of Noga Eshed, or the public professions of faith and belief in God of Dana International. Although the above figures may practice Judaism to varying degrees, their interest—and that of others—in the tension between their Jewishness and sexual minority status represents a vital contribution to Israeli culture generally and its Jewish components in particular.

Media Madness

To understand the evolution of Israeli lesbian and gay culture, it is necessary, I believe, to first understand the role of the Israeli media (both mainstream and lesbian/gay) in these developments. The journey of the Israeli media, print and electronic, on lesbian and gay issues has provided an important underpinning first for lesbian and gay political advances and later for cultural visibility. The smallness of Israel, and the high level of concentration in its media, has enabled gays and lesbians in these fields to play an important role in shaping evolving perceptions of gays and lesbians as well.

An important caveat is in order before proceeding: much of the cultural and media visibility is directed at gay men rather than lesbians. Although lesbian culture and issues are also becoming more visible in Israeli society, the existence of a patriarchal society and the more limited financial resources available to women conspire to render women less visible in the evolving media and cultural discourse on gay issues.

The media have done much to raise public consciousness about gay issues. From 1991 onward not a week seemed to go by without one of Israel's major newspapers, if not several, devoting major quantities of ink to gay issues and personalities. One daily, *Davar* (later known as *Davar Rishon*), even devoted two pages of its weekend section every week to gay and lesbian news and commentary until its demise in May 1996. Even more remarkably, the news coverage and editorial commentary have been largely positive, save for sensationalist coverage of murders *al reka homoseksuali* (on homosexual background), the phrase used to describe pick-up murders of gay men.

Edward Alwood, the author of *Straight News*, a look at how the American media have covered news about gay people, writes that "the stories chosen, sources interviewed, placement selected, language and descriptions used, and many factors that are a part of everyday journalism influence what people consider important or unimportant. When society faces a problem, the media suggest a proper response."[4] The Israeli media have been applying their influence to suggest Alwood's "proper response."

The evolution in Israeli media attitudes toward homosexuality and gays and lesbians differs from other models, however. As Amit Kama, former executive director of the Aguda and a doctoral candidate in communications at Tel Aviv University points out,

> Israel is rather unique in the ways its public sphere incorporated gay men and their issues. . . . Between 1988 and 1993 the Israeli public sphere underwent a tremendous transformation. . . . What makes the Israeli case intriguing is the abruptness of the shift and the permeable quality of the illusory boundary between these eras: a pendulumlike oscillation can be demonstrated by singular instances.[5]

The shift has been radical indeed. Just as the 1988 decriminalization of certain homosexual acts gave a top-down stamp of approval to the country's lesbian and gay community, so too does it seem to have given a green light to the media to pursue the "gay story," in turn creating further visibility and legitimacy.

As Kama notes, early Israeli media coverage of gay issues was replete with stereotypes and sinister overtones. A 1962 cover story in the sensationalist weekly *Ha-Olam ha-Ze*, since defunct, proclaimed, "Underground on the Seaside Promenade," against a grainy darkened photo of men cruising for companionship in the Mediterranean evening. The article's opening paragraph continues in a similar vein:

> A secret underground exists in Israel. This underground is established and organized, already operating for a number of years. It includes a few thousand active members in all parts of the country. Included in it among others: a government minister, a senior official in the Foreign Ministry, a few famous intellectuals, a number of officers in the

UN Emergency Force stationed in Israel, journalists, artists, and rich industrialists.[6]

In a society preoccupied at that time with nation building, such a story, dealing with a small minority, was remarkable. Although sensationalist in its tone, the article was exceptional for its time, against the silence that Israeli society placed over any discussion of homosexuality. Moreover, the collectivist ethos that prevailed in Israel at that time until well into the 1980s would decry such individualistic behaviors as pursuing one's true sexual orientation at the expense of the collectivist imperative to be fruitful and multiply.

One can date the beginnings of more positive gay images in the media to the late 1980s, when the Tel Aviv weekly *Ha-Ir* began running a chronicle of a gay man's life written by "Moshe," the pseudonym that the now openly gay editor of *Ma'ariv*'s culture section, Gal Ochovsky (partner of *Florentin* producer Eitan Fox), used to chronicle his life with Fox and his thoughts about life as a gay man in Israel. He wrote about reserve duty, how the hot Tel Aviv summer affects one's sex drive, and how he and the wife of his partner's best friend conspire with each other against their mates. Amit Kama notes in his look at media portrayals of Israeli gay men, "The narrator. . . and his lover represented the epitome of the Israeli mainstream society. Both were law-abiding citizens who function in conformity with what is implicitly expected in our society."[7] But such images were important in balancing out the negative views of gay people, the only other ones to which Israelis were previously exposed.

The column was all the more remarkable for the period in which Ochovsky wrote it—the mid to late 1980s, when Israel's sodomy law was still on the books and gay activism was still a clandestine affair. But *Ha-Ir* was consciously the voice of trendiness, trying to effect a more worldly pose and smash various taboos, including homosexuality. Moshe/Ochovsky's column was perhaps the first mainstreaming of gay voice, in which gay people could speak directly to the wider public, educating heterosexuals about gay issues while also creating a model of sorts for gay people. While the column had entertainment and gossip value, Ochovsky acknowledged to me the wider social role his work played in showing how a gay couple lived and in trying to create parallels with the lives of heterosexual counterparts his own age.

The other seminal event in mainstream news media treatment of lesbians and gay men was the decision of *Davar*, the organ of the Histadrut

Labor Federation—Israel's virtually all-encompassing labor union—to publish in its weekend section two pages of lesbian and gay news, culture, and debate from Israel and abroad from 1991 until the newspaper's demise in 1996. I spent one morning talking with one of the shapers of gay images in the media, the avuncular Tzvi Marom, the founder and former editor of *Davar*'s weekly "Homogeni" column of gay and lesbian news and opinion. Marom, a sixty-eight-year-old retired journalist, and his wife, Shula, a psychologist, welcomed me warmly to their art- and antique-filled apartment in Tel Aviv's Bavli neighborhood. Marom served as my editor when I wrote for six months for his "Homogeni" column about gay developments in the United States. Our meeting that morning was part interview, part homecoming, since we had previously known each other only through telephone calls and faxes.

The Israeli press, he says, enjoy a large readership and is "energetic enough to push the country forward." It is also a monopoly operation, he explains. Three large families—the Moseses (*Yediot Achronot*), the Nimrodis (*Ma'ariv*), and the Schockens (*Ha'aretz*)—serve as the country's media barons and inevitably have interests "that aren't exactly professional." Their media control extends increasingly into television as well as publishing and competing chains of local weeklies.

This vertical concentration of media power enables a few to effectively shape the country's agenda and bring prominence to issues of interest to those wielding that power. And that agenda is quite liberal. While the religious have their own newspapers and, thanks to pirate radio, their own broadcasting media, the mainstream Israeli media lacks a conservative organ. Right-wing Israelis have been left to issue bumper stickers about "hostile media," or even the *Tishkoret*—Lying Media—a play on words with the expressions for media, *tikshoret*, and lie, *sheker*. It is true that the dailies all have at least a token conservative columnist, but they amount to window dressing. The two major tabloids, *Yediot Achronot* and *Ma'ariv*, pursue what I would call consensus politics and try to keep to the center of the political spectrum, feinting left or right as the issue warrants, in their editorial policies. Although their readership probably tilts toward the right of Israeli politics, the sensibilities of the two dailies' reporting staffs are strongly to the left, a bias that is reflected in their sometimes alarmist political coverage. *Ha'aretz*, which began as a newspaper of the bourgeoisie at a time when the glories of socialism were the order of the day in Israeli society, today is firmly to the left in both its reporting and editorial line. Marom recalls that newspapers once were more politicized, but that the collectivist values once promoted in *Davar* and the even more left-wing *Al ha-Mishmar* (also defunct) have "moderated and merged into the secular consensus."

As Israeli society's collectivist ethos has worn down, the country's media have become more aggressive and sensationalist. Shmuel Meiri, the *Ha'aretz* journalist, links media aggressiveness to the trauma Israelis absorbed during the 1973 Yom Kippur War, when they saw their country's cherished security certainties go up in flames. Since then, he says, "there've been no limits on what to cover. Even security secrets. Once, the press never would have published the name of the head of the Mossad. The Israeli press today plays without a referee. It has no responsibility to anyone. It reports everything it hears, without considering the consequences."

A change in editors at *Davar* prompted Marom to consider launching his column on gay and lesbian issues. The new editor, Yoram Peri, told the paper's journalists, recalls Marom, that "we should be waving the social flag." By this, Marom explains, Peri was referring to the rights of women and Arabs, and to issues associated with poverty in Israeli society. With respect to the gay community, Marom tells me that "I saw that we did not know a fairly large population. There simply was no awareness [about these issues]." He freely admits a more commercial motive as well: gay issues were a sure-fire circulation booster.

I asked Marom about complaints I had heard from some Israeli gays— that the image of gays in the media is too "straight" and that the press focuses on individuals in its coverage rather than the community as a whole. "There is a lot of empathy in the press for 'straight' gays. The image is that gays are like anyone else." As for the focus on individuals, he freely admits that "it's not dealt with in coverage as a collective group. The process is very slow." But he is quick to defend the media's approach and what has occurred in Israeli society: "Today, you can go into the workplace and run into gay people. You can't get thrown out of work anymore because of your sexual orientation. Rights are what's important."

And has the gay community absorbed some of the social progress engendered by the reams of sympathetic press coverage? No, says Marom, who sees nothing special about that—the wider Israeli public has not in his view absorbed such momentous changes as the growth of the religious population or even the murder of Yitzhak Rabin. He sees a cultural war going on that in his view has become more acute: "The secular public is still the majority, but recent developments haven't pushed it to act. We won't go out to the streets to demonstrate against the religious." Why, I ask. "There's a 'privatization' of Israeli society going on. Once there were large political groupings politically and large companies economically. Today, people don't belong to groups, to big foci. Even after the Rabin murder, one hundred thousand people went out into the streets—and then went home."

The government-run radio and television have moved a bit more slowly than the country's print media, but they too have progressed. Israel Television runs gay feature films, including such Israeli classics as *Drifting, Amazing Grace,* and *Time Off,* without a murmur of public protest. Israeli television has also produced gay-themed sitcoms, ranging from *Streit ula-Inyan* ("Straight and to the Point"), about a woman and her gay housemate, to *Siton,* which featured a story line about a man whose wife learns that he's gay. There is also the hugely popular (and crass) *Ramat Aviv Gimel,* an Israeli *Dallas* with a visible, albeit smarmy, gay character. And, of course, there's *Florentin.*

Israel Television's weeknight newscast, *Mabat,* typically doesn't give much coverage to gay and lesbian issues, but when it does, it's clear where its sympathies lie. In 1995, when the ultra-Orthodox succeeded in torpedoing an effort to extend spousal benefits to same-sex couples across the board, their rhetoric became quite sharp. Chaim Yavin, Israel's Walter Cronkite (who stepped down from his anchor position in 1997, only to return in September 1998), proceeded to interview one of the ultra-Orthodox rabbis responsible for the inflammatory rhetoric and accused him on the air of engaging in "incitement." Coming as it did only six weeks or so after the Rabin assassination, Yavin's intent and sympathies were clear.

Yavin's temporary successor, the twenty-something Geula Even, similarly gave sympathetic coverage to gay issues. When transsexual singer Dana International brought home a Eurovision victory for Israel in 1998, *Mabat* went all-out, explaining to viewers what those rainbow flags joyful lesbian and gay Israelis were waving in Rabin Square at a spontaneous victory celebration were: "the flag of the international gay movement."[8]

The 1993 launch of a commercial channel, Channel 2, also had a positive effect on coverage and public discussion of sexual minorities. Professor Shmuel Leiman Viltzig, coordinator of the communications program at Bar-Ilan University, could tell *Yediot Achronot,* in that newspaper's retrospective look at the first five years of Channel 2's life, that

Channel 2, with all its commercialization and Americanization, has made us more tolerant, liberal, and open toward the stranger and the other. The moment that Dan Shilon (host of a popular talk show program) invites a transvestite to the studio and talks respectfully with him, there's a social effect. Dana International wouldn't have been accepted by the public in such a manner six or seven years ago. Now we're more open toward minorities, but the price is heavy: if a minister sits next to a transvestite, it means the minister's equal to the transvestite, and the transvestite's equal to the minister, and the meaningful differences between principal and trivial disappear.[9]

In parallel with the development of commercial television and cable, there has been a similar growth in commercial radio stations, some of which now broadcast programs directed at gay listeners. Radio Tzafon broadcasts a weekly program called *To the North with Pride,* featuring everything from an interview with lesbian poet, singer, and performer Shez to perspectives and stories of a gay soldier. Aguda chair Menachem Sheizaf has his own weekly program devoted to gay issues on Radius, another local radio station.

Gay Journalists, Gay Message

Lesbian and gay journalists have openly shaped the way in which media present gay issues to the Israeli public. While Edward Alwood could write that the emergence of gay and lesbian journalists from the closet "was one of several unrelated but simultaneous developments that changed the long-standing antigay tone of the news media,"[10] in Israel the influence of this factor has been particularly acute. The high degree of media concentration ensures that a few openly gay and lesbian journalists and editors can have a significant impact on how gay issues reach the public. All three Israeli dailies have well-placed gay editors and writers. Thus, at *Yediot Achronot*, there is Avner Bernheimer, a writer and editor for the *Seven Days* weekend supplement, while, over at *Ma'ariv,* Gal Ochovsky edits the paper's cultural section. The newspapers also have their share of lesbian and gay reporters, many of whom are out.[11]

Bernheimer's position as editor is a particularly influential one, for even in Israel's concentrated newspaper market, *Yediot Achronot* stands out—its weekend edition reportedly enjoys a 66 percent market share. The change in Israeli media coverage of the lesbian and gay community, he says, came through the efforts of individual journalists and editors to change that coverage. "We went through a period where we were dictating—you couldn't write a bad word about gays. Every word in an article would be checked over ten times." Bernheimer even admits that there were more than a few stories written about gays that lacked a shred of objectivity, because editors feared being politically incorrect. But he's not apologetic: "If there's only one type of gay presented today, it's because of years of miserable gays, of quotes that all gays want to be women. We're not a country that's so enlightened that you can allow a freak show."

While I was interviewing Bernheimer at Tel Aviv's Café Bialik, a trendy watering hole off of Allenby, one of his colleagues saw him and came over to say hello. Ranen Mosinzon reports on music and culture for *Seven Days,* having previous worked for the weekly *Tel Aviv,* and is herself openly lesbian. One of the noticeable trends in mainstream media coverage of gay issues is its tendency to focus on men. Stories on lesbian issues are few and far between. While admitting that there is not enough coverage, she contended, as a journalist, that "there's not much to write about. Very few women are willing to come out." From her own position as a culture reporter, she knows what she's talking about. In the field of popular music she ticks off the names of two prominent female singers who have kept their closet doors tightly nailed shut. At the same time, however, lesbians are subject to a media double standard. When coverage of gay male issues was beginning to take off, use of pseudonyms or first names was common. It would seem that lesbians should enjoy similar treatment rather than measuring their community against the progress and visibility that gay men already have built for themselves.

Mosinzon, almost predictably, was critical of the organized lesbian community represented by KLAF: "The community is very closed and has few activities of any value." As for *Klaf Chazak,* a magazine that raises a lot of interesting serious issues, she was dismissive: "It leaves it in the ghetto, in a circle of three people." Needless to say, she was not a member of KLAF. Not that she's apolitical. Commenting on the Weizman affair, she told me that "when Ezer Weizman opened his mouth, it pissed me off. It was even worse that he said what he said to high school kids." And Mosinzon won a badge of honor from *Ha-Zman ha-Varod* for an article on the Israeli pop group Ice Nine, in which she challenged the group's hesitancy to admit to the gayness of one of their songs, "With Him Forever," which became a big hit in the summer of 1997.

Although, as Alwood points out, journalism has often strived for a "neutrality" that excludes the voices of the marginalized, journalists with whom I spoke readily admitted to trying to shape coverage of lesbian and gay issues. Nor did they see a conflict between their own homosexuality or lesbianism and their ability to cover the community effectively. On the contrary. As Mosinzon put it to me, "What makes a journalist good is not objectivity but the ability to get into a subject. You *should* write about the type of people you know well, although not just." Shmulik Ben-Menachem, a gay reporter for one of the Hebrew dailies who requested a pseudonym, told me that "gays can do a better job covering the community because of the access they have. Gays can write about other gays, so long as they leave their biases behind." The same reporter admitted, à la Avner Bernheimer, that "perhaps [gay journalists] give a discount to the community. We're more sympathetic. Sometimes we'll tell white lies. We'll say there were 'thousands' at an event rather than 'two thousand.' It doesn't disturb readers." While such an approach has been effective for lesbian and gay Israelis, it is not without its problems. It suggests that, if gays were not volunteering to cover their community, Israeli media coverage might not have developed as well as it has. The existence of solid coverage in Israeli dailies of gay issues owes much to journalists and editors like Gal Ochovsky and Avner Bernheimer who pushed their editors for stories on the issues. Bernheimer told me that he "had to initiate things. Most of my straight colleagues deal with different issues." Ochovsky puts a slightly different spin on things, albeit with a touch of hyperbole: "Ten people in the Israeli media do it. We've gotten to the point where we can shape things. Everyone knows everyone."

The Growth of Gay and Lesbian Media

In an article in the November 1991 issue of *Maga'im* gay poet Ilan Sheinfeld wrote about the media's then new interest in the lesbian and gay community. He first noted that the press learned from its first interviews with gay people that lesbian and gay issues were a surefire circulation booster. He stated that

> the updated image of the homosexual, as he appears in the Israeli press, is one that is mixed and evolving, according to the quality of the newspaper. The optimist will believe that [increased coverage] will lead to the growth of a gay culture on the periphery. The pessimist will claim that [such coverage] will lead to assaults on gays in every gathering place in Israel.[12]

Neither Sheinfeld's optimist nor his pessimist has won the battle. With such extensive mainstream coverage of gay concerns, indigenous gay and lesbian media and culture have been slower to develop, but the increased coverage has created greater understanding of gay issues among the wider public rather than persecution.

The problem that media internal to the lesbian and gay community have in Israel is in trying to carve out a niche in the face of mainstream media whose coverage of issues of interest to the community continues to widen. If anything, the mainstream media, with their greater resources, more frequent publication and broadcast schedules, and openly gay journalists and editors, can do a better job of bringing the day's news to lesbian and gay readers.

Yediot Achronot's Avner Bernheimer puts the problem thus: "The market in Israel is very small. Gays read newspapers here just like anyone else. They see the ads in *Yediot Achronot*. Moreover, the mainstream press writes a lot about the topic, both politics and culture. It's a hot issue right now. As a result, the gay press here deals mostly with internal issues."

Both *Ha-Zman ha-Varod* and *Klaf Chazak* have implicitly recognized that fact and focus on what they do best—serve as a platform for discussions of issues within the community. *Ha-Zman ha-Varod* ran a series of articles dealing with couplehood, both gay and lesbian. The variety of perspectives presented was particularly important in a country where settling down two by two has a certain inevitability to it, and challenges to that cultural norm are rare. *Klaf Chazak*, for its part, devoted a significant portion of one issue to Mizrachi lesbians and the ways KLAF could be more inclusive of such women. These types of articles are important in shaping a community and its values and further constitute the types of issues that mainstream media likely would not cover.

KLAF for many years has put out *Klaf Chazak*. The first time I saw an issue, back in 1991, it was little more than a bulletin. Today readers enjoy a magazine format, with a color cover and glossy paper, featuring interviews with leading Israeli women such as cosmetics manufacturer-turned-politician Penina Rosenblum, articles on being both Mizrachit and lesbian, sports, and culture. Its advance to magazine format demonstrates the growing visibility of lesbian issues in Israel.

Israeli gay media made some significant advances in 1996 with the launching of *Ha-Zman ha-Varod*, a gay and lesbian monthly produced in newspaper format and edited by Ya'ir Kedar.[13] In terms of its quality, it marked a significant step forward for the gay Israeli press. Kedar, sporting a brush cut, greeted me in the apartment he shares with his boyfriend. He was dressed all in black—this on a sweltering day in Tel

Aviv. His home is also the office of *Ha-Zman ha-Varod*, and a Macintosh computer, on which he designs the paper each month, sits in one of the rooms. Kedar earns his living as a nightclub promoter, and he's full of enthusiasm for the "queer scene" developing in Tel Aviv clubs, where, he says, young gays, lesbians, and transsexuals freely mix and collaborate.

Kedar, an earnest guy, is also quite shrewd. I come to this epiphany after listening to him chart out for me the economics and goals of *Ha-Zman ha-Varod*. The paper, he says, "is a basis for building community. It's for the entire community. It is strongly against homophobia and has sparked a debate over approaches to people in the closet (the paper believes in coming out, but does not generally favor outing)." In the beginning its coverage of lesbian issues was weaker than is the case today. The paper, too, has given increased visibility to drag queens, transvestites, and transsexuals. But its inclusiveness is not perfect. Rarely are there articles or discussion about gay and lesbian Palestinians or religious Jews, pointing out some of the limits to diversity in the Israeli gay community. As shall be seen in chapter 8, while it may be chic or politically correct in the Israeli gay community to concern oneself with sexual minorities like transsexuals, it is much less so when it comes to gay and lesbian Palestinians. Similarly, while *Ha-Zman ha-Varod* once ran a cover story about "spirituality" and gays and lesbians, the article dealt with Eastern mystical spirituality rather than Judaism. The newspaper has yet to run a feature about lesbian and gay religious Jews.

In terms of content, the paper is fairly straightforward. There are news articles, cultural columns, a few personal columns, and letters to the editor. The reporting style is relatively balanced, *except* when it comes to egregious homophobic comments from public figures. Thus, the late education minister, Zevulun Hammer, earned the paper's wrath on more than one occasion. The November 1996 issue featured the heads of Hammer and fellow National Religious Party MK Chanan Porat superimposed on two hunky nude male bodies locked in embrace. Following the minister's affidavit in the *Open Cards* suit, in which he declared homosexuality a "moral flaw," Kedar published the quote above a pig on the cover of the May 1997 issue. I asked Kedar about this, in light of the way in which portraying an Orthodox minister as an unkosher animal might be perceived. Kedar fixed me with a smile and replied, "We considered placing a yarmulke on the head of the pig, but decided *that* would be going too far." Touché.

Although the writing is straightforward in *Ha-Zman ha-Varod*, it has an ideological goal. While Israeli society tries to teach gays and lesbians that they are individuals rather than a community, *Ha-Zman ha-Varod* celebrates distinctiveness and the notion of a pansexual community embracing lesbians, gay men, bisexuals, drag queens, and transsexuals. His paper celebrates a more in-your-face homosexuality than Israel—and even gay and lesbian Israelis—have been used to until recently. Typical of this approach are the pages of coverage that *Ha-Zman ha-Varod* devoted to the riots that broke out in May 1998 when the police tried to close the Wigstock event at 7:00 P.M. at the beginning of the Jewish Sabbath. For Kedar and his newspaper, such a spontaneous demonstration, which the newspaper linked to the heightened gay assertiveness following Dana International's victory in the Eurovision Song Contest, is the type of communal self-confidence and "we don't give a damnism" that Israeli gays, lesbians, and members of other sexual minorities should be cultivating.

These media attempts to create lesbian and gay space in turn reflect the development of other Israeli gay and lesbian cultural media. Liora Moriel takes a expansive and democratic view of gay and lesbian—especially lesbian—culture. She emphasizes that it is artificial and limiting to define culture only by those works that can be found in a bookstore, performed in a public theater, or displayed in a public art gallery or museum. Many works do not get such public exposure, she notes, due to economic constraints, particularly with respect to women's and lesbian culture. She points to the development of lesbian potlucks, picnics, lectures, and women performing poetry and songs before audiences of women. A bar scene has also developed, filled primarily with Mizrachiot seeking the love of other women, along with a café scene, best exemplified by Minerva, a café-bar-art gallery that opened in Tel Aviv in 1998. Although perhaps culture with a small *c*, Moriel contends that that such developments have been pivotal to the development of lesbian life in Israel and should be dissected with the same care one would use in examining a work of published literature.

At the same time, Moriel concedes that the development of an indigenous lesbian culture with a capital *C* has been much slower. *Hot Night*, performed and published in 1994, and the women's cultural evenings that took place at the Aguda as a predecessor to the development of this first anthology of lesbian poetry, prose, and songs constituted a serious effort to lay the underpinnings of such an indigenous culture.

Are there Israeli elements to lesbian culture in Israel, I asked Moriel. Moriel points to the fact such culture appears in Hebrew and reminds me that this is something that women have only done for the past century, since until Eliezer Ben-Yehuda revived Hebrew as a living language, only men had access to its riches and its use. "The fact that lesbians use a genderized language means that you have to be very out to create lesbian material, especially love songs," she notes. The other specifically Israeli element is the use of biblical allusions, common to both gay and lesbian creative efforts, as well as those of the wider culture.

Ziv for her part rattles off a few cultural indicia: the army ("It's a [form of] national worship and a national reality"), the relationship to physical surroundings, the Mediterranean atmosphere. Sharon Ne'eman's "No'a and Inbar," published in the Israeli lesbian anthology *Hot Night*, demonstrates the pervasiveness of military life, even on the lesbian subculture. Her song portrays a lesbian's relationship with two straight woman friends whom she has known since childhood, including their period of military service:

With No'a and Inbar I went to the army
I still didn't know what was . . . love
But No'a had already started up with Gadi, a classification
    officer;
Inbar, every day on another hitched ride, caught another lay
Inbar went to the platoon commanders and No'a to the police;
I straight to . . . Nili! The medics course commander!
Ouf, how much I learned, late at night
And little by little I got the last laugh on No'a and Inbar.[14]

Toward a Literary Promised Land

What ultimately distinguishes today's lesbian and gay Israeli writing is 1) that, for the time being at least, it cannot take place in a well-developed gay or lesbian world; and 2) after a period where gay cultural output reflected the isolation and social marginality in which lesbians and gay men lived, new works are presenting gay heroes—characters who are well-adjusted, well integrated into the wider society, and coupled (or at least looking for Mr. or Ms. Right).

Yotam Reuveni's *In Praise of Illusion* was one of the first modern Hebrew story collections to deal so explicitly with homosexuality. His grim writing portrayed an equally grim world for Israeli gay men of the time: "You stand in the Central Bus Station in Tel Aviv, going out and cruising between the platforms in the entrance hall and returning to the bathroom. Stealing a glimpse of those urinating. Whoever looks at you is yours. Immediate, telegraphic, lightning agreement."[15] The world he portrayed in his writing was one of anonymous, almost obsessive sex, where men with homosexual feelings were disconnected from each other, save for brief encounters in which they obtained temporary sexual release.

This world, of course, still exists, and public parks like Tel Aviv's Independence Park are among the few demarcated gay spaces that exist, even today. Yossi Avni's *The Tibetan Book of the Dead* reveals its Israeliness in its descriptions of Tel Aviv's Independence Park, a place not only geographic but metaphysical for Israeli gay men:

> Yaki's getting married. As soon as I got the invitation, my legs carried me to the park (Tel Aviv's Independence Park). Out of old habit, my legs carried me to the park's paths of loneliness, to the path looking out onto the beach and the foam of the waves and the distant lights of Jaffa. . . . How many times I strolled alone, along the crowded streets, promising myself that I no longer would go to the park, and how many times my legs carried me there anyway. I would walk the city streets and think—where are those 5 or 7 percent that statistics talk about; that if 5 or 7 percent live and breath on this earth—why do I see only those miserable half-people, crazed with loneliness.[16]

The centrality of Independence Park and its counterparts in other Israeli cities, not only as a place to meet men for sex but also to visit with friends, perhaps is a leitmotif of Israeli gay male culture. The geographic beauty of the place and the importance it plays in male social life figure strongly in a number of Israeli written works and films.

The despair expressed in Reuveni's stories, or even the more recent work of Yossi Avni, stands in contrast with some more recent works. Perhaps the first true mass-appeal gay novel hit bookshelves in March 1997. Titled *Does Your Mother Know?* by journalist Yaron Freed, the novel portrays the tangled love and family lives of three journalists working at a close-to-failing Tel Aviv newspaper: Ofer, the gay protagonist, who falls for Alon ha-Chayalon (best translated as "Roy the Soldier Boy") during a stint of reserve duty and who seduces an air-conditioner repairman in the paper's offices, Iris, "the Israeli champion in short-term love affairs," and Eli, a star columnist who moves from a paper in the south of Israel to the big time of Tel Aviv. Great literature? Hardly. Entertaining? Extremely.

What is remarkable about *Does Your Mother Know?* is its presentation of a new type of gay man—one who has already come out, to both family and work mates, and whose homosexuality is taken for granted. As gay as Ofer is, however, he actually is very much part of the Israeli consensus. Although unlucky in love, he ultimately decides to have a child with Galit, a woman whom he meets and who falls for him, thrilling his mother and, by extension, the wider society, for whom to be "fruitful and multiply" is a national imperative.

Moreover, one never sees him at a gay bar and barely in a cruising park. Rather, his only contact with other gay men is with those he happens to meet by chance—on reserve duty, or the air-conditioning repairman at his office. His lack of ongoing contact with other gay men serves to underscore the social isolation that many Israeli gays feel. It also, again, shows the lack of a physical gay community in Israel represented by bars, stores, and other places of entertainment.

A 1998 novel, Yossi Waxman's *My Darling Alexandria*, represents another step in the development of a gay Hebrew genre. The novel follows three Israeli gay men—Moshik the Rebbetzin,[17] Dani, and Dani's partner, Shlomi—as they explore Alexandria, Egypt's Mediterranean port and resort where an amalgam of cultures mingle: Ancient Greece, Italian colonists, the American wife of an Egyptian hotel owner, Egyptian gigolos, and, of course, the Israeli trio. For Waxman it was important to portray three ordinary Israeli gay men, each with his own human defects. In fact, "ordinary" sums up the way he likes to portray himself. As the sub-headline in a January 1998 *Ha'aretz* profile about him and his just released novel declared, "As a homosexual, Yossi Waxman is completely straight. He's married for twelve years to his partner, lives a square life, doesn't feel persecuted, and doesn't wave any flags."[18]

If anything, perhaps the most negative character, although very real and ultimately very touching, is Moshik the Rebbetzin. The Rebbetzin grew up in a religious household and his constantly cruising for sex, fueled by the guilt he feels over his homosexuality, stands in contrast to the stable couplehood of Shlomi and Dani throughout the book. As Dani screams at him during one argument, "Stinking *dos* (a pejorative name for the ultra-Orthodox) who gets fucked in public toilets. . . . Stinking *dos*. . . . Go pray to your miserable God."[19] As Shlomi contrasts his life with that of the Rebbetzin:

> Sometimes I tried to put myself in the Rebbetzin's place. To think like her. To understand what pushes her. . . . Maybe the lack of love, of simple affection, daily, to return home in the evening to warm soup and a pair of enveloping hands. And perhaps because she doesn't love her-

self, maybe there lies the reason for her scattered untiring energy. She throws herself into all types of screwed up holes out of panic, out of the honest, true fear of her divided reality.[20]

The wild, free, but tormented life experienced by the Rebbetzin, in which he flirts with every passing Egyptian man in Alexandria, is foreign and completely undesirable to the stable, settled Shlomi. As with Yaron Freed's Ofer, the settled gay man is new and revolutionary in a society where it was difficult until recently to live openly as a gay person, let alone in a gay couple.

Which is what makes Israeli poet Ilan Sheinfeld's work stand out. Arriving for my appointment to interview him at his office in Tel Aviv's Neve Tzedek neighborhood, a warren of streets that has become popular with artists in recent years, I was nervous. My friend, Adib Jarrar, who set up many of my interviews for me, warned me that I had best obtain his most recent volume of verse and be familiar with it. Nor was I encouraged by an article about Sheinfeld in the February 1998 issue of *Ha-Zman ha-Varod*. The article by Gur Rozen painted Sheinfeld as a bit of a megalomaniac, impatient, and a carrier of grudges.

Sheinfeld in person proved to be the opposite of his portrayal in *Ha-Zman ha-Varod*. What I found was a very bright, personable, and engaging man. What most impressed me about him (my own bias here) was that he was engaged with his Judaism in a way few secular Israelis would admit today. Judaism for him was not a topic in which he engaged separate from the rest of his life. Rather, he had a constant internal dialogue going between his Judaism and his homosexuality. Add to that the power and richness of his Hebrew and the hot gay erotic poetry he composes in that ancient/modern language and you have a central cultural figure. In addition to his writing, Sheinfeld has taught and served as cultural editor of *Al ha-Mishmar*, a now defunct left-wing daily affiliated with the Mapam Party. At the time we met he was working on a doctorate on homosexuality in Hebrew poetry and had launched a small press to publish gay and lesbian works, including books for the children of same-sex families. He has since published his first novel, *Shedletz*, which moves between the Polish shtetl and modern Israel and contains a gay protagonist.

What stands out in his work is how he revels in the tension between his Jewishness and his homosexuality, as well as the eroticism of the poems he writes about his life with his partner, photographer Adi Ness. Born in 1960, Sheinfeld was brought up in a tradition-minded family. Both his parents were Holocaust survivors, and he grew to appreciate the power and beauty of Jewish prayers as he accompanied his father to synagogue. Against such a family background, coming out was not easy for Sheinfeld. When he discovered his homosexuality, his connection to Jewish tradition left him ashamed, he told me, toward God, his parents, and the Jewish people.

The interest in things Jewish is a rarity among many secular Israeli writers, and even more so in lesbian and gay circles. For Sheinfeld, however, it's a basic necessity. As he told me, "A people that doesn't respect its culture cannot be a people." Many of his poems employ biblical allusions and older forms of Hebrew. He dates his more recent poems according to the Hebrew calendar because "I want to put gay culture into the Jewish life cycle. I want to be part of the Jewish life cycle. I use Gregorian dates for poems where I do not want to be part of that cycle—like my poems about war."

One can get a sense of this tension between a same-sex identity and a Jewish upbringing in Sheinfeld's poem "Tashlich." "Tashlich" is the ceremony during the High Holy Days in which Jews symbolically cast their sins into a body of water as they repent their transgressions of the previous year:

My hands glide over my body; My love for my body
Which will grow older and go to its death as a rooster in my
    father's hands;
    That is my exchange.[21] That is my atonement.
My body is moist from semen,
And I do not take it to the ritual bath;
I love all the discharges of my love.
    That is my exchange. That is my atonement.
I stroke the face of a companion, for the bristles
Of his erect face I am yearning, for the rubbing of his body
    on mine;
    That is my exchange. That is my atonement.
To roll together like two stones of open fields, landing
In his thighs as he moves inside me, receiving in me the burdens
    of my love;[22]

"Tashlich" suggests that the basic human needs and couplings of same-sex love are one ongoing penitential act. As with Sheinfeld's sometimes conflicted dialogue between his homosexuality and his attachment to Judaism, the poem can be read in two ways: same-sex love as a means of purifying oneself from the internalized homophobia accumulated over a lifetime, with the sexual act as a means of casting out such self-hatred and thereby celebrating one's love. Alternatively, Sheinfeld may be taking a dimmer view, suggesting the sinfulness that Orthodoxy attributes to homosexuality. When he writes that "my body is moist with semen / And I don't take it to the ritual bath," he is suggesting that there is no place in Judaism for a man like him, who delights in his body and those of other men. His sin is so great that even the ritual bath that Jewish men and women immerse themselves in cannot purify him of his transgressions.

Many of Sheinfeld's other poems borrow religious themes or language, such as his poem "B'reishit" (Genesis) or "Matir Asurim" (Redemption of prisoners), which borrow from the Torah or Jewish ritual prayers. More powerfully, his latest book of poems is called Karet, Hebrew for "excommunication." The poem by the same title deals with powerful emotions of being the child of Holocaust survivors and again focuses on a serious issue of identity for Israeli society:

> Take me if you can back to Europe's gas chambers
> To the ovens that burned your names, which did not reach the
>   fire but smelled it —
> I'm the genetic experiment, I'm the survivor of Auschwitz
> I'm the son of the twisted punishment of your stolen childhood.[23]

The nexus of Jewish, Israeli, and gay identity also preoccupies him. While there is a growing number of Israeli lesbian and gay cultural figures exploring the meaning of their sexuality and its connection to broader Israeli identity, adding Jewish to that mix is rare. In a poem titled "My Identity" Sheinfeld writes:

> My identity is all those things that save me from uncertainty and
>   the detachment of a cold rest in a foreign city:
> Homosexuals, Jews, authors. Three minority groups whose sites
>   I pursue in London.
> Every bar seems to me like a homeland, although I'm not a
>   follower of its citizens. Every hint of a man's Jewishness in the
>   street, in the library, frees up great comfort.[24]

What is remarkable about this poem is how it stands as a counterpoint to the Zionist ideal of the New Jew. The New Jew was not supposed to seek out his identity among the Jews of the Diaspora, and his relation with them was superior to say the least. Yet Sheinfeld does not negate the Diaspora but seeks out other private personal identities—author and homosexual—that early Zionist pioneers would have decried as distractions from the challenges of nation building.

Another barrier Sheinfeld broke down was bringing a vivid self-affirming homoeroticism into Hebrew literature. In tandem with wider social changes in Israeli society toward greater acceptance of individualism, injection of the personal into one's writing has become legitimate. Sheinfeld dates these changes to the 1970s but notes that acceptance of erotica itself within Hebrew literature has been longer in coming. As he put it, "There are things in erotica that I've dared publish only in the past four years."

Sheinfeld's erotic poetry includes paeans to both men and women. Although he identifies as gay, he also loves women and at various times had seriously considered getting married. But, in recent years, especially since his relationship with photographer Adi Ness (they're monogamous), his homoerotic poetry has been a significant accomplishment, made all the more interesting because much (but not all) of it takes place in a domestic setting. In "A Waterfall of Innocence," he writes: "You sit and pet our dog, stretched out under your head, and I look at you, stunned, seeing you suddenly, a waterfall of innocence, a man of tenderness, part of your soft skin upon which I'll prey in a bit."[25]

The poem begins with a scene of domestic quietude, only to see the narrator at the end turn to the language of an intense hunt, in which he'll seize his partner with longing and lust. In another poem, "Fountains of Pleasure," he turns more explicit about the raw physical pleasures of same-sex coupling:

As it is impossible to wait any longer for the pleasure
And it is impossible to contain the pleasure
Of your penis that fucks my body
And shoots fountains of pleasure into my throat
And widens my halo to a brilliant canopy
To an envelope of skin of two
And makes us into one fragile and airy
Strengthened so greatly by the pleasure of love—
How much I would give now for cunt
While you rub your kingdom inside me and hold
And hold my mouth so it will not shout its desire for cunt

For cunt, for cunt, for cunt without leaving you outside with the
  bloody feeling
Of someone who gave me such a pure homosexual creation
Without a cunt to consume you in it, my beloved, to swallow you
  in its teeth,
In its juice, in its imaginary sheath. But only for the desire
Shall I add—and Blessed is God who did not create me a
  woman.[26]

Here Sheinfeld combines the joys and lusts of life with his partner with
an explicit pining for some of the joys of sex he experienced once with
women, only to end his poem on a startling Jewish note, recalling the
morning prayers that Jewish men recite. One of those prayers, "Blessed is
God who did not create me a woman," is a prayer of thanksgiving that
Jewish men recite for having to observe all God's commandments
(women in Orthodox Judaism are exempt from a number of commandments). Yet there is obvious double meaning here; were Sheinfeld a
woman, he would not be able to experience the sexual pleasure he receives in his lover's arms.

Obviously, a variety of gay male literary work has found a commercial audience in Israel in recent years. *Ha'aretz* noted the phenomenon in
1997, and the accompanying changes in the style of gay male writing—
"more liberated, whole, the tendency to describe the gay world as drea-
ry, difficult, and painful has disappeared."[27] Lesbian literature has not
yet enjoyed the same renaissance or public interest. Amalia Ziv told
Ha'aretz that "lesbian writing . . . requires the existence of a lesbian
world: meeting places, events, festivals, and in Israel, as opposed to
Western countries, such experience is practically nonexistent."[28] While
the media certainly gives greater play to stories about gay men out of
both arguable sexism and the ability of more economically established
men to take the risk of coming out publicly, the lesbian community for
years has presented art and literature about the lesbian experience internally and, through feminist conferences, externally as well.

In 1998, Noga Eshed made a Hebrew first—the commercial publication of a book of lesbian short stories. Eshed arrives at Minerva, a lesbian café and bar tucked away off of teeming Allenby Street, with a chic
scarf around her neck, a sign of the years she spent living in Paris. Her
collection, *Queen Bees' Nectar*, tells simple stories of women's lives. The
world presented is an intimate one, which is not surprising, considering
Amalia Ziv's analysis of the impact of the lack of lesbian space in Israel.

Her stories unfold against the backdrop of private parties and the occasional bar, not at the annual Lesbian and Gay Pride events in Israel or feminist conferences. Some of them take place within wider society, such as in a kibbutz. In that respect, Eshed's writing is not all that different from the works of Israeli gay male writers who also lack a strong community in which to develop their characters. But lesbians lack even public preserves like Tel Aviv's or Jerusalem's Independence Park.

In her story "Biology" the narrator, Na'ama, explains why lesbians lack an Independence Park of their own, as she recalls her conversations with gay men she's met when strolling through the park: "So I have to explain to them that, in general, it begins with the matter of organs. We aren't them. With them, it's like the Wild West: hanging out, stopping, taking it out, and falling on each other's sword. And we, of course, are the King's daughter. Inside."[29] With that last sentence, she deftly moves into Jewish tradition, where Psalms 45:14 sets forth the traditional dictate about the proper place of women, "The honor of the King's daughter is inside." She thus links the traditional invisibility of lesbians in Israel to powerful undercurrents of Jewish tradition.

But Eshed's "Biology" also describes a changing lesbian Israel in her recounting of a scene at a lesbian bar: "Look, my friend once met her young son's baby-sitter there. High school students, soldiers out of uniform, postarmy. The best of the youth fills the place. Still, I've got a slight fear that I'll meet a student there, one of my students. But I decided: If it happens, so what. It's after office hours."[30]

Not that Eshed feels compelled to conform to a set of political expectations about the presentation of lesbians. Eshed put it to me thus: "I write as a person who creates, without a commitment to anyone. I'm made up of many things. I'm the sum total of myself and my worldview. I chose to write about what I wanted. It's a first in Hebrew. It's not a romantic novel, it's not a portrait of the community." Typical of her stories is "On the Burning Fire," which follows a group of women together on a weekend getaway at a country house. As they sit down to eat, Nira recites a blessing for the Sabbath and the group of friends gathered round: "Blessed are You, Lord our God, Ruler of the universe, blessed are all of you, our dear friends who've come here, and more blessed than all of us today are our hostesses, Tzipi and Zohara, and may there be a blessing on this house, may there be in it only light and L-O-V-E! And Shabbat shalom."[31] Eshed explores intimate and homely details, from food preparation to the permutations in the women's relationships. Some of the women are coupled, some were previously married to men, several have children, and one, somewhat improbably, is an ultra-Orthodox lesbian from B'nei Brak, an ultra-Orthodox town outside of Tel Aviv.

A more assertive, self-affirming example of increasingly visible lesbian Israeli culture is *Zushi Bar,* a lesbian theater presentation organized by KLAF members that looks at the day-to-day loves and lives of lesbian feminists. As the flier for the show put it: "When the theater group was established in 1996, its goal was to bring together lesbian women through the medium of theater and propose to the women, most of whom had no prior experience in theater, a new method of expression for their personal experience as lesbians in Israel and thus bring about authentic lesbian art." Israel being such a young country, people often talk of firsts, as in "the first Jewish army in 2000 years." *Zushi Bar* is a similar first: bringing the first-person voice of Israeli lesbians to the wider public. I attended one of the show's performances in Jerusalem. Fifteen women were involved in acting and staging the show, many of whose skits took place against the backdrop of a lesbian bar. Such public presentation of lesbian space, and bringing that space to the attention of a wider public, both gay male and heterosexual, marks an important milestone in making lesbian Israeli artistic work more universal and accessible.

Another important work for a community trying to find its voice is *A Different Dictionary*, a collaboration between Aguda executive director Gil Nader and Dr. Michael Glozman, of the Tel Aviv University Department of General Literary Theory. The impetus for the work was a discussion between Nader and Glozman about the treatment of homosexuality in various Israeli dictionaries and encyclopedias. Published in 1996, the work is multifaceted, containing reprints of letters to and from dictionary publishers concerning the treatment of homosexuality in various Israeli dictionaries as well as multiple definitions of words used in the language of sexual orientation (authored by various writers and community figures), along with poetry and photography. The existence of the dictionary is crucial to community building. *A Different Dictionary* gives gays and lesbians the ability to reclaim language and define their world.

Such multimedia work is a specialty of Nader's, a tall, long-haired man who looks as if he could have walked off the set of *Hair*. In 1997 he mounted an exhibition titled *House Calls* at Kibbutz Bari. He visited with kibbutzniks and gave them avocado facial mask treatments, during which they talked about society's tolerance, and that of the kibbutzim in particular, toward The Other. Nader: "The facials are a way to get people to relax but also constitute intimate contact." The masks also constitute a metaphor for the need of many gays and lesbians to hide who they are. Another of Nader's projects, exhibited in September 1997, involved giving such facials to stall owners in Tel Aviv's Carmel Market and to the wealthy in Ramat Aviv Gimel. Nader screened for me some of the videos of his experiences administering facials and talking with his subjects, among them one man who talked of his wife's lesbianism, as well as several others who talked about their attitudes toward homosexuality. A butcher in the market told Nader that he knows homosexuals. That they're educated, they're good people, but they "have a problem in life—something got messed up, but they manage. It's not at my expense and it doesn't bother me." This man, speaking from behind the counter, then added the Israeli clincher: "One homosexual is worth a thousand *charedim* (ultra-Orthodox) who defile Memorial Day."

Nader's art deals with the essence of Israeli identity. As shown in earlier chapters, even after half a century, Israel's identity is still a work in progress. The early sureties and national ideology provided by the state's Zionist founding parents has given way to competing identities, ethnic, ideological, religious, and sexual. Nader explores the interplay between sexual orientation and broader Israeli identity. He also uses his art to break down stereotypes, both about gays and segments of Israeli society that themselves are the subject of social stereotypes like the Mizrachim of the Ha-Tikva Market—or the wealthy inhabitants of Ramat Aviv Gimel. Nader admitted to some nervousness about going to the Ha-Tikva Market, a place that for him initially represented a conservative, even intolerant, segment of Israeli society. Instead, he found that people were warm and attentive, and really thought about the issue of homosexuality. Conversely, he also learned a lot about the reality of Ramat Aviv Gimel. He went with his own stereotype that people would open up their homes to him and his questions. The homes of the rich, he found, were private spaces in which people do not wish to reveal who they are.

The Musical Closet

In Israeli music homosexuality is everywhere—and nowhere. It's an open secret that some of the country's most revered singers are lesbian or gay, but closet doors remain tightly shut. Other musicians write gay-themed songs and then some of them try to run away from any inference that they themselves are gay, or even that their songs are gay. In the summer of 1997 the pop group Ice Nine performed at Pride Day in Tel Aviv just before the release of their first album, which contained a clearly gay-themed song, "With Him Forever." It's a sweet upbeat song that soon had the country humming along. The lyrics of the first verse and chorus were as follows:

> I wanted him to show his love for me with a kiss.
> Maybe it just seemed to me, certainly it only seemed to me, that when he smiled at me, I felt it happen.
> I want to live with him forever, then certainly I'll make him my husband,
> We'll live like husband and wife.[32]

One of the group's singers, Nimrod Rotem, gave an interview to a Haifa suburban weekly, *Arei ha-Mifratz*, in which he was asked about the song. Rotem's attempts to distance himself from any personal meaning to the song is typical of how Israeli musicians, despite progress in other areas of Israeli culture, try to distance themselves from gay messages:

INTERVIEWER: Let's go on to Controversy Number 2.

ROTEM: Oh, the song about gays.

INTERVIEWER: *Gevald!* Gays!

ROTEM: Yeah, *gevald*. It's simply a great love song dealing with two men. Many people would be happy if I waved some flag whose flagpole I don't even want to get near.

INTERVIEWER: What you're saying is that many people would be happy if you were gay?

ROTEM: Yeah. Many people would prefer that I sing it and shout here, I'm a proud gay who's come out of the closet and sings a song about gays. But that's not the way it is. I wrote a love song that for me was very nice, and I've done my share. Now, let everyone take the song and do whatever he wants with it.[33]

In recent years a growing number of heterosexual-identified singers have included gay-themed songs in their albums. Singer Si Heiman, known for her left-wing views on many issues,[34] included a song in her third album called "Come Out of the Closet." In it she exhorts a young gay man that "if you have a home and a great love, find the strength to go for it." In another one of her songs, "Graffiti Tel Aviv 89," she sings about Yonatan Danilovitz, the gay El Al flight attendant who successfully sued the airline for equal benefits for his partner. The lyrics are full of wordplays like "Tnu ladayal l'hitromem el al ("Let the flight attendant soar"—the Hebrew slang for faggot, *mitromem*, comes from the verb *l'hitromem*, to rise; *el al*, "skyward," is the name of the Israeli national airline).[35]

The rock group Carmela, Gross and Wagner included three arguably gay-themed songs in its first album: "Until the Disease Is Cured," "Wet and Hot," and "Women Writing Poetry." "Wet and Hot" was audacious for its time, presenting sexually charged longing for an athlete: "And then suddenly I got a sexual orgasm / And then I suddenly touched the winner's trophy / And up until then I'd seen it only in pictures of players / And then suddenly I touched my love, my man, my man."[36] The band's lead singer, Eran Tzur, told *Nativ Nosaf* that he fully meant to include homoerotic lyrics in the songs: "Of course I meant it. I'm not gay, but, without connection to my identity, the subject interests me. The issue, from a public standpoint, is another sacred cow that must be smashed."[37]

The band's lesbian erotic song, "Women Writing Poetry," penned by Amalia Ziv, is actually a rather dark piece:

Women writing poetry
are something sticky sweet
like molten brown sugar
out of a colorful cookbook
showing each other their verse
they seem to be comparing breasts
standing in front of the large bedroom mirror.
Nipple brushing against nipple,
goosebumps against goosebumps,
self-hatred against self-hatred.[38]

Ziv told me that she had written the poem when she was eighteen. At the time, she recounted, via e-mail, she didn't intend the poem as a lesbian poem; rather, the picture she carried was of two girls comparing their breasts. When Carmela, Gross and Wagner set the poem to music, however, it was received as lesbian and became meaningful to people as such.

Not that there are no "out" musicians from the community. In the early 1990s rock singer Sharon Ben-Ezer and her band, Pollyanna Frank, came roaring out of the closet. Ben-Ezer, who resides in London, released her album, *No Choosing*, and ignited a minor media sensation at the time. One newspaper headlined an article about her, "I'm Not a Freak." Ben-Ezer's lyrics were sexually charged and powerful. Take for example her song "Ziva": "I don't care if your name's distorted or if it sounds like the name of a disease [note: *ziva,* spelled differently in Hebrew, means "gonorrhea"] / It makes me feel pretty good and that's what matters / And your chest is something fantastic."[39] Not only was her music about sexy powerful women but it was very political as well—a guaranteed explosive combination in Israel. One song in English, "Dykes and the Holy War," proclaimed, "And I'll beat my own drum / Don't be fooled: I'm not sweet, I'm a nicely wrapped bomb / All revolutions are alike / None will enter my door / Guess what they'll do to us dykes / When they'll win their holy war."[40] In effectively denouncing nationalism as patriarchal, Ben-Ezer is calling into question the basis for reestablishing Israel and the primacy of Jewish nationalism in Israeli identity. As such, her radical feminist and lesbian outlook is indeed subversive. Ben-Ezer is *not* a child of the Consensus like other Israeli artists. Her social critique can be harsher, however, precisely because she lives abroad.

Viva La Diva: The Journey of Dana International From Koksinel to "Our Transsexual"

Another subversive on the Israeli music scene is none other than transsexual singer Dana International. Unlike Ben-Ezer's fierce political music, International is all sweetness and light. Her story condenses into one person the way in which Israeli society and culture have undergone a sea change concerning sexual minorities. Born Yaron Cohen, a boy who grew up in a traditional Mizrachi Jewish family in Tel Aviv, International discovered Tel Aviv's gay scene while still in her early teens. One night at a club, she met music impresario Ofer Nissim. Soon she was performing in drag at Tel Aviv gay spots, imitating one of Israel's most well-known singers, Ofra Haza. In her early twenties she had a sex change operation in London. Back in Israel, she recorded her first song, "My Name is Not Saida," a parody of a song by Whitney Houston, "My Name Is Not Susan." The song became a hit, and soon came her first album, *Dana International.* International, who sings in Hebrew, Arabic, English, and bits of pidgin French and Italian, became a hit with the country's youth.

Her songs, however, are subversive on both religious and national levels. Her second album contained a remake of the religious song "Dror Yikra" (Proclaim Freedom) to a catchy dance beat. In interview after interview International has noted that she grew up in a traditional Mizrachi household and that she believes in God. Moreover, she defends her right to sing traditional songs. Asked about that musical choice in one interview, International actually said that "the connection to Judaism is very important and it's too bad that the young today are not closer to it. Shabbat songs are wonderful. I sang them at home, and I can sing them and get excited by them no less than some bearded cantor."[41]

Israel's religious establishment has fallen all over itself trying to figure out what to do with her. One rabbi allegedly issued a halachic ruling that men could listen to her songs.[42] Deputy Health Minister Shlomo Benizri prefers to call her an "abomination" and "worse than Sodom and Gomorrah." In appropriating Jewish religious music for her repertoire, International is doing more to challenge Orthodox control of Judaism than most of Israel's secular majority. She also is helping spread the beauty of Jewish tradition in ways that Israel's rabbinical establishment wouldn't know how to do.

International is also subversive on both the national and Middle Eastern levels. In addition to remakes of religious songs, she has done remakes of old popular hits like "There Are Girls," standing them on their head in the process. In a sense she is deconstructing Zionism itself, taking the songs of Israel's early collective pioneering years and turning them into a unique individual statement of self.

Ofer Nissim, International's manager, told me at our late-night interview that bootleg copies of her albums have sold over 5 million copies in the Arab world. Her embrace of Arabic is rare in a society that has traditionally disdained Arab culture as "primitive." And if Israel's religious establishment doesn't know how to deal with International, Israel's Arab neighbors are equally frustrated. Considering that sex is not a subject of polite conversation in the Arab world—most certainly not in popular music—International's lyrics serve to scandalize and titillate Arab audiences, all the more so because many of them are in the Arabic she learned at home. In "My Name Is Not Saida" she declares, "Ana ḥuriya" (I am a free woman), and later purrs, "Ana ḥarmana"—Arabic for "I'm horny."

The cultural challenge presented by International has created a cottage conspiracy industry that accuses Israel of sending her to corrupt the Arab nation. A pulp paperback published about her in Egypt is titled *A Scandal By the Name Saida Sultan: Dana the Israeli Sex-Singer.* The book jacket proclaims:

After having failed to invade our society militarily, today they have entered our houses by disseminating their poison through the arts— which make up a society's existence and value. They have fabricated a

Jewish prostitute and called her "Dana International" for her to send her moans and disgraceful words from the City of a Thousand Minarets to invade all Arab cities and impose her crazy artistry on people's taste.[43]

Against these religious, national, and Arab-Israeli barriers, International has struggled and overcome them all. An article in the Israeli youth magazine *Rosh Echad* recounts how Nissim tried to get her an appearance on a Friday evening TV program, only to be told initially that "it's not appropriate for someone [female] who was once a [male] someone to appear on the Sabbath on State Television."[44] She was taunted with cries of *koksinel* (a derogatory word for transvestite) at one concert she gave in Beer Sheva, and religious protestors forced her to curtail one performance at Tel Aviv's Luna Park during Passover.

From those marginalized beginnings International has moved steadily toward the Israeli consensus, which ultimately embraced her. She has been chosen as "Singer of the Year" and, I'm told, even appeared on children's TV shows. But her road to first place in the Eurovision Song Contest has turned her into "our transsexual."

A short word of explanation about the Eurovision is necessary for American readers. As Nohav, the queer boy in Eitan Fox's latest film, *Gotta Have Heart,* put it: "I feel sorry for those Americans . . . they've got everything: New York, McDonald's, Hollywood, Madonna, Tom Cruise, and Chelsea, Clinton's daughter. But what's all that without the Eurovision?" The contest was established thirty-something years ago as a way of promoting greater European unity and cultural exchange. Israel, included in this European grouping, has performed quite well over the years. In 1978, Yizhar Cohen's song "Abanibi" won first place for Israel, and Gali Atari brought the country another victory the following year with her song "Halleluyah." Above all, however, the Eurovision is about kitsch, and, for gays outside the United States, the annual event is a gay cultural event.

Dana International first sought Eurovision stardom in 1995, when she competed in Israel's Pre-Eurovision Song Contest, itself a monument to polyester, kitsch, and wacky bad taste. Her song, "Laila Tov Eiropa" (Good night, Europe), took second place. At the time there was talk that prejudice stood in the way of her victory in the contest.

She decided to try again for a berth in the 1998 contest, slated to take place in Birmingham, England. In the meantime, however, Israel had changed the way it selected its entry for the contest. In 1997 an official

Israel Broadcasting Authority (IBA) panel met in Caesarea, charged with the weighty task of selecting a singer and a song to represent Israel. On the panel sat openly gay journalists Gal Ochovsky and Itzik Yosha as well as a Likud representative from the IBA, Gil Samsonov. The race quickly came down to International and singer Arkady Duchin, a veteran of the Israeli rock group The Friends of Natasha. The Likud's Samsonov said, "I admit that, in my car, I prefer one of Arkady's CDs. But it's clear that for the Eurovision, for three minutes on the stage, Dana has a much greater chance."[45]

Her Eurovision song entry, "Diva," was a catchy pop tune in which she sings about strong women throughout history—Aphrodite, Cleopatra, and Queen Victoria. The song was also very much about International and her ambitions: "a woman larger than life."

On May 9 International took to the stage, after a week during which she became the talk of Birmingham, England—indeed, of all Europe. Wherever she went, she was mobbed with attention. The European media, like its Israeli counterpart years earlier, couldn't get enough of her and her interesting life story.

Her victory, against tough competition from Malta, was assured when Macedonia, the last country to vote, gave eight points to Israel, ten to the United Kingdom, and twelve to Croatia (had Macedonia's twelve points gone to Malta, Malta would have won the contest). International's victory was both a national victory for Israel and a transnational victory for sexual minorities. She took to the stage in Birmingham in her parrot dress designed by French designer Jean-Paul Gaultier, waving the blue and white Israeli flag and declared, "I love you all. See you next year in Israel."

What happened next was a real cultural turning point. Gays and lesbians, joined by ordinary Israelis filled with national pride, spontaneously crowded Tel Aviv's Rabin Square to celebrate the Israeli victory. Israel Radio went live to Rabin Square and played "Diva" over and over again, all night long. The 4 A.M. newscast reported that "throngs gathered in Rabin Square singing, dancing, and waving Israeli flags. Members of the gay community are also there, waving the movement's flag."

The next morning, on Sheli Yechimovitch's radio show, *It's All Talk,* Deputy Health Minister Shlomo Benizri, who had denounced International's selection months earlier, took to the air to declare that the Eurovision interested him "like the weather in Antarctica" and said that International had won because of her "gimmick." Meanwhile, Education Minister Yitzhak Levy, a member of the National Religious Party, congratulated International publicly but not in person. He said in a statement that her victory "brings honor to Israel and puts Israel on the map of Europe." Israel Television's *Mabat* newscast broadcasted a piece that tied International's victory to the broader cultural struggle between religious and secular, between Holy Jerusalem and the fleshpots of Tel Aviv. The report included this analysis: "That night, joy in Birmingham. The next day: the government coalition in danger." The report spliced scenes of ecstatic and shirtless gay men dancing in Tel Aviv's Rabin Square with clips of ultra-Orthodox Jerusalem Deputy Mayor Chaim Miller repeatedly intoning, "There will not be a Eurovision contest in Jerusalem."

The politics of International's victory were tricky shoals for the Netanyahu government to navigate. Israel's citizenry takes the contest seriously and feels great national pride when an Israeli singer succeeds. So, on the one hand, a nationalist government like Netanyahu's should have felt immediate pride in International's victory. But there were the religious coalition considerations to take into account as well. Netanyahu was truly betwixt and between. Torn between two imperatives, Netanyahu instructed one of his media spokesmen, Shai Bazak, to telephone International and congratulate her in his name. Meanwhile, the Knesset Education Committee convened to congratulate International, praise her contribution to Israeli culture, and make her an honorary roving ambassador.

Her victory created new tests of tolerance. Israel Television journalist Yo'av Toker covered the Eurovision from Birmingham and, in the aftermath of International's victory, bestowed a kiss on her. To kiss or not to kiss became an almost existential question, an issue of acceptance versus tolerance, as former Asiron chair Chagai El-Ad analyzed it for me. Minister of Tourism Moshe Katzav *did* kiss her, in effect bestowing an official stamp of approval on sexual minorities. Once again, Israeli society took a potentially revolutionary situation and mainstreamed it, with Dana becoming part of the consensus in just a few short years.

International's victory and the public reaction to it took on added significance, coming only two weeks after the ultra-Orthodox had succeeded in censoring the central pageant celebrating Israel's jubilee. Thus, in many ways, International was but another front in the ongoing culture war between the religious and the secular. Many secular commentators took great joy in shoving International's victory in the face of the religious, eager to revenge the humiliation that the religious had inflicted on Israel's jubilee celebrations. Israel Television's often raucous debate program, *Popolitika*, took on the meaning of International's victory on May 11, 1998. A poll commissioned for the program showed that

59 percent of the Israelis surveyed were proud of International's victory, while only 17 percent were not. The same 59 percent felt that her victory would lead to increased understanding of gays and lesbians in Israel, admittedly blurring the lines between transsexuals and gays and lesbians in the process.

The *Popolitika* panel was stacked in this instance. There was one ultra-Orthodox journalist, Yonatan Shreiber, battling the rest of the panel, consisting of Aguda chair Menachem Sheizaf (who put a Rainbow flag on the table), Gil Samsonov, openly gay radio host Ofer Nachshon, and MK Yael Dayan. They essentially ganged up to pummel the ultra-Orthodox representative. Right off the bat, *Popolitika* host Tomi Lapid told Shreiber, in the oft-repeated Israeli refrain, that "if I had to choose between a gay son and one like you, I'd choose the gay son."

Pink Cinema

Israeli cinema has broadly paralleled the changes in Hebrew literature to address gay themes. The late filmmaker Amos Gutman was the first to make a gay Israeli movie. *Drifting*, very much autobiographical, followed a young filmmaker who was trying to make a film about being gay in Israel. The film, shot in gritty black and white, added to the film's grim atmosphere. If anything, Gutman's film was a slap in the face of the Zionist ideal. Instead of imagery of masculine soldiers, Gutman showed a grim demimonde of miserable gays. Moreover, in another slap at Zionism, Gutman's protagonist is seen submitting sexually to an Arab, implicitly challenging Israeli dominion over the Arabs. He portrayed an uncertain conflicted community that came out only under cover of darkness, terrified of exposure. Many of those involved in shaping the community's image, including poet Ilan Sheinfeld, did not particularly love Gutman, feeling that he should have made more positive art at a time when healthy gay images were so lacking in Israeli society.

Filmmaker Eitan Fox is at the opposite end of the spectrum. His first film, *Time Off*, chronicled a young soldier named Yonatan's growing awareness of his sexual orientation and his conflicted relationship with his unit commander, Erez, who turns out to be gay himself. Although he flirts with the female unit clerk, one soldier says to another, "I think our lieutenant has an earring."

If Gutman's films portrayed disturbed, alienated, self-hating homosexuals, Fox's characters are all-Israeli. Both commander and enlistee in *After* are wholesome Israeli men on break for a day in Jerusalem before heading up to Lebanon. The commander singles out Yonatan for harassment, perhaps perceiving him to be gay and wanting to strengthen his own masculine self-image by picking on someone softer. The denouement of the film occurs when Yonatan is strolling through Jerusalem's Independence Park and spies his commander going into a public bathroom where he engages in heated, raw sexual congress with another man, as Yonatan listens from the neighboring toilet stall. In the heat of passion the commander drops his military ID on the floor and inadvertently leaves it there, leaving Yonatan to discover it.

This event makes Yonatan late getting back to the unit's bus, and his commander singles him out for punishment, a series of public push-ups in front of his fellow troops, when Yonatan refuses to detail why he was late. In frustration, he finally throws down the commander's ID and yells, "Dai!" (enough). That moment forever changes the dynamic between commander and enlistee.

Fox's latest film, *Gotta Have Heart*, is his most queer film to date. Yet this film, too, ultimately shows how Israeli gays are comfortably part of the Consensus. Fox's film shows in a sweet way how the importance of family and settling down with a mate in Israeli society does not exempt gay people. Produced as part of a Channel 2 series of films called Short Stories About Love, the film takes place in a mythical small town where everyone turns up for what seems to be daily regimens of folk dancing. Everyone but Gur, a cute, strapping young man who's recently completed his military service in the IDF's paratrooper unit, who always stands by the side watching. He shows up with his friend, Mitzi, a young woman who knows that Gur's gay.

Playing opposite Gur is Nohav, a seventeen-year-old bleached blond wisp of a young man dressed in colorful flamboyant clothes. Nohav is an enthusiastic folk dancer who leads the class in new dances that he choreographs to the beat of European pop tunes. The contrast with the straight-looking, straight-acting Gur is immediate.

The object of everyone's affections and lust in the film is Marito, a tall, dark muscular man with a big Star of David around his neck. Mitzi is ecstatic when Marito asks her one night to dance the evening's last dance. When Gur scolds her that Marito is not good husband material, she shoots back, "Well, what about fantasies?" calling into question for a moment Israeli family values. But the ever practical Gur tells her that "you can't realize fantasies in a place where everyone knows everyone from kindergarten on."

One night at folk dancing Nohav and Gur get to talking. When Gur admits that "I actually like the Eurovision," Nohav invites him over to see his collection of Eurovision contest records. Gur tells him of his dream of getting admitted to the Bezalel Art Academy, where he hopes to study architecture. Nohav tells him in turn of his dream, of dancing with the man he loves at a Eurovision Song Contest and living happily ever after. Gur sanctimoniously tells him that Nohav's dream won't come true because "you're different. You have to accept that you won't get married, you won't have kids. At most you'll have everyday miracles, like a match in the dark at a moment when you least expect it."

When Gur is admitted to Bezalel, the class instructor congratulates him and tells him he must, this night, choose a partner and dance. From the middle of the dance floor, Marito fixes him with his erotic gaze and says, "Come! Dance with me." Gur looks back at him and tells him, "Sorry, but I've already promised this dance to someone." He strides across the floor to Nohav and asks him for the dance. As they dance, a dream sequence ensues, with Nohav in a paratrooper uniform. The two twirl round and round, through different stages of their lives, living out Nohav's dream of living happily ever after with the man he loves.

Later, at the ice cream stand, Mitzi reminds Gur of his promise to have a child with her if she's not married by the time she's thirty-five but then despairs, "You'll have a partner, you'll be a couple." Although he claims to Mitzi that he can't describe the man of his dreams, he tells her, "There'll be somebody, eventually. Why should only I be alone?"

Thus, rather than present alienated gay men, Fox presents different types of gay men—from the effeminate Nohav to the straight-acting Gur—with a common dream: to meet the man of their dreams and live happily ever after. If they can bring a child into the world with a female friend, so much the better. Gur and Nohav happily find their way into the Israeli consensus. Fox's imagery is very important in an Israel where everyday life for gay people is finally beginning to catch up to all the political and legal changes.

As the legal and political gains of lesbians and gay men solidify, it is likely that the ideological range of art, literature, and film produced commercially will increase as well. It may also then become possible to explore gay and lesbian identity in its own right, divorced from the outside impact of Israeli society's own struggles over identity issues.

6

Hereinafter, the Boyfriend: Same-Sex Families in Israel

Is being apart from a same-sex partner easier than being apart from an opposite-sex partner?
—Israeli Supreme Court in *Danilovitz v. El Al Israel Airlines, Ltd.*, 1994

Equality demands not only the removal of the formal obstacle that prevents homosexual couples from enjoying monetary benefits. It additionally demands a reevaluation of the rationale behind legal recognition of couplehood period.
—Hebrew University lecturer Alon Harel, *Tat-Tarbut*, 1996

Before coming out of the closet to various friends in Israel, invariably I would face the Question when going to visit them and their families. Why aren't you married yet? If not that, then the variant: Do you have a girlfriend? Everywhere you look in Israel, you see couples and families. I remember attending a concert by pop singer Miki Gabrielov at the Sultan's Pool in Jerusalem in the summer of 1988 by myself—and feeling completely out of place. No one among my fellow law school graduates on a tour of Israel wanted to attend, and I decided to set off alone. I sat down on the lawn and looked around me. Everyone seemed to be sitting in twos, male-female twos. It was as if Noah's Ark had come ashore outside the walls of the Old City instead of on Mount Ararat.

This presumption of heterosexuality, and the importance that Israelis have traditionally attached to settling down and starting a family, affects not only coming out of the closet but also forming same-sex relationships. This in turn influences other aspects of gay life in Israel, particularly gay politics. I do not believe that, in an Israeli context, it is mere coincidence that many of those who have come out publicly have partners, or that those who are single proclaim their availability to Israeli newspapers.[1] Nor is it a coincidence that the Israeli lesbian and gay rights movement has enjoyed a string of family-related victories in recent years, victories that meet with a fair amount of understanding from the wider secular public.

Perhaps most notably, the ethic of sexual liberation, present in many gay male communities abroad, barely exists in Israel. Not to say that all gay men or lesbians want to settle down necessarily into exclusive relationships; from discussion with the many Israelis I met, there is variety on that score. But the notion of casual sex as a way of life—as something political—thus far remains alien to the gay Israeli way of thinking. Instead, while individual gays and lesbians might play the field, the societal ethic of *mishpachti'ut* (familyhood) influences gay life and politics.

Sexual liberation, dependent on infrastructure like bathhouses and a large critical mass of people to foster both variety and anonymity, cannot thrive well in a small country with an even smaller gay community. A cartoon by Itzik Rennert in the first issue of *Ha-Zman ha-Varod* showed just how difficult wild anonymous sex could be in Israel. The top of the cartoon stated: "Finally, after 2,000 years, a darkroom has opened in Israel, a place of anonymous desires and zippered lays." The scene in the darkroom is anything but anonymous, however. One voice calls out, "Say, were you in Brigade 7? Operations sergeant?? That's it. I thought the name sounded familiar." Another exclaims, "Come here, aren't you Shiri Mualem's brother?"[2]

In a society where young people have traditionally faced tremendous pressure to marry, gay men and lesbians are not exempt from those pressures in a double sense. First, the pressure to marry, be fruitful, and multiply keeps some homosexuals and lesbians from their true sexual orientation or leads them to discover their sexual orientation after they have married and produced children. Second, the Noah's Ark–like emphasis on settling down two by two creates strong pressures on singles of whatever sexual orientation. While Israelis are marrying later than used to be the case, remaining single as a heterosexual, particularly a heterosexual woman, is still a difficult social option. As for lesbians and gay men, it is not unusual that they similarly want to marry, to find a suitable partner and build a life together. As David Michaeli, a graduate student who has participated in a gay studies reading group, told me, "It was important to me to have a boyfriend. Otherwise, why be gay?" He has been together with his partner, Amit, for eight years.

What is mishpachti'ut? Simply put, it is an emphasis on family and bringing children into the world. It is the constant drumbeat in the ears of Israelis that getting married and having children is something close to their national duty. Some of this stems from Judaism's emphasis on family life, but it also relates to the ongoing Arab-Israeli conflict and the perceived need to produce more Israelis to counter Arab demographic trends.

While the concept does not yet explicitly encompass same-sex couples, the wider secular public is increasingly comfortable with same-sex couples who comply with the social norm of life à deux. In this social climate growing (albeit still small) numbers of lesbians and gay men are raising children, a phenomenon that does not appear to inspire instinctual opposition from heterosexual Israelis.

Considering the role that religion plays in Israeli civic life, a topic examined at length in chapter 3, one would think that issues of "family" would be the last that activists would dare to raise in the Knesset, in the courts, and in the media. In fact, family-related issues have been the greatest source of lesbian and gay activists' success and also, going forward, their greatest challenge.

Family law in the Jewish state is a complicated field, even setting aside the question of same-sex families. As noted in chapter 3, civil marriage does not exist in Israel, although such marriages contracted abroad are recognized. The fact that eligibility for marriage is determined by religious law has created a large group of individuals unable to marry Jewishly for all sorts of arcane reasons. These include, for example, certain men thought to descend from the priestly *Kohen* class who seek to marry divorcees. But as former Israeli Supreme Court Justice Chaim Cohen (who in the 1970s ran into the above-mentioned Jewish religious restriction) stated in one opinion, "For those for whom the law deprives of the right to marry, the law does not bar them from loving each other, from living together, and from reproducing: the right to conduct a marriage is taken from them, but the right to live is not taken from them."[3]

The result: a classic Israeli compromise called *yedu'im ba-tzibur* (literally "those known in the community")—a close relation of common-law marriage, an institution that has been disappearing from American jurisprudence. ACRI attorney Hadas Tagari, who works on legal issues for KLAF, told me that the institution of yedu'im ba-tzibur in fact stems both from the large numbers of casualties suffered during Israel's War of Independence and from large numbers of couples who, steeped in the socialist ideology of the early Zionist pioneers, refused to undergo religious ceremonies for ideological reasons.

The new state sought a way to recognize and provide for the partners of the war's casualties, creating a whole body of law around this new status. The concept crept into more and more of Israel's social welfare laws and ultimately defined the rights of children born to yedu'im ba-tzibur as equal to those of children born to a legally married couple.[4] One significant difference between yedu'im ba-tzibur and their legally married counterparts is in the dissolution of relationships. Those who are yedu'im ba-tzibur can unilaterally leave their relationship, while the legally married are subject to the jurisdiction of rabbinical or family law courts.[5] It is doubtful whether, in today's Israeli political climate, such an institution could be created de novo; Israel's religious parties today likely would not stand for it.

To qualify as yedu'im ba-tzibur, says Tel Aviv attorney Amnon Ben-Dror (who served for a time as counsel for Adir Steiner), a couple must demonstrate to a court that they have such indicia of a shared life as joint bank accounts and property, the existence of private partnership contracts, and that they socialize together. Rather than seeking recognition for gay marriage (a futile effort considering the explicitly religious underpinnings of marriage and the lack of civil marriage), Israeli activists have been working to win status as yedu'im ba-tzibur for same-sex couples, an institution for which many gay activists would love to extend heartfelt thanks to the country's religious parties.

Legislative recognition of lesbian and gay relationships has been difficult, however, because of the role that Israeli religious parties play in government coalitions. In 1994 Knesset Member Dayan introduced legislation that would have amended a series of laws to explicitly include same-sex couples. The legislation came close to passing, until Israel's religious parties threatened to bring down the government over the issue. No one is under any illusion that such legislation will pass any time soon.

While legislative progress remains stymied, Israeli gays and lesbians have achieved some success within government and quasi-government bureaucracies in obtaining recognition of same-sex relationships. In perhaps the earliest victory for same-sex couples in Israel, former Aguda chairs Liora Moriel and Susan Kirshner petitioned Magen David Adom, the country's Red Cross, to be able to store blood for each other in the event of surgery, as family members are able to do. Magen David Adom approved such blood storage for lesbian couples but, due to concerns about AIDS, declined to do so for gay men.

Tal Weisberg-Bloch, who suffered a serious fall in 1993 that caused substantial injury to one of his legs, similarly has achieved some partner rights by going through bureaucratic channels. As a person deemed partially disabled, Weisberg-Bloch is entitled to purchase a car tax-free, no small consideration in a country where auto levies can total the value of the car. The law, he says, limits the persons entitled to drive such a vehicle and begins "The disabled and his wife . . . " Weisberg-Bloch went to the National Insurance Office and said, "I don't have a wife. I have a

[male] partner." The matter went to the National Insurance legal adviser, and Weisberg-Bloch eventually won the right for his partner, Yoel, to drive the vehicle. He told me that, at this point, were he ever unemployed, he would apply for unemployment compensation and demand the sum due to a married individual. He estimates that he would enjoy similar success.

In July 1998, echoing Weisberg-Bloch's earlier request, *Ha-Zman ha-Varod* reported that the same-sex partners of new immigrants would be entitled to use their partners' tax-free automobiles. The case arose in 1995 when a gay couple complained about the issue to the Aguda. The two had been summoned to the Customs House in Jaffa, after Customs received information that the partner was using the immigrant's car. After Dan Yakir of ACRI brought a formal complaint against Customs, the latter turned the issue over to the government legal adviser. The legal adviser was asked to rule whether the term *ben-zug*—partner—could define same-sex partners. In consultation with the Ministry of Justice, the regulations were modified to allow "household members," rather than just "partners," to drive new immigrants' automobiles. The criteria for defining "household member" included indicia of couplehood like a common residence and a joint bank account.[6]

Even more surprising was a March 1998 ruling by the Israeli Civil Service Commission announcing a readiness in principle to grant pension benefits to the surviving same-sex partners of state employees. In a letter from Reuven Boimel, director of the Pensions Department in the Civil Service Commission, to a lesbian school teacher who had inquired about whether her partner of fourteen years would be eligible for her pension upon her death, the Civil Service Commission interpreted the Civil Service Law (Pensions) as applying to "a male or female partner, including a male/female common law spouse, without any consideration of the sex of the partner."[7] The letter concluded as follows: "After your death, relying on the request or requests presented to the Custodian (the Custodian for Pension Payments, the Chief Accountant, Ministry of Finance), the Custodian will decide on the entitlement to a pension. In the case of a common-law spouse of the pensioner receiving a pension, the status of the partner will be examined without connection to the sex of the partner, as a common-law spouse."[8] No one has come forward to test this ruling yet, so it remains to be seen whether it will be implemented, or whether a future government may refuse to honor it.

While working through administrative channels has achieved some progress for same-sex couples, the Israeli legal system has provided truly fertile ground for beginning to equalize the status of same-sex couples with that of their heterosexual counterparts in Israel. The cornerstone for those successes has been the Israeli Supreme Court's ruling in 1994 in *Danilovitz v. El Al Israel Airlines, Ltd.* A three-judge panel held 2–1 that El Al had violated its own collective bargaining agreement with its employees when it denied one of its star flight attendants, Yonatan Danilovitz, a free ticket for his male partner, as the airline granted to the partners of its heterosexual employees, married or otherwise. The Tel Aviv Regional Labor Court, which first heard Danilovitz's suit, defined his relationship as follows: "Plaintiff claims that he has engaged in homosexual relations with another person of the same sex (hereinafter, 'the boyfriend') since July 1979. . . . He and his boyfriend have a joint household as partners, including shared residence in a private apartment that was bought by them through joint effort."[9]

When the case reached the Supreme Court in 1994, following rulings in Danilovitz's favor by both the regional and national labor courts, Justices Aharon Barak and Dalia Dorner held that Israel's Equal Workplace Opportunities Law, which bars discrimination on the basis of sexual orientation, combined with El Al's collective bargaining agreement, required El Al to treat Danilovitz equally and equitably and grant him the tickets for his partner.

The Supreme Court opinion's language says much about the principles that the court system deems worthy of upholding. Not only is equality "a basic principle of Israeli law," said the justices, but at the heart of this principle is the right of "every person to develop his body and mind as he sees fit. . . . Its meaning is 'equality before the law' and the neutrality of the law in the face of differences between persons."[10] Getting to the heart of the matter, the Supreme Court declared that "an employer must take a neutral stance toward his workers' sexual orientations. . . . Thus, if a benefit is given to an employee who has an ongoing permanent relationship with a woman, it must grant the same benefit to an employee who has an ongoing permanent relationship with another man."[11]

The Israeli Supreme Court displayed a remarkable sensitivity toward the nature of same-sex relationships, asking, "Is being apart from a same-sex partner easier than being apart from an opposite-sex partner? Is a shared life between members of the same-sex different from the standpoint of sharedness and fellowship, and conduct of the social unit, from a shared life between members of the opposite sex?"[12]

Although legal observers initially felt that the *Danilovitz* decision would have limited impact because of its reliance on El Al's collective bargaining agreement, the *Danilovitz* case in fact has had substantial effect on jurisprudence affecting same-sex couples. Professor Uzi Even sued Tel Aviv University in the Tel Aviv Regional Labor Court for a number of benefits for his spouse, Amit Kama: 1) plane tickets for Kama to accompany him on sabbatical, as the university grants the heterosexual spouses of its employees; 2) exemption from tuition and the right to use university facilities; and 3) recognition of Kama's rights to his pension upon his death.[13] The university prevaricated, seeking to wait until the outcome of *Danilovitz*. In fact, Tel Aviv University quickly acceded once the Supreme Court issued its ruling in that case. Tal Yarus-Chakak made a similar demand for tuition for her partner in 1996.[14]

In addition to the Tel Aviv District Court's opinion in the *Steiner* case, which cited *Danilovitz* in support of its ruling, a Haifa magistrate's court in June 1997 relied on the *Danilovitz* decision to support its holding that same-sex couples were covered by the scope of the Law for the Prevention of Family Violence. In the Haifa case, as reported by *Ha'aretz*, a lesbian sought a restraining order against her alcoholic partner, barring her from their jointly owned apartment.[15]

Family-related case law has come so far in Israel that I wasn't all that surprised to open up the tabloid *Yediot Achronot* one day to read that a gay man was suing his former partner for half of the ex's property. The man, a state employee in his thirties, claimed that he and his ex-partner, "a senior academic," had lived as common-law spouses and maintained a joint household throughout their years together; the two allegedly had a relationship agreement stipulating that if they broke up the property acquired during their relationship would be split between the two of them equally.[16] The day after this report there came a follow-up: the Ramat Gan family court sent the suit to the court's family arbitration division, despite the academic's contention that the court had no standing to hear the case, as Israeli law did not recognize the plaintiff as a family member.[17]

It obviously is no accident that the biggest successes of Israeli gay and lesbian activists have centered on family-related issues, and that those couples were leading rather "traditional" lives. ACRI attorney Dan Yakir told me that "it was important that couples were living a certain model," meaning that they shared a household, were entwined financially, and appeared straight looking.

Hebrew University law lecturer Alon Harel wrote an incisive critique of this state of affairs in *Tat-Tarbut*. In his article, titled *Gay Rights in Israel—A New Era?* Harel writes that

Yonatan Danilovitz and his partner were an ideal couple from the standpoint of the gay community. They were presented in the court opinions of the majority judges as partners who had a deep emotional relationship and had a financial partnership that characterizes heterosexual couples. But not all couples who have a deep emotional and intimate relationship have such financial partnership. In this respect, the typical gay couple is different from a heterosexual couple. . . . Equality demands not only the removal of the formal obstacle that prevents homosexual couples from enjoying monetary benefits. It additionally demands a reevaluation of the rationale behind legal recognition of couplehood period.[18]

When I asked Harel about this, he reiterated to me the value that couples such as Danilovitz and his partner can play as a stepping stone to fuller equality but continued to express concern to me about the wider oppression of other sexual minorities, and of couples who do not live according to the models that judges ascribe to couples.

But just as the mainstream approach to activism has led to growing acceptance of all sexual minorities, so too may legitimization of "mainstream" same-sex relationships ultimately give rise to acceptance of other types of couple relationships that deviate from the mainstream norm. Moreover, the conditions for couplehood as currently established by the Israeli legal system are not unreasonable ones. As Israeli society continues to become more open, more same-sex couples likely will begin living together. There is nothing innately gay about couples not living together or not commingling finances and the like. If gay and lesbian couples in Israel do not necessarily live according to the models of couplehood subscribed to by the Israeli judiciary, it is more because of the level of societal homophobia that prevented same-sex couples until recently from living accordingly.

A different critique comes from Ruth Ben-Yisrael's treatise on equality in the workplace. The Law on Compensation for Lay-Offs as amended in 1993 states that "the law will view as a lay-off the resignation of an employee to move his residence at the time of marriage to a community in Israel where his partner lives."[19] As she notes, however, the law discriminates against same-sex couples who, as in *Danilovitz,* must first demonstrate that they live together and share other indicia commonly associated with couplehood; a same-sex partner would first have to leave his or her job, forfeiting compensation under the Law on Compensation for Lay-Offs, before being able to prove the existence of the relationship.

Marriage, no matter how short or short-lived, constitutes immediate proof of the existence of a "permanent" relationship. The real discrimination against same-sex couples is not that they need to live together. It's that there is no way for them to record their relationship officially through some administrative procedure that would constitute unassailable proof of the relationship.

Judging from a recent advertisement in *Ha-Zman ha-Varod*, more couples may in fact be living according to the judicial definition of couplehood. The advertisement, for insurance, tells the story of Ronen and Shai: "A couple in their forties. Ronen's a publicist and Shai works as a renovations contractor. One day Shai was hurt on the job and broke his leg in a manner that does not allow him to continue to work. Ronen and Shai's lives have changed beyond recognition. . . . Had they known that they, too, have rights, they would have been able to prepare for the situation."[20] While the Israeli gay press in the past has contained advertisements from attorneys offering their services in drafting partnership agreements, the above advertisement suggests the next stage: same-sex couples not merely sharing an emotional commitment but a financial one as well. Israeli society, through judicial decisions and admiring profiles in the media, is increasingly broadcasting the message that, for those with a same-sex orientation, couplehood is a desirable social option to which society will extend at least qualified support, if not necessarily enthusiasm.

Ha-Zman ha-Varod ran a special on same-sex couplehood, Israeli style, in December 1997. Writer Oren Kaner presented an article titled "I Went Out Looking for Gay Couplehood . . . I'll Be Right Back," in which he wrote that "the strong gut feeling of many is that more and more gays are choosing the couple option and are successful in keeping it. Quietly, in one-on-one conversations, two-on-two conversations, or on long phone calls, a sort of Oral Law is developing."[21] The rest of the article went on to discuss the same issues that same-sex couples have been discussing for years, whether in Israel, North America, or Europe—how to divide household tasks when there are no preset role models, monogamy versus nonmonogamy, and whether life in a couple is somehow imitative of heterosexual norms.

Ma'ariv cultural editor, Gal Ochovsky, had a fitting sidebar column in that same issue, "It's Not So Easy to Be Gay (and It's Also Not So Hard)":

Once, in those days, there was a feeling that we've got to show them. That we can do it too. As if, what? Where's it written that two men can't have a healthy, ordinary monogamous relationship to the point of boredom? After some more time passed they began to get used to the idea that gays can. That some of them even give up countless wild lays to build a warm nest. The world seemed like it was advancing toward some normalization, until someone decided that it's not possible to have everything. That gays in a couple are basically a challenge to the beautiful life on the wild margins. . . . Suddenly a couple of men with an apartment and thoughts of kids are the red flag on the dance floor. The New Right. A type of cheap collaborator-ism[22] with the Old Order.[23]

Ochovsky concludes his piece by arguing that "gays haven't invented anything new in couplehood. The straights have already tried everything, documented everything, and a large portion of them have found a reasonable balance between their sweet fantasies and thin reality."[24]

Alongside the disparate voices on couplehood, including Amalia Ziv's article on the issues that two women face in forming and maintaining a relationship, *Ha-Zman ha-Varod* has been running monthly columns by *Yediot Achronot* journalist Avner Bernheimer called *Double Bed,* about life with his partner. The columns describe their courtship, how they cope with reserve duty, or how the World Cup turns them on sexually, in pieces like "When My Husband Sleeps."

In the same December 1997 issue of *Ha-Zman ha-Varod* that dealt with couplehood, Bernheimer wrote about his partner's sleeping habits:

"Can I hug you?" he asks me in his sleep and already moves toward me, leaving me barely 20 centimeters of mattress while on his side there's a meter completely free. I push him over to his side, just so I can hug him afterward myself. He's already sleeping on his stomach, and I'm already curled up against him and drape my left arm on his shoulders, which have widened in the past year in the gym.[25]

I asked Bernheimer when we met whether he intended to serve as a role model of sorts for the community, setting forth an example of life à deux as Gal Ochovsky had done in his *Boys/Moshe* columns nearly a decade previous. He said that *Ha-Zman ha-Varod* editor Ya'ir Kedar had suggested it for such purposes but that he had done it as a chance to try his hand at writing something personal. In fact, the banal (but usually amusingly exaggerated) scenes from everyday life that Bernheimer sets out for his readers do provide gays and lesbians with a vision for life in a couple.

As for the debate about couplehood itself, Bernheimer, who was refreshingly blunt in our interview, pronounced it "a stupid debate. No one's forcing them to be in a relationship." He added tellingly, "To be in a couple is a measure of your self-acceptance as a gay person." What he means is that, in an Israel where anonymity is lacking, being able to live openly with a same-sex partner constitutes conclusive proof of integration of one's homosexuality or lesbianism. While there are the beginnings of a community debate on the nature of same-sex couplehood, influenced by trends picked up from overseas, the dominant voices in the debate still favor a gay/lesbian version of mishpachti'ut. In a society that until recently kept gays and lesbians on the margins of Israeli life, what is revolutionary is not anonymous sex in Independence Park, the lot of gay men for many years, but living openly as a couple.

Not that Israeli society has decreed total acceptance for same-sex couples. A recent effort to launch a campaign for civil marriage has been notable for its refusal, thus far, to include same-sex couples, with legal scholar and Meretz MK Amnon Rubinstein adamant that rights for same-sex couples should be guaranteed through some mechanism other than marriage. Were civil marriage ever to become a reality and Rubinstein's position enshrined in law, the legal status of same-sex couples might even *worsen*.

Until recently, living openly as a same-sex couple was an almost utopian ideal. In 1990 Simcha Mizrachi, today a social worker, presented her thesis for her masters degree in social work, "Same-Sex Couples: Coping with Stigma."[26] For her thesis she studied five gay and five lesbian couples. She wanted to determine how same-sex couples coped with the need, for almost all the couples studied, to be closeted in a homophobic society. The couples had been together for five years or more. Her study underscored the social forces against which gay people needed to struggle to preserve their relationships.

Mizrachi studied a number of aspects of the couples' lives: their interactions with the world outside of the couple unit, how their families accepted their homosexuality, the couples' sex lives, and how they divided up household roles. She asserted that

> stigma constitutes the main factor that influences all aspects of the lives of the same-sex couples in the study. Stigma influences not only the interaction outside the couple with heterosexual society but also the couples' relation as couples and their relationships with the gay/lesbian subculture. All the other differences between the study subjects such as

social status, economic status, ethnic origin, outlook, specific personality, and sex of the study subjects are dwarfed in the face of life under
stigma and express themselves only in the same areas of life where the
influence of stigma is lessened.[27]

Mizrachi found that all the couples she studied were closeted in at
least some aspects of their lives. She noted that all the couples attached
a high value to their relationship, that they considered their relationship
to be special, and that such self-imputed value was necessary to ensure
the survival of the relationship in the face of the social pressures they
faced. Her study points out a few factors unique to Israel that can influence same-sex couples' lives: money from families was one of the more
interesting factors. She writes that, in Israel,

> it's customary "to set up" the young couple for marriage. Family mem-
> bers from both sides meet and discuss the financial aspects of purchas-
> ing an apartment[28] and furnishing it, obtaining all the couple's needs
> whether by purchasing or receiving them from other family members.
> It's clear to everyone that the couple needs its privacy, without regard
> to the age of the partners. It's also acceptable for families to help a sin-
> gle son or daughter above a certain age to buy an apartment for
> him/herself.[29]

Mizrachi found at the time however that, even among couples where one
set of parents knew of the relationship and accepted it, "There was no
recognition of the couple's need for housing. . . . In four cases, three male
couples and one female couple, the parents gave a sum of money as assistance to purchase the apartment. The giving of the money was always
and unambiguously for the individual, who was also entitled to a government mortgage because of [his/her] age, and not to the couple."[30]

The lack of such elementary social support from family required a
same-sex couple, living in such close proximity to family, to be especially close to withstand the social opprobrium that they faced. Living without such social supports was very difficult, because of the close family
ties that are customary and the small distances in Israel that make seeing
one's family virtually obligatory. As Mizrachi herself concluded, the
siege-type situation in which her couples lived created a feeling of "us
against the world" that ultimately helped strengthen the couple in the
face of the social pressures brought on by living as a closeted same-sex
couple in a homophobic society.

Mizrachi told me that the notion of "family is very traditional here. The ongoing wars require it. You can't forget the Holocaust. Gays and lesbians receive this same education." She added that choosing bachelorhood is considered strange by most Israelis—"Whoever wants to live alone is viewed as strange. An article that appeared once in the press about straight couples who didn't want children caused a big shock." Because Israeli society has undergone substantial change with regard to homosexuality since she wrote her thesis, it seems more likely that lesbian and gay couples today have at least the possibility of social support from family and heterosexual friends that did not exist previously. That said, couples still appear to be the minority within the lesbian and gay community. Activists commented to me that most people remain single. The Jerusalem branch of KLAF once surveyed its members on the issue and found that over 60 percent of the women were single.

Tal and Avital Yarus-Chakak are very much the idealized couple, à la Danilovitz, if one uses the factors outlined above as a yardstick. The two women live with their three young sons, aged six, three, and four months, in an upscale Ramat Aviv high-rise. Their apartment looks out on the local country club and is quite spacious by Israeli standards, with tasteful modern furniture and the requisite electrical and audio-visual appliances. The two women have been together for over eight years. Tal tells me that "when we met, we both wanted kids. For us, it was a question of timing." Timing was obviously still a happy factor in their household, as they periodically went to check on their four month old during our interview.

The two say that they were pioneers, for at the time that they began planning to become parents, they knew only one couple that had had children through artificial insemination, although they knew other lesbian mothers who had had children while heterosexually married. As they both told me, "We read books and had some support from our families. We also had confidence."

The Yarus-Chakaks alternated as birth mothers during their three pregnancies. For their third pregnancy Tal took on the Ministry of Health and its regulations requiring "unmarried" women to undergo psychiatric evaluation as a condition for receiving artificial insemination. Joining her in this suit was an unmarried heterosexual woman with a male partner who similarly wanted to become pregnant through artificial insemination treatments. Their case reached the Israeli Supreme Court and, in another victory for the developing body of gay law, the Ministry of Health agreed to repeal the discriminatory regulations, even before the justices heard the case. Attorney Dori Spivak indicated to me that Supreme Court president Aharon Barak urged the ministry to repeal the regulations rather than have the court hear the case.

During their first pregnancy the Yarus-Chakaks used a private doctor, and the regulations on artificial insemination at the time were not clear. The second time, Avital served as the birth mother and actually did undergo an interview with both a psychiatrist and a social worker. And the third time—the proverbial charm—Tal succeeded in getting the regulations repealed.

The couple must love either litigation or lawyers, because they applied to the courts for a second-parent adoption in which the nonbiological mother would be recognized as the child's other legal parent. In December 1998 the court granted them second-parent guardianship, with the adoption petition to be heard later.

The Supreme Court will not be able to evade the second-parent adoption issue for long, however. In response to a new lawsuit, the Israeli Supreme Court demanded in April 1999 that the Ministry of the Interior explain its refusal to permit two lesbian mothers, Ruthi and Nicole Brenner-Kadish, to both be registered as a child's mother (the two were seeking recognition of a joint adoption approved in California). The Shas-controlled Ministry of the Interior contended that a child could not have two mothers. ACRI attorney Hadas Tagari, who represented the couple before the Supreme Court, told me that ACRI's position was that the ministry had no discretion to refuse to recognize and record the adoption. Although some of the justices appeared open to ACRI's arguments, Tagari cautioned that the road to a favorable decision was still long. During court arguments, the justices appeared to accept the need to protect the child by recognizing the adoption, but still seemed wary of creating broad new precedents.

Is Israel undergoing a "gayby" boom? The signs are everywhere, although parenthood still remains uncommon for same-sex couples. Tami, the Haifa activist who spoke at Nesher High, as well as the Yarus-Chakaks, sees growing numbers of lesbians bearing babies. For gay men the options are more limited, although Devora Luz of Tehila, the support group for parents of gay people, indicated to me that her son was exploring adoption options. Younger gays and lesbians whom I interviewed often volunteered their desire to have children sometime in the future.

Symptomatic of the trend is an article that appeared in *Ha'aretz* in April 1998 about a group called Horut Acheret (Alternative Parenting).

The group matches up straight women and gay men, with a few lesbians thrown into the mix—groups that do not marry out of choice, lack of luck in finding the right spouse, or sexual orientation. The group is run by two heterosexuals, Racheli Bar-Or, a social worker and psychotherapist, and Gidi Shavit, who holds a master's degree in social work and marriage counseling. Bar-Or started up the group about six years ago, after seeing the struggles of her women friends raising children as single parents, on the one hand, and the yearnings of her gay male friends to have children, on the other, many of whom she felt would make excellent fathers. Bar-Or told *Ha'aretz* that the notion was pretty revolutionary: "To take the Jewish-Israeli mania for 'be fruitful and multiply' and stand it on its head. You want children? Please. Whoever wants to be a parent, without any connection to his ability or desire to live with a partner, can realize his right to parenthood."[31]

Ro'i, age thirty-five, one of the gay men interviewed for the feature, pointed out some of the uniquely Israeli aspects (in his view) of a program like Horut Acheret:

> Neither in Europe nor in the United States is there anyone who can imagine a combination like this. The gays are concentrated in ghettos in Paris, in Amsterdam, and every place else, they shop in the same clothing stores, eat in the same restaurants, basically closed off from the rest of the world. They can't even begin to think about raising kids. In Israel, in contrast, familyhood is so strong, and the society so small, that maybe we gays have outgrown to an extent our gay experience. When I talked about it with someone in Paris, he almost choked. But in Israel, the responses are mostly enthusiastic.[32]

Meanwhile, Ro'i also reported enthusiastic responses from his parents. The relationships that form from the groups are not without their problems, judging from the article. The straight women sometimes fall for the gay fathers of their children, and the gay men sometimes even get jealous of their childbearing partners' heterosexual boyfriends.

Having children as a gay man or lesbian in Israel often grants greater legitimacy in the eyes of family, friends, and the wider society. Social pressures to have children are as strong as the pressures exerted on people to marry, perhaps even more so. As Mizrachi pointed out to me, Israel's ongoing security problems and the memory of the Holocaust, which destroyed six million Jews, one million of them children, makes having children an almost national duty, like reserve duty for men. Being gay or lesbian and having children, while not common, is not innately radical in Israel. Rare, yes. Controversial? No (or at least, not yet). The broad social support for parenthood seems to extend, increasingly, to lesbians and gay men as well.

Dori Rivkin, an American-born social science researcher in Jerusalem, has a daughter with her partner, also of American origin. She described an acceptance of her and her partner as lesbians that she says would be lacking if they didn't have a child. What she portrayed was at least as much reinforcement of the importance of parenthood as it was implicit unsaid acceptance of Rivkin's and her partner's relationship. When her partner was pregnant, they began receiving presents from their workplaces. Their neighbors in an apartment block in a working- and middle-class neighborhood in Jerusalem populated predominantly by Mizrachim have never said the "lamed word"—for lesbian—but often make remarks like, "It's much better with two mothers." As Rivkin put it, "Having a child puts lesbianism into a niche. It's very mainstreaming." The expectations regarding having children are so strong that having only one child is stigmatizing. Rivkin laughingly tells me, "We get asked when we'll have a second child." The government also provides support to "single parents." Her partner received a special grant when their daughter was born.

She mused about the lesbian-feminist politics of parenthood. For her having children was both "revolutionary and mainstreaming. I enjoy the privileges parenthood gives me. I like a society that supports children and supports having children." Workplaces, she said, are flexible about accommodations when it comes to children—"In Israel a child is everyone's problem. You can cancel a meeting because your child is sick." Though both she and her partner take their daughter to the pediatrician together, and it is her partner who is officially the "mother," the two women make it clear to doctors and day care personnel that they are raising the child together. As for how she expects teachers to deal with same-sex families, Rivkin says she doesn't expect the schools to explicitly discuss and promote acceptance of same-sex families but, by the same token, expects that teachers will do nothing to embarrass her daughter because of the type of family that she has.

Tal Yarus-Chakak also casually admitted that "the fact that we have children makes us more palatable to wider society." She and her partner say that "we present ourselves as two mothers to doctors and educators, and we want equal treatment." The only discrimination they say they've encountered, even indirectly, was when they wanted to place their oldest child in a gifted program. He had to have an interview with a psychiatrist, who claimed that there *might* be problems for the child because of his family structure.

Their children call Tal and Avital *ima* and *imaleh* (mom and mommy). How do the children perceive their family? Tal: "In Israel, there's Family Day, and the kids tell about their families at school. The oldest can explain things very clearly." They also take part in a social group for gay and lesbian parents, which enables the children to meet others who have the same family structure.

The Yarus-Chakaks perhaps are lucky. They live in Ramat Aviv, the upscale epicenter of the Western-looking secular sector of Israeli society. If there is anywhere in the country that would be tolerant—even accepting—of same-sex couples and their offspring, it is Ramat Aviv. But Rivkin too has experienced at least partial acceptance in a much more conservative milieu. The acceptance is remarkable, as it is not too many years ago that gays and lesbians with children faced a lot more social opprobrium. Marcia Freedman, the American-born lesbian former Knesset member recounts the problems her daughter faced in school[33] in her memoir, *Exile in the Promised Land*: "There was a rumor spread by one of Jenny's teachers that we had orgies at the house and that Jenny participated. She was ostracized by her classmates. Only a few friends remained loyal. Like me, she was branded a pervert."[34]

And when Tal Weisberg-Bloch divorced his wife seven years ago, after coming to terms with his homosexuality, his wife actually wanted to give him custody of the children. The psychologist who had to submit a report to the rabbinical court was adamant that he would not recommend that Weisberg-Bloch receive custody, contending that such an arrangement would be disastrous for the children and might "make" them gay.

The children of same-sex couples may face greater social pressures as they grow older. On one of the early episodes of the Aguda's short-lived cable TV show, *Proud to Present*, which dealt with gay and lesbian families, Ziv Sofer, one of Avi Sofer's two children, recounted how, in his adolescence, he told only his closest friends that he had a gay father, choosing whom to tell in part based on how people reacted to gay issues generally. Today he is completely open about his father, feeling that whoever wants to know him needs to know about his father as well. Both of Sofer's children marched with him in the 1998 Pride Parade.

The tenth anniversary issue of *Klaf Chazak* contained interviews with the children of lesbian mothers. They seemed to mirror Sofer's experiences. The children interviewed, aged nine to twenty-two, had no outward problems about their mothers' lesbianism but were not eager to share the fact with their peers either. Some had told a few friends, but the younger ones did not want the information widely known. Generally, as the children matured, they worried less about sharing the information and, like Avi Sofer's son, viewed such acceptance as important in their social relationships.[35]

During Tal Weisberg-Bloch's visit with his two sons, Ben and Or, aged fourteen and eleven, to Washington in July 1997, I got to observe at least one gay-headed family over a period of several days. Over a game of pool one night (at which I was no match for the two boys), followed by a more substantial interview a few nights later between computer games and Internet surfing, I tried to get a sense of how the Weisberg-Bloch children deal with having a gay father.

On the one hand, they are quite matter of fact about their father's gayness. If their father said something unusually corny or dumb, one or both of the boys would fix him with a look that bespoke exasperation and bemusement, and say, "Tishtaki, tipsha!" (Be quiet, stupid woman). I asked Weisberg-Bloch about it, and he told me that the kids saw him and his partner interact the same way and picked up on it.

Or told me that he first "knew" that his father was gay at the end of second grade. "I had seen him with Yoel (Weisberg-Bloch's partner), but this was the first time we had ever really discussed it." Ben chimed in, "We didn't know what it (their father's homosexuality) really meant. We knew it was a man loving another man but didn't understand what else was connected with it."

I asked them what else in their view was connected with their father's gayness. Ben jumped right back in: "You can't talk about it with friends. You can't say that your dad has a partner. You have to say he's unmarried." Both of them told me that they worry about the consequences if all their classmates knew their father was gay. Or: "If you tell the wrong person, it will be all over the place within a day."

Both of Weisberg-Bloch's sons in fact have told their closest friends that they have a gay dad. These friends have been uniformly supportive and have kept the information confidential. The boys chose whom to tell on the basis of who they felt could keep the information to themselves. Some of these friends have even gone with the boys to spend the weekend at Weisberg-Bloch's. One of Ben's friends had met Weisberg-Bloch before Ben confided that his father was gay. The friend, according to Ben, "didn't see it as a big deal. He said to me, 'I've met your dad before and this doesn't change anything.' "

Ben and Or think that it may be easier to tell friends as they get older. Ben: "I think it will be easier. People will be less childish. There are those who learn about differences faster than others."

Is there discussion of gay issues in their schools in Herzliya, a well-to-do suburb of Tel Aviv? Not at all, reply the two of them, who had just finished fifth and eighth grade respectively when we met. Or did say that his class had spent part of the year studying about "difference," but the subject did not include sexual difference. He adds, "No one in Herzliya is teaching us that *homo* is okay, that someone gay is different but like us." But Or several months after our initial talk actually approached his father and asked him to come lecture on gay issues at his school, because he was tired of the ignorance of some of his fellow classmates. The boys have seen growing social acceptance of gay people and it seems to have given them confidence.

The two brothers struggle with how to deal with schoolyard use of words like *faggot* and *homo*. Ben: "If they call someone *homo*, it bugs me and I'll sometimes say, 'Do you know what *homo* is?' " But they do not push things too far, because, as Or points out, the schools are full of cliques, and all it takes is for a group of students to label someone as "uncool" to bring about a lot of harassment and isolation. And gay taunts are not the only ones thrown around between students. Or told me of a Russian girl in his class named Katya. Another boy teases her with lines like "Katya drowned in the bathtub" (it rhymes in Hebrew).

It's getting late and there are more video games to play on our computers, so I try one last question: What do they think about their father's activism? Ben says he wishes his father wasn't quite so active in gay politics, "because if the wrong person sees it, it will spread all over school." And, in fact, Weisberg-Bloch declined an opportunity to run for city council in Haifa on the Meretz list because his children did not want to see him become so public as a gay man. Interview concluded, they open the door and Ben goes to hug his father, who's lounging on the sofa in the living room.

7

Out on the Farm:
Gay Life in the Kibbutzim

Most researchers have written with amazement about the lack of homosexuality in the kibbutz.
—Yosef Shefer, *Introduction to the Sociology of the Kibbutz*, 1977

Concerning homosexuality, it's difficult not to see the decisive influence of the bisexual children's houses—which allow from infancy onward ongoing physical contact with children of both sexes, which lessens the danger of alienation and sexual fears.
—Dr. Mordechai Kaufman, *Kibbutz*, 1990

It was a March night and my friend, Ilan Vitemberg, was driving me northward in his Volkswagen Beetle (a 1970s Beetle, not one of the newly issued ones designed to appeal to the sixties nostalgia of the middle aged). We headed out of Kiryat Chaim, a northern seaside suburb of Haifa, through the other *krayot* (townships) that blended one into the next with their shopping malls and apartment blocks, past Acre and Nahariya, along the coastal road. Soon enough signs appeared announcing the end of Israel, the Lebanese border. Ahead of us in the distant darkness loomed an Israeli military base that sits astride the conflict-ridden border, illuminated, antennae bristling, in the night sky. We turned off the road and chugged up a hill (the Beetle had seen better days) until we reached the barbed wire perimeter of Kibbutz Rosh ha-Nikra, where soldiers asked us what our business was before admitting us into the settlement.

Kibbutz Rosh ha-Nikra, situated right on Israel's ever tumultuous border with Lebanon, seems to be an unlikely place in which lesbians and gay men would willingly settle down, much less thrive. Yet, in the early 1990s, the kibbutz was very much in the spotlight of the Israeli media, and not because of the delicious avocados and bananas it grows for export.

In a 1991 article titled "The [Female] Kibbutz Secretary Has a Girlfriend, The [Male] Kibbutz Secretary Has a Boyfriend,"[1] the Tel Aviv weekly *Ha-Ir* told the story of Nurit Barkai, the then current kibbutz secretary, and life in the settlement with her American-born girlfriend. Not only was the kibbutz secretary lesbian, but her successor was a gay man who lived in the settlement with his male partner. Kibbutz members were not happy to see their kibbutz's name in print, but the article helped trigger discussion of gay issues within the kibbutz movement.

The fortunes of the kibbutzim, Israel's great collectivist experiment, and Israel's gay community are intertwined in ways that might not be apparent at first glance. The kibbutzim reflect the tremendous evolution in Israeli society's values over the last ten to twenty years, an evolution that in turn fostered the emergence of Israel's lesbians and gay men from the margins. Israel's founders sought to build an egalitarian collectivist society in which a New Jew would flourish. These New Jews would derive their sense of self-worth from physical labor, redeeming the land with their own hands, rather than work in the bourgeois occupations that they or their families had engaged in back in Europe or other places of exile. As Amnon Rubinstein, a Knesset member and academic put it in his recent book, *From Herzl to Rabin: One Hundred Years of Zionism*, "The symbols of the hated Diaspora—Yiddish, the city, the despised ways of earning a living—were pushed to the margins, and the symbols of the New Jew inherited their place—Hebrew, settlement, working the land and physical labor, connection to nature, healthy rootedness."[2]

The kibbutzim became one of the essential building blocks of the Zionist movement in Palestine, prior to Israel's independence in 1948. Members of the kibbutzim created a politically aware, self-sufficient society and served as the vanguard for redeeming and safeguarding outlying areas of settlement. Like the Jews of America, their societal impact exceeded the 2–3 percent of the population they numbered at their height. Israeli commentator Nachum Barnea noted in an August 15, 1997, column that

> their value weight was huge. First, as a model for correct living, for proper fulfillment. The kibbutz ideal, so it was acceptable to think, constituted the newborn State of Israel's greatest contribution to the world. Second, as a breeding ground for the elites. Tens of thousands of Israelis, perhaps hundreds of thousands, passed through the kibbutz and what they absorbed there followed them through their lives.[3]

The founders of the early kibbutzim set up communities where private property did not exist—not even the clothes on their backs belonged to them as individuals. It was perhaps the best embodiment of Marx's adage, "From each according to his abilities, to each according to his needs." In the early days of statehood there were fierce debates on whether members should be able to accept reparations from Germany for their suffering during the Holocaust or whether any such proceeds should be turned over to the collective, for the benefit of all.

There were also deep splits among the kibbutzim in the early 1950s over whether to criticize Stalinism in the Soviet Union and over the Ben-Gurion government's shift in Israeli foreign policy from nonalignment to close alliance with Western Europe and the United States. Families divided over these issues, and some kibbutzim broke apart. A 1992 book by Israeli journalist Karmit Gai titled *Journey to Yad Channa* recounts the split that afflicted Kibbutz Yad Channa, the only communist (as opposed to socialist) kibbutz in Israel, over these deeply felt ideological issues, viewed from her perspective as a young girl. Today, such ideological hairsplitting seems archaic, perhaps quaint, but it was deadly serious business for kibbutzniks at the time.

Beyond the matter of private property, the kibbutz movement experimented greatly in the social realm, as well. Children lived apart from their parents in their own communities, where they imbibed the collectivist ethos. An article in *Ha'aretz* about the history of, and changes in, seventy-five-year old Kibbutz Afikim could note that the children "were the children of the entire kibbutz," and the collective, rather than the parents, chose a name for each child.[4] Women were supposed to be liberated through collectivist child-rearing, since it would free them from the burdens of raising their own. Most of the kibbutzim disdained organized religion and reinterpreted many Jewish festivals to fit Zionist ideology and the importance of redemption through labor. As Rubinstein notes:

> Shavu'ot became the holiday of the bringing of the first fruits of the harvest—and not the festival commemorating the giving of the Torah; Hanukkah was the festival of the Macabees' heroism, who liberated from foreign yoke, with almost no mention of the religious significance of renewed worship in the Temple. . . . And [there were] completely new holidays as well—the birthdays of Herzl and Bialik, and of course—the first of May, the workers' holiday.[5]

A minority of the early kibbutzim even disdained the institution of marriage. As Rubinstein recalls, ritual circumcision of their children and burial according to Jewish tradition were the only threads binding these early pioneers to the traditions of their Diaspora past. Despite their striking out on a new path, it is unlikely that any of the early pioneer theorists and builders of the kibbutz movement embraced same-sex love as a laudable ideal. In fact, in thrall to the glories of socialism and the new society they were trying to create, some of the early pioneers viewed sexuality as a distraction. In the early days of Kibbutz Afikim, at an assembly called to discuss "love and relations between young men and women," one of the members declared that "love between the sexes need not occupy the central, dominant place in life" and labeled free love a "victory of biological, animalistic urges."[6]

Consistent with their reinvention of themselves as New Jews and their reinterpretation of Judaism, the kibbutzniks saw themselves as a breed apart, the apotheosis of the New Jews. As sociologist Oz Almog notes, "There reigned a feeling of social superiority in the kibbutz movements, which viewed themselves as the leading cultural force in pre-state Jewish society."[7] They viewed the inhabitants of Jewish towns and cities in Palestine, and later in Israel, as pampered bourgeois denizens. So superior was their way of life that the problems of a "decadent" outside world were not supposed to exist within their settlements. Consider a 1977 book on the sociology of the kibbutz:

> The kibbutz is known in Israel and the world as a social framework in which phenomena of deviance known in modern society do not exist. There's no crime in the kibbutz, there are no people addicted to drugs or alcohol, and incidents of suicide and mental illness are few—thus claims the accepted point of view. . . . Nonetheless it's necessary to assume that because of the strict character of social supervision within the kibbutz and because of the high level of most members' identification with the values of the kibbutz, which do not contradict the values of Israeli society, there are few violations of law, certainly less than in other social frameworks.[8]

As for homosexuality, it, too, was assumed to be highly rare. The same sociology text claimed that

> most researchers have written with amazement about the lack of homosexuality in the kibbutz. We do not have any established knowledge regarding that, mainly because it is much easier to prove the existence of a certain phenomenon than to prove its lack of existence. It may be that the strict social supervision of the kibbutz succeeds in

driving out such phenomena, while they are still in their infancy, without the fact of their existence entering into public consciousness, but it may also be that the assigned character of the kibbutz, which leaves relatively little leisure time and little privacy . . . prevents the appearance of homosexuality.[9]

New Jews were not supposed to be gay or lesbian, certainly not in the kibbutzim.

Thirteen years later, in 1990, Dr. Mordechai Kaufman, then head of the Family and Child Treatment Station at the Kibbutz Seminar (an educational institute in North Tel Aviv) could still tell the weekly newspaper *Kibbutz* that the alleged lack of homosexuality among kibbutzniks stemmed from the fact that "the children grow up, are cared for in children's houses, in a bisexual society. Boys and girls are together from the first moment and there are plenty of possibilities for contact between the sexes."[10] If this was the view of a respected doctor, coming to terms with one's sexual identity in the confines of the kibbutzim could not be easy.

These old views have begun to yield to new ideas about the place of gays and lesbians, reflecting the evolution in views underway in Israeli society as a whole. The end of collectivist certainties and the blossoming of a more individualistic ethos have changed both the kibbutzim and the lives of Israeli lesbians and gay men.

Nurit Barkai of Kibbutz Rosh ha-Nikra welcomes us into her cottage. The kibbutzim have come a long way since their ascetic early days, and Barkai, an attractive and trim woman, steps into a small modern kitchen to prepare the ubiquitous Nescafé. Drawings of women, along with Meretz and animal rights stickers, decorate the walls. The kibbutz, she tells us, was established in 1948 just after Israel's War of Independence by a group of native-born Israelis.

Barkai is considered nobility of sorts in the kibbutz as her parents were among Rosh ha-Nikra's founders; they were eighteen at the time, and her father had served in the Palmach, an elite prestate Jewish military force. The kibbutz grew in its early years by taking in Nachal groups, a military unit that combined military service with settlement in outlying areas of the vulnerable new state. Youth groups brought their members to live in the settlement at the age of fourteen. Later, the kibbutz began taking in members of Ha-Bonim, a Diaspora Zionist youth group. Today, the kibbutz has roughly 250 members, plus 200 children below the age of eighteen, along with another 50 who are students and soldiers.

Economically, Kibbutz Rosh ha-Nikra reflects the changes that have buffeted the kibbutzim. The kibbutzim originally were agricultural communities, and members rarely worked on the outside. But that is no longer the case. As a recent work looking at some of the winds of change blowing through the kibbutz movement could note, "For years, the kibbutzim had received much direct and indirect assistance, due to the national tasks they fulfilled. In addition, much of this assistance stemmed from close ties between the kibbutz movement and the ruling Labor Party, which formed every Israeli government until 1977."[11] The aid enabled them to get involved in new industries. From agriculture, Kibbutz Rosh ha-Nikra has diversified into tourism (kibbutzniks run the cable car at the nearby grottos) and agricultural cloning. In addition, many members today work outside the kibbutzim, as educators, academics, and managers. Barkai herself is a human resources coordinator. Her salary, like that of other kibbutzniks who work outside the settlement, goes back to the kibbutz. Barkai is philosophical about the sea change that working outside of the kibbutz represents: "A profession is part of a person's personality. Today, there's more communication and discussion about finding satisfying work." The economic transition for the kibbutzim to a less insular, more modern economy has not been an easy one. Many of the collectives started up industries they knew nothing about. They sank deeper into debt, until the government had to take over most of the country's banks in the 1980s when they faced collapse because of their high loan exposure to the kibbutzim as well as stock market speculation.

Barkai enjoyed growing up in the communal environment of the children's house. At eighteen she spent a year in Tel Aviv serving as a counselor to youngsters, a very common experience for kibbutz young people, She was supposed to preach the virtues of kibbutz life to her young charges and inspire them to live the Zionist dream by returning to the pioneering virtues that built the state. By her early twenties, she was married and had a child (her son today is twenty-three). Although she had not felt "different" as a girl, the way many gays and lesbians feel growing up, she recalls having questions about attractions to women. She made a vow to herself at the time she was pregnant "that I might still investigate [lesbianism]."

Her first experience with another woman came in the form of a female volunteer. The two worked together and, she laconically recalls, "it happened. We were together for a week while my husband was on reserve duty. Twenty years ago, the kibbutz didn't know what 'gay' and 'lesbian' were. Friendship with another woman wasn't considered strange." For

Barkai, that affair changed her life. She was studying at the Wingate Sports Institute at the time and had a romance with another woman there. Within the following two years she concluded that she would have to divorce her husband. He had found out about her lesbianism and, for a time, they tried to make things work. But after much effort, they decided to separate and share child rearing. Her ex-husband ultimately left the kibbutz.

Barkai's next dilemma was whether to stay at Rosh ha-Nikra or, like many kibbutzniks who realize that they are lesbian or gay, leave the kibbutz. At the time, she was "deep in the closet," to use her words, and feared the prospect of effectively coming out to three hundred people, for, if she came out, word would get around quickly. As a child of Rosh ha-Nikra's founders, Barkai was very attached to her home; her ex-husband had been from another kibbutz, and they had even lived there for a year, but she had insisted that they return to Rosh ha-Nikra. She believed strongly in the kibbutz ideology. She defined herself to me "as a socialist and a feminist. I need a worldview, to commit to a social message."

Ultimately, her love of kibbutz life pushed her to come out—and remain. She first came out to her sister, and asked her sister to tell her parents, so that they would not hear it through gossip. But when she then decided to tell a friend of her sister's, she knew that word would get out. In an intimate society like the kibbutz, everything is subject to discussion, especially the lives of fellow kibbutzniks. In many ways kibbutz life is akin to life in any small provincial town where talk and gossip are part of the social fabric that binds residents together.

Barkai was not the first in her kibbutz to come out, however. That honor went to Chesi, a man who had used his divorce to announce his homosexuality a few months earlier. He had met another married kibbutznik, David, through their participation in a regional choir, and the two had fallen in love. His coming out unnerved the men of Kibbutz Rosh ha-Nikra. Barkai didn't have as many unpleasant experiences in that respect because the kibbutz, she says, is a macho environment and women are allowed masculine behaviors, although the opposite is not the case. Barkai had reason to be concerned though. She worked as a teacher and principal at the time and feared negative reaction to her working with children, although she says she never encountered any problems on that score and she continued to teach while her son studied at the school.

Around this time, she met Nicole Brenner, an American volunteer at the kibbutz with whom she fell in love. They moved in together and, when Brenner planned to move to the U.S. for a year to complete her degree in women's studies at Berkeley, Barkai asked the kibbutz to allow her to accompany her, at kibbutz expense, as her partner. The kibbutz agreed, effectively setting a precedent for the future. When they returned to Rosh ha-Nikra, the question arose as to what Brenner's status would be—full membership or something else.

As is the custom in the kibbutzim, a General Meeting was convened, and the issue discussed. One man, recalls Barkai, said that he was proud that Kibbutz Rosh ha-Nikra had a gay and a lesbian couple living in the settlement. The kibbutz membership voted to make Brenner a member. When Chesi wanted to make his partner, David, a candidate for membership, there was yet another discussion. By this time Barkai was already kibbutz secretary. But this vote proved more contentious. A member stood up and declared his concern that same-sex relationships do not last and that there would be a constant influx of new gays and lesbians, as couples broke up and then met new partners. The difference in the two couples experiences suggests the ways in which male homosexuality can be perceived as more threatening to people than lesbianism and the greater willingness people can feel to openly express their homophobia toward gay men.

Barkai readily concedes a number of advantages she had, advantages that call into question, as will be seen, just how much the kibbutzim have changed in their attitudes toward homosexuals. First, she had "a record," as she put it. She had grown up in the community, made that community her home, and demonstrated her commitment to the values of the kibbutz movement. Although some might view her lesbianism as a blot on that record, it wasn't a big enough blot to negate her many accomplishments. And although the kibbutz is officially an equal society, with no class divisions, the reality is different. As a daughter of two of Kibbutz Rosh ha-Nikra's founding members, she was the equivalent of Americans who could trace their ancestry back to the Mayflower, a recognized member of a social elite. This also helped her, and the kibbutz as a whole, in dealing with her lesbianism.

My friend Ilan Vitemberg, who was raised on Kibbutz Meggido, in the Jezreel Valley, gave me some additional perspectives on growing up gay on a kibbutz. Unlike Barkai, Vitemberg, like many other twenty- and thirty-somethings, has left the kibbutz in search of a different life. While Barkai offered me the viewpoint of someone deeply committed to the kibbutz vision, Vitemberg offers a darker picture. The beginning of the end for the kibbutzim, he recounts, came when "the Yom Kippur War shattered Israeli society's sacred cow—the myth of the sabra's superiority. Before the war, kibbutzniks were the elite and *yordim* (a pejorative term for emigrants) were the scum of the earth. Everything became a question mark. People wanted to find their voice."

"The rise of the Likud to power in 1977 actually developed the country," he continues, but it brought inflation, which in turn ultimately destroyed the kibbutzim. But the change in power, he recalls, "ended a hegemony where there were only three radio stations, all broadcasting the same news bulletin, and one television network."

Vitemberg illustrates how consumerism began to enter the kibbutzim and how this triggered more fundamental changes in kibbutz society. "In my kibbutz, people started getting private telephones in 1985. Before that, there were only public phones and one in the kibbutz secretary's office. There was no privacy. If you wanted or needed to make a call overseas, you had to request permission from the kibbutz secretariat. The secretary would actually stand there while you made your call, so you had to be aware of what you were saying."

Other changes, such as VCRs, led to the demise of film screening for the entire kibbutz, and television discouraged socializing and even led to the demise of the famed kibbutz general meeting (some kibbutzim began broadcasting such meetings over closed-circuit television). These changes unraveled the distinct social fabric of kibbutz life, with members involved in each other's lives in ways both good and bad. As people retreated to their remote controls and kitchenettes, they simultaneously received greater exposure to the outside world and grew more distant toward each other.

Vitemberg's former kibbutz is affiliated with the Ha-Shomer ha-Tza-'ir youth movement, which established a network of kibbutzim that created in 1927 the Ha-Kibbutz ha-Artzi federation, ideologically the most radical of the three kibbutz movements.[12] "When I was growing up, we got only one newspaper in the kibbutz," the now-defunct *Al ha-Mishmar*, the ideological organ of Ha-Shomer ha-Tza'ir, whose masthead proclaimed "For Zionism, Socialism, and the Brotherhood of Peoples." If you wanted a newspaper, that is what you read.

The kibbutzim have seen other economic changes over the years, changes that presaged the development of personal autonomy. Vitemberg tells me that the kibbutzim used to distribute a set number of "points" that could be used respectively to purchase clothes, books, and sundries. The points were not interchangeable. In other words, the kibbutz would decide for you what you needed and how much of it you needed. Later,

Meggido and other kibbutzim began giving their members a general budget that kibbutzniks could use in the manner they saw fit. With some personal control over money, kibbutzniks today constitute yet another marketing niche. When Vitemberg and I had lunch with his parents, the dining hall at Kibbutz Meggido was festooned with banners for Nestlé and Osem[13] products, like the peanut butter–flavored Bamba chips so popular with Israeli children (and me). I could only imagine the founding parents of the kibbutz movement turning over in their graves, as the society for which they had struggled surrendered to the siren song of Nestlé's Quik and Bamba.

In the traditionally collective environment of the kibbutzim, gay people did not count. While Nurit Barkai could report that kibbutz members did not feel particularly threatened by her lesbianism, kibbutz boys and men were subject to more rigid and traditional social roles (as Barkai herself asserted) While the kibbutzim could experiment with women's roles, there was no similar experimentation with male roles or the social construction of masculinity.

Vitemberg winced a bit as he recalled the "kibbutz male ideal" that had made his youth quietly hellish: "You were supposed to be both a fighter and a lover of classical music. You were supposed to be both intellectual and macho. To be part of the consensus, you were supposed to have both these traits. If you chose only cultural pursuits, you were outside the consensus."

A permissive attitude toward sex reigned, especially for boys. Boys, Vitemberg remembers, were encouraged to have girlfriends and sleep with them. On top of it, there was no privacy, so "you could be in your room while your roommate was having sex on the bed on the other side of the room—this was perfectly acceptable." But that laid-back approach to sex went only so far. The tenth commandment of Ha-Shomer ha-Tza'ir youth was "sexual purity," which meant, he says, that "you don't go to prostitutes and you're not gay."

Vitemberg went to high school at a regional kibbutz high school called Shumriya that served four kibbutzim. The kibbutzim, he says, saw the Summerhill School as an ideal—a place where children would have control over their lives—and Shumriya reflected that ethos. His school, he says, equally emphasized studies, culture, and work. "It was good, because you could develop culturally. I took guitar, dance, and drama classes. But I couldn't confront who I was sexually."

At the age of sixteen Vitemberg went to see a psychologist to discuss his feelings for men. The school psychologist sent him to Oranim, the psychology center for the kibbutzim, where the psychologist analogized homosexuality to thumb sucking. "She said, 'Once you sucked your thumb, right?' I said, 'Yes.' 'Do you now?' she asked. 'No,' I replied. 'It's the same thing with homosexuality—it's something that sometimes happens in youth. As soon as you have a girlfriend, you'll get over it.'"

Vitemberg did get a girlfriend, for four years, in fact. But during military service he began to accept himself. Today he surveys his former high school in disbelief. "My institution's been merged into another one. There's cable TV. Gay lecturers have been invited to lecture. You can have your own room there. Sometimes I feel angry that I didn't have the chance to love—it's a really brutal thing they did."

For Vitemberg's parents, immigrants from Argentina, coping with their son's homosexuality in a kibbutz setting was traumatic. Only with the passage of years and their son's temporary exile to the United States were they able to come to terms with the news. They had long seen "gay tendencies" in their son—they noticed that he liked dancing and cutting hair—and had consulted educational advisers, who counseled that adolescent sexual orientation was still in formation and that it was by no means definite that their son was a homosexual. Even though he had girlfriends, their concerns were not eased. Vitemberg's father, Hershel, has an earthy—sometimes coarse—sense of humor, and said to me that they thought that the girlfriend he had during his army service was ugly and told him so. His mother interjected that "Ilan was upset—he was trying to please us."

The Vitembergs found out about their son's sexual orientation because they opened a letter he had left sitting out. "It was the end of the world for us," his father recounted in the living room of their cottage, as he plied me with enough coffee and cake to add a few pounds to my frame. "We were educated a certain way—gay jokes. We didn't know any gays."

His parents kept hoping for a while that he was bisexual, and when Ilan wrote them during a trip in Latin America after his army service that he had met Peter, his future partner, in Guatemala, they didn't think much about it. Like many other parents, the Vitembergs brought closure to their difficulties with their son's sexual orientation. Today, notes his mother, "everybody knows about it in the kibbutz, but they don't want to talk about it. For a long time, we didn't want to talk about it either with anyone in the kibbutz." When I met the Vitembergs for the first time, on Ilan's recommendation, during a 1991 trip to Israel, they did not want me to mention to other kibbutzniks that I was gay, let alone that their son was.

In fact, when Vitemberg married his partner Peter just outside Washington, D.C., two years ago, his mother recounts that "we didn't ask the kibbutz for money to attend the ceremony, although we could have. Instead, we told the kibbutz that we wanted to travel to Washington to attend his graduation ceremony from college," which took place a week before the wedding. The Vitembergs then debate between themselves whether Kibbutz Meggido would have paid for them to attend their son's wedding. His mother said yes, but his father wasn't as sure, and besides, he didn't want to ask. A few months after our interview, in a sign of how much they had changed, they formally applied to the kibbutz for the grant that it gives members when one of their children get married. The kibbutz granted their request, giving his parents four thousand shekels.

While the kibbutzim increasingly seem willing to accept lesbian and gay members who grew up in the settlement or who became members before they came out of the closet, it is very difficult to apply to be a kibbutz member as an openly gay man or lesbian. Vitemberg experienced this firsthand when he and his partner applied to different kibbutzim. Vitemberg wanted to teach children in one of the kibbutzim. Kibbutz Rosh ha-Nikra, the home of the openly gay and lesbian former kibbutz secretaries, "didn't want to deal with it," says Vitemberg. Another kibbutz, Metzer, actually sent a letter to the parents telling them of Vitemberg's sexual orientation. As Vitemberg himself admits, "It's still harder for a gay kibbutznik, because kibbutzniks are a 'different people.' It's a closed society in which it's tough for someone who is different."

Neil Harris, British-born, lives today as an openly gay man in Kibbutz Tuval, located near Karmiel in the western Galilee. The kibbutz has a dairy farm, chicken coops, a kiwi plantation, and a seminar center that specializes in a kind of "Outward Bound" leadership training and team-building exercises and in Arab-Jewish relations. I first met Harris at one of those seminars as a twenty-five-year-old law school graduate. I remember looking at the cute British seminar leader with an earring wondering if he could possibly be gay. At the time, I didn't think such a thing was possible in a kibbutz. A decade later I had my answer.

Harris immigrated to Israel in 1979 as a twenty year old with a group of friends who were going to join a kibbutz. Zionism didn't particularly motivate him, but the notion of collective living was exciting and besides, he laughs, "England was shit." After language and agricultural training, Harris set off to help establish Kibbutz Tuval. Thirty-five people founded the kibbutz, one-third of them British, one-third South African, and one-third Israeli. At its peak, Tuval had 120 members.

Today, the number is substantially less, but, in an economic innovation, the kibbutz has been selling plots of land to nonmembers attracted by a rural lifestyle. Twenty-seven private houses are being constructed, although Harris insists there's a centralized plan governing the development, presumably to keep Tuval a rural attractive place. Twenty members work outside the settlement in everything from speech therapy to graphic arts.

Harris defined himself as bisexual when he first moved to Israel. He had trained to be a welder and was also destined to be Tuval's first secretary. Rumors began spreading that he was bisexual, but no one thought it was possible because he was a welder. When he finally came out, he recalls, "the Israelis were freaked, at first, but soon became bored with it."

Harris was married to a woman for five years, by whom he has a child. He slowly came to an awareness of the strength of his same-sex attractions, divorced, but remained in the kibbutz because of his son. Today, the kibbutz, he says, is perfectly fine about same-sex couples, and he believes that a same-sex couple from outside the settlement could be admitted as members. At Tuval, he says, slipping into promotional mode, they're looking for people with initiative and entrepreneurial skills rather than blue-shirted workhands. But as Ilan Vitemberg's experience suggests, applying as an openly gay person to a kibbutz, even when, in his case, he grew up in such a community, is risky.

For all the sexual permissiveness and rhetoric about the "brotherhood of peoples," the kibbutzim were quite conservative about homosexuality. Vitemberg remembers quite well the 1990 *Kibbutz* article about gays in the kibbutzim and a further rejoinder three months later from Dr. Mordechai Kaufman. In the original article Dr. Kaufman attacked the idea of bringing in gay lecturers from the outside to speak about homosexuality and the discrimination that lesbians and gay men faced in Israeli society. He attacked the figure that outside lecturers used about the number of homosexuals in the kibbutzim (6 or 7 percent of the population) as "imaginary, Tales of 1,001 Arabian Nights."[14] So enraged was Kaufman about gay lecturers that he accused those speakers of coming to lecture "with the clear goal of expanding their ranks by influencing adolescents who are at the stage of looking for a self-identity. . . . It recalls the types of methods used by missionary sects seeking to capture souls."[15] He was quick to deny any antigay animus, however:

> There is no debate between me and the homosexual organizations on
> the equal worth and equal rights of every human being. I have always

fought, and continue to fight, against any discrimination: black or white, Jew or Palestinian, homosexual or heterosexual. . . . I'm against any discrimination against homosexuals, whether in the city or on the kibbutz, because I don't judge or value human beings according to their sexual orientation.[16]

Based on his professional experience, Dr. Kaufman claimed that the percentage of gays and lesbians in the adult kibbutz population was no greater than .5 percent. Why the low percentage? The membership policies of most of the kibbutzim discriminate against singles, whether gay or straight. He wrote that "the possibility that a gay couple will apply to the kibbutz and seek to be accepted as a 'family' is rare and not relevant statistically." Dr. Kaufman asserted that the "truth" is that gays tend not to want to apply and/or remain in kibbutzim—there's a "negative chemistry" between gays and an intimate society, he wrote, where the "unassailable focus" is the family and child rearing. Furthermore, the kibbutz isn't ideal for looking for a same-sex partner; it requires leaving the kibbutz to go to meeting places in urban centers where gays congregate, at the expense of kibbutz life. Finally, the lack of privacy in kibbutzim made it very difficult for homosexuals to remain in the closet, thus presenting another reason why gays and lesbians are not interested in kibbutz life.[17]

The article concluded with a warning not to open the "gates of the kibbutzim" to gay lecturers, which would only "cause damage in a field that requires psychological expertise and knowledge," and that the kibbutz newspapers should not serve as "an effective shelter for homosexual organizations." He urged only that the kibbutz public use the Kibbutz Family Counseling Center, "the earlier the better."[18]

I interviewed Dr. Kaufman by telephone from his kibbutz, Ramot Menashe, where he has retired. Truth be told, Dr. Kaufman sounded a bit befuddled as we spoke. He kept repeating, "It's no more, no less" throughout the interview. He claimed to me that, while kibbutz values in general have changed, they had not done so with respect to homosexuality. He insisted that the number of gays in the kibbutzim had not grown, that "they build their community outside the kibbutz."

The Family and Children Counseling Station once headed by Dr. Kaufman has changed a lot, however. First, in economic terms, more and more of its patients come from outside the kibbutzim. The station seems to take a different view of homosexuality as well. I spoke by telephone with Dr. Ora Zamir, a clinical psychologist, at the station. While Dr. Kaufman was convinced that environmental factors explained the alleged lack of homosexuality in the kibbutzim, Dr. Zamir said that today biological factors seemed to provide a better explanation for the development of sexual orientation. "Homosexuality no longer is considered deviant or unhealthy, as it once was defined," she added.

I asked her how the station's psychologists would treat a gay patient today. Her response: "We'd discuss whatever issues the patient brings with him. We wouldn't try to change a person's sexual orientation. If a person was confused about his sexual identity, we'd explore those issues." As for the desirability of bringing gay lecturers to kibbutzim, she said that the station does not take a position, but added: "There's debate about whether to teach about issues like drugs or sex, for fear of giving legitimacy to certain things."

Things are changing the most, in fact, with the young generation of kibbutzniks. Whereas homosexuality was once the great unmentionable, kibbutz schools, like those in the cities, are beginning to encourage discussions of gay issues. In Harris's view the kibbutz schools have the most liberal approach to sex education.

One morning I journeyed to the Meggido Comprehensive High School, into which Ilan Vitemberg's kibbutz high school was merged and which today serves a number of kibbutzim in the Jezreel Valley. Ilan and I strolled through the grounds—low-rise buildings, gardens, and large stretches of verdant lawn. We asked one teenage boy directions to the building we were searching for and got a deep-voiced, confident response that sounded as if it were coming from the vocal chords of a battle-tested military commander. "An example of the kibbutz male ideal," quipped Vitemberg. Nine educational advisers from various schools in the area, most, but not all of them, serving kibbutzim, came together to share perspectives with me on how they deal with gay issues in the kibbutz schools.

One adviser recounted how the kibbutzim used to encourage sexual experimentation before marriage and how a smaller minority viewed sex as food—a hunger that should be satisfied with a minimum of fuss. Today, although they acknowledged that high school students certainly engaged in sex, they felt that youth were more cautious than their elders, mainly because of fear of AIDS and pregnancy. There was no stigma attached to early sexual relations, however.

Most began considering gay issues in response either to professional workshops they attended and/or because of gay and lesbian students who came out in their schools. Nurit, an adviser at Zorea, recalled a student who had come out four years previously to the entire school. It made her realize, she said, that she had always educated gay and lesbian students in a kibbutz setting. Raising the subject is not necessarily easy, she added. For some students, in the midst of adolescence, the whole issue is very threatening.

Meggido High, along with the other schools represented at the meeting, made use of the Education Ministry's booklet on sexual orientation, although the kibbutz setting, it was generally agreed, presented special problems. In the kibbutz education system there is lots of opportunity to discuss issues but less opportunity to experience them firsthand; for the students it's very "in" to discuss controversial issues like homosexuality, but the advisers were quite uncertain whether all the discussion led to practical acceptance of gays and lesbians. One of two male advisers present, Dani, added that if the students have to deal with an actual openly gay or lesbian person, the issue can be discussed and internalized better.

A Meggido adviser, Nira, said that kibbutz education is not open, that, while it is changing, the toughness that kibbutz society traditionally encouraged still exists. Her generation, she said, rebelled against the notion that expressing emotion or crying were signs of weakness. "All the *besederi'ut* [everything is okayism] led us to deny the existence of gays. We're like any society—we have troubles. Even in elementary schools, there are kids picking on other kids whom they perceive to be gay." Ora, another adviser, said that "the gap is between declarative and practical acceptance in the kibbutzim. Many choose to come out outside the kibbutz. Those whom we know about don't live full lives. They shut down."

I asked those present what they saw as the goal of their discussions of gay issues in the kibbutz schools. And, here, things got interesting. Nira said that the goal was "to break down stigmas." Hadar, another adviser, said that the goal should be to enable gays "to merge into society." Nira chimed in, "Jews are a community. Gays are not." A spirited discussion then ensued between me and Ilan Vitemberg on the one hand, and the advisers on the other, as to why lesbians and gay men want to define themselves as a community—a discussion that by this point in my trip to Israel was nothing new to me, having heard it from Knesset members, the Parents and Friends of Lesbians and Gays group, educators, and gays and lesbians themselves. It struck me as ironic that kibbutz educators, part of a community that deliberately prided itself on its difference from the wider society, would have a hard time seeing lesbians and gay men define themselves as a community and emphasizing any distinct features they felt they had. But their view was not a kibbutz-specific one; it pointed to the difficulties Israelis still have in relating to gays and lesbians as a group as opposed to individuals with a minority sexual orientation.

The advisers with whom I met at Meggido High seemed simultaneously committed and conflicted. The kibbutzim had come to embrace greater individualism as contact with the wider society and economic pressures led to wholesale changes in their communities; human and civil rights for all were definitely part of the kibbutz creed in the 1990s, a continuation of the universal message of equality that the early pioneers espoused.

After my morning at Meggido High, I spent the evening at the Jezreel Valley Regional Council building outside of Afula with members of Ha-TAKAM, a youth group primarily for gay kibbutzniks (the name means "gay residents of the kibbutzim and moshavim" but also stands for one of Israel's kibbutz movements, the United Kibbutz Movement). The building is part of an impressive complex of government and recreation facilities situated out in the middle of nowhere. There are seven young people present, all of them young men, four of them kibbutzniks, one serving in the Nachal in one of the area kibbutzim and two from the town of Nazareth Ilit. At first glance, these kids seem a world apart from their counterparts in the youth groups that I saw in Tel Aviv, Haifa, and Jerusalem. They somehow seemed less carefree. When Ilan and I enter, they're in the midst of a group exercise—to pick a flower out of the bunch lying on the table and tell what they like about it. When my turn came, I dutifully picked a flower and said I liked it because it was my spouse's favorite color, purple, and it made me think of him.

As I talked with the group's facilitator, Kobi (a pseudonym), the tough exteriors began to open up and reveal pretty ordinary teenage boys. Kobi said that the Afula group didn't have the same awareness of sexual orientation issues as did, say, the Tel Aviv group, whose members even bring their straight friends along. Living in rural settlements, they didn't have easy access to the same wide spectrum of gay life. He himself didn't expect to stay in the kibbutz, even though he really liked kibbutz life. For him, the dream was to live in a moshav, a quasi-communal settlement where individuals own their homes and land but market their output collectively, and he wanted to do so with a future boyfriend or partner.

Two other young men at the group were boyfriends; the older of the two, Amos (pseudonym), aged seventeen and a half years old, had come out in school. Were there any difficulties doing that, I asked. "None at all. People know you. They ask questions for a week, and that's it." Amos said he had no desire to stay in the kibbutz, but for reasons having nothing to do with his homosexuality. Rather, he wanted to experience life outside the bubble that still is kibbutz life in many settlements.

His boyfriend, Gilboa (again, a pseudonym), was shorter, dark, and muscular, with moussed hair. He and Amos had met in the group and had been dating for three weeks at that point. He had come out in his kibbutz, similarly not reporting any great difficulties. He often traveled to Amos's kibbutz (where Amos has his own room) and has met Amos's parents as well. Unlike his boyfriend, Gilboa really wanted to stay in the kibbutz after completing his military service. He liked horses and sports, and everything seemed hunky-dory. Gilboa turned serious for a moment and said, "Fifteen years ago, it wouldn't have been possible to come out in a kibbutz. Israel and the kibbutzim are more open today. It's due to the media." Did living in the city, with its higher numbers of gays and lesbians, have any appeal? "*Ma pitom* [What are you talking about]? I don't want to live in a ghetto."

In such a changing environment, gay people have been coming out—and remaining--within kibbutzim, although it is still not easy. They do so for the same reasons as their heterosexual counterparts—a belief in the special mission of the kibbutz and its ideology or, in other cases, because it is the only life they've ever known.

The decline of the kibbutz movement in Israeli society presaged the growth of a culture that gives greater autonomy to the individual, a culture in which sexual difference could find expression, and a lesbian and gay rights movement could advance—even in the previously rigidly conformist confines of the kibbutz. Thus, while the connection surely would vex Dr. Kaufman, the change in values within Israeli society at large, and in the kibbutzim in particular, has thrown the kibbutz and the gay community together—for better or for worse.

8

Twice Marginalized: To Be Gay and Palestinian in Israel

Will you persist in these lewd acts which no other nation has committed before you? You lust after men instead of women. Truly you are a degenerate people.
—Quran 7:80–81

What type of Arab society do we want to build? We want to build an Arab society in which there is respect for human beings, for their bodies, for their sexual orientation."
—MK Azmi Bishara to the Knesset, February 4, 1997

It is 12:30 A.M. on a warm June evening in Jerusalem and I am walking behind my friend, Lutfi al-Mi'ari (a pseudonym), as he gives me a tour through the darkened paths of Independence Park, a meeting place and cruising ground for many Jerusalem gay men. In the distance, from one of the hills, one can see the illuminated walls of Jerusalem's Old City. The scene is admittedly striking, but I cannot quite get over my American discomfort with being in a darkened city park in the middle of the night, with male shadows darting along the paths or disappearing into groves of trees.

We enter a fenced-off area, just down the hill from the Jerusalem Sheraton. Tombstones in varying states of neglect and decay, their Arabic inscriptions visible, lie scattered on the ground. In a mixture of anger and resignation, al-Mi'ari recounts to me the history of this place: "This land that we're standing on used to all belong to the *Waqf*, the Muslim religious trust." After the war and the establishment of Israel, forever seared into Palestinian consciousness as *an-nakba*,[1] the Catastrophe, the Israeli government took over vast amounts of Palestinian property, even from Palestinians who did not leave the country during the fierce conflict that broke out between Jews and Arabs and who became Israeli citizens.

Israel's Declaration of Independence, which set out the founding parents' putative aspirations for the new state, declares that "the State of Israel . . . will maintain complete social and political equality for all its citizens regardless of religion, race, and sex and will guarantee freedom of religion, conscience, language, education, and culture."[2] Although Arabic is an official language and formal equality of one person, one vote is guaranteed, discrimination against Palestinians remains rampant—despite efforts under the governments of Yitzhak Rabin and Shimon Peres to close some of the social gaps between Jewish and Arab citizens. Their land use and ability to plan their communities is limited by the fact that most land in Israel is owned by either the state itself or the Jewish National Fund, neither of which wants to grant extensive lands to the country's Arab population. Their schools receive a fraction of the funding received by Jewish schools, and fewer resources are devoted to health care and infrastructure as measured against funds received by Jewish towns and cities. Because they are not drafted into the military, Palestinians in Israel cannot obtain many social benefits available to those performing military service, including mortgage subsidies and admissions preferences to institutions of higher learning. Many job announcements require military service as a credential, a back door way of discriminating against Arabs.[3] The constant tension in Israel's identity as both a democracy and a Jewish state comes into play most strongly in its relationship with those Palestinians who effectively cast their lot with the state in 1948 and remained behind, becoming step-citizens in the process.

Al-Mi'ari faces reminders of some of the humiliations visited on Israel's Palestinian minority every time he visits Independence Park and sees the remnants of what he says was once a large Muslim cemetery. "When the city 'renovated' the park a couple of years ago, more of the graves were covered over. I've even seen people having sex on some of the tombstones."

Even the gay men strolling the park and the Muslim dead lying in eternal rest underneath cannot escape the cold political and public relations calculations of the Arab-Israeli conflict. Al-Mi'ari complains, with a certain justification, that "the Israelis are always bringing up the desecration of Jewish graves on the Mount of Olives by the Jordanians (between 1948 and 1967). But look at what they've done here to an Arab cemetery. They've destroyed a huge gravesite and obliterated evidence of the Palestinian presence." Not that the destruction of the Muslim cemetery is unique. Other Palestinian cemeteries, mosques, and villages also have met this fate.

Lutfi al-Mi'ari was born in one of Israel's major cities after the birth of Israel in 1948. His family was among the minority of Palestinians who did not flee or were expelled in the turmoil and war surrounding the birth of the Jewish state and the Palestinians' subsequent nakba. Following high school, he enrolled in the Hebrew University of Jerusalem and graduated with a degree in the social sciences. He later obtained a masters degree overseas and today works in the nonprofit sector for an organization that promotes democracy and pluralism in Israel.

Despite his academic and professional success, life in Israel is complex at best, painful at worst, for al-Mi'ari and his fellow Palestinian citizens, as our tour of Independence Park illustrates. Palestinian citizens of Israel enjoy de jure political equality, in that they can vote and participate in the political process. But, until 1966, Israel placed them under a military government that restricted their movement and freedom, making a mockery of the professed aspirations of the Declaration of Independence.

In addition to the difficulties inherent in being a Palestinian citizen of Israel, al-Mi'ari is also gay. Gay Palestinians on the one hand identify with and participate in their people's struggle for equality within Israel and independence for the Palestinians in a state alongside Israel. But they cannot express their sexual identity openly within the Palestinian community in Israel. Al-Mi'ari and other gay and lesbian Palestinians would face social ostracism among many Palestinians were their sexual orientation known. Yet, as much in Israel's gay community as in Israeli society in general, al-Mi'ari faces social marginalization and prejudice because of his Palestinian identity.

Renewed contact with Palestinians in the Occupied Territories after 1967, coupled with the inequality they face within Israel, led Palestinian citizens of Israel to identify more strongly with their siblings there, with a concomitant alienation from the State of Israel and their Jewish fellow citizens. A seminal event in the growing alienation was Land Day, a day of demonstrations and strikes called to protest government-sponsored land confiscations from Palestinians. In 1976 police shot dead a number of Arabs protesting those expropriations, and injured tens more. The anniversary since has become the major event on the political calendar of Palestinian citizens of Israel. A similar occurrence in the town of Umm al-Faḥm in September 1998, when the IDF sought to confiscate agricultural lands for a firing range and police again injured scores of protesters, only reinforced Palestinians' feelings of second-class citizenship.

Another factor encouraging their alienation is the unwillingness of successive Israeli governments to give them an effective voice and stake in governmental affairs. Although Palestinians are elected to the Knesset, both within Zionist parties such as Meretz and Labor, as well as through

Arab political parties, no Arab has ever been a minister in an Israeli government, nor has an Arab party been invited to be a formal part of a government coalition.

The closest that state of affairs ever came to changing was during the late Prime Minister Rabin's tenure in the early and middle 1990s, when his government was only able to survive because of the external support of the Arab parties in the Knesset; Rabin even appointed Labor Party MK Saleḥ Tarif and Meretz MK Walid Sadik, both Palestinians, to serve as deputy ministers. But this state of affairs only added to the bitterness of Israeli Arabs. On the one hand, Rabin refused to give them a true seat at the table. On the other hand, the opposition vociferously attacked Rabin for relying on the support of Arabs to gain approval of the Oslo Accords in the Knesset, with some Knesset members from the right going so far as to declare that Arabs had no place voting on matters of such critical national importance.[4] After Rabin's assassination the Arabs' dissatisfaction only grew when Shimon Peres ran an election campaign that took their support for granted. He further alienated them by launching an ill-fated Lebanese incursion designed to make him look like more of a *bitchonist*, a man dedicated to Israel's security.

Moreover, Israeli Arabs are invisible in the ongoing national conversation. To use author David Grossman's term, they are truly "present-absentees." Even among portions of the left, Palestinian citizens of Israel do not truly count as Israelis, a nationality that in the eyes of most of the public is synonymous with Jewish. As Israeli scholar Benjamin Beit-Hallahmi could note, "Israel is the only state in the modern world in which citizenship and nationality are two separate, independent concepts."[5] Palestinians in Israel possess Israeli citizenship, but the nationality line in their domestic Israeli identity cards reads "Arab."

This unwillingness to integrate Palestinian citizens of Israel, formally and symbolically, has sparked a counterreaction from many Arabs, the most visible symbol of which is visits by Palestinian members of the Knesset to neighboring Arab countries such as Syria. Instead of serving as possible bridges between the two societies, some Arab MKs use their visits to meet with Palestinian rejectionist organizations and engage in the type of anti-Israeli rhetoric that is already passé for Israel's partner to the peace process, the Palestinian Authority.

In May 1998 *Ha'aretz*'s Ari Shavit, a well-known left-wing journalist, interviewed Chadash-Balad MK Azmi Bishara, a Palestinian, about his vision for the future and how he balanced the tension in his identities. Bishara's responses were revealing and, at times, bordered on the seditious. Asked about the ritual loyalty oath to the state that he as a Knesset member took, Bishara declared, " 'Loyal to the State of Israel?' What do you mean loyal to the State of Israel? To the founding values on which it was established? To the Judaization of labor? To redemption of the land?"[6] With more than a little chutzpah, Bishara also refused to recognize that there was a worldwide Jewish people entitled to a nation of its own, stating that "I think that Judaism is a religion and not a nation, and the Jewish community in the world has no national status. I do not believe that this community has a right to self-determination."[7] The coup de grâce of the interview was his declaration that "it's impossible to say 'I'm both a proud Arab and a loyal Israeli.' It's nonsense."[8] If so, Israel's rejection of its Arab citizens in the first five decades of its existence has sown such bitterness.

But alienation from Israel is not the complete story. After Israel's founding, those Palestinians who remained had to adapt to new realities. Their previously agricultural-traditional way of life confronted the Western and increasingly urban ways of the new state. As their agricultural way of life began to change, they became a part of the Israeli workforce and economy, although they faced discrimination. They fought assimilation, wanting Israel to reflect their existence and culture as Palestinians. Writers like Emil Habibi have expressed the struggle of Palestinians in Israel to preserve their culture and identity. And there have been authors like Anton Shammas, a Christian Palestinian who writes in Hebrew. In laying claim to Hebrew as a non-Jewish Israeli citizen, Shammas is mounting a challenge to preconceived notions of what it means to be Israeli.

This chapter took me as a gay American Jew, who considers himself a Zionist and is proud of many facets of Israeli society, on a journey to places I had never previously ventured. In it I confront some of my own subtle stereotypes as a Westerner and as a Jew toward Palestinians as I try to analyze, dispassionately, what I saw and heard. Although this chapter concerns those gay Palestinians who are Israeli citizens, my journey brought me into contact with gay Palestinians from East Jerusalem, the West Bank, and the Gaza Strip. As double outsiders (East Jerusalem Palestinians carry Israeli identity cards although most are not Israeli citizens) and triple outsiders (West Bank and Gaza Palestinians are not Israeli citizens or residents and most today live under the jurisdiction of Yasser Arafat's Palestinian Authority), their contacts with the Israeli gay and lesbian community are layered with that much more difficulty.

My journey to examine the status of gay Palestinians in Israel also took me to Palestinian feminists. A look at the status of Palestinian women in

Israel, who labor under many of the same cultural, political, and national disabilities as their gay siblings, sheds light on the problems of Arab gays. Although I certainly tried, I did not personally speak with Arab lesbians, despite the help of several individuals in this regard. Here, again, the status of women in Arab society in Israel is a useful marker for examining the world that Palestinian lesbians must navigate. Because Arab women must struggle fiercely for autonomy and equality as both Palestinians and women in Israel, the ability of Arab lesbians to live even closeted lives within Palestinian society in Israel is even more limited than that of heterosexual women *and* gay men generally.

While I cannot say that it is easy to develop a gay identity, as Westerners and most Israelis would understand that notion, such individuals exist, even if Palestinian society requires them to hide their sexual orientation. Not surprisingly, those individuals with gay identities tended to be better educated and/or had lived overseas, which in turn influenced their own analysis of their sexual identity and any political implications that might flow from it. Equally important is that gay Palestinians, whether Israeli citizens, residents of East Jerusalem, or citizens of the future Palestinian state being built in Gaza and portions of the West Bank, have greater contact with Israelis.[9]

Palestinian society in today's Israel is heterogeneous and dynamic. It consists of Muslims, Druze (an offshoot of Islam), and Christians, urban residents and villagers. Socioreligiously, there are secular and Islamist outlooks competing for the allegiance of Arabs in Israel. Politically, Palestinian citizens of Israel occupy a wide spectrum. They vote for Arab nationalist parties reflecting secular and Islamist outlooks as well as for Zionist and even ultra-Orthodox Jewish religious parties (the latter because of funding that some ultra-Orthodox parties have been selectively directing at certain Arab communities). Despite the variety of outlooks and debate on many issues among Palestinian citizens of Israel, there has been very little public discussion of homosexuality or gay and lesbian political issues.

Islam and Homosexuality

One key to beginning to understand the approach of Palestinian society in Israel toward homosexuality is religion. Most Palestinians in Israel are Muslims, with smaller minorities of Christians (relatively more tolerant toward homosexuality, with emphasis on "relatively") and Druze (very conservative toward homosexuality). Islam, like Orthodox Judaism, does not approve of homosexual acts.

Jim Wafer's chapter on "Muḥammed and Male Homosexuality," in *Islamic Homosexualities*, notes that the Quran contains seven references to the story of Lot, and the "people of Lot," and that the destruction of Lot's inhabitants was due to homosexual behavior.[10] The Quran states in one passage, "Will you persist in these lewd acts which no other nation has committed before you? You lust after men instead of women. Truly you are a degenerate people."[11] The Quran takes a particular position regarding homosexual relations between Muslims, stating: "If two men among you commit a lewd act, punish them both. If they repent and mend their ways, let them be. God is forgiving and merciful."[12] Yet Wafer contends that this verse suggests a lenient attitude toward homosexual relations among believers, in contrast to the specific penalty of one hundred lashes for fornication.[13] What is not clear from a reading of the Quran is whether early Islam recognized the existence of individuals attracted constitutionally to their own gender and lacking any attraction to the opposite sex. Some of the verses, such as those condemning men who leave their wives for other men, suggest situational same-sex attractions rather than the type of gay identity and lifelong homosexual attraction in existence today in Western societies.

Like Judaism, Islam has also developed commentaries on its holy book, called the Ḥadith, that constitute exegesis on the views of Muḥammed. One set of commentaries mentioned by Wafer denounces anal intercourse, declaring, "Whenever a male mounts another male, the throne of God trembles; the angels look on in loathing and say, Lord, why do you not command the earth to punish them and the heavens to rain stones on them?"[14] Another Ḥadith called for the stoning of participants in anal intercourse. Yet another set of commentators contended, according to Wafer, that homosexuality does not merit any punishment because of another Ḥadith stating, "Muslim blood can only be spilled because of adultery, apostasy, or homicide."[15]

Punishment for homosexual relations under Islamic law requires either four witnesses who have seen the "key enter the keyhole" or a confession by the accused four times. As one writer points out, under such exacting standards for conviction, penalties for same-sex relations are rarely carried out.[16]

While the concept of "gay identity" is just beginning to make inroads in the Arab world, same-sex relationships are reputedly quite common. As with Hebrew, there is no native, nonjudgmental term for individuals who love members of their own sex. The most common expression in Arabic is *liwaat*, a word derived from the Arabic word for Lot, Lawt, whose travails, recounts the Quran, triggered God's wrath against Sodom and Gomorrah. One gay Palestinian in Jerusalem helped translate the Hebrew University lesbian and gay student group's posters into Arabic and, after much consultation, came up with the term *mutamathillin jinsiyan*, literally, "those who are the same sexually," from the Arabic root word *mathala*, to be the same or like.[17] It remains to be seen whether this expression will ever catch on in Arabic public discourse in Israel.

Rather than using identity discourse, the Arabs' notion of homosexuality has traditionally looked more to the active/passive dichotomy in sexual pairings to determine their worth. One isn't so much homosexual as characterized by the role assumed in a sexual act. A man who takes the active role with another man does not face the same social opprobrium that a man taking the passive role in sexual relations would receive.[18] In certain circumscribed contexts, as among adolescents and young adults, discreet same-sex relations may be tolerated. Some of those I interviewed contended that stereotypically effeminate homosexuals were tolerated, albeit as the butts of jokes and disdain, as they could be viewed as "mistakes of nature." A masculine openly gay man, however, would face substantial social opprobrium and sanctions.

The Palestinian Politics of Homosexuality

The Palestinian establishment in Israel traditionally has not been terribly receptive to gay issues. I sought to interview Palestinian MKs for this chapter to ascertain their views on homosexuality and Israel's increased tolerance of lesbians and gay men. Two of them, Azmi Bishara of Chadash-Balad and Saleḥ Tarif of the Labor Party, ultimately did not consent to interviews (more on Bishara later), the former because of travel plans[19] and the latter simply failing to respond. But MK Tawfiq Khatib of the Arab Democratic Party–United Arab List readily consented and spent forty-five minutes forcefully expounding his view of homosexuality. Our interview, at the beginning of a five-week sojourn in Israel, gave me ample evidence of the problems that gay Arabs face in their own society.

Khatib's office is located in a mobile home attached by a covered walkway to the main Knesset building. The rather modest and distant quarters suit the marginal status of Arab Knesset members in the Israeli national dialogue. His party, the United Arab List, is Islamist in outlook and ran in alliance during the last national elections in 1996 with the Arab Democratic Party, established by Abdel Wahab Darawshe, a former

Labor Party MK who broke away from Labor over the Palestinian cause. Unlike the secular Chadash-Balad, which is made up of both Jews and Arabs (even though most of its support comes from Palestinians), the ADP-UAL is the voice of Arab nationalism with an Islamist accent. One of its leaders, Abdel Malik Dahamshe, is a leading figure in Israel's Islamic Movement and brought the movement into Israeli electoral politics after much internal debate over such participation.

I knocked on Khatib's door and introduced myself in the best Modern Standard Arabic I could muster. Modern Standard Arabic is actually never spoken except in newscasts and formal speeches (or between educated Arabs whose respective spoken dialects are not easily intelligible), and Khatib, like other Palestinians I spoke with in Israel, looked a bit bemused by my overly formal speech. I told him that I was an American Jew writing a book about gays in Israel. To make sure he understood the nature of the book, even with my mediocre Arabic, I threw in "gays and lesbians" in Hebrew. After a bit more back and forth in Arabic as he hospitably prepared me some Arabic coffee, we switched to Hebrew for the remainder of the interview.

"I oppose it (homosexuality) on principle," began Khatib. "Religion is a way of life. When God created man, He created limits to live within. If they are broken, it leads to disaster. A society that legitimizes this will be destroyed. I fear that we'll be in a situation like that which Lot confronted (in the story of Sodom and Gomorrah). God will bring down his wrath on such a society." As is the case in Judaism, Islam sets rules for every moment of one's waking day. For an observant Muslim like Khatib, religion and state cannot be separated.

How should Arab society view homosexuality, I asked. "You won't find any Muslim who believes in Islam as a way of life who can give legitimacy to homosexuality." I asked Khatib if it was difficult for him to reconcile his religious beliefs with the fact that he lives in a country, and serves in a parliament, that has banned discrimination against gays in many walks of life. He had a very certain reply: "The Knesset makes mistakes. It should try to correct this mistake as soon as possible. If [MKs] can't see the catastrophe they're bringing because of this, they shouldn't be in the Knesset."

And how do you view individual gay people, I ventured. "I view a person who's gay as deviant. I won't shoot him. He should get treatment. It's a disease. The problem is in giving it legitimacy." When I mentioned that I knew gay Palestinians and that they reported on the difficulty they experience within Arab society because of their homosexuality, MK

Khatib retorted that "I'm glad they realize that [Arab] society rejects them as deviants. They should feel like strangers in our society."

Turning to the status of Arabs generally in Israeli society, Khatib told me that Israel has to decide what it wants: "If they can't live with another people in their state and want to be Jewish, they need to say it. Or if they want Arabs to be integrated as Arabs, that's fine. Once Israel called us *Aravei Yisrael* (the Arabs of Israel), but it became clear that we weren't Israel's Arabs. Israel then pushed further and said, 'You're not equal, you're Arabs. You're citizens, but not exactly Israeli.' " He added: "I'm a citizen, I'm Arab, and I need to avoid assimilation. Jews should understand this. They were *ahl al-kitab* [people of the book] in the Arab world"—a minority that, due to its adherence to monotheism, was accorded special protection and religious/cultural autonomy under Muslim rule.

Perhaps at the other end of the Palestinian political spectrum with respect to homosexuality is MK Azmi Bishara, a self-described liberal from Chadash-Balad, and a prominent proponent of declaring Israel "a state of all its citizens." Addressing the Knesset in 1997 during a debate on amending the country's libel law to prohibit, among other things, maligning another person on the basis of that person's sexual orientation, he stated that the amendment was "praiseworthy." He then asked: "What type of Arab society do we want to build? We want to build an Arab society in which there is respect for human beings, for their bodies, for their sexual orientation, etc., for the freedom of women, respect for women, and for her right to control her body."[20] Bishara's remarks suggest a willingness to fight for a pluralistic Palestinian society that will respect differences among its members. His call for tolerance of those with different sexual orientations was singular in its clarity. The contrast with MK Khatib's worldview is evident and points to the range of outlooks on social questions within Palestinian society in Israel.

The reality is more complicated, however, and shows the ways in which divisions in Israeli society prevent what might be a far-reaching alliance between marginalized groups that would include both gays and lesbians and Palestinians. Simply put, the primary issue that determines political alliances in Israel is the peace process and security issues. Although shifting alliances among Knesset members on social issues are developing, particularly because of growing secular-religious tensions, social issues, including equality and civil rights, remain a marginal matter for most Knesset members. Moreover, the merits of particular social issues cannot be easily divorced from their often Zionist context.

When I stopped by Bishara's office seeking an interview, Bishara's par-liamentary aide put it bluntly: "We don't see a possible alliance between 'oppressed minorities.' Why did gays first go with the army, the nuclear reactor in Dimona (a reference to Uzi Even's probable work in the years before the IDF took away his rank and security clearance because of his homosexuality), and the Jewish National Fund (a reference to the fight that Israeli gays and gay Jews abroad waged against the JNF to force it to hang a plaque in the Lahav Forest acknowledging the trees that gay and lesbian Jews had contributed)?"

In other words, the very issues that have brought Israeli Jewish gays safely into the fabled consensus ensure, at a minimum, suspicion from the country's Arab leadership. Another point of contention for Bishara's aide was her perception of the country's gay leadership as overwhelm-ingly Ashkenazi and male.

Bishara's fellow party member in the Fourteenth Knesset, MK Tamar Gozhansky, a Jew, had her own take on discussion of gay issues in her party and among Palestinians in Israel. Taking me through a far-reach-ing analysis of Israeli politics and the strata of Arab society in Israel, Gozhansky told me that the leadership of Chadash-Balad was against "all discrimination" but could not at this juncture single out sexual ori-entation. Arab society, she continued, "views homosexuality as some-thing foreign, and I can't turn it into an issue on the public agenda of the party." The fact that Palestinians in Israel lived in concentrated areas of the country only reinforced traditional ways of life, in her view. Gozhan-sky tries to tread carefully on gay issues, on which she personally has been active in the Knesset: "I try not to be patronizing. You can't dictate [on these issues] but you can debate." She also wanted to avoid being in a position of seeming to advocate the alleged superiority of the West with regard to attitudes toward homosexuality.

A Palestinian civil rights attorney, Ḥassan Jabarin, from Adala, a legal organization working for the civil rights of Israel's Palestinian mi-nority, offered me a different perspective on how Palestinians view the gay community. Within the gay community, he said, the existential threat against the community as a whole is stronger than against, say, the women's community, thereby blunting deeper debate and discourse over the connection between sexual orientation and broader Israeli and Zionist identities. The struggle for existence as gay people supersedes the national and religious differences that otherwise divide them. In the feminist community, in contrast, national identity is a crucial ingredient and thus that movement's politics are problematic. Jabarin pointed to the support of some Jewish feminists for Likud Communications Minister Limor Livnat, because she is a woman, while ignoring her right-wing views about the Arab-Israeli conflict. Arab feminists cannot feel part of a movement that fights for a woman's right to serve in the Israeli air force, he told me. Moreover, Arab women belong to a larger national collective and to a culture. They are not excluded from Palestinian society, although they face rigid social roles and expectations, themselves the subject of growing discussion among Palestinians. Thus, Arab women can and do express their identities as both Palestinians and women in Israel.

An Arab homosexual, in contrast, is compelled to hide his sexual orientation and identity within Arab society. "He can't find his place in his society," said Jabarin. They "have no access. No newspapers. No place of their own." The fact that gay identity has what Jabarin called "a transnational component" makes integration between Jewish and Arab gays that much easier. He speculated that the gay community had a number of mixed Jewish-Arab couples, higher perhaps as a percentage than in the country as a whole.

Part of the problem facing Palestinians in Israel stems from what Jabarin labeled the impoverishment of Arab society in the country. The establishment of Israel in 1948 led to the exodus of most of the Palestinians' intelligentsia. Moreover, Israel did not want to see a rich Arab culture develop, fearing a sense of Arab separatism.

Thus, MK Bishara's rhetorical question to the Knesset—"What kind of Arab society do we want to build?"—is likely to remain at least partially unanswered until Israel arrives at some type of peace settlement with the Palestinian people, thereby perhaps equalizing the status of Palestinian citizens of Israel.

Contact with Israeli society has influenced the evolution of Palestinian society in Israel in many ways, but the influence on attitudes toward sexuality has been minimal. Arabs in Israel have adopted significant aspects of Israeli consumer culture and are certainly exposed to looser sexual mores through Israeli television and print media, which they consume, but that exposure has not yet altered Palestinian society's conservative sexual standards, although it clearly has impacted individuals. It may be that their precarious status in Israeli society leads Palestinians to cling to familiar social structures and roles as a means of preserving their traditions as well as resisting Israeli and Western influences politically and culturally.

Palestinians in Israel come into greatest contact with the more Westernized values of Israeli society in mixed workplaces and at the country's universities. While these foci have had some influence on attitudes toward women, and toward sexuality, the influence has not yet radically transformed Palestinian society. Thus, while there are growing numbers of Arab women studying in Israeli universities, Palestinian feminist activists complained to me that, for many, the only acceptable fields of study remain teaching and social work as a consequence of social attitudes about what type of work women may engage in outside of the home.

Palestinian Feminism and Gay Rights

The socioeconomic and sociopolitical obstacles confronting Palestinian women in Israel are certainly daunting. They include high levels of illiteracy, despite Israel's formal guarantee of education to all its citizens, minimal health care facilities, employment discrimination and unequal wages as both Arabs and women, and patriarchal social structures within Palestinian society in Israel.[21]

One of the fundamental issues confronting Palestinian women in Israel is violence—even murder—within the family, euphemistically referred to as "family honor killings." A 1997 report submitted to the United Nations states that Israeli women's organizations have documented fifty-two cases of Palestinian women murdered by their families in the name of family honor in the previous seven years. A woman can be murdered for reasons of family honor because she had premarital or extramarital sexual relations, was raped, or violated social codes and thereby shamed her family. It is the men in the Palestinian family who determine what constitutes acceptable and unacceptable standards of behavior for their wives and daughters. As noted in the 1997 report, "Palestinian society approves of family honor killings and absolves the murderer of personal responsibility for his crime. The murderer is seen as a victim of society, which expects and even pressures him to act in order to 'clean' the family's name."[22]

For Arab feminist organizations today in Israel, ending these killings—and the attitudes that make them possible—is a major priority. Iman Irani-Kandalaft of As-Siwar, the Arab Feminist Center for Support of Victims of Sexual Violence, talks of fighting "all the social phenomena that oppress me as a woman. I want to change the environment in which women live." Like Israeli Jewish feminists in the 1970s, Palestinian feminists have had to battle the silence that surrounds domestic violence in Palestinian society. They have worked to create greater awareness of the problem among Palestinians. As-Siwar runs a twenty-four-hour hotline and puts advertisements in Arabic newspapers like *Kul al-Arab* and *Al-Ittiḥad*. With much struggle, the group has taken its message to social workers, the police, politicians, and the schools. The latter in many ways is the most difficult institution to reach. Irani-Kandalaft: "We go to the schools and encounter great ignorance. They don't know basic things [about sexuality]. We have to start with the ABCs." The schools, whose curriculum is dictated by the Israeli Ministry of Education, fear that allowing feminists (let alone gays and lesbians) in to talk about family violence, and the basic sexual issues and inequality behind the phenomenon, would somehow encourage permissiveness.

As-Siwar takes no "official" position on homosexuality. As Irani-Kandalaft frankly admits to me, "We can't. We need to give legitimacy to more basic issues, which will encourage women to be more public and then come out." Asked to compare the status of gays in Palestinian society to the status of women, Irani-Kandalaft speculated that, in certain respects, gay Arabs might have greater freedom because of their ability as men to move around more freely, while Arab women, because of strong social traditions, lived in more circumscribed circumstances.

In fact, the family honor killings against which As-Siwar struggles can and do encompass sexual orientation. Irani-Kandalaft mentioned a case widely reported in the Israeli media in late 1997 involving a young lesbian couple, one Jewish and the other Palestinian. The two women had met in a shelter for battered women in Haifa, to which each had fled individually after being sexually assaulted by family members. The shelter refused to allow them to live together and they left to live on the streets of Tel Aviv.[23] Because the Palestinian woman's family threatened to kill her for bringing shame on the family, the two women ultimately fled overseas.[24] KLAF members helped raise money for the two women to build a new life together abroad.

A similar group, Al-Badil (The Alternative)—the Coalition Against Family Honor Killings, operates out of Nazareth, Israel's largest Arab city. Na'ila Awwad, one of the group's organizers, spoke with me in the group's spare offices on a quiet side street. One obstacle, she said, to greater activism against family violence is the ineffectiveness and/or unwillingness of the Israeli police to deal with the issue. Awwad, who works as well with another Nazareth-based organization called Women Against Violence, recalled fears in 1997 that there was an informal blacklist of women targeted for murder being circulated. Included in the list were women who work or study outside the home and whose male family members were opposed to such independence. Al-Badil sent a letter to Internal Security Minister Avigdor Kahalani, who never responded. When MK Salah Salim raised the issue with the minister at the group's request, Kahalani's reported response was that "this is the Arab mentality." The indifference of the police makes it difficult for women to come forward and complain about the abuse they suffer. Making a formal police complaint in some cases triggers family honor killings as a result of the public exposure—and perceived shame—that such complaints bring on the family as a whole. To prove her point, Awwad recounted the story of two sisters from Umm al-Fahm, a town abutting the West Bank, who were sexually assaulted at home. When they went to the police, their brothers killed them.

Like Irani-Kandalaft, Awwad sees a need for basic sex education at schools to begin combating the problem of family violence. Although some Arab schools teach "family life courses," students are not taught the basic notion that one has the right to control one's body and that no one else has the right to touch a person sexually against his or her will. Awwad contended that Arab women "are viewed as bodies, not persons with minds and opinions of their own."

Dealing with problems like family violence requires confronting both national/political and societal issues. On the one hand, family violence stems from patriarchal mores in Palestinian society that seek to restrict women's movements and autonomy. On the other hand, one cannot look at the problem in isolation from broader problems of Arab-Jewish relations. Awwad pointed out that of thirteen battered women's shelters in Israel, only one is for Arab women. This dichotomy in resources, so reflective of the sociopolitical realities that Palestinian citizens of Israel face in their daily lives, further marginalizes Arab women's problems. It would be easy to say that if Israel provided more resources for the "Arab sector," the problem of family violence would be less severe. But that is only partially true. While greater resources are necessary, groups like As-Siwar, Women Against Violence, and Al-Badil must continue to struggle with their own society's attitudes toward the problem.

Nabila Esbanyoli, a Palestinian feminist in charge of the At-Tufula Women's and Childhood Center, is at work trying to develop a stronger women's community within Palestinian society as well as more open sex education curricula. In 1997 Esbanyoli had published a book in Arabic for parents dealing with early childhood sex education, what she called in our interview "holistic sex education." While her book does not discuss homosexuality per se, it is, she says, aimed at creating support for a child's individual choices, including choices related to sexual orientation. As she put it, "where sex education introduces the notion of choice, it can introduce acceptance of others and different orientations."

Esbanyoli herself met lesbians for the first time in the United States rather than in Israel. While personally supportive of lesbians' and gay men's struggle for equality, she notes that "I speak of different sexualities [in my work], but I can't go out to demonstrate on this issue if there are no lesbians around. As long as there isn't a group of Palestinian lesbians coming out, the issue simply won't be as pressing."

Like Azmi Bishara's parliamentary assistant, Esbanyoli isn't enamored of all she sees within Israel's gay and lesbian community. While lesbians have developed social consciousness through their involvement with feminist politics and, in fact, have played an important, if largely unacknowledged, role in the Israeli peace movement, gay men have declined to connect their oppression with other forms of oppression in Israeli society. As Esbanyoli sees it, "Gay men did not try to break sacred cows. They didn't call into question social roles. The gay community tried to destroy stereotypes by showing that gay men can be like other men. They went for social acceptance, not social change." And to achieve social acceptance, gay men pursued issues like serving in the IDF, which Palestinian feminists see as an agent of both patriarchy and national oppression.

Like Irani-Kandalaft, Esbanyoli believes that gay Palestinians have fewer problems in Palestinian society than women, especially lesbians. "Men have their social spaces—you can go out. Women's space is confined to the home. If two men go out together to the forest [to have sex], no questions will arise. If two women are seen going somewhere alone, there are questions."

This comparison of oppressions is superficial in certain respects, however. While men in general—gay men included—may have greater freedom of movement within Palestinian society in Israel, they face other difficulties, namely, the inability to be public in their identity because of a realistic fear of the social opprobrium they would reap. So restricted are Arab women's roles and freedoms that Palestinian feminists could conceive of Arab gay men as possessing freedom because they could move about to satisfy their sexual needs. I personally found such an analysis depressing. The oppression of Palestinian gays and lesbians stems not from their inability to have sexual relations but from their inability to lead open lives within both Palestinian and Israeli societies.

In this comparison of oppressions Arab lesbians, unfortunately, occupy the bottom rung of the ladder. Writing in *Klaf Chazak*, a twenty-two-year-old Palestinian lesbian, Mansiya (a pseudonym that means in Arabic the "forgotten one"), notes: "Although I grew up in a very open and liberal home that did not distinguish between Jew and Arab, Muslim and Christian, and man and woman, the fact that Israeli society discriminates between Arab and Jew and the conservative Palestinian-Arab society discriminates between man and woman has created many dilemmas for me."[25]

Palestinian women, in contrast, while still sharply restricted by conservative social mores, have carved out social and political space. The existence of organizations like As-Siwar, Al-Badil, and the At-Tufula Center attests to the creation of a domain where Arab women can meet, collaborate, and build a vision for their future. This progress has not come cheaply, and many feminists have paid a personal price for raising such sensitive social issues. Yet they and their ideals have become a small part of the Palestinian social and political dialogue in Israel. Should their progress continue, feminists like Esbanyoli, Awwad, and Irani-Kandalaft may be able to speak out for their silenced lesbian sisters.

Small Signs of Change

Even in generally conservative Palestinian society the political successes of Israel's gay community may be bringing modest progress. In the September 1996 issue of *Ha-Zman ha-Varod*, there was a survey, the first in several years, of Knesset members' attitudes on gay rights. MK Abdel Malik Dahamshe of the ADP-UAL, asked whether he would act to advance the rights of gays and lesbians in Israel, stated, "If they're attacked as human beings, then yes. I'm against discrimination."[26] While hardly pro-gay, Dahamshe's response may indicate awareness among Arab politicians in Israel that equality for gay people cannot be dismissed derisively.

AIDS ultimately may serve as a means to increase the discussion of sexual orientation issues among Palestinian citizens of Israel. In the town of Shefaram I met Nazieh Kabha, director of the Department of Health Education and Promotion at the Galilee Society, a Palestinian group struggling for improved health and educational services for Arabs. Kabha recalls how AIDS has made a growing number of Arabs realize that gays and lesbians exist, after years "where we wanted to suppress [discussion of the topic]. We didn't want to think [gays and lesbians] exist. It deals with dangerous behaviors." The Galilee Society conducted a survey of Palestinian professionals—doctors, teachers, and social workers—on AIDS-related issues that uncovered a high level of ignorance. Professionals, he said, linked AIDS to risk groups like gays, rather than to risky behaviors.

The lack of awareness of such issues stems, as Palestinian feminists also pointed out, from the absence of basic health and sex education in Arab schools in Israel. Kabha felt that a special committee was needed that would have awareness of the needs of Arabs in Israel, since the Ministry of Education if anything perpetuated ignorance of such matters. That is a widespread complaint, echoed by Palestinian politicians and feminists alike. Thus, calls have grown for "autonomy" for the Palestinians of Israel in educational and cultural matters. Feminists felt that this would help advance their issues, but it seems to be a risky bet. With growing conflicts between Islamist and secular Arabs within Israel, it is unclear whether Arab control of educational content would promote more progressive approaches to sensitive social issues like sex education.

The Galilee Society tries to get the word out on what constitutes risky behaviors as well as on how to minimize one's risk. Because the reality is that Palestinian society in Israel is actually quite heterogeneous, Kabha says that it's impossible to present one message for AIDS education, and the group must tailor its message for different audiences—a Christian urban versus a Muslim village audience, or even a Muslim city versus a Muslim village public.

Because AIDS can pass from one person to another through certain same-sex sexual acts, the Galilee Society has had to gingerly raise sexual orientation issues as well in its presentations, thereby becoming one of the few efforts in Palestinian society to begin dealing with these questions in any meaningful way. "The word *gay* is still scary," notes Kabha, but the group tries to encourage tolerance and acceptance of gays as they are.

Still, like the efforts of Palestinian feminist organizations, work on AIDS-related issues among Palestinian citizens of Israel is a struggle. The group, in collaboration with the Israel AIDS Task Force and Doctors for Human Rights, puts out an Arabic-language pamphlet setting out the rights of persons with HIV and AIDS. The Galilee Society presented a day-long seminar in 1997 dealing with AIDS in the Arab sector, including a discussion of AIDS and gays (presented by a physician specialist) as well as personal testimony from an Arab person with AIDS.[27] The stigma that persons with AIDS face in Palestinian society is akin to the stigma faced by gay Arabs generally. Kabha read to me excerpts from the testimony of an Arab person with AIDS at that workshop: "My relatives and friends distanced themselves from me, as they believed that AIDS could come from a few meters away and that they should stay away from me. The social worker initially was supportive, but when he knew why I was there, he too distanced himself. My father kicked me out of the house."

Gay Palestinian Organizing

Gay Palestinians in Israel must navigate through this sociopolitical no-man's land. Some live in Arab society in Israel while hiding their sexual orientation. They may marry but engage in extramarital same-sex relations. A small number tries to blend into the wider Israeli society, sometimes cutting themselves off from their families and their Arab culture in the process. Yet others live their gay identities on a selectively open basis, struggle for their rights as Palestinians, and have substantial contact with Israeli society, gay and mainstream.

At Tel Aviv's Pride Day I asked Yasser, a Palestinian from Jerusalem, whether he had any problems with going to such an Israeli event as a Pride Day at Gan Meir, complete with Israeli pop songs. "No, they're (Israeli gays) not like other Israelis. They're more open." In fact, Yasser and several of his friends were planning to move to Tel Aviv, because there was better gay nightlife there than in Jerusalem.

Over the years there have been a few articles in the Israeli gay press on being both Palestinian and gay. These articles tend either to express Israeli hopes for peace with their neighbors or reinforce stereotypes about Arabs. Two examples: in advance of the Madrid Peace Conference in 1991, the August 1991 issue of *Maga'im* included an article titled "The Brotherhood of Peoples,"[28] which discussed where to meet gays in Damascus, Amman, Riyadh, and Cairo. In contrast, the October 1993 issue of *Maga'im*, published a month after the signing of the Oslo Accords between Israel and the Palestine Liberation Organization, contained an article about a gay Palestinian from Gaza titled "Hamas Would Murder Me If They Knew I Was Gay."[29]

It would be easy to turn this chapter into a litany of such sensationalist stories. But that is not the entire story. Some Palestinians do become involved in the Aguda and other Jewish gay groups. Contact with Israeli society and its lesbian and gay community have led to changes for gay Arabs: for example, the short-lived establishment of a youth group for gay Arabs under the auspices of the Aguda's Haifa branch.

The group started up in February 1998 because of the efforts of a young Arab gay man, Munir (a pseudonym), whom I had met at Pride

Day back in June 1997. When he came out, Munir was assaulted with the knowledge of his parents—the concept of family honor again comes into play in a lesbian/gay context. Munir fled his home for Jerusalem, where he remained for several months. He eventually returned home to an uneasy truce: "I returned, because I have to help my parents. It's part of the Arab mentality. I have to help my mother, even at the expense of my feelings."

Munir decided to try to establish a support/social group for gay Arabs out of a wish to help others avoid the difficult years he'd faced. He recounted calling the Aguda at the age of fifteen hoping to receive concrete support. Instead, he says he was met with indifference, not even receiving a referral to a support group.

The group, which lasted but a few months, was primarily social and, says Munir, was designed to give its participants a sense of confidence and self-worth. Munir's effort was certainly pioneering and, like many pioneering efforts, faced a host of obstacles and struggles. The young men attending Munir's group must deal with the fact that they cannot easily disclose their identity in Palestinian society, discrimination by Israeli Jewish gays, as well as elementary questions such as shelter (some of them have fled their families' homes). In contrast, the participants in other youth groups for gay Israeli Jews that I attended discuss issues like when to come out or how to cope with the army, or even broader gay political questions.

The Monday evening I attended the group, while in Haifa, there were five young men present, listening to Dana International and other dance music. They were clearly there to escape their problems for a couple of hours, in the company of others who faced the multiple challenges of living as gay Palestinians in the State of Israel. While the Aguda publicized the group's activities in *Ha-Zman ha-Varod* and in local Hebrew weeklies, Munir said that it was too early to attempt to advertise in Arabic, as the group needed more time to form and develop strength.

A couple of the attendees agreed to talk to me in a side room where we could escape Dana International and discuss things freely. One young man named Hani (a pseudonym), aged sixteen, announced that he was considering taking hormones and becoming a woman. He goes to clubs in Haifa dressed as a woman, and everyone in those clubs knows him as such. Another seventeen-year-old young man, Fathi, has a twenty-one-year-old Jewish boyfriend who, he claims, is afraid of him because he's an Arab. Fathi dropped out of school over a year ago because other students were harassing him because of his perceived sexual orientation. He currently works and shares an apartment with two other roommates. The stress of dealing with his sexual orientation causes him to break out in tears unexpectedly.

Fatḥi, as a Druze, intends to enlist in the IDF in the coming months and is looking forward to the experience. "I feel Israeli. I belong to this country and I have to defend it. It (army service) will make me feel more like an ordinary person." I got the feeling he may have been telling me this because I'm Jewish, but, on the other hand, many Druze do serve enthusiastically. Fatḥi's mother and sister already knew of his sexual orientation, and Fatḥi said he knew of other gay Arabs whose parents accept them. In his view, "It's a generational matter. Once, parents would murder their gay kids [in the name of family honor]. Arab society slowly will come around to accepting it. They see it already among Jews."

The trauma of coming out at a relatively young age in a society that is still hostile to homosexuality immediately drives a wedge between young gay Arabs and Palestinian society as a whole. Munir recounted to me how coming out caused him "to deny the Arab part of me. I didn't want to be persecuted a second time." As for Fatḥi, "The Arabs are the ones giving me a hard time." Some of their comments might have been a defense mechanism against having to hide their sexual orientation in Arab settings. Clearly, the difficulties these young people face delight Knesset Member Khatib, who said that he wants young Arab gays to know that their society rejects them.

But Israeli gays were scarcely more welcoming. Munir recalled being rejected once by a potential boyfriend because he was Palestinian, and Fatḥi's boyfriend apparently feels some discomfort because he is Arab. In their desire to be accepted by their gay Israeli Jewish counterparts, or perhaps because I myself am Jewish, they tried to accentuate the positive. They all were of the opinion that gay Israeli Jews were more accepting of Arabs because of their experiences as homosexuals, which places them in the category of persecuted minority as well. Hani wants "Arab and Jewish gays to accept each other—we're all homosexuals." While they may want to fit into Israel's gay community by downplaying their Arab identities in favor of the "transnational gay identity" that attorney Ḥassan Jabarin sees, the feeling is not necessarily reciprocated by gay Israeli Jews.

Gay Israeli Jews tie their gay identity very much to their broader Israeli identity. By doing so, and by emphasizing their commitment to such emblems of Israeliness as service in the IDF, they indeed have bought their entry into the Israeli consensus. That is not to say that the response to gay Arabs is uniformly hostile. It is not. Gay Arabs readily participate in community events, and the establishment of a youth group for gay Arabs within the Aguda clearly was a significant event. That it happened in Haifa is no accident. Haifa has a significant Palestinian population and, compared to the rest of Israel, has experienced less Jewish-Arab communal tension. Moreover, it serves as a gateway to the Galilee, with its numerous Arab towns and villages.

For the Haifa youth group to succeed, it would have needed a lot more resources than it received. While Munir wanted to give its participants a safe space in which they could explore their identity and escape from the pressures of home, or the streets and parks where many of the group's attendees hang out, there were clearly needs that the format could not satisfy. Munir himself was a young man with no specialized training in dealing with the issues aired by the group's participants. While the social aspect of the group served an important purpose, the problems that many of its participants brought with them around their sexual identity, as well as basic needs like shelter, suggested the need for more professional support.

If the young gay Arabs in Haifa are trying to make their way in the world, their somewhat older counterparts in Jerusalem do not have the same difficulties. Back in Jerusalem I meet three young gay Palestinians, Nimr, Hussein, and Ali, all residents of East Jerusalem ranging in age from twenty-six to thirty-two. At their age, they've all grown up knowing nothing but Israeli control of *al-Quds*, as Jerusalem is known in Arabic. The three are not terribly fond of Israelis and view them and the institutions that the gays among them have established in quite utilitarian terms. At the same time, they have a highly developed sense of gay identity, the product largely of travel abroad rather than contact with their Jewish cousins on the other side of the city. We spoke in English, in which they are quite fluent, thanks to education in private church-affiliated schools in Jerusalem.

The three had all told at least some members of their immediate families of their sexual orientation. The socioeconomic milieu in which they all grew up, complete with private education, was relatively open and liberal. Although some family members know, it is not a subject of ongoing discussion and does not exempt them from family pressure to get married, although the "pressure" sounds more formalistic than actual.

Communication with their gay Israeli counterparts exists but cannot be considered apart from the broader political situation in Jerusalem and the ongoing Arab-Israeli conflict. Nimr felt that, on the one hand, Israelis look down on him as an Arab, while, at the same time, "we think we're better than they are." Class distinctions probably have a lot to do with Nimr's attitudes, as he grew up in a comfortable middle-class environment. Israeli society, with its directness, surface egalitarianism, and sometimes charming/sometimes infuriating vulgarity, strikes many Arabs as uncouth and uncivilized. Hussein for his part said that he would have little contact with Israelis were he not gay.

Despite their sense of difference from, and resentment toward, Israelis, all three, when asked how they identify themselves, stated that they see themselves as gay. Their Palestinian identity is a given. That they can do so stems from their exposure to the West, and its notions of gay identity, and their economic background rather than their interactions with gay Israelis. Although they have a highly developed sense of gay identity, it does not extend to politics. Gay politics in Jerusalem necessarily has a lot to do with Israeli politics, in which they have no desire to take part. Ali does, however, volunteer for the Israel AIDS Task Force in Jerusalem and Nimr and Hussein both patronize gay clubs and attend events like Pride Day and the Wigstock festival in Tel Aviv.

Although they are unhappy living under Israeli rule, none of the three said they expected Jerusalem to be part of any future Palestinian state. As Ali put it, "It's not worth hoping for something that isn't going to happen." At best, contended Nimr, the city might eventually be shared in some way by Israel and the future Palestinian state.

Love Across the Divide: Same-Sex Relationships Between Jews and Palestinians

Amidst the conflict between Jews and Arabs, both in Israel itself as well as in the West Bank and Gaza Strip, there are some gay men who fall in love across the national and ethnic divide. *Yediot Achronot* published an article in November 1995 about a gay couple, with one of the men a Jew who immigrated to Israel and the other a Palestinian from Gaza.[30] Despite the pressures of the intifada, the two have managed to build a life together. In fact, one of the last acts of the late Prime Minister Yitzhak Rabin, in his role as defense minister, was to approve permanent resident status in Israel for the Gazan (although the story erroneously made it appear as if that was the end of the matter), so that he could continue to live with his Jewish Israeli partner.

I spoke with the Jewish Israeli partner, David (a pseudonym), at their home in a Tel Aviv neighborhood once populated by drug addicts but now welcoming many new immigrants. He met his partner, Salaḥ (also a pseudonym), ten years ago. "Before the intifada, young Palestinians came from the Occupied Territories to work. They had contact with Israeli society, and part of this was contact between Jewish and Arab gays."

The intifada, and paradoxically, the peace process, forced David and Salaḥ to take some fairly drastic measures. "With the beginning of negotiations, there were more difficulties, because the concept of 'two states for two peoples' began to take hold, and terrorist attacks created a situation in which Palestinians could not come to Israel to work," remembers David.

He wrote a letter to Rabin and to Meretz MK Yossi Sarid asking for permanent residency for Salaḥ so that he could live legally in Israel. This was not an easy matter, because Salaḥ was married to a Palestinian woman in Gaza and the two had children. David and Salaḥ decided not to ask for permanent resident status for Salaḥ's wife and children—and Salaḥ actually divorced his wife—to increase the chances that his application would be approved.

David recalls that "it took a long time. We needed the approval of the Interior Ministry and the Defense Ministry. Contrary to the *Yediot Achronot* story, the matter was not finalized at the time of Rabin's assassination, although he had given his approval. I was scared because the Interior Ministry passed into the hands of the ultra-Orthodox." The process was still ongoing, as of our interview in June 1997, but Salaḥ had received temporary resident status and David was confident that there were only some bureaucratic procedures standing in the way of Salaḥ's permanent resident status. Salaḥ, reported David, at least had social security and could join the country's main health cooperative, Kupat Cholim.

Not that it is easy for gay Jews and Arabs to meet, fall in love, and develop a relationship in Israel. Along with the stresses that exist for any couple, and the additional difficulties of being a gay couple in a heterosexual society, the Israeli-Palestinian conflict is never far away. David Shipler's 1986 book, *Jews and Arabs: Wounded Spirits in the Promised Land*,[31] tried to explore the terrain of love between Jews and Palestinians in Israel. The titles for his chapters on this subject: "Sexual Fears and Fantasies" and "The Sin of Love."

Shipler reported that Jews in Israel viewed Arabs as sexual studs, out to seduce Jewish women as their only way of screwing the State of Israel. Many Arabs have similar stereotypes about Jews. The Egyptian press, despite Egypt's peace with Israel, regularly trumpets stories about supposed Israeli efforts to corrupt the morals of Egyptian women.

Gay Jews and Palestinians in Israel are prisoners of the same stereotypes. One of the interesting motifs in an early gay Israeli feature films, *Drifting,* was the readiness of the protagonist, who wanted to make a film about being gay in Israel, to submit to the desires of a group of Palestinians living nearby in an abandoned house. Not only was the protagonist—a young gay Israeli Jew—willing to submit sexually to Palestinians, he even brought them food and bandaged the wounds of one of them (the implication being that the Palestinians were terrorists on the lam). His behavior simultaneously reinforced stereotypes about homosexuality among the Arabs and symbolized the wider political struggle between Israelis and Palestinians.

A cartoon in the winter 1996 issue of *Tat-Tarbut* stood some of this sexual stereotyping on its head. Titled "Love in the Shadow of the Intifada," Itzik Rennert's cartoon tells the story of Roni and Yusuf, who meet on the outskirts of Jenin, in the West Bank, where Roni is doing reserve duty. One minute Yusuf is lobbing stones at Roni and the next minute, after a charged look passes between them, they're having sex, with the Israeli soldier as the active partner. When Roni's Orthodox family discovers the truth (Roni tries to disguise his beloved as an Orthodox woman), the two of them flee to New York, where they get jobs in a sex club and their show, "The Jewish-Arabic Conflict Show" (with Roni still playing the active role), becomes a smash hit.[32]

Sergei Baitelman, a Kiev-born Israeli who made aliyah to Israel in 1991, in one of the first waves of Russian immigration following the collapse of the Soviet Union, began life in Israel in a West Bank settlement. Today, after a number of life changes, both political and sexual, he also has a Palestinian boyfriend. He met Samir (a pseudonym), a twenty-four-year-old Palestinian Christian from Beit Sahour (again, at Baitelman's request, I have changed certain details) in Jerusalem's Independence Park. When they first met, Samir claimed that he was from East Jerusalem rather than from the West Bank. As trust grew between the two of them, Samir revealed his true place of residence. Samir described his family to me when I interviewed him nine months later as lower middle class; yet his family invested in private education for him. In addition to his fluent Hebrew, he speaks both English and German.

Because Samir is neither an Israeli citizen nor a resident of East Jerusalem, he cannot legally enter Israel without a permit, the result of the Israeli policy of collective closure of the West Bank and Gaza. Baitelman: "He stays with me for periods of time. He cleans houses and helps take care of an elderly man. I'm trying to get him a work permit and marry him to an Israeli—Jewish or Arab. I'll leave Israel, if necessary, to be with him. I want to be happy, and he brings me happiness. I won't yield on this." Samir subsequently told me that Baitelman had even contacted MK Yael Dayan for help in getting permanent residence for Samir. The composition of the current government, she said, made that impossible. Samir has since succeeded in obtaining a permit entitling him to at least work in Israel.

David claims that he and Salaḥ do not experience problems as a mixed couple within the gay community, perhaps because Salaḥ has always had Jewish friends and has blended in well. Baitelman feels differently: "My friends have said, 'This is trouble. Don't put too much of yourself into this.' Even gay Israelis are not tolerant. They view [relationships between Jews and Palestinians] as problematic." Samir says that the concerns of Baitelman's friends dissipated as they got to know him. And, in fact, I ran into them one weekend in Jerusalem's Old City, where they were sightseeing with some of the other members of the Asiron, the Hebrew University lesbian and gay student group.

The Middle East conflict is present in both David's and Baitelman's relationships, but not in severe form. To reach across the divide between Israelis and Palestinians and see someone as a human being, rather than a representation of the enemy, requires a humanistic outlook. David and Baitelman have been to Gaza and Beit Saḥour respectively to see where their partners grew up. Samir, claimed Baitelman during our first interview, "hates Arafat and doesn't like Muslims. He'd like to see Israel give citizenship to all Palestinians." Samir, when I interviewed him alone, readily confirmed Baitelman's statement: "I always said I don't want to be Palestinian. I don't feel so great in the Palestinian community. Because of the situation, there are a lot of pressures. You can't do anything, you can't feel free. I feel free here in Israel, even when I was working here illegally." Samir's attitudes of dissatisfaction with Palestinian society were the sharpest that I heard among the Palestinians I interviewed. But they did not reflect a love for Israel, I think, as much as they reflected relief at being able to live more freely as a gay man.

The most interesting mixed Jewish-Arab gay couple I met was Sami, thirty-seven, and Ehud, twenty-eight (both pseudonyms—I've also altered other aspects of their identities to respect their desire for privacy), a doctor at an Israeli hospital and doctoral candidate in political science, respectively, who live in an upper-class Tel Aviv neighborhood. Both men are strikingly handsome and they and their quite posh apartment at first glance could be an advertisement for the guppie lifestyle. They've been a couple for two and a half years.

While in other mixed couples I met it was the Arab partner who had to undergo Israelization and live life largely on Israeli Jewish terms, in Sami's and Ehud's relationship there appeared to be a lot more give and take and discussion concerning each other's national identities and how these are expressed within the relationship. Sami grew up in the mixed Arab and Jewish town of Lod, outside of Tel Aviv. Although he attended a Jewish kindergarten, a fairly rare state of affairs for most Palestinians in Israel, he subsequently attended an Arab high school. At Tel Aviv University, where he studied medicine, Sami gravitated toward Arab students and Palestinian political causes, as his disillusionment with Israeli treatment of the Palestinians grew.

Although he had dated women even in high school, Sami had had same-sex experiences during the same period. At the age of twenty-six he had his first boyfriend, but continued to feel some attraction for women. A relationship with a woman six years later almost led to marriage. Yet, in his late twenties, he confided his attraction to men to a cousin, his sister, and his mother.

Ehud grew up in Rechavia, an upper-class neighborhood in Jerusalem. He, too, dated women but began coming out to people at the age of twenty. He served in a combat unit as a medic and continues, for the time being, to perform reserve duty. Since the age of twenty-two he's been completely open and has taken an active role in gay community organizations.

Sami is not out of the closet in the workplace and, unlike his partner, is not actively involved in gay community activities. The relationship with Ehud led him nevertheless to come out to his father, who comes from a more traditional background than his mother. It wasn't easy, he recounts, and the father at first did not want Sami to bring his Israeli Jewish boyfriend to the family home, a state of affairs that lasted only one week. A few of Sami's relatives have married Israeli Jews, and he told me that he "tried to draw parallels between the queerness of our relationship and that of others in the wider family."

Like most Israeli Jews, Ehud doesn't speak Arabic and had never given much thought to the problems of Palestinian citizens of Israel before meeting Sami, even though his family's politics were fairly liberal by Israeli Jewish standards. He admitted to me that "I didn't know what I was getting into." Sami interjected at that point that Israeli Jewish kids don't grow up learning in the Israeli school system about the government's land confiscation and other discriminatory policies. For Ehud, their first Israeli Independence Day as a couple was difficult. He had always been used to celebrating the day and putting up an Israeli flag—"But for Sami, it's a tragedy, and I didn't celebrate for the first time."

Being gay and sharing his life with an Israeli Jewish man has similarly led Sami to look at Israeli society differently than might have otherwise been the case. He remained sharply critical of Israeli policies toward the Palestinians both in Israel and the Occupied Territories but he also admired the Western liberal strands of Israeli society, strands that he would like to see develop more strongly in Palestinian society. In fact, he decries the Israelization that Palestinian society has undergone as largely superficial: "Israelization is in form rather than in essence. It's a process of external symbols. Tolerance and pluralism haven't penetrated. Arab society hasn't absorbed them. Rather, it's absorbed the material."

The two men then get into a debate about where Israeli society is headed, both on gay issues and more broadly. While both agree that it's the Israeli elite that has bought into gay issues, they disagree about the impact. Ehud sees the impact as shallow, as a surface political correctness. As he put it, "The country isn't Tel Aviv, it isn't the left. The elites may be ready to deal with it intellectually, but not from the stomach." Sami, in contrast, sees an important role for elite institutions such as the court system in setting a "tone" for the country to follow. More broadly, Sami sees a cultural synthesis developing in Israeli Jewish society between its Western and Eastern elements, contending that "Israel can't continue to live as a Western foreign implant" in the Middle East. Ehud sees this as a virtual disaster, complaining that " 'Mediterranean' isn't romantic for me. It means becoming more like Teheran. There's a cultural war going on here."

Their relationship, I think, enjoys this level of give and take on political and cultural issues because they, unlike some other Jewish-Arab gay couples, meet on equal footing. Sami has succeeded in the Israeli system, and both he and Ehud are highly educated. Moreover, as an Israeli citizen, Sami can effectively fight for his rights, unlike gay Palestinians who are not Israeli citizens and grew up in the Occupied Territories. In contrast, David and Salaḥ have very different educational backgrounds, with Salaḥ working in a more menial profession than David.

Israeli Gay and Lesbian Attitudes Toward Palestinians

In a country wracked by conflict, long-term intimate relationships between gay Jews and Palestinians are obviously an exception. Gay and lesbian Palestinians in Israel must cope with occasional hostility, or at least suspicion, from their Jewish counterparts. A particularly egregious example occurred in early 1999, when three gay men were murdered in pick-up killings in Tel Aviv. Gay party promoter Shimon Shirazi told the weekly *Tel Aviv* that "I can't believe this is coming from Jews. The Arab sector is always the threat. . . . There are Jews who love to have sex with Arabs, and now they'll have to be more cautious."[33] More subtly, many of those I interviewed spoke of Israeli gays as if they were all Jewish. For them, the Arabs are effectively invisible.

Ultimately, the predominant attitude is one of indifference rather than virulent hostility. For years Israel liked to create the perception that Israelis were yearning for peace and interaction with their Arab neighbors. The reality is a great deal more complicated, however. Yes, Israelis stormed the pyramids in Egypt and the ancient city of Petra in Jordan when those borders opened up, thirsty to see sites long denied them. But real cultural interaction and understanding with the Arab world? Forget it.

The Israeli gay and lesbian community has this same mindset. Even *Ha-Zman ha-Varod*, which prides itself on its inclusiveness, rarely has printed anything about gay Arabs, let alone a detailed cultural piece about homoerotic Arabic poetry or regular news about gay Arab organizations overseas. It's as if Arabs do not exist. Which is why Yossi Waxman's *My Darling Alexandria* was so remarkable. It portrayed Israeli Jews—gay ones at that—with an interest in Arab culture and the Arabic language. It showed them as individuals who could learn something from the Arabs and relate to them on a human level.

From my outsider's gay American Jewish perspective, this is a most interesting state of affairs. The organized gay and lesbian movement in America is constantly grappling, albeit not always successfully, with the issues of diversity and cultural pluralism. How to incorporate people of color into organizations, how to ensure that organizations attain gender parity, how to make events accessible to the differently abled, whether to include bisexuals and transgendered individuals—these and other issues are the subject of constant discussion and debate. Moreover, many American gays and lesbians believe that the common bond of a shared sexual orientation, or sexual minority status, can overcome barriers posed by race or religion.

This debate has not yet reached Israel, at least with regard to relations with gay Palestinians. While most of the activists I met held centrist or left-wing political views, they don't necessarily translate their professed beliefs into change on this particular issue. Although in the abstract they

may support equality for Palestinian citizens of Israel, within their organizations they are only beginning to take steps to include Arabs. Liora
Moriel did point out to me that, when she was Aguda chair, there was a
Palestinian board member of the Aguda for the first time ever. Unfortunately, she recounted, he mysteriously disappeared, and rumor had it
that he had died of AIDS.

The Aguda, until the advent of the Haifa youth group, did not offer any
services geared to the needs of gay Palestinians. Not that the youth group
formed as a result of the Aguda's initiative. It came together through the
efforts of Munir. Once the group was established, the Aguda did not appear to take any steps that might have ensured its long-term success.

Amit Kama, the former executive director of the Aguda, once claimed
in a conversation with me that no Arabs would show up, even if the effort was made. Avi Sofer, the former chair of the Aguda, told me that it
is "impossible" to reach this segment of the Israeli population. There is
no doubt that such outreach is difficult, but the Aguda conducts outreach to other hard-to-reach segments of Israeli society, such as Orthodox Jews. And when Israel began absorbing waves of Russian immigration in the early 1990s, the Aguda included a page of Russian-language
information in *Nativ Nosaf* and other publicity materials it issued. Never
has there been Arabic-language information in the Aguda's publicity,
even though Arabic is an official language in Israel and there are, in fact,
Palestinian members of the Aguda. The Aguda did advertise in its
newsletter for Arabic speakers in the spring of 1998, but, thus far, the
materials remain in Hebrew only, although the sign on the office door is
now in Arabic as well as Hebrew and English.

The failure to provide such outreach is part of the Israeli gay rights
movement's tendency to work for social acceptance, not social change,
and is that much more glaring because the Aguda does not consider itself a "Jewish" organization. Its name—the Association of Gays, Lesbians, Bisexuals, and Transgenders in Israel—suggests that it aims to represent the interests of all sexual minorities, whatever their national
background, not just those of Israeli Jewish gays and lesbians. An example of how un-Jewish the Aguda at times considers itself to be is the 1994
European-Israeli Regional Conference of Gay and Lesbian Jews. Although ostensibly a conference for gay and lesbian Jews, the Aguda ad-
vertised the conference in Hebrew in Israel as an "international gay and
lesbian conference," with no reference to Jews! My friend Lutfi al-Mi'ari
attended the conference, as did a couple of other Palestinians. The conference in terms of content was actually quite Jewish—from the work-

shops, to the services for the Jewish Sabbath, to the Israeli folk songs, disappointing the Palestinians present who, on the basis of the advertising, expected something different.

The gay and lesbian groups in Jerusalem have been making greater efforts—and progress. Both the Asiron and Jerusalem Open House in Jerusalem say that they are committed to including Arabs in their activities. As mentioned earlier, the Asiron's posters now contain the group's name in Arabic. Asiron chair Sa'ar Natanel proudly noted to me, "We're the only Jewish group on campus to use Arabic in our advertising. Even peace groups don't do it." Its web site now offers a virtual bookstore in conjunction with Amazon.com; among the books offered are some dealing with Islam and homosexuality.

Over at the Jerusalem Open House, whose colorful bumper stickers proclaim its existence in Arabic as well as in Hebrew and in English, Jerry Levinson recalled with excitement a recent visit by gay Jordanians to the Open House. And in October 1998 a Palestinian from East Jerusalem was elected to the Open House's board. That such dialogue and interaction find a home under its roof remains noteworthy in a city so polarized along national, political, ethnic, and religious lines. Those steps certainly are positive, but whether the Open House or other Israeli gay organizations can attract significant Palestinian membership remains to be seen; at the least, it would require programming directed to their needs, just as the Open House already offers programming and counseling aimed at gay ultra-Orthodox Jews, Russian immigrants, and gay and lesbian youth. Moreover, the Jerusalem Open House, although committed to a pluralistic vision of Jerusalem that includes gay Arabs, and with a Palestinian board member, remains quite Israeli in its outlook, celebrating Israel's Independence Day and Jewish festivals without, as yet, any Palestinian religious or cultural programming. In a city beset by national tensions, the Open House is not yet a neutral zone where gays from both sides of the city can meet on a level playing field.

As for KLAF, it is ideologically committed to the creation of a diverse lesbian organization. However, KLAF, like the Aguda, has not attracted many Palestinian members, although, as activists recounted, the organization supports Palestinian self-determination and works on its own, as well as through the wider feminist movement, on peace and equality issues. Tal Yarus-Chakak points out that it is not surprising that KLAF has only one Palestinian member, because "they do not have the same issues." Moreover, Yarus-Chakak feels frustrated with the slow acceptance of lesbian issues among Arab feminists generally: "Arab feminists don't relate well to us. It's clear to us that it is a difficult issue. It makes us angry sometimes—we've given a lot to the Palestinian cause, but they have not made the same contribution back to us."

Her point is interesting: those who engage in coalition-type politics arguably have the right to expect some level of support in return. Furthermore, lesbian feminists who are struggling to change patriarchal, sexist, and homophobic attitudes have a legitimate complaint: that they should not have to downplay their identity or aspirations any more than they would expect the Palestinians to do. Yet presumably KLAF's pro-Palestinian stance stems from a broad feminist worldview, one that should support Palestinian aspirations for an independent state on their own merit. And after interviews with Palestinian feminists it became clear that the issue of organized Palestinian feminist support for lesbian and gay rights causes is not a simple matter, due to the social and political confines in which they operate in Palestinian society in Israel. As Palestinian feminism still must struggle against deep-rooted patriarchy within Arab society, it may not be possible to seek the type of quid pro quo politics that Israeli lesbians have every right to demand from their heterosexual Jewish counterparts in the wider Israeli feminist movement.

Future Prospects for Gay and Lesbian Palestinians in Israel

Several factors will influence the future position of Palestinian gays and lesbians in Israel. The most significant one is the peace process. Peace between Israel and its Arab neighbors will generally improve the status of Palestinians in Israel. It would accelerate their integration into Israeli society, even as they maintain their Palestinian identity and culture. This in turn might create an opening for the beginnings of public discussion on homosexuality within Palestinian society.

The progress of Palestinian feminists may also ultimately have a positive impact on the lives of gay and lesbian Palestinians. The more they can reach Palestinian society with the message that women are equal, the more Palestinian society may become open, bit by bit, to discussions about sexuality, including homosexuality.

Social change in the Arab world could have a similar beneficial impact. There are the beginnings of gay organizing in the Arab world, as the visit of Jordanian gays to the Jerusalem Open House points out, as does the existence of expatriate gay Arab groups like the Gay and Lesbian Arabic Society, a group with branches in several U.S. cities. Social changes in Arab countries toward homosexuality could have a beneficial impact on discussions of homosexuality among Palestinians in Israel by presenting an Arab face to such an identity. Of course, the influences of the wider Arab world may thwart more open discussion of gay issues among Palestinians in Israel, if conservative Islamist attitudes spread. And while Palestinian citizens of Israel today have strengthened their ties with their siblings in the West Bank and Gaza, it is doubtful that changes in attitudes toward homosexuality will come from a newly independent Palestine. The new state will confront a host of challenges, and there likely will be a struggle between secular and religious camps over the character of that state.

In the meantime, however, gay and lesbian Palestinians find themselves, to use a Hebrew expression, "between hammer and anvil"—forced to remain largely silent about themselves among Palestinians and subject to discrimination as Arabs in Israeli society. Perhaps naively, Sergei Baitelman argued to me that, when peace comes, Israel might serve as a positive example for Arab gays and lesbians in the to-be-born Palestine and in other neighboring countries. Perhaps. But considering the intense suspicion that Israel still evokes today in the Arab world—even in countries, such as Egypt and Jordan, that have signed formal peace treaties with the Jewish state—looking to Israel as a source of inspiration could actually complicate, if not hurt, gay Arab causes in the eyes of their people. It is more likely that the walls of suspicion and indifference that have separated lesbian and gay Jews and Palestinians *within* Israel finally may crumble further. As we Jews say each year at Passover, *Dayeinu.* It would be enough.

Conclusion:
Kadima—Looking Ahead

I wheeled the baggage cart filled with the jetsam and flotsam of five weeks in Israel into Ben-Gurion Airport late one Friday night to head back to Washington, D.C. I'd spent my last evening in Israel in the company of my friends Gil Nader and Motti Porat at Abu Nasser's on the Hill, a seafood restaurant in Jaffa housed in an ornate villa and festooned with colored lights that looked like some kitschy Middle Eastern fantasy. We stuffed ourselves silly on stuffed calamari accompanied by plate after plate of Arabic salads, and finished up with baklava and Arabic coffee. Only in Israel would I have eaten such an unkosher dinner on a Friday night, the beginning of the Jewish Sabbath. But it was delicious, God forgive me. It seemed a strangely appropriate way to end a trip to Israel.

From Abu Nasser's, we made our way to He/She, a gay bar located on the edge of Tel Aviv's Carmel Market, for a drink, but nothing much was happening at that relatively early hour, so we drank up and left. Then, off to the airport, down the Ayalon Highway to Highway 1, past the billboards proclaiming "Together in Pride, Together in Hope," the official slogan for the upcoming jubilee celebrations.

Once in the terminal, I waited for my turn with airport security. All around me the security personnel were going through the Air Canada passengers' luggage intently, questioning people at length. My turn came and I said "Shalom" to the security guard. She asked me if I spoke Hebrew and, when I replied in the affirmative, we were off and running.

How long were you in Israel?

Five weeks.

What were you doing here?

I was researching a book on Israel's lesbian and gay community.

That had the desired effect. "Really?" she asked. "Tell me about that. It sounds fascinating." So we chatted a little bit about *Between Sodom and Eden* and she finally turned to me apologetically and went through the usual laundry list of questions: Where's your Hebrew from? Where did you go in Israel? Who packed your suitcase? Did anyone give you anything to take to someone?" Then, she slapped a couple of stickers on my bags, passport, and ticket, indicating I'd been questioned, and wished me a *n'siya tova*. Bon Voyage.

No sooner had I returned to Washington than events began to happen at a speed unusual even for Israel: the Israeli Civil Service Commission announced at least a theoretical readiness to grant pensions to the surviving same-sex partners of state employees, the Wigstock riots erupted, Michal Eden came in second place in the Meretz primaries, ultimately giving her a seat on the Tel Aviv City Council in November 1998, the first gay pride parade in Israeli history took place, and the Netanyahu government finally collapsed under the weight of its accumulated contradictions, with elections set for May 1999. As I sat completing this book over that period, I realized just how much the gay community was advancing at an accelerated pace and developing its own self-confidence, even as the broader political picture looked bleak, with secular-religious tensions spiking and Prime Minister Netanyahu wrecking the peace process.

Even as these wider battles go on, there is much to be optimistic about. The lesbian and gay community has not only continued to enjoy virtually uninterrupted political progress, but it has finally begun to internalize the notion that the attitudes of Israeli society toward gays and lesbians have changed substantially. Until the demonstration against President Weizman in 1996, that was not the case; the legislative and legal strides had not yet sunk in. Although a number of activists would disagree with me, the community today does not need enemies to coalesce.

The story of Israel's lesbian and gay community is largely a success story. The question does arise, however, as to what is the appropriate standard or standards for measuring success. Some would argue that, because gay and lesbian identity is a construct involving more than physical/emotional attraction to one's own sex, one should look at whether a strong rooted community, with a distinct culture, exists. Others might look to the strength of homophobia in society at large. And yet others would look to whether legal impediments to equality for gays and lesbians have disappeared. I will consider each of these arguments in turn.

Rooted gay community   This standard for judging the success of Israel's lesbian and gay community is problematic because of its underlying American assumption: that a gay neighborhood or territory is appropriate across cultures and represents a model to which gay people everywhere should aspire. But even under this standard the Israeli story today is an increasingly successful one. Compared to five years ago, there has been a dramatic increase in gay and lesbian Hebrew-language cultural output. More and more artists, writers, and musicians are defining the Israeli lesbian and gay experience through a variety of artistic media. Moreover, the community itself *is* growing, a phenomenon reflected in the membership growth of organizations, the development of new organizations (including a new group for sexual minority youth called No'ar 2000), the growth of restaurants, cafés, and bars offering diverse leisure options, the spread of lesbian and gay organizing to smaller towns, people coming out of the closet at a younger age, and even the growth in the number of pages and advertising space in *Ha-Zman ha-Varod* and *Klaf Chazak*.

But notions of community likely will continue to differ from those of other Western societies. Simply put, the notion of community will continue to be more loosely defined in Israel. Geography, the relative lack of anonymity, close family ties, and small numbers all will continue to conspire to make the establishment of a gay neighborhood in Israel problematic. Moreover, even as people are coming out at an earlier age, young gay and lesbian Israelis have yet to adopt a separatist ethos. The values inculcated in the educational system and through military service ensure an integrationist future for most Israeli gays and lesbians.

Israeli lesbians and gay men are developing their own forms of identity, rooted in the notion of a minority battling for full civic equality and acceptance, developing a culture but still integrated into the larger web of Israeli life, both institutionally and at a personal level. In some ways, as I argued in chapter 5, this synthesis is very Jewish. As Jews adapted their religion to the reality of exile, so, too, are Israeli lesbians and gay men adapting how they live their sexuality to the realities of their country.

Homophobia Some may contend that gay and lesbian Israelis have achieved only illusory success, as substantial homophobia, or at least homo-ignorance, continues to exist in Israel. Although I would agree that homophobia certainly remains a problem, there are a couple of reasons why I do not accept this argument. First, homophobia has lessened in a short period of time, in response to legislation and judicial decisions and the social changes that these have accelerated. Efforts in some schools, the education on gay issues offered by the Israeli media, and even the instructive value of laws and judicial decisions, all provide concrete examples of this. Moreover, when public figures today issue homophobic utterances, their remarks typically garner swift condemnation.

Second, from everything I have seen, homophobia in Israel is less virulent than in some other countries. The level of physical antigay/lesbian violence is low. Polling data suggest that, while young people by a narrow margin may harbor negative attitudes toward gay people, those attitudes do not necessarily translate into support for discrimination against gays and lesbians. Efforts in the educational system and the media should cause prejudice to drop even further in the future.

A crucial piece in all this may be the fragmented opposition to gay rights in Israel. Most of that opposition in the political realm comes from religious politicians. This has proved to be a benefit for gay rights activists operating in a mostly secular society where the dictates of religious parties are increasingly resented and feared. Moreover, religious politicians themselves have not organized any sustained opposition to gay rights, both because of other priorities but also because, I believe, of Judaism's proportionate response to the issue: while Orthodoxy does consider homosexual behavior to be a sin, it recognizes that no one is perfect. The religious have managed to preserve their outlook on homosexuality while coexisting with progress for gay people.

In any case, complete or even substantial eradication of homophobia should not be the standard for measuring lesbian and gay success. Here I offer my perspective as a Jew living in the Diaspora. Anti-Semitism continues to exist in the United States, Canada, and in Western Europe (in my activist capacities I've met lesbian and gay European Jews who have as many issues about coming out Jewish as they do about coming out gay and lesbian). Yet no one would argue that North American or Western European Jews do not live largely successful and free lives today, both as individuals and as members of a minority group, despite the stubborn existence of anti-Jewish attitudes in some quarters. It is necessary, of course, to continue to fight against homophobia, but that ongoing struggle should not lead to a conclusion that the Israeli gay and lesbian experience is not, today, largely a success. Just as Jews have continued to monitor and combat anti-Semitism, so, too, will gays and lesbians in Israel fight homophobia.

Removal of legal impediments   In examining whether the Israeli case is successful, I would argue for measuring success by the extent to which the state treats lesbian and gay citizens as equal to heterosexual ones. Legislation and judicial decisions can provide gays and lesbians with the tools to defend themselves against unequal treatment and discrimination. This type of progress, I would argue, is particularly important in areas where a large critical mass of gays and lesbians does not exist.

The removal of legal impediments certainly has been crucial in the development of Israel's gay and lesbian community. It was the Knesset's 1988 repeal of the country's sodomy law that sparked methodical public gay and lesbian activism. Moreover, laws and judicial decisions in Israel constituted a stamp of approval from on high that gave more and more gay and lesbian individuals the courage to come out publicly in a country that offered little anonymity.

There are those who would argue that the political and legal successes of Israeli activists are the product of little more than assimilationism, a success achieved by adopting heterosexual norms and presenting gays and lesbians as no different from heterosexuals. Even if this is the case, so what? Until recently, Israeli gays and lesbians, including activists, were largely integrationist in their outlook. They saw their goal as achieving equality within their society, not trying to remake it. The path they chose was tailored to the realities of Israeli society and the immediate needs of gays and lesbians in that society. In such a struggle most any means are legitimate to achieve the goal of making gays and lesbians equal to heterosexuals, including putting the most likable face on gays and lesbians for legislators, judges, and the wider public.

The success in shaping the public tone on gay issues owes much to what in retrospect was the "results-oriented" strategy pursued by activists in the late 1980s to mid-1990s, as well as those who preceded them in laying the foundations of lesbian and gay organizing in Israel. They succeeded in winning support for a series of incremental legislative and legal steps that have brought the community where it is today.

In fact, the success of that approach today is enabling different visions of what it means to be a lesbian or gay Israeli to emerge. Those changes have provided growing numbers of gays and lesbians with the security to live openly. As the community grows, so, too, do the options and visions for designing an open gay or lesbian life. The strategies pursued by Israeli activists have ultimately provided gay and lesbian Israelis with choices as individuals, something they did not have previously.

I admit that all the rapid change makes it difficult to predict how events will unfold in the future, but my bottom line prognosis is this: the Israeli lesbian and gay community should continue to advance politically, legally, and socially. But such progress is contingent on wider forces in Israeli society having little to do with the gay community per se. As the preceding chapters have demonstrated, the Israeli lesbian and gay community has benefited from three conflicting trends in Israeli society: 1) the decline of collectivist norms, in which allegiance to the broader nation and society is being supplanted by the growth of individualism and narrow, sectoral political and cultural interests; 2) the opening up of Israel to the wider world socially, culturally, and intellectually; and 3) the tribal notion of Israeli Jews as one family.

The growth of the Israeli lesbian and gay community rests uneasily astride these trends. While the emergence of a lesbian and gay political bloc, proven by the success of Michal Eden in the Meretz primaries, owes much to a political system and culture that has turned the Knesset into a battleground of rival publics, the gay community in many ways remains a subgroup of Israeli society's traditional elites. But the future fortunes of that group are uncertain. I believe that they rest, ultimately, on a resolution of the Arab-Israeli conflict; as many of the politicians I interviewed pointed out, the end of that conflict will change the Israeli political map and rearrange the country's social and political priorities.

On balance, I would be cautiously optimistic. The secular public, still a majority, has begun to battle religious coercion more vigorously in recent months. It is clear that the famed status quo cannot endure. It was one thing when the ultra-Orthodox wanted state support to maintain their unique way of life within their own communities. It is quite another when that same population demands imposing its way on the rest of the nation.

While the status quo may ultimately meet its demise, the religious may yet emerge victorious ideologically. Whereas secular groups devoted to Jewish studies have become more popular in recent years, including in some portions of the lesbian and gay community, the secular Jewish public, by self-definition, has been unable to struggle for Judaism itself. They start the battle with the increasingly radicalized Orthodox and ultra-Orthodox at an ideological disadvantage because they have effectively conceded the definition of Judaism to these groups. The only "true" Judaism for too many secular Israelis is that defined by a group that developed its Jewish way of life several centuries ago in the shtetls of Poland and Russia. The inability of the secular public to fight for Judaism itself, as opposed to fighting the political power of the ultra-Orthodox, is a tragedy for the State of Israel. Against that backdrop it is encouraging to see a group like Mo'ach Gavra in Jerusalem bringing together secular and religious lesbian and gay Jews to study Jewish texts, but I fear that those efforts are but drops in the bucket.

The lesbian and gay community in Israel has created a fascinating synthesis between subcultural identity and its wider national identity. The small size of the country and its ongoing struggles over identity do not facilitate separation or alienation from wider national issues, or from its culture. Thus, it is not surprising that mainstream pop stars flocked to perform at the 1998 Pride Day or that the event ended with the singing of Israel's national anthem. Nor is it shocking that filmmaker Eitan Fox could use a traumatic national event like the Rabin murder to explore a facet of gay identity. Israeli lesbian and gay cultural and political identity is heavily invested in the existing order rather than in tearing that order down.

Ultimately, Israel offers another example of how gay politics and community can develop. While not necessarily a model for other countries, because of its unique political circumstances, Israel does show how a gay community need not develop along the lines suggested by American theorists and models. Israel, along with its lesbian and gay activists, has produced its own unique synthesis of politics and community, one that offers a lot of advantages, certainly to the gay and lesbian Israelis who increasingly benefit from the changes their society has undergone on sexual orientation issues.

April 1999

Afterword

The throngs in Tel Aviv's Rabin Square were rocking to the beat of Israeli pop groups like Mashina on the night of May 17, 1999. At 10 P.M. Israel's two television networks had released exit polls showing One Israel leader Ehud Barak besting Benjamin Netanyahu in the elections for prime minister by margins of up to 17 percent—a crushing defeat. Such a victory margin was unheard-of in Israel, whose 1996 election was decided by a mere thirty thousand votes, a fraction of 1 percent of the vote total.

As the news sank in, ordinary Israelis began streaming to Rabin Square to celebrate—and commemorate. Although Barak was the flesh-and-blood winner, many of the revelers were crying, "Rabin won," and viewed the elections as a belated affirmation of the late prime minister's path toward peace with the Palestinians and the Arab world. Rabin Square, which had assumed virtual iconic status for many liberal secular Israelis, by midnight was awash with Israeli flags, One Israel party banners, photos of the murdered prime minister, and, as I spied it on CNN, at least one proud gay rainbow flag. A few days later, Israeli commentator Nachum Barnea would note the "demonstrative" affection of gay couples at the victory celebration.

The 1999 Israeli elections only underscore the political and social changes in Israeli society that have facilitated the development of a gay and lesbian community. The decline of collectivism and the growth of individualism were reflected in the swearing-in ceremony of new Knesset members on June 7, 1999, presided over by former prime minister Shimon Peres, who declared, "Democracy is not only the right of every citizen to be equal, but the equal right of every citizen to be different."

While the rise of individualism has benefited lesbian and gay Israelis, it had a less seemly side: an election campaign where, in a shameless spectacle, party members acted like free agents, maneuvering between parties—and even across the political spectrum—all in the name of getting a good spot on a Knesset list. Thus, Tzomet MK Modi Zandberg, not known for his dovishness on the Arab-Israeli conflict, abandoned Tzomet (which was disintegrating, in any event) to hook up with the pro-peace process Center Party. When he failed to place high enough on the Center Party list, he left the Center Party and joined the militantly secular Shinui party, itself a split-off from Meretz, placing fifth on the list. His jockeying paid off, and he was duly sworn in as a member of the Fifteenth Knesset. The Mizrachi former Likud foreign minister David Levy, betrayed by Netanyahu one time too many, embraced his former ideological nemesis, One Israel, the successor to the much-maligned Labor Party. And so it went.

The decline in collectivist values and Zionist ideology reflected itself in other small incidents. While, in years past, Israeli political parties had tried to appeal to Russian voters by subtitling their television campaign ads in Russian, the 1999 elections marked the first time that parties like One Israel (the bloc headed by Labor Party leader Ehud Barak) and the Likud ran ads on national television in Russian—with subtitles in Hebrew. Israel's founders, who had relentlessly preached, "Ivri, daber Ivrit" (Jew, speak Hebrew), must have been turning over in their graves.

The growing prominence of an individualistic ethic not surprisingly reflected itself in party advertisements and themes. One stanza of Meretz's ad declared, "Meretz—I rely on myself." Meretz, some of whose roots were in ideological socialism, now represented individual freedom and rights. One Israel ran a campaign based on pocketbook issues, namely, the Netanyahu government's sorry economic performance. One particularly memorable ad declared, "Under Netanyahu, one hundred thousand Israelis have lost their jobs. Why should he keep his?"

The traditional big questions of war and peace played bit roles, with religious and ethnic tensions rising to the fore. This, too, underscored how tribal and personal identity politics were changing the priorities and coalitions of Israeli politics. Balad MK Azmi Bishara became the first Arab to run for prime minister of Israel; Bishara openly admitted that he

had no chance of, or interest in, winning but wanted to put issues dear
to the country's Palestinian citizens on the country's agenda. No Israeli
Jewish political leader or party would do so, beyond occasional lip service. In fact, no sooner had Ehud Barak won election as prime minister
than the modus operandi of refusing the country's Arab leadership a
place at the cabinet table returned with a vengeance, infuriating Palestinians who had voted for Barak overwhelmingly.

The Palestinians, the religious, and the Russians were not the only tribes
flexing political muscle in these elections. The 1999 elections showed how
a secular "tribe" was coalescing in response to religious coercion. Blunt-
spoken *Popolitika* talk show host Tomi Lapid left the small screen to lead
the Shinui party to six seats in the Knesset, all on the basis of its antireligious coercion message. To the tune of light, up-tempo music usually employed by advertisers to sell laundry detergent and such, Shinui's TV ads
declared, "There's a torch for the secular" (Lapid means "torch" in Hebrew) and, "Judaism is for everyone, we're sick of giving in."

Gay issues, though, were all but invisible in the campaign, as befits a
political cause that has racked up great achievements but remains marginal to the discourse of most Israeli political parties. Meretz was the
only major party to include a gay rights plank in its platform (the pro-
marijuana legalization party, Green Leaf, also adopted an unabashedly
pro-gay stance), and it trumpeted its pro-gay stand in a colorful supplement in *Ha-Zman ha-Varod*. Its campaign jingle seemed to contain a
subtle pitch aimed at gay and lesbian voters, with singers crooning about
being "free to love." But when I asked Meretz's openly lesbian Tel Aviv
City Council member, Michal Eden, about the ad, she said that, while
appealing to gay voters, it was also meant to appeal to Israelis of all
stripes unable to marry under Jewish law.

Ha-Zman ha-Varod, with Eden's help, attempted to interview the three
leading candidates for prime minister, One Israel leader Ehud Barak, former Netanyahu defense minister and Center Party leader Yitzhak Mordechai, and Netanyahu. The requests never received a response, positive or
negative, from the three candidates' campaigns, suggesting that while gays
are gaining power at the municipal level, Israeli politics are not yet ready
to treat gays as a voting bloc akin to the Russians, the Mizrachim, the
ultra-Orthodox, and the Palestinians on the national level. Aguda chair
Menachem Sheizaf could care less whether candidates responded to interview requests. As he put it to me three weeks after the election, "We know
where they all stand and what they've done."

While group politics and tensions, symbolized by Mizrachi alienation and growing tension between Russian and Mizrachi/religious voters, played a strong role in the elections, Israeli gays and lesbians, despite their progress, are only beginning to gear up for competition at the national level; I believe this likely will change in future elections. Uzi Even, in fact, won the number 13 spot on the Meretz list, even if not high enough for a realistic shot at election. News reports indicated, however, that Even might yet make it into the Knesset if Meretz ministers in Barak's new government resign their Knesset seats to make room for others, like Even, further down on the list.

Either Even or Michal Eden stands a good chance of becoming the first openly gay or lesbian Knesset member in the next round of elections, in any event. When I spoke with her a week before the election, Eden told me that she was seriously considering such a future run.

Against the backdrop of postelection political drama, lesbian and gay Israelis marked the 1999 Pride season with ever expanding events. Haifa held its first Pride festival, with five hundred in attendance at a local park. Tel Aviv led off with another parade, this one funded by the Tel Aviv municipality to the tune of 100,000 shekels (roughly $25,000) under the slogan "From Tel Aviv with Pride." The city hung rainbow flags along Ibn Gavriol, one of Tel Aviv's main thoroughfares, to mark the event, which drew numerous heterosexuals and their children, attracted by the colorful floats and dance music, and performances by renowned singer Yehuda Poliker and, of course, Dana International.

The new mayor of Tel Aviv, Ron Chuldai, a former fighter pilot and school principal, began his political career years earlier with his foot in his mouth, declaring in a newspaper interview that the sight of two men kissing made him sick. He took his licks over that, but, running to replace Tel Aviv Mayor Roni Milo in 1998, he succeeded in convincing the gay community that his views had changed. Once elected, Chuldai appointed Adir Steiner, one of the first figures in the gay community to be convinced that Chuldai indeed was a changed man, to the position of municipal spokesman.

Lesbian and gay Israelis had much to celebrate, following Ehud Barak's victory in the race for prime minister. A Netanyahu victory would not have placed gays and lesbians in any immediate political danger, seeing that gay issues are not a major preoccupation of the Likud or even the religious parties. But any government he formed would have had a deleterious impact on the role of the Israeli Supreme Court, the ultimate protector of gay—and civil—rights, and led to even more influence for religious parties.

Like his predecessors, Barak himself seems likely to remain personally quiet on gay issues. The ten-point guidelines that he and his party drew up for coalition negotiations mentioned the need to improve the status of women, as well as Israel's Palestinian minority, but contained no discussion of sexual orientation issues. Menachem Sheizaf was confident that Barak would be good for lesbians and gay men, no matter whom he chose as his coalition partners. If Barak formed a government without the ultra-Orthodox, the gay community could expect progress on legislation further equalizing the status of same-sex couples. But even if he included the ultra-Orthodox in his coalition, Sheizaf estimated, One Israel and Meretz would probably control ministries that matter to lesbians and gay men, such as the ministry of education.

Barak's new government, whose contours became clear in the final days of June 1999, gives lesbian and gay Israelis cause for hope. Meretz MK Yossi Sarid received the post of education minister, ensuring that gay efforts to reach young gay and straight people with a message of tolerance and support will continue unabated. Although there undoubtedly will be battles with the three religious parties that make up part of Barak's new government—Shas, the National Religious Party, and United Torah Judaism—they will be fighting more pressing battles, even as they make their ritual public threats and denunciations. An early indication of this can be seen in religious reaction to the 1999 Eurovision Song Contest in Jerusalem. When contest organizers announced plans to film Dana International singing the Sabbath hymn "Dror Yikra" against the backdrop of the Tower of David, ultra-Orthodox leaders threatened to bring out their followers to block such "desecration." In the end, no outraged ultra-Orthodox showed up, the filming proceeded as scheduled, and International performed to the usual enthusiasm; she famously tripped on her dress, though, as she presented first prize to the Swedish winners.

Israeli gays and lesbians, in any event, will not sit quietly waiting for the government to take care of them. Rather, they will continue to push the courts, the Knesset, and the bureaucracy for their rights. The continued growth of the community, reflected even in the publication of a flood of lesbian and gay books in 1999, ensures that the lesbian and gay community will find itself ever more rooted in the Israeli mosaic and prepared to demand its due. The Barak era points to continued progress and growing acceptance for Israeli lesbians and gay men politically and the continued growth of gay and lesbian community institutions.

July 1999

Glossary

ADP-UAL Arab Democratic Party–United Arab List. A bloc consisting of the Palestinian nationalist Arab Democratic Party and the Islamist-oriented United Arab List. The creation of the UAL followed debate within Israel's Islamic movement over the legitimacy of participating in Israeli electoral politics.

Aguda The Association of Gays, Lesbians, Bisexuals, and Transgenders in Israel. Formerly known as the Society for the Protection of Personal Rights. Founded in 1975.

Aliyah 1) Immigration to Israel; 2) the honor of being called upon to recite blessings before and after the reading of the Torah in synagogue.

Ashkenazi Plural: Ashkenazim, Ashkenaziot. Jews whose roots are in Western, Central, and Eastern Europe.

Association for Civil Rights in Israel ACRI. An Israeli organization working on civil rights issues, including gay and lesbian civil rights issues, in Israel.

Bela Do'eget A group working on AIDS advocacy and service issues within the Aguda.

Chadash-Balad An alliance of two parties. Chadash, the Democratic Front for Peace and Equality, is a Jewish-Arab communist list. Balad, the National Democratic Alliance, is an Arab nationalist faction. In the 1999 Israeli elections the two parties' alliance dissolved, and each ran independently for the Knesset.

Dover Tzahal The Israel Defense Forces Spokesman's Office.

Gei'ut A group of gays, lesbians and bisexuals working on gay issues within the Meretz Party. Founded in 1996.

Halacha Jewish religious law.

Ha'aretz Israeli daily newspaper with strong liberal leanings, including on gay issues.

Ha-Asiron ha-Acher The Other 10 Percent: the Gay/Lesbian/Bisexual Student Union at the Hebrew University of Jerusalem.

Ha-Zman ha-Varod   An Israeli monthly for gays, lesbians, bisexuals, and trans-gendered people. Established by Ya'ir Kedar in 1996, the paper ceased publication in May 1999. The Aguda is slated to resume its publication in August 1999.

Israel AIDS Task Force   Israel's primary AIDS service organization.

Israel Defense Forces   IDF. Its Hebrew acronym, *Tzahal*, stands for *Tzava Hagana l'Yisrael*.

Jerusalem Open House   Jerusalem's Gay/Lesbian/Bisexual/Transgender Community Center.

KLAF   The Lesbian-Feminist Community. Israel's principle lesbian organiztion. Founded in 1987 by Chaya Shalom.

Klaf Chazak   Monthly publication published by KLAF.

Knesset   The Israeli parliament. The Knesset has 120 members, with elections scheduled every four years, unless the parliament votes no-confidence in the government or the prime minister decides to call early elections. The Knesset can dissolve itself with an absolute majority of 61 of the 120 members. The Knesset can depose the prime minister under the new system of direct election of the prime minister by a vote of 80 Knesset members.

Labor   One of Israel's principal political parties, with a center-left orientation. Espouses a mostly progressive stance on gay issues but at times has displayed diffident attitudes. One of its Knesset members, Yael Dayan, has made gay rights a centerpiece issue.

Likud   One of Israel's principal political parties, with a center-right orientation. Significant pro-gay legislation has passed when it has been in power, although the party itself does not take strong positions either for or against gay concerns.

Ma'ariv   Israel's second largest daily newspaper.

Meretz   A left-wing party made up of three factions until the 1999 Israeli elections: Citizens Rights Movement, Mapam (socialist in orientation), and Shinui (liberal in the European mode). Highly supportive of gay civil rights concerns.

Mizrachi   Feminine: Mizrachit; plural: Mizrachim, Mizrachiot. Jews whose origins are in the Middle East, North Africa, or Asia. Used since the 1970s by Jews from Muslim cultures protesting the inequality they faced in Israeli society at the hands of the Ashkenazi elites. Although Israelis often use this phrase interchangeably with *Sephardi, Mizrachi* has become the preferred term.

MK   Member of Knesset.

Moledet   A far-right party that advocates for the "transfer" of Arabs from the West Bank and Gaza, and for eternal Israeli control of those territories. One of its two Knesset members, Beni Elon, is on record in support of antidiscrimination measures against gays as individuals.

National Religious Party   A nationalist Orthodox political party advocating for settlement of the West Bank. Unlike its ultra-Orthodox counterparts who denouce gay rights while doing little in practice to stop gay advances, the National Religious Party used its control of the Ministry of Education in the Netanyahu government to try, unsuccessfully, to ban a program on Educational Television about lesbian and gay youth.

New Israel Fund   A fund-raising body that directs funds to organizations working for civil rights, women's rights, religious pluralism, and Jewish-Arab cooperation. The New Israel Fund also has been active on gay civil rights concerns, providing grants to the Aguda, the Jerusalem Open House, and the
Israel AIDS Task Force.

One Israel   Political bloc established by Labor Party leader Ehud Barak in the
1999 Israeli elections consisting of Labor, Gesher (a Mizrachi populist party),
and Meimad (a moderate religious party).

Orthodox/Ultra-Orthodox   The Orthodox are those Jews who adhere strictly to
Jewish law. The ultra-Orthodox, who comprise a variety of sects, share the
strict devotion of the Orthodox, but shun to a greater extent the influences of
modern society. The ultra-Orthodox also believe that Zionism is a form of
heresy, as only the coming of the Messiah can bring about the rebirth of a
Jewish state.

Sabra   Native-born Israeli.

Sephardi   Plural: *Sephardim*. The term originally designated the Jews expelled
from Spain during the Inquisition (*Sepharad* is "Spain" in Hebrew), who dis-
persed throughout the Mediterranean to Italy, Greece, Turkey, and North
Africa, but also to Flanders, Germany, and the New World. For European
Jews, the term came to designate all Jews from Arab and/or Muslim countries.
The term is often interchangeable with *Mizrachi*, although the latter is the preferred term.

Shas   A populist ultra-Orthodox party supported primarily by religious and traditional Jews of Middle Eastern and North African background.

Shinui   A liberal party in the European mode. Until the 1999 elections, part of
the Meretz bloc. In the 1999 Israeli elections, it transformed into a militantly
secular party under the leadership of Tomi Lapid.

Tzomet   A secular right-wing party, one of whose Knesset members, Eliezer
"Modi" Zandberg, has been a fairly vocal supporter, but not leading advocate, of gay civil rights concerns. Went out of existence in the 1999 Israeli
elections.

United Torah Judaism   An Ashkenazi ultra-Orthodox political party made up of
two factions: Agudat Yisrael and Deqel ha-Torah..

Yediot Achronot   Israel's largest daily newspaper.

Yedu'a ba-Tzibur   Plural: *yedu'im ba-tzibur*. The Israeli version of common-law
marriage. Its origins in Israeli law stem from the lack of civil marriage in Israel, leaving many Israeli Jews unable to marry within the country because
they do not meet various requirements of Jewish religious law. The institution
of *yedu'im ba-tzibur* grants most, but not all, the rights of marriage.

Appendix

The following is a list of some of the gay and lesbian organizations and organizations working to advance gay rights in Israel that are discussed in this book.

Association of Gays, Lesbians, Bisexuals and Transgenders in Israel
P.O. Box 37604
Tel Aviv 61375
http://www.geocities.com/westhollywood/stonewall/2295

Association of Gays, Lesbians, Bisexuals and Transgenders in Israel—
Haifa Branch
Nordau 6
Haifa
http://www.geocities.com/westhollywood/5574

Association for Civil Rights in Israel
Bialik 12
Tel Aviv 63324

Asiron (Hebrew University Gay and Lesbian Student Group)
P.O. Box 6916
Jerusalem 91068
http://www.poboxes.com/asiron

Israel AIDS Task Force
P.O. Box 56110
Tel Aviv 61561
http://www.iatf.org.il

Jerusalem AIDS Project
P.O. Box 7956
Jerusalem 91077
http://www.aidsnews.org.il

Jerusalem Open House
P.O. Box 33107
Jerusalem 91037
http://www.poboxes.com/gayj

KLAF—Jerusalem
P.O. Box 26221
Jerusalem 91261

KLAF—Tel Aviv
P.O. Box 22997
Tel Aviv 61228
http://www.aquanet.co.il/vip/klaf

New Israel Fund
1625 K St., N.W.
Suite 500
Washington, DC 20006
USA
http://www.nif.org

No'ar 2000 (Gay/Lesbian Youth)
P.O. Box 37413
Tel Aviv
http://www.noar2000.co.il

Orthodykes
http://www.orthodykes.org

Tehila (Parents and Friends of Lesbians and Gays)
http://www.poboxes.com/tehila

Tzahal Bet (Gay/Lesbian Youth Group)
http://members.xoom.com/zahalb

World Congress of Gay, Lesbian, and Bisexual Jewish Organizations
P.O. Box 23379
Washington, DC 20026–3379
USA
http://www.wcgljo.org/wcgljo

Notes

Introduction: How a Nice Gay Jewish Boy Came to Write This Book

1. Wallach, "Hebrew," *Forms*, pp. 17–18 (in Hebrew).

2. Years before activists tried to spread usage of *aliz*, they had tried to popularize the terms *na'imim* and *na'imot*, literally "those who are pleasant," or, more loosely, "those who give pleasure."

3. The *Lexicon of Hebrew and Military Slang* defines *homo* as "an abbreviation of homosexual" and gives as an example: "In my eyes, anyone who's openly gay is a real man." Sela, *Lexicon of Hebrew and Military Slang*, p. 52. But, as Haifa University academic Yuval Yonai notes, "In the past it was a curse directed at gays or straight men who behaved in a manner considered effeminate." In Glozman and Nader, *A Different Dictionary*, p. 47.

4. *Gan Ha-Ir v. Horowitz*, T.A. 319/90, P.D. Ha-Shalom 2 (1991) at 139, in Rubinstein, *Constitutional Law of the State of Israel*, 5th ed., p. 328.

5. *Divrei ha-Knesset*, June 1, 1994, p. 7781 (in Hebrew).

6. Ibid., p. 7784.

1. Together in Pride, Together in Hope: Lesbian and Gay Politics in Israel

1. I first heard the remarks, courtesy of the internet, on Israel Radio's 2 P.M. newscast.

2. Itamar Eichner, "Weizman's Returning Us to the Darkness of the Middle Ages," *Yediot Achronot*, December 22, 1996, pp. 8–9 (in Hebrew).

3. Weizman still has a lot to learn about the issue, judging from remarks he made in April 1998 to *Yediot Achronot* during a Passover interview. When asked about his apology to gays, Weizman replied,

Look, I'm at the Reali High School and they give me questions and I see there's a question about homos. What should I do? Not answer, or say *putzkelach-mutzkelach* I understand you? So I said I prefer that a woman want to be a woman, and a man want to be a man, is that wrong? Afterward, a few guys from the gay club at the Hebrew University came to me. We talked, I said that perhaps there were a few matters I didn't understand, and I'm sorry about that. Out of great happiness, some homos recently came to me, and they even wanted me to stand at the head of a conference of homos. So I said thank you very much. Why shouldn't I do it? How's it different, say, from a conference of cancer victims that I was invited to head?

> Shlomo Nakdimon and Ruth Yuval, "I've Got a Position Description:
> I Head the Country," *Yediot Achronot/Seven Days* (U.S ed.),
> April 10, 1998, p. 18 (in Hebrew).

4. Zo Artzeinu ("This Is Our Land") was a militant right-wing coalition that in the summer of 1995 engaged in massive acts of civil disobedience to protest the Oslo Accords with the Palestinians.

5. D'Emilio, *Sexual Politics, Sexual Communities*.

6. The Mantra provides only a partial explanation for why gay people have won a number of important battles in a short period of time. None of the Israelis I interviewed could offer an explanation for why a "heterosexist" society would bother to take up the gay rights mantle, particularly in the early stages, when the Israeli gay and lesbian community maintained a low public profile. Other explanations for the remarkable political and legal progress, discussed later in this chapter, do demonstrate, however, that the mantra—the absence of virulent societal homophobia—fosters a social climate in which gay causes can advance.

7. The informal and close-knit nature of Israeli society reflects itself, among other ways, in the nicknames that many Israelis carry. Many of the nicknames date from childhood, others from army days. Thus, even in the press, former prime minister Netanyahu is "Bibi," MK Eliezer Zandberg is often "Modi Zandberg," and the head of the IDF's Central Command, Moshe Ya'alon, is just as often known as "Bugi."

8. *Divrei ha-Knesset*, February 10, 1993, p. 3202 (in Hebrew).

9. Ibid., p. 3203.

10. Ro'i Shenhar, "Poll of Knesset Members," *Ha-Zman ha-Varod*, September 1996, p. 3 (in Hebrew).

11. In November 1997 the Tel Aviv City Council agreed to provide 100,000 shekels (roughly $27,000 at the time) annually to lesbian and gay organizations in the city.

12. Sheizaf's optimism stands in marked contrast to that of other gay and lesbian activists in the community who tended toward pessimistic predictions about the future of gay political and legal gains in the Netanyahu era. What was interesting about the pessimism, however, is that it was not connected to the Ne-

tanyahu government's anticipated actions on gay-related matters per se. Rather, it has much to do with the feared erosion of the traditionally secular values of Israeli society.

13. Law for the Prevention of Sexual Harassment, *Sefer ha-Chukim* 1661, March 19, 1998 (in Hebrew).

14. Stenographic Protocol, 189th Session, 14th Knesset, March 10, 1998, p. 184 (in Hebrew).

15. Ibid.

16. Rayside, *On the Fringe: Gays and Lesbians in Politics*, p. 218.

17. Ari Shavit, "Matan's Reserve," *Ha'aretz* (Weekend Supplement), September 11, 1998, pp. 20, 22 (in Hebrew).

18. Labor Party Young Guard Advertisement, *Maga'im*, August 1991, p. 10 (in Hebrew).

19. "What Did They Say?" *Maga'im*, September 1991, p. 11 (in Hebrew).

20. *Gei'ut*, no. 1, February 1997 (in Hebrew).

21. Tom Segev, "One Issue Politics," *Ha'aretz*, December 27, 1995, p. 1B (in Hebrew).

22. Michal Eden, "For a More Equal Tel Aviv: Municipal Platform for the Gay Community" (draft), March 1998 (in Hebrew).

23. "Michal Eden: For a More Equal Tel Aviv" (in Hebrew).

24. Eden might have placed first had two gay candidates, Marc Tennenbaum and Lior Kei, not thrown themselves into the race at the last minute. I was not surprised to see Tennenbaum competing in the primaries at the last minute. At the Pet Café opening, in March, I witnessed a confrontation between him and Eden in which he accused her of not seeking his input sufficiently. Although he claimed when I saw him at a lesbian-gay Jewish conference in Paris in May 1998 that his candidacy would not hurt her chances, other activists did not see it that way. Activist Hadar Namir told me after the election in a telephone interview that he had been working against Eden in the days leading up to the primaries.

25. Ben-Simon, *A New Israel*, p. 25 (in Hebrew).

26. Adi Golani, "Meir Ariel Surrenders: I'm Leaving the Stage," *Yediot Achronot* (U.S. ed.), September 25, 1998, p. 4 (in Hebrew).

27. Spivak and Yonai, "Between Silence and Condemnation."

28. Dani Lachman, "And to Where Shall We Lead the Pride?" *Ha-Zman ha-Varod*, July 1998, p. 11 (in Hebrew).

29. The National Steering Committee on AIDS includes representatives from the Ministries of Health and Education, the IDF, Magen David Adom (the country's Red Cross), the National Union Health Fund, and nongovernmental organizations like the Israel AIDS Task Force.

30. In fact, Ben-Yishai suggested that financial and publicity issues were at the root of the disagreement with the Israel AIDS Task Force, since "a group that doesn't grow isn't doing its work."

31. Tzvi Ben-Yishai, "National AIDS Policy of Israel," in Inon I. Schenker, Galia Sabar-Friedman, and Francisco S. Sy, *AIDS Education* (New York: Plenum Press, 1996), p. 82.

32. Levy believes that the statistics regarding Ethiopian Jews are indeed accurate, because they undergo mandatory testing upon arrival in Israel.

33. Mark Ariel, "Don't Go with Him?" *Maga'im*, October/November 1987, p. 20 (in Hebrew).

34. Levy and Shneider, *Life with AIDS*.

35. Oren Kaner, "AIDS in Israel. A Gay Disease," *Ha-Zman ha-Varod*, March 1997, pp. 3–5 (in Hebrew).

36. Yanetz, *Oops*.

37. Bela Do'eget, *Sex Between Men*.

38. Society for the Protection of Personal Rights, *On Homosexuals in Israel*, p. 2.

39. Or Maroni-Paner, "KLAF and the Mizrachi Lesbians," *Klaf Chazak*, Winter 1998, p. 7 (in Hebrew).

40. Sharoni, *Gender and the Israeli-Palestinian Conflict*, pp. 96–97.

41. Safran, "Alliance and Denial," p. 8.

42. Ibid., p. 26.

43. Anonymous, "Straight Women and Lesbians in the Feminist Struggle in Israel," *Chad Pa'ami*, Summer 1998, p. 41 (in Hebrew).

44. The term *present-absentees* comes from a book by Israeli author David Grossman about Palestinian citizens of Israel. He, in turn, adapted the phrase from Israeli laws dealing with property left behind by Palestinians who fled or were expelled in the 1948 War of Independence.

45. Anonymous, "Straight Women and Lesbians," p. 42.

46. The term *ars* usually refers to tough-talking Mizrachi young men.

47. In the early years of the state, young sabras sometimes called Holocaust survivors "soap."

48. Shmulik Ben-Menachem, "Don't Call Me Gay," *Chad Pa'ami*, Summer 1998, p. 47 (in Hebrew).

49. Michal Lebertov, "Wanting to Go Nuts," *Ha'aretz* (Weekend Supplement), August 15, 1997, p. 50 (in Hebrew).

50. For a comprehensive account of the Aguda's activism leading up to the 1988 sodomy law repeal, see Yuval Yonai, "The Law Regarding Homosexuality: Between History and Sociology," 4 *Mishpat u'Mimshal* 531 (1998) (in Hebrew).

51. Ibid.

2. Yotzim m'ha-Aron: Coming Out

1. The name is a humorous play on words with the Mona Lisa, whose visage adorns many of the group's advertisements, roughly translating from the Hebrew as "much gaiety."

2. Almog, *The Sabra*, p. 359.

3. Yuval Yonai, "The Law Regarding Homosexuality: Between History and Sociology," 4 *Mishpat u'Mimshal* 531, 545 (1998) (in Hebrew).

4. Amir Somkai-Fink, "Coming Out Slow," *Ha-Zman ha-Varod*, May 1997, p. 4 (in Hebrew).

5. Lorentz prepared the booklet, titled *Same-Sex Orientation (Homosexuality and Lesbianism),* with Chava Barnea, national supervisor for Sex Education and Family Life in the Ministry of Education. The booklet was sent to all high school advisers and educators in the secular school system.

6. There are several state-supported education systems within Israel: *mamlachti* (State-Secular), *mamlachti-dati* (State-Religious), and schools for Druze and Arab students. In addition, the ultra-Orthodox run their own educational institutions, some of which receive state support.

7. I visited two high schools in Israel, Nesher and the Meggido Comprehensive High School. I was asked not to mention the name of the specific school where the exercise was conducted.

8. Even-Kama, "Some Children Are Zig-Zag."

9. Ibid., p. 19.

10. Ibid., pp. 20–23.

11. Yaron London and Gaia Koren, "Conservative Youthful Dreams," *Yediot Achronot* (Weekend Supplement) (U.S. ed.), September 25, 1998, p. 18 (in Hebrew).

12. Tzachi Cohen, "Are Israeli Youth Racist?" *Yediot Achronot* (24 Hours), July 23, 1997, pp. 14–15 (in Hebrew).

13. Weishut, "Prejudice of Homosexuality."

14. Lesbian and gay activists complained to me that the Ministry of Education distributed the booklet on a one-time basis rather than sending it every year to schools. Some even contended that the booklet had been removed from circulation by the new, more conservative Likud government, where politicians from the National Religious Party headed the ministry until the 1999 Israeli election. When asked about these accusations, Barnea became rather exasperated, saying that she had told the Aguda that the booklet was still very much available and that anyone who wanted to order copies from the Ministry of Education could do so. In December 1998 the Ministry of Education, following its exclusion of KLAF from a fair devoted to "tolerance," announced, as a sop to angry activists, that it would be reprinting and distributing the booklet.

15. Barnea and Lorentz, *Same-Sex Orientation (Homosexuality and Lesbianism).*

16. Ibid., p. 38.

17. Ibid., p. 39.

18. In Israel, says Alon Harel, senior lecturer in law at the Hebrew University Law School, citizens possess the right of direct appeal to the Supreme Court with regard to governmental administrative action. He noted to me that "people see it as a basic right, and it would be very difficult to change."

19. Shmuel Meiri, "Hammer Rejects Supreme Court Compromise Proposal Concerning Broadcast of Program about Homosexuals," *Ha'aretz,* August 6, 1997, p. 6A (in Hebrew).

20. The other two justices participating in the hearing, Supreme Court president Aharon Barak and Justice Dalia Dorner, also coincidentally had been on the panel issuing the *Danilovitz* decision and had ruled for the flight attendant.

21. "The Victory," *Ha-Zman ha-Varod*, July 1997, p. 3 (in Hebrew).

22. "Response Brief from Respondent #1," in "Minister of Education v. Gays," *Ha-Zman ha-Varod*, May 1997, p. 3 (in Hebrew).

23. Not all gay Israelis saw the Supreme Court ruling in such a favorable light. Hebrew University Law Lecturer Alon Harel, for one, saw a significant difference in how the public and the media perceived the victory versus the actual language of the Supreme Court's decision. Harel saw a certain retreat from the broad, supportive rhetoric of the 1994 *Danilovitz* decision as well as a lack of elemental legal reasoning in the decision; the court failed to apply principles of reasonableness and administrative law in evaluating Hammer's refusal to broadcast the program. Alon Harel, "The Courts and Homosexuality—Dignity or Tolerance?" 4 *Mishpat u'Mimshal* 785 (1998) (in Hebrew).

24. *Society for the Protection of Personal Rights of Gays, Lesbians, and Bisexuals in Israel v. The Minister of Education, Culture, and Sport*, BAGATZ 273/97 (September 21, 1997), p. 1 (in Hebrew).

25. Ibid., p. 5. The reference to "outside the encampment" is from Numbers 5:1–4, when God ordered the Israelites to remove lepers from their midst in order to protect the purity of the ceremonial camp.

26. Shai Kerem, "Diva," *Rosh Echad*, December 7, 1997, p. 8 (in Hebrew).

27. Chanan Greenberg, "Two Knights," ibid., p. 10 (in Hebrew); Gad Chernovilsky, "God is Great," Rosh Echad, November 30, 1997, p. 10 (in Hebrew).

28. Michal Zilkha, "Personal Advice," *Ma'ariv Lano'ar*, August 29, 1996, p. 47 (in Hebrew).

29. Not that the issue did not make her nervous. Ezra was the only public figure with whom I spoke who refused to let me record our interview.

30. "It's O.K. to Be Different," *Kishkashta* (Nesher: Nesher High School, 1998), p. 8 (in Hebrew).

31. "Ahlan wa-Sahalan," ibid., p. 6 (in Hebrew).

3. The Personal Is the Political: Judaism and Gay People in Israel

1. Jacob Emden, "Hanhagat Leil Shabbat," *Siddur Beit Ya'akov* (Lemberg: David Balaban, 1904), cited in Kaufman, *Love, Marriage, and Family*, p. 131.

2. Talmud, Tractate Yavamot 62B.

3. Rabbi Isaac of Corbeil, *Sefer Mitzvot Katan*, in Kaufman, *Love, Marriage, and Family*, p. 216.

4. Ibid., p. 217, n. 38.

5. Leviticus 18:22.

6. Sifra on Leviticus 18:3, in Rosner, *Sex Ethics in the Writings of Moses Maimonides*, p. 120, n. 44.

7. Gunther Plaut, *The Torah: A Modern Commentary* (New York: Union of American Hebrew Congregations, 1981), p. 1497.

8. Talmud, Tractate Sanhedrin 58A.

9. Talmud, Tractate Kiddushin 82A.

10. See note 6 above.

11. Shulchan Aruch, Even ha-Ezer 24:1, in Kaufman, *Love, Marriage, and Family*, pp. 140–141.

12. Talmud, Tractate Sanhedrin 9B.

13. Talmud, Tractate Shabbat 66A.

14. Ibid., 66B.

15. Talmud, Nedarim 51B

16. Tosafot, cited in Alpert, *Like Bread on the Seder Plate*, p. 27.

17. Tzvi Marx, "A Blessing Over Differences," *Jerusalem Report*, April 6, 1995, p. 51.

18. Deuteronomy 23:2.

19. Marx, "A Blessing Over Differences," p. 52, n. 17.

20. Ibid.

21. Anat Meidan, "Secular, But," *Yediot Achronot/Seven Days* (U.S. ed.), September 22, 1996, p. 14 (in Hebrew).

22. Ibid., p. 15.

23. Limor Nisani, "Shoshana Damari Doesn't Want to Wish You Anything," *Ha-Zman ha-Varod*, October 1998, p. 11 (in Hebrew).

24. Geffen, "Good Morning Iran," *Hollowed*.

25. Elbaum, *Elul Time*, p. 10.

26. Arye Kaspi, "The People Chose Palma de Majorca," *Ha'aretz* (Weekend Supplement), September 13, 1996, p. 13 (in Hebrew).

27. Einat Berkovitz, "The Amidror Report," *Yediot Achronot/Seven Days* (U.S. ed.), April 24, 1998, p. 19 (in Hebrew).

28. Tova Tzimoki, "Eichler Won't Be Prosecuted For Comparing Secular to Nazis," *Yediot Achronot* (U.S. edition), February 5, 1999, p. 6 (in Hebrew).

29. "Breachers of Morality," *Ha-Tzofe*, February 4, 1993, p. 2 (in Hebrew).

30. Moshe Ishun, "And They Shall Not Be Ashamed," *Ha-Tzofe*, February 5, 1993, p. 3 (in Hebrew).

31. Dov Elbaum, "From Zion Shall Go Forth Impurity," *Yediot Achronot/Twenty-four Hours*, December 1, 1994, p. 2 (in Hebrew).

32. Ibid.

33. Ibid.

34. Letter from Rabbi Raphael Frank, Office of the Chief Rabbi of Israel, September 14, 1998 (in Hebrew).

35. Lili Galili, Moshe Reinfeld, Gabi Zohar, and Shachar Ilan, "Yossi Sarid, Yael Dayan, and Gay Representatives to Meet Today with Weizman," *Ha'aretz*, December 23, 1996, p. 7 (in Hebrew).

36. David Tamar, "To the Rabbis of Israel," *Ha-Tzofe*, September 26, 1997, n.p. (in Hebrew).

37. Levy, *The Ultra-Orthodox*, pp. 123–124.

38. Talmud, Tractate Chagiga 16A.

39. Elbaum, *Elul Time*, p. 81.

40. Talmud, Tractate Sanhedrin 44A.

41. Itzik Yosha, "Why the Religious Were Silent," *Tat-Tarbut*, Summer 1995, p. 37 (in Hebrew).

42. Yerach Tal, "Uzi Even to Run in Meretz Primaries," *Ha'aretz*, December 26, 1995, n.p. (in Hebrew).

43. Yitzhak Shilat, "Barren Justice—The Moral Failure of the Supreme Court," *Nekuda*, February 1995, p. 23 (in Hebrew).

44. Yosha, "Why the Religious Were Silent," p. 37.

45. In recent years ultra-Orthodox efforts to set up footholds in previously secular neighborhoods have sparked strong secular resistance.

46. Shachar Ilan, "MK Porat Proposes Economic Rights for Same-Sex Couples," *Ha'aretz*, August 14, 1998, n.p. (in Hebrew).

47. Alex Libak, "Our Land," *Ha'aretz* (Weekend Supplement), p. 3 (photograph; caption in Hebrew).

48. Almog, *The Sabra*, p. 128.

49. Ibid., p. 131.

50. "Congregation Ga'avat Yisrael," *Nativ Nosaf*, Spring 1994, p. 4 (in Hebrew).

51. Ronen Pa'ari, "The Story of King Achashveroshu," *Ha-Zman ha-Varod*, March 1998, p. 10 (in Hebrew and club argot).

52. The name of the parade means "Until He Did Not Know" and refers to the Purim tradition of drinking until one can no longer distinguish between Haman and Mordechai.

53. I had hoped to raise that idea—and other questions—with Beit Daniel's rabbi, Meir Azari, personally, but he was heading abroad when I called and couldn't make time. Only when I was back in the U.S. did I learn that Azari had headed to a confab of Reform rabbis in London where he argued against the American Reform movement's agreeing to conduct marriage ceremonies for same-sex couples. His reason: it would hurt the Israeli Reform movement's efforts to gain recognition as a legitimate branch of Judaism in Israel.

54. Sigalit Shachor, "God Created Me a Sinner," *Yediot Achronot/Seven Days* (U.S. ed.), April 26, 1996, p. 39 (in Hebrew).

55. Ibid.

56. Smadar Partush, "Friends from Another Planet," *Yediot Achronot/Twenty-four Hours*, April 29, 1997, p. 11 (in Hebrew).

57. *MARAM Resolutions Concerning Its Relation to Partners of the Same Sex*, n.d. (in Hebrew).

58. The quorum of ten Jews (ten *male* Jews in Orthodox circles) necessary for a service.

59. Shachar Ilan, "According to the Law of Moses and Rabbi Yoel," *Ha'aretz*, July 1, 1997, p. 3B (in Hebrew).

60. Shaul Shiff, "Hypocrisy . . . ," *Ha-Tzofe*, February 20, 1998, p. 2 (in Hebrew).

4. *Gays with Guns: Gays in the Military, Israeli Style*

1. The IDF drafts Bedouin and Druze young men. The Druze are Arabs but practice a religion that is an offshoot of Islam. On rarer occasions, the IDF has accepted Christian and Muslim Arab volunteers.

2. Sagi Green, "The New Israelis," *Ha'aretz* (Fiftieth Independence Day Supplement), April 29, 1998, p. 42 (in Hebrew).

3. Gal, *A Portrait of the Israeli Soldier*, p. 59.

4. K-31–11–01 Service of Homosexuals in the IDF, Manpower Division Standing Orders, September 1986 (in Hebrew).

5. Gal Ochovsky, "Called Up Suddenly, as Usual," *Ha-Ir*, January 9, 1987, p. 37 (in Hebrew).

6. *Divrei ha-Knesset*, February 10, 1993, p. 3206 (in Hebrew).

7. K-31–11–01 Service of Homosexuals in the IDF, Manpower Division Standing Orders, 1993 (in Hebrew).

8. Yo'av Ze'evi, "Discrimination Has Ended," *Bamachane*, June 16, 1993, pp. 8–10 (in Hebrew).

9. Gal, "Policy and Practice in the Israeli Defense Forces," p. 184.

10. In recent years top Israeli generals have pursued political careers upon retirement from the IDF. Thus, former defense minister Yitzhak Mordechai was ardently wooed by the Likud Party (Labor unwisely spurned his overtures), and jumped to the head of the Center Party that ran in the 1999 elections, while Ehud Barak catapulted into the role of foreign minister in Shimon Peres's government, before becoming the chair of the Labor Party. In 1998 IDF chief of staff Amnon Lipkin-Shachak retired, announced he was running for prime minister, but ultimately took a back seat to Mordechai.

11. Yo'av Tadmor, "General Staff Regulation 1332.14 in the U.S. Military States: Gays—Out," *Bamachane*, February 13, 1993, p. 11 (in Hebrew).

12. Twenty centimeters is just under eight inches.

13. *Eliezer v. Chief Military Prosecutor*, Case No. 40/95/A (Military Appeals Court 1995) at 2 (in Hebrew).

14. Ibid. at 7.

15. Ibid. at 8.

16. Ibid.

17. Ibid.

18. Ibid.

19. Kaplan, *Coping Strategies of Homosexuals in Combat Service*.

20. His interviewees served in infantry units, the armor corps, gunner units, missile boats, and the elite fighter pilot training course.

21. Girls in Israel have a similar ceremony called bat mitzvah, which, in contrast to the ceremony in the United States, they celebrate at the age of twelve.

22. Kaplan, *Coping Strategies of Homosexuals in Combat Service*, p. 3.

23. Ibid., p. 6.

24. Gal, *A Portrait of the Israeli Soldier*, p. 40.

25. Kaplan, *Coping Strategies of Homosexuals in Combat Service*, p. 6.

26. Ibid., p. 7.

27. Ibid.

28. Even-Kama was upfront about his sexual orientation when he enlisted. It struck me as perhaps a bit homophobic that the IDF would post him to one of

the Women's Corps training bases. He claimed, however, that he saw no homophobia on the IDF's part.

29. "Green? It Suits Me!" *Ha-Zman ha-Varod*, April 1998, at 3 (in Hebrew).

30. *CHEN Translates Charm: CHEN—the Israel Defence Force's Women's Corps* (Israel: IDF Spokesman's Office, 1980), cited in Gal, *A Portrait of the Israeli Soldier*, p. 47.

31. See *Alice Miller v. Minister of Defense et al.*, BAGATZ 4541/94, P"D MT(4)94, cited in Ben-Yisrael, *Equality of Opportunities*, pp. 372–413.

32. Michal B., "Lesbians in the Military," *Klaf Chazak*, Spring/Summer 1997, p. 34 (in Hebrew).

33. Ibid., p. 35.

34. Ibid.

35. Lior El-Chai, "The Commanders Called Me Homo Over the Loudspeaker—And My Life Became Hell," *Yediot Achronot* (U.S. Edition), August 16, 1996, p. 16 (in Hebrew).

36. Ariela Ringel-Hoffman, "Out of Eleven Reservists, Nine Evade," *Yediot Achronot* (Weekend Supplement) (U.S. ed.), October 17, 1997, pp. 8–10 (in Hebrew).

37. Eitan Haber, the head of the Prime Minister's Office, told *Ha'aretz* several years later that Rabin was influenced to change the military's policy toward homosexuals not by ideology but by his "warm acquaintance" with Maisel. Shmuel Meiri, "The IDF's Pride Parade," *Ha'aretz*, August 12, 1997, p. 2B (in Hebrew).

38. *Steiner v. Compensation Officer*, B-8/94 (Appeals Panel Under Law for Families of Soldiers Who Perish in Battle (Compensation and Rehabilitation) 1950) (1995), at 22 (in Hebrew).

39. Ibid.

40. Ibid. at 24.

41. *Steiner v. Israel Defense Forces*, A-Sh 369/94 (Standing Army (Pensions) Appeals Panel, Tel Aviv District Court) (1997), at 1 (in Hebrew).

42. Ibid. at 1–2.

43. When *Ha-Zman ha-Varod* publicized the settlement in August 1998, it seemed to do so with very little enthusiasm. It spoke of how many felt that Steiner had been leading a "personal" battle, rather than one for the community. Avi Barak, "Steiner Affair: The End," *Ha-Zman ha-Varod*, August 1998, p. 2 (in Hebrew).

5. Media, Culture, and Visibility

1. As if the connections were not clear enough, Channel 2 ran advertisements for its special, "Two Years Since the Murder," in the midst of this particular episode.

2. Ezrachi, *Rubber Bullets*, p. 22.

3. Amalia Ziv, "The Literature Not Yet Written That Is Waiting to Be Written," *Tat-Tarbut*, Summer 1995, p. 20 (in Hebrew).

4. Alwood, *Straight News*, p. 6.

5. Kama, "From *Terra Incognita* to *Terra Firma*."

6. "The Homosexuals," *Ha-Olam ha-Ze*, February 7, 1962, p. 12 (in Hebrew).

7. Kama, "From *Terra Incognita* to *Terra Firma*," p. 17.

8. Israeli newspapers likewise explained the meaning of the rainbow flag and then began running many of their gay-related stories with either a picture of the flag itself or a rainbow border around the article.

9. Eilat Regev and Yehuda Koren, "The National Sweetener," *Yediot Achronot/ Seven Days* (U.S. ed.), September 18, 1998, pp. 10–11 (in Hebrew).

10. Alwood, *Straight News*, p. 15.

11. Equally significant, a number of lesbian and gay political leaders have come from the media—Liora Moriel (*Jerusalem Post*) and Itzik Yosha (*Yediot Achronot* and radio) are but two examples.

12. Ilan Sheinfeld, "Gays in Black and White," *Maga'im*, November 1991, p. 8 (in Hebrew).

13. The paper published its last issue under Kedar's leadership in May 1999, and temporarily closed, with the Aguda slated to resume its publication in August 1999.

14. Sharon Ne'eman, "No'a and Inbar," in Moriel, *Hot Night*, p. 11.

15. Yotam Reuveni, "Conjectures on the Death of Pier Paolo Passolini," *In Praise of Illusion*, p. 8.

16. Yossi Avni, "The Tibetan Book of the Dead," in *Grove of the Dead Trees*, p. 19.

17. Rebbetzin usually refers to the wife of a rabbi. In Waxman's book, it is a playful feminized reference to Moshe's religious upbringing.

18. Shiri Lev-Ari, "I'm Not a Sad Gay," *Ha'aretz* (Weekend Supplement), January 23, 1998, p. 50 (in Hebrew).

19. Waxman, *My Darling Alexandria*, p. 239 (in Hebrew).

20. Ibid., p. 218.

21. The verse "This is my exchange" refers to the Orthodox custom of "kaparot"—twirling a rooster or chicken around one's head (a reminder of sacrifices in the Temple in Jerusalem)—as a symbolic atonement and exculpation of one's sins.

22. Ilan Sheinfeld, "Tashlich," *Tashlich*, pp. 24–25.

23. Sheinfeld, "Excommunication," *Karet*, p. 79.

24. Sheinfeld, "My Identity," ibid., p. 55.

25. Sheinfeld, "A Waterfall of Innocence," ibid., p. 61.

26. Sheinfeld, "Fountains of Pleasure," *Tashlich*, p. 63.

27. Dana Gilerman, "The Bookshelf," *Ha'aretz*, August 7, 1997, p. 1D (in Hebrew).

28. Ibid.

29. Noga Eshed, "Biology," *Queen Bees' Nectar*, p. 66.

30. Ibid., p. 70.

31. Eshed, "On the Burning Fire," ibid., p. 95.

32. Ice Nine, "Want to Live With Him Forever."

33. Sharon Segel, "I Admit It: I'm an Ego Maniac," *Arei ha-Mifratz*, September 26, 1997, p. 81 (in Hebrew).

34. Her song, "Shooting and Crying," released during the intifada, was banned from play on Galei Tzahal, the popular Israeli army radio station.

35. Si Heiman, "Graffiti Tel Aviv '89," *Working on the Road.*

36. Carmela, Gross and Wagner, "Wet and Hot," *Black Flower.*

37. "Wet and Hot," *Nativ Nosaf,* December 1991, p. 6 (in Hebrew).

38. Carmela, Gross and Wagner, "Women Writing Poetry," *Black Flower.*

39. Polianna Frank, "Ziva," *No Choosing.*

40. Poliana Frank, "Dykes and the Holy War," ibid.

41. Shai Kerem, "I Wouldn't Dare Put a Transvestite at the Top of the Charts," *Yediot Achronot/Seven Days,* December 2, 1994, p. 57 (in Hebrew).

42. Orthodox Judaism forbids men from listening to women singers, as it might drive men to impure distractions. Lest one laugh, this ruling caused a headache for Israeli president Ezer Weizman on the occasion of his second inauguration. Weizman had planned to have a mixed Israeli military choir perform during the ceremony in the Knesset. The religious parties raised a hue and cry, threatening that they would have to boycott the ceremony if the choir's women performed. The final compromise: the choir performed discreetly during the reception following the ceremony.

43. Al-Ghitti, *A Scandal by the Name Saida Sultan.* For the Arabic translation, I would like to thank a Norwegian graduate student of Arabic, Geir Skogseth, who maintains a comprehensive web site about Dana International at http://d1o202.telia.com/u222600821/Geir%20Site/Geir/Geir_Danna_1.html.

44. Shai Kerem, "Diva," *Rosh Echad,* December 7, 1997, p. 8 (in Hebrew).

45. Gal Ochovsky, "The Success and Gaultier's Parrot," *Ma'ariv* (Weekend Supplement) (U.S. ed.), May 15, 1998, p. 27 (in Hebrew).

6. Hereinafter the Boyfriend: Same-sex Families in Israel

1. A December 1997 article in *Yediot Achronot's Seven Days* weekend supplement about designer Yuval Kaspin was typical of this approach. The headline: "If It Interests You, I'm Available Too." The article teaser went on to state: "Designer Yuval Kaspin wants to fall in love. He's searching for a boyfriend, who'll be not just bread and butter for him, but shrimps as well." Tzachi Cohen, "If It Interests You, I'm Available Too," *Yediot Achronot/Seven Days* (U.S. ed.), December 12, 1997, p. 32 (in Hebrew).

2. Itzik Rennert, "Comics," *Ha-Zman ha-Varod,* September 1996, p. 6 (in Hebrew).

3. *Isaac v. Ministry of the Interior,* BAGATZ 353/70, in Rubinstein, *Constitutional Law of the State of Israel,* 3d ed., p. 153.

4. Ibid., p. 151.

5. Ibid., p. 152.

6. Dori Spivak, "Precedent: Customs to Recognize Gay-Lesbian Couplehood," *Ha-Zman ha-Varod,* July 1998, p. 2 (in Hebrew).

7. Letter from Reuven Boimel, director of the Pensions Department, State of Israel Civil Service Commission (January 1, 1998) (in Hebrew).

8. Ibid.

9. *Danilovitz v. El Al Israel Airlines, Ltd.*, Case No. MT/3–1503 (Tel Aviv-Jaffa Regional Labor Court 1993), p. 1 (in Hebrew).

10. *El Al Israel Airlines Ltd. v. Danilovitz*, BAGATZ 721/94 (Israeli Supreme Court 1994), pp. 6, 9 (in Hebrew).

11. Ibid., p. 14.

12. Ibid., p. 12.

13. Ben-Yisrael, *Equality of Opportunities*, p. 993.

14. Ibid.

15. "A First: Israeli Court Recognizes Female Couple as Family Unit," *Ha'aretz*, June 3, 1997, p. 1 (in Hebrew).

16. Yechzakel Adiram, "Homosexual Sues Former Boyfriend for Half of His Property, Totaling Millions," *Yediot Achronot*, March 16, 1998, p. 11 (in Hebrew).

17. Karni and Adiram, "Homosexual Couple Sent to 'Mediation,'" *Yediot Achronot*, March 17, 1998, p. 17 (in Hebrew).

18. Alon Harel, "Gay Rights in Israel: A New Era," *Tat-Tarbut*, Winter 1996, pp. 41–42 (in Hebrew).

19. Ben-Yisrael, *Equality of Opportunities*, p. 1023.

20. Advertisement placed by Dudu Naftali, *Ha-Zman ha-Varod*, July 1998, p. 20 (in Hebrew).

21. Oren Kaner, "I Went Out Looking For Gay Couplehood . . . I'll Be Right Back," *Ha-Zman ha-Varod*, December 1997, p. 5 (in Hebrew).

22. The acronym that Ochovsky used for "collaborator," *mashtap*, is usually used to describe those Palestinians who collaborated with the Israeli occupation of the West Bank and Gaza Strip.

23. Gal Ochovsky, "It's Not So Easy to Be Gay (And It's Also Not So Difficult)," *Ha-Zman ha-Varod*, December 1997, p. 5 (in Hebrew).

24. Ibid.

25. Avner Bernheimer, "When My Husband Sleeps," *Ha-Zman ha-Varod*, December 1997, p. 9 (in Hebrew).

26. Mizrachi, "Same-Sex Couples Coping with Stigma."

27. Ibid., p. 174.

28. In Israel the rental housing market is almost nonexistent. The government provides mortgage assistance for many segments of the population, such as soldiers and new immigrants, and parents also expect to help their grown children finance the purchase of their first apartment.

29. Mizrachi, "Same-Sex Couples Coping with Stigma," p. 125.

30. Ibid.

31. Channa Kalderon, "Seeking Partner for Childbirth," *Ha'aretz* (Weekend Supplement), April 29, 1998, p. 30 (in Hebrew).

32. Ibid., p. 32.

33. Freedman was not out of the closet while she served in the Knesset. In fact, it was during those years that she was beginning to recognize her attraction to women.

34. Freedman, *Exile in the Promised Land*, p. 207.

35. Or Maroni-Paner and Michal Levy-Nachum, "My Mother's a Lesbian: Children of Lesbians Speak," *Klaf Chazak*, Spring/Summer 1997, p. 10 (in Hebrew).

7. Out on the Farm: Gay Life in the Kibbutzim

1. Ran Reznik, "The [Female] Kibbutz Secretary Has a Girlfriend, the [Male] Kibbutz Secretary Has a Boyfriend," *Ha-Ir*, March 29, 1991, p. 32 (in Hebrew).

2. Rubinstein, *From Herzl to Rabin*, p. 43.

3. Nachum Barnea, "The Kibbutz Has Gone," *Yediot Achronot* (Weekend Supplement), August 18, 1997, p. 3 (in Hebrew).

4. Asaf Anbari, "What Did the Stork See?" *Ha'aretz* (Weekend Supplement), October 23, 1998, p. 24 (in Hebrew).

5. Rubinstein, *From Herzl to Rabin*, p. 45.

6. Anbari, "What Did the Stork See?" p. 20.

7. Almog, *The Sabra*, p. 125.

8. Shefer, *Introduction to the Sociology of the Kibbutz*, pp. 208–209.

9. Ibid., p. 209.

10. Arik Bashan, "Comrades, I'm a Homosexual," *Kibbutz*, January 31, 1990, p. 5 (in Hebrew).

11. Rozner and Gatz, *The Kibbutz in an Era of Changes*, p. 14.

12. The three movements are TAKAM (United Kibbutz Movement), Ha-Kibbutz ha-Artzi, and the small Ha-Kibbutz ha-Dati, the religious kibbutz movement.

13. Osem is one of Israel's two major food conglomerates.

14. Bashan, "Comrades, I'm a Homosexual," p. 5.

15. Ibid.

16. Ibid.

17. Ibid.

18. Ibid.

8. Twice Marginalized: To Be Gay and Palestinian in Israel

1. In Arabic certain letters such as *nun* and *sin* do not take the regular form of the definite article *al* in front of them; rather, a double consonant is used, as in *an-Nakba*.

2. Declaration of Independence (1948), in Rubinstein, *Constitutional Law of the State of Israel*, 3d ed., p. 28.

3. Arabs drafted into the IDF still face discrimination and anti-Arab attitudes, both in the military itself and in the job market.

4. Similarly, in 1998, when Prime Minister Netanyahu toyed with holding a referendum on the second redeployment required by the Oslo Accords, a number of politicians suggested setting the necessary approval threshold at 60 percent, or higher, to cancel out any impact from the Arab vote.

5. Beit-Hallachmi, *Original Sins*, p. 90.

6. Ari Shavit, "Citizen Azmi," *Ha'aretz* (Weekend Supplement), May 29, 1998, p. 26 (in Hebrew).

7. Ibid., p. 23.

8. Ibid., p. 26.

9. I am not suggesting by using this phraseology that these will be the ultimate borders of a future Palestinian state, but Israel is not apt to withdraw from all of the West Bank, and border adjustments between Israel and the future Palestinian state are likely.

10. Jim Wafer, "Muhammed and Male Homosexuality," in Murray and Roscoe, *Islamic Homosexualities*, p. 88.

11. Quran 7:80.

12. Ibid., 4:15.

13. Wafer, "Muhammed and Male Homosexuality," p. 89.

14. Ibid., p. 89.

15. Ibid., pp. 89–90.

16. Jehoeda Sofer, "Sodomy in the Law of Muslim States," in Schmitt and Sofer, *Sexuality and Eroticism in Moslem Societies*, p. 132.

17. The term is not yet widespread, and it remains to be seen whether it will catch on. In my own Arabic studies I once came across a similar expression— *Ahaadii al-jins* (literally, "one sex")—in a Voice of America newscast in Arabic.

18. James T. Monroe, "Abu Bakr's Naughty Son," in Wright and Rowson, *Homoeroticism in Classical Arabic Literature*, p. 120.

19. MK Bishara also failed to respond to a letter seeking his views.

20. *Divrei ha-Knesset*, February 4, 1997, Knesset Internet site.

21. Working Group on the Status of Palestinian Women in Israel, *The Status of Palestinian Women Citizens of Israel* (Submitted to the United Nations Committee on the Elimination of Discrimination Against Women, 17th Session), July 1997, pp. 23–55.

22. Ibid., p. 63.

23. Iti Asher, "Jewish-Arab Lesbian Couple Living in Trash Bins in Tel Aviv Fear for Their Lives," *Ma'ariv*, December 9, 1997, n.p. (in Hebrew).

24. "Liz and Nurit: A Story of Two Women," *Klaf Chazak*, Winter 1998, p. 25 (in Hebrew).

25. Mansiya, "A Forgettable Story About an Arab Lesbian Girl," *Klaf Chazak*, Spring/Summer 1997, p. 14 (in Hebrew, with Arabic headline). Some Jerusalem lesbians attempted to put me in contact with "Mansiya." But, almost in allegorical fashion, she had moved and left no forwarding address or telephone number.

26. Ro'i Shenhar, "Poll of Knesset Members," *Ha-Zman ha-Varod*, September 1996, p. 3 (in Hebrew). When I raised Dahamshe's comments with his fellow party member, Tawfiq Khatib, Khatib professed great surprise and said that he would have to check out those remarks with his colleague.

27. Galilee Society, "Instructional Day on AIDS in Arab Society in Israel," February 12, 1997 (in Arabic).

28. "The Brotherhood of Peoples," *Maga'im*, August 1991, p. 11 (in Hebrew).

29. Ido Tzafrir, "Hamas Would Murder Me If They Knew I Was Gay," *Maga'im*, October 1993, pp. 10–11 (in Hebrew).

30. Itzik Yosha, "Israeli and Palestinian, A Love Story," *Yediot Achronot/Twenty-four Hours,* November 5, 1995, p. 4 (in Hebrew).

31. Shipler, *Arab and Jew.*

32. Itzik Rennert, "Love in the Shadow of the Intifada," *Tat-Tarbut,* Winter 1996, p. 63 (in Hebrew).

33. Ziv Cohen, "Community Under Siege," *Tel Aviv,* February 7, 1999, at http://www.tam.co.il/news1.html (in Hebrew).

Bibliography

Academic Articles and Papers

Ben-Yishai, Tzvi. "National AIDS Policy of Israel." In Inon I. Schenker, Galia Sabar-Friedman, and Francisco S. Sy, *AIDS Education*. New York: Plenum, 1982.

Even-Kama, Yossi. "Some Children Are Zig-Zag." Paper submitted at Tel Aviv City High School D, 1996 (in Hebrew).

Gal, Reuven. "Policy and Practice in the Israeli Defense Forces," in Wilbur J. Scott and Sandra Carson Stanley, eds., *Gays and Lesbians in the Military: Issues, Concerns, and Contrasts*. New York: de Gruyter, 1994.

Harel, Alon. "Gay Rights in Israel: A New Era?" 1 *International Journal of Discrimination and the Law* 261 (1996).

Kama, Amit. "From *Terra Incognita* to *Terra Firma*: The Logbook of the Voyage of the Gay Men's Community Into the Israeli Public Sphere." 38(4) *Journal of Homosexuality* 133 (in press).

Kaplan, Dani. *Coping Strategies of Homosexuals in Combat Service—Construction of Walls and Their Breach in the Stronghold of Masculinity*. Jerusalem: Van Leer Institute, 1997 (in Hebrew).

Mizrachi, Simcha. "Same-Sex Couples Coping with Stigma." Master's thesis, Tel Aviv University, 1990 (in Hebrew).

Safran, Channa. "Alliance and Denial: Feminist Lesbian Protest Within Women in Black." Paper submitted in partial fulfillment of the requirements for the degree of Master of Arts, Simmons College, 1994.

Spivak, Dori and Yuval Yonai. "Between Silence and Condemnation: Construction of Gay Identity in Legal Discourse in Israel 1948–1988." *Sotziologiya Yisraelit* 1(2) (in press) (in Hebrew).

Weishut, Daniel J. N. "Prejudice of Homosexuality: A Study of Israeli Students." *Israel Journal of Psychiatry and Related Sciences* (in press).

Yonai, Yuval. "The Law Regarding Homosexuality: Between History and Sociology." 4 *Mishpat u'Mimshal* 531 (1998) (in Hebrew).

Anthologies

Kaner, Oren, ed. *Not Nature's Way*. Tel Aviv: Society for the Protection of Personal Rights, 1994 (in Hebrew).

Moriel, Liora, ed. *Hot Night*. Tel Aviv: Society for the Protection of Personal Rights, 1994 (in Hebrew).

Razuani-Pur, Chaim, ed. *Chad Pa'ami*. Jerusalem, 1998 (in Hebrew).

Books

Almog, Oz. *The Sabra—A Profile*. Tel Aviv: Am Oved, 1997 (in Hebrew).

Alpert, Rebecca. *Like Bread on the Seder Plate*. New York: Columbia University Press, 1997.

Alwood, Edward. *Straight News*. New York: Columbia University Press, 1996.

Avni, Yossi. *Grove of the Dead Trees*. Tel Aviv: Zmora-Bitan, 1995 (in Hebrew).

Balka, Christie and Andy Rose. *Twice Blessed: On Being Lesbian, Gay, and Jewish*. Boston: Beacon, 1989.

Beck, Evelyn Torton Beck, ed. *Nice Jewish Girls: A Lesbian Anthology*. Boston: Beacon, 1989.

Beit-Hallahmi, Benjamin. *Original Sins: Reflections on the History of Zionism and Israel*. New York: Olive Branch, 1993.

Ben-Simon, Daniel. *A New Israel*. Tel Aviv: Arye Nir, 1997 (in Hebrew).

Ben-Yisrael, Ruth. *Equality of Opportunity and Prohibition of Discrimination in Employment*. Tel Aviv: Open University, 1998 (in Hebrew).

Boyarin, Daniel. *Carnal Israel: Reading Sex in Talmudic Culture*. Berkeley: University of California Press, 1993.

— *Unheroic Conduct: The Rise of Heterosexuality and the Invention of the Jewish Man*. Berkeley: University of California Press, 1997.

D'Emilio, John. *Sexual Politics, Sexual Communities: The Making of a Homosexual Minority in the United States, 1940–1970*. Chicago: University of Chicago Press, 1983.

Elbaum, Dov. *Elul Time*. Tel Aviv: Am Oved, 1997 (in Hebrew).

Eshed, Noga. *Queen Bees' Nectar*. Tel Aviv: Sifriat Poalim, 1998 (in Hebrew).

Ezrachi, Yaron. *Rubber Bullets*. New York: Farrar, Straus and Giroux, 1997.

Freed, Yaron. *Does Your Mother Know?* Tel Aviv: Yediot Achronot, 1997 (in Hebrew).

Freedman, Marcia. *Exile in the Promised Land*. Ithaca: Firebrand, 1990.

Gai, Karmit. *Journey to Yad-Channa*. Tel Aviv: Am Oved, 1992 (in Hebrew).

Gal, Reuven. *A Portrait of the Israeli Soldier*. Westport: Greenwood, 1986.

Al-Ghitti, Mohammed. *A Scandal by the Name Saida Sultan: Dana the Israeli Sex-Singer*. Cairo: Arabic Center, 1995 (in Arabic).

Glozman, Michael and Gil Nader. *A Different Dictionary*. Tel Aviv: 1996 (in Hebrew).

Grossman, David. *Present Absentees*. Tel Aviv: Ha-Kibbutz ha-Me'uchad, 1992 (in Hebrew).

Heilman, Samuel. *Defenders of the Faith: Inside Ultra-Orthodox Jewry*. New York: Schocken, 1992.

Kaufman, Michael. *Love, Marriage, and Family in Jewish Law and Tradition*. Northvale: Aronson, 1992.

Landau, David. *Piety and Power: The World of Jewish Fundamentalism*. New York: Hill and Wang, 1993.

Levy, Amnon. *The Ultra-Orthodox*. Jerusalem: Keter, 1989 (in Hebrew).

Likosky, Stephan, ed. *Coming Out: An Anthology of International Gay and Lesbian Writings*. New York: Pantheon, 1992.

Moore, Tracy. *Lesbiot*. London: Cassell, 1995.

Murray, Stephen O. and Will Roscoe. *Islamic Homosexualities*. New York: New York University Press, 1997.

Noibach, Keren. *The Race: Election 1996*. Tel Aviv: Yediot Achronot, 1996 (in Hebrew).

Rachlevsky, Sefi. *Messiah's Donkey*. Tel Aviv: Yediot Achronot, 1998 (in Hebrew).

Raphael, Lev. *Journeys and Arrivals: On Being Gay and Jewish*. Boston: Faber and Faber, 1996.

Rayside, David. *On the Fringe: Gays and Lesbians in Politics*. Ithaca: Cornell University Press, 1998.

Reuveni, Yotam. *In Praise of Illusion*. Tel Aviv: Achshav, 1979 (in Hebrew).

Rosenblum, Doron. *Israeli Blues*. Tel Aviv: Am Oved, 1996 (in Hebrew).

Rosner, Fred. *Sex Ethics in the Writings of Moses Maimonides*. Northvale: Aronson, 1994.

Rozner, Menachem and Shlomo Gatz. *The Kibbutz in an Era of Changes*. Israel: Ha-Kibbutz ha-Me'uchad and University of Haifa Press, 1996 (in Hebrew).

Rubinstein, Amnon. *Constitutional Law of the State of Israel*. 3d ed. Tel Aviv: Schocken, 1980 (in Hebrew).

— *Constitutional Law of the State of Israel*. 5th ed. Tel Aviv: Schocken, 1996 (in Hebrew).

— *From Herzl to Rabin: One Hundred Years of Zionism*. Tel Aviv: Schocken, 1997 (in Hebrew).

Sela, Uri. *Lexicon of Hebrew and Military Slang*. Ramat Gan: Prologue, 1993 (in Hebrew).

Schmitt, Arno and Jehoeda Sofer, eds. *Sexuality and Eroticism Among Males in Moslem Societies*. Binghamton: Harrington Park, 1992.

Scott, Wilbur J. and Sandra Carson Stanley, eds. *Gays and Lesbians in the Military: Issues, Concerns, and Contrasts*. New York: de Gruyter, 1994.

Segev, Tom. *1949: The First Israelis*. New York: Henry Holt, 1998.

Sharoni, Simona. *Gender and the Israeli-Palestinian Conflict*. Syracuse: Syracuse University Press, 1995.

Shefer, Yosef. *Introduction to the Sociology of the Kibbutz*. Israel: Rupin Agricultural College Press, 1997 (in Hebrew).

Sheinfeld, Ilan. *Ara'i*. Tel Aviv: Tammuz, 1988 (in Hebrew).

— *Karet*. Tel Aviv: Shufra, 1997 (in Hebrew).

— *Lines to a Friend in Parting*. Tel Aviv, Aleph, 1987 (in Hebrew).

— *Tashlich*. Tel Aviv: Tag, 1994 (in Hebrew).

Shipler, David. *Arab and Jew: Wounded Spirits in a Promised Land*. New York: Times, 1986.

Tubali, Shai. *Body Language*. Jerusalem: Keter, 1996 (in Hebrew).

Tzifer, Beni. *Turkish March*. Tel Aviv: Am Oved, 1995 (in Hebrew).

Wallach, Yona. *Forms*. Tel Aviv: Ha-Kibbutz ha-Me'uchad, 1987 (in Hebrew).

Waxman, Yossi. *My Darling Alexandria*. Jerusalem: Keter, 1998 (in Hebrew).

Wright, J. W. Jr. and Everett K. Rowson, eds. *Homoeroticism in Classical Arabic Literature*. New York: Columbia University Press, 1997.

Films

Gotta Have Heart, produced by Eitan Fox, screenplay by Gal Ochovsky, 39 min., Al Ahava, 1998, videocassette (in Hebrew).

Don't Cry for Me, Edinburgh, produced by Erez Laufer, 78 min., Erez Productions, 1998, videocassette (in Hebrew and English).

Drifting, produced by Amos Gutman, 80 min., 1983, 35 mm (in Hebrew).

Time Off, directed by Eitan Fox, Film Project 1990, 1990, videocassette (in Hebrew).

Government Documents

Divrei ha-Knesset

K-31–11–01 Service of Homosexuals in the IDF, Manpower Division Standing Orders (1986) (in Hebrew).

K-31–11–01 Service of Homosexuals in the IDF, Manpower Division Standing Orders (1993) (in Hebrew).

Law for the Prevention of Sexual Harassment 1998/5758, Sefer ha-Chukim (March 19, 1998) (in Hebrew).

Regulations for the Prevention of Sexual Harassment (Employer Obligations) 1998/5758 (Version Approved by Knesset Committee for the Advancement of Women's Status) (August 5, 1998) (in Hebrew).

Transcript of Session of Committee for the Advancement of Women's Status (June 17, 1997) (in Hebrew).

Judicial Decisions

Danilovitz v. El Al Israel Airlines, Ltd., Case no. MT/3–1503 (Tel Aviv-Jaffa Regional Labor Court 1993) (in Hebrew).

El Al Israel Airlines Ltd. v. Danilovitz, DB"A NG/3–160, PD"A 66 339 (National Labor Court 1993) (in Hebrew).

El Al Israel Airlines Ltd. v. Danilovitz, BAGATZ 721/94, P"D 88 (5)(749) (Israeli Supreme Court 1994) (in Hebrew).

Eliezer v. Chief Military Prosecutor, Case No. 40/95/A (Military Appeals Court 1995) (in Hebrew).

Gan ha-Ir v. Horowitz, T.A. 319/90 P.D. Ha-Shalom 2 (1991) (in Hebrew).

Society for the Protection of Personal Rights of Gays, Lesbians, and Bisexuals in Israel v. Minister of Education, Culture, and Sport, BAGATZ 273/97 (Israeli Supreme Court 1997) (in Hebrew).

Steiner v. Compensation Officer, B-8/94 (Appeals Panel under Law for Families of Soldiers Who Perish in Battle (Compensation and Rehabilitation 1950) (1995) (in Hebrew).

Steiner v. Israel Defense Forces, A-Sh 369/94 (Standing Army [Pensions] Appeals Panel) (Tel Aviv District Court) (1997) (in Hebrew).

Magazines and Newspapers

Al ha-Mishmar
Arei ha-Mifratz
Bamachane
B'Meretz
Davar Rishon
Du'et
Ha'aretz
Ha-Ir
Ha-Machane ha-Charedi
Ha-Olam ha-Ze
Ha-Tzofe
Ha-Zman ha-Varod
Jerusalem Report
Kibbutz
Klaf Chazak
Kol Chaifa
Kol ha-Ir
L'Isha
Ma'ariv Lano'ar
Maga'im
Nativ Nosaf
Nekuda
Rosh Echad

Tat-Tarbut
Tel Aviv
Tzafon ha-Ir
Yated Ne'eman
Yediot Achronot

Music

B'not Pesia. *Can't Be.* Hed Artzi compact disc (1997) (in Hebrew).
Carmella, Gross and Wagner. "Until the Disease is Cured." *Black Flower.*
    Nana Disc (1991) (in Hebrew).
—— "Wet and Hot." *Black Flower.* Nana Disc (1991) (in Hebrew).
—— "Women Write Poetry." *Black Flower.* Nana Disc (1991) (in Hebrew).
Geffen, Aviv. *Hollowed.* Hed-Artzi compact disk (1998) (in Hebrew).
Heiman, Si. "Come Out of the Closet." *Working on the Road.* NMC audio-
    cassette 465981–4 (1990) (in Hebrew).
Ice Nine. "With Him Forever." *The Beginning of the Right Life.* NMC com-
    pact disk 20270–2 (1997) (in Hebrew).
International, Dana. *Danna International.* I.M.P. compact disk 2004 (1993) (in
    Hebrew, Arabic, and English).
—— *Diva.* I.M.P. Dance compact disk 2048 (1998) (in Hebrew, Arabic,
    English).
—— *Umpatampa.* I.M.P. Dance compact disk 2012–2 (1994) (in Hebrew, Ara-
    bic, English).
—— *E.P. Tampa.* I.M.P. Dance compact disk 2022 (1995) (in Hebrew, Arabic,
    English).
—— *Maganona.* Helicon Records compact disk HL8143 (1996) (in Hebrew,
    Arabic, English).
Polianna Frank. "Dykes and the Holy War." *No Choosing.* Third Ear audio-
    cassette (1990).
—— "Ziva." *No Choosing.* Third Ear audiocassette (1990) (in Hebrew).
Poliker, Yehuda. "Melting in the Rain." *The Child Within.* NMC Music com-
    pact disk 20158–2 (1995) (in Hebrew).

Pamphlets

Association of Gays, Lesbians, and Bisexuals in Israel. *There's Life After AIDS.*
    Tel Aviv: Association for Gays, Lesbians, and Bisexuals in Israel, 1998 (in
    Hebrew).
— "Information Sheet." Tel Aviv: Association of Gays, Lesbians, and Bisexuals
    in Israel (in Hebrew).
— "Israel Update." Tel Aviv: Association of Gays, Lesbians, and Bisexuals in
    Israel.

Barnea, Chava and Dalia Lorentz. *Same-Sex Orientation (Homosexuality and Lesbianism)*. Jerusalem: Ministry of Education, Culture, and Sport, 1995 (in Hebrew).

Bela Do'eget. *Sex Between Men and the Risk of Infection with AIDS: The Guide to Safe Sex*. Tel Aviv: Bela Do'eget, 1997 (in Hebrew).

Galilee Association: *Rights and Privileges of Persons with AIDS and HIV*. Shefaram: Galilee Association, n.d. (in Arabic).

Galilee Association. *Study Day on AIDS in Arab Society in Israel*. Shefaram: Galilee Association, 1997 (in Arabic).

Gei'ut. Israel: Gei'ut/Meretz, 1997 (in Hebrew).

Levy, Patrick and Ricardo Shneider. *Life with AIDS: A Guide for Treatment of People Living with HIV/AIDS*. Tel Aviv: Israel AIDS Task Force, 1996 (in Hebrew).

"Michal Eden: For a More Equal Tel Aviv" (1998) (in Hebrew).

Society for the Protection of Personal Rights. *On Homosexuals in Israel: Background and Facts*. Tel Aviv: Society for the Protection of Personal Rights, 1983 (in Hebrew).

Yanetz, Uri. *Oops*. Tel Aviv: Bela Do'eget, n.d. (in Hebrew).

Television Programs

Closing Out the Week with Amnon Levy, Israel Television Channel 1.

Florentin, Channel 2.

Mabat, Israel Television Channel 1.

Open Cards, Israeli Educational Television.

Tekuma, Israel Television Channel 1.

Yoman, Israel Television Channel 1.

Zehu Ze, Israeli Educational Television and Channel 2.

Index

ADP-UAL, 23, 222, 223, 231
AIDS: caseload, 37; demographics of, 38; education against, 38–9; media and, 39–40; Palestinian education efforts on, 231–33; impact on gay political strategy, 11, 40–41, 56
Al-Badil, 228–29, 231
Al ha-Mishmar, collective values of, 149, 205
Almog, Oz, 59, 102, 200
Alwood, Edward, 146, 151, 152
Ariel, Meir, 35
Ariel-Yoel, David (Rabbi), 113; ceremony for lesbian couple, 110–11; on Torah and homosexuality, 111
As-Siwar, 227, 229, 231; position on homosexuality, 228; *see also* Feminists, Palestinian
Association for Civil Rights in Israel (ACRI), 36, 70–71
Association of Gays, Lesbians, Bisexuals and Transgenders in Israel (Aguda), 6, 17, 24, 43, 53, 55, 80, 93; and AIDS, 41; community center of, 7; growth of assertive activism, 34–35; in Haifa, 50–51, 75–76; lecture service of, 61, 80; and *Open Cards*, 70; services for gay Arabs, 244–45; and transgender issues, 54–55; women's participation in, 47; and youth groups, 76–77
Avni, Yossi, *see Grove of the Dead Trees*
Awwad, Na'ila, 228, 231; on family violence, 228–29; on need for sex education, 229

Baitelman, Sergei, 239–40, 247
Bar-Lev, Chaim (MK), 29
Bar-Zohar, Michael (MK), 29
Barak, Ehud, and Adir Steiner, 137; impact of on gay concerns, 258–59; 1999 election victory of, 255; role in military policy change, 118; *see also* Labor Party; One Israel
Barkai, Nurit, 198; kibbutz experience of, 201–4, 206; on military, 133
Barnea, Chava, 25, 69, 271n14; *see also Same-Sex Orientation (Homosexuality and Lesbianism)*

Barnea, Nachum, 198, 255
Beer Sheva, gay life in, 51–52
Bela Do'eget, 37, 41
Ben-Dror, Amnon, 181
Ben-Ezer, Sharon, see Music
Ben-Simon, Daniel, 32
Ben-Yishai, Tzvi (Dr.), 37–38,
    269n30
Ben-Yisrael, Ruth, 185
Bendel, Ehud (Rabbi): analogy
    between place of gays and place
    of women in Conservative
    Judaism, 111; on homosexuality,
    112; on image considerations,
    112; on same-sex couples, 112
Benizri, Shlomo (MK), 23, 99; on
    Dana International, 171, 173
Bernheimer, Avner, 124, 151, 153; on
    AIDS coverage, 39; on coverage
    of gay/lesbian issues, 151–52;
    reserve duty of, 124–25; on role
    of gay press, 154; on same-sex
    couplehood, 187–88
Bishara, Azmi (MK), 218, 222, 226;
    on gays, 224; on identity of
    Palestinians in Israel, 219; on
    Jews as nation, 219; prime
    ministerial candidacy of, 256–57;
    see also Palestinian citizens of
    Israel

Carmela, Gross and Wagner, see
    Music
Center Party, 22, 49, 256, 257,
    275n10
Chadash-Balad, 19, 218, 223, 224
Chad Pa'ami, 52
Chief Rabbinate, views on homo-
    sexuality, 95; see also Judaism
Chuldai, Ron, 258
Collective values, 33, 42, 54, 71, 78,
    147, 148, 253; and gay/lesbian
    culture, 144; and kibbutzim, 198–
    99, 201; and military service, 115;
    and 1999 elections, 255–56; see

also Individualism; Kibbutzim;
    New Jews; Zionism
Coming out: impact of family on,
    59–60; impact of geography on,
    59–60; role of religion in, 83
Conservative Judaism, 85: and
    homosexuality in Israel, 111–13
Culture, gay and lesbian: and
    factionalization of Israeli society,
    143; growth of, 250; impact of
    lack of gay ghettos on, 144;
    interaction with Judaism, 145; as
    part of Israeli consensus, 143;
    relation to decline of collective
    values, 144; see also Literature,
    gay/lesbian; Music

Dahamshe, Abdel-Malik (MK), 223,
    231
Danilovitz, Yonatan, 94, 99, 168,
    183, 185; and Tehila, 79
Danilovitz v. El Al Israel Airlines,
    138, 183–84, 185
Davar: collective values of, 149;
    reporting on gay issues of: 145,
    147–48; see also Media,
    mainstream
Dayan, Yael (MK): 17, 22, 26, 27,
    29–30, 50, 94, 117, 122, 133,
    175; on gay representation in
    Knesset, 29, 32; and IDF
    treatment of gays, 18–19; impact
    of legislation on public attitudes,
    18; legislative progress under
    Likud governments, 18; and Yad
    Vashem incident, 9
D'Emilio, John, model for gay
    community development, 15–16
Does Your Mother Know? as repre-
    sentation of new gay image, 158–
    59; see also Literature, gay/lesbian
Drifting, see Gutman, Amos

Eden, Michal, 13, 15, 49, 249, 253,
    257, 269n24; on Ashkenazi-

Mizrachi relations in gay/lesbian community, 50; city council race of, 30–33; electoral strategy of, 31–32; Knesset prospects of, 258; political platform of, 31; and Wigstock Riots, 34

Educational system: approach to gay identity of 58–59, 66, 77, 80; flaws in approach to gay issues, 78; views on normality of homosexuality, 68–70

El-Ad, Chagai: on Asiron activities and organization, 52; on coming out, 60; on community image, 36; reserve duty of, 136; on Weizman affair, 14

Elbaum, Dov, see Elul Time

Eliezer v. Chief Military Prosecutor, 125–26

Elites: connection of gay community to, 32–33, 253; support for gay rights, 11, 14, 19, 57, 140

Elon, Beni (MK), 25, 95; on antigay discrimination, 20; on gay rights as partisan issue, 20; on Open Cards, 21; on religious prohibitions against homosexual relations, 20; on same-sex families, 20–21; on sexual harassment law, 25

Elul Time, 93, 97; see also Literature, gay/lesbian

Equal Workplace Opportunities Law, 17, 28, 183

Esbanyoli, Nabila: on gay/lesbian rights, 230; on gay mainstream strategy, 230; on sex education approaches, 229–30; on social consciousness of lesbians, 230; on status of gays versus women in Palestinian society, 230; see also Feminists

Eshed, Noga, 143, 145; and Queen Bees' Nectar, 164–66

Eurovision, 35, 56, 65, 172–74, 259

Even, Uzi, 14, 122, 133, 136; on antigay harassment in IDF, 135; foster child of, 66, 72; and IDF policy on gays in military, 117–18; masculine image of, 36; 1996 Knesset race of, 29–30, 98–99; 1999 Knesset race of, 258; suit against Tel Aviv University for partner benefits, 184

Even-Kama, Yossi, 68; high school survey of, 66–67; military service of, 129–30, 275–76n28; and Open Cards, 71–72

Ezra, Devora, 61, 272n29; on gay identity, 77–78

Ezrachi, Yaron, 144

Family honor killings, 227–29, 234, 235; and lesbians, 228

Feminism: and lesbians, 46; North American origins of, 42; and Palestinian cause, 42–43; politics of, 43

Feminists, Palestinian, 219–20; and family honor killings, 227–29; impact of on gay rights, 246; relations with wider feminist movement, 226; see also Al-Badil; As-Siwar; Women Against Violence

Flinker, Ilana, approach of to gay and lesbian youth, 64–65

Florentin, 65, 141–43

Fox, Eitan, 143, 143, 254; and mainstream portrayal of gays, 175–77 ——works: Gotta Have Heart, 172, 176–77; Time Off, 150, 175–76; see also Florentin

Freed, Yaron, see Does Your Mother Know?

Freedman, Marcia, 42–43, 194, 279n33; impact of U.S. immigrants on Israeli feminism, 42

Gafni, Moshe (MK), 91, 94

Gal, Reuven, 132; on centrality of

military service, 115; on integration of soldiers with civilian life, 121; military unit as extended family, 128; see also Israel Defense Forces

Galilee Society, AIDS education efforts of among Palestinians, 231–33; see also AIDS

Gay/Lesbian community, 56; lack of ghettoes, 250; spread to smaller towns, 50–54

Gay/Lesbian identity: and connection to Israeli identity, 235, 254; development of, 33, 250; educators' views of, 58–59, 66, 77–78, 212–13; parents' views of, 79–80

Gay/Lesbian religious Jews, 104, 107–9; see also Judaism

Gay rights as electoral issue, 26–27, 257

Geffen, Aviv, 92

Gei'ut, 14, 28–29

Gemara, 88, 92

Gozhansky, Tamar (MK), 19; on Palestinian attitudes toward gays, 225

Greenberg, Steve (Rabbi), 103

Greenblad, Terry, 42

Grove of the Dead Trees, 158

Gutman, Amos, 143; Drifting, 150, 175, 239

Ha-Asiron ha-Acher (Asiron), 14, 24, 52; activities and organizational structure of, 52; and Jerusalem Pride, 52; outreach to gay Arabs, 245

Ha-Ir, 117, 147

Ha-Olam ha-Ze: article on gay pride, 4; 1962 article on gays, 146–47

Ha-Tzofe, 94, 96, 97, 113

Ha-Zman ha-Varod, 30, 32, 36, 60, 71, 105, 130, 154, 160, 186, 231, 234, 250, 257; and AIDS, 41; Michal Eden column in, 32; and

gay Arab issues, 243; as platform for community building, 155, 156; and Wigstock, 34

Ha'aretz, political orientation of, 148; see also Media, mainstream

Haifa, gay and lesbian community in, 50–51

Hammer, Zevulun, 155; and Open Cards, 70–71

Harel, Alon, 271n18; on couplehood, 184–85; on homophobia, 16; on Open Cards ruling, 272n23

Harris, Neil, 208–9, 211

Hebrew, terms of for gay and lesbian, 3–4, 267nn2–3

Heiman, Si, see Music

Hillel, Shlomo (MK), 29

HOD, 102, 107, 108, 109

Homophobia, 16–17, 250, 251–52, 268n6; in IDF, 123, 133–35

Hot Night, 47, 157

Ice Nine, 152, 167–68

Individualism, 33, 40, 42, 73, 100, 120, 201; and gay rights, 43, 253; and kibbutzim, 201, 203, 214; in literature, 144, 163; and 1999 Israeli elections, 255–56; reasons for, 54; see also Collective values; Kibbutzim; New Jews; Zionism

International, Dana, 55, 73, 106, 143, 145, 154, 234, 259; career struggles of, 172; as catalyst for Wigstock riots, 35; childhood of, 170; 1998 Eurovision victory of, 173; and 1999 Eurovision, 259; popularity of in Arab world, 171–72; reactions to victory of, 173–75; religious attitudes of, 170–71

Irani-Kandalaft, Iman, 227, 230, 231; on sex education among Palestinians, 228; on status of Arab gays versus women, 228; see also Feminists

Islam, attitudes toward
homosexuality of, 220–21
Israel, collective values of, 27, 78,
198, 201, 252; identity of, 27–28;
political tribalization of, 32, 253;
see also Collective values;
Individualism
Israel AIDS Task Force, 37–38, 40–
41, 232, 237; see also AIDS
Israel Defense Forces (IDF), 114;
educational role of, 123; harassment of gays in, 123, 134–35;
and lesbians, 132–34; policies on
service of gays and lesbians, 115–
19, 122–24, 129–32; publicity on
policy change in military ranks,
119, 126; reserve duty evasion,
136; role of in Israeli society,
114–15, 275n10; service of lesbians in, 132–34; spousal benefits
for same-sex partners of soldiers,
137–40; and women, 132

Jabarin, Ḥassan, 225, 235; on status
of Arab gays in Palestinian society,
226; on transnational nature of
gay identity, 226, 231; see also
Palestinians, gay and lesbian
Jerusalem, gay/lesbian life in, 52–54
Jerusalem Open House, 80; outreach
to Palestinians, 53, 245; as
symbol of pluralism, 54; work
with women, 53
Judaism: attitudes toward homosexuality, 86–90; attitudes toward
sexuality, 84–86, 97; attitude
toward sin, 98–99; gay/lesbian
attitudes toward, 100–102, 103,
113; gay/lesbian explorations in,
103–7; and Israeli politics, 90–92;
Israeli practice of, 91; and
personal status issues, 90; see also
gay/lesbian religious Jews

Kabel, Eitan (MK), 22–23

Kabha, Nazieh: on AIDS education,
231–32; on need for autonomy
for Palestinian education, 232
Kama, Amit, 14, 55, 184; foster
child of, 66, 72; on importance of
legal changes, 55; on media
coverage of gay issues, 146–47;
on outreach to gay Arabs, 244;
religious attitudes of, 101
Kaplan, Dani, 15, 133, 136; book on
gays in IDF combat units, 126–
29; harassment of gays in military,
135; impact of military service on
gay identity, 128; on reserve duty
evasion, 136; see also Israel
Defense Forces
Karmil, Devora, 67–68
Kaufman, Mordechai, 201, 209–10,
214; see also Kibbutzim
Kedar, Ya'ir, 154–55, 156, 187,
277n13; see also Ha-Zman ha-
Varod
Kedmi, Ya'akov (Justice), 71, 72
Kerem, Shai, approach of Israeli
youth press to homosexuality,
73–74
Khatib, Tawfiq (MK), 23, 222, 235,
281n26; on homosexuality, 223–
24; on status of Palestinian
citizens of Israel, 224
Kibbutzim: attitudes toward homosexuality, 200–1, 209, 210–14;
attitudes toward marriage and
sexuality in, 199–200, 206;
attitudes toward religion, 199; as
building block of state, 198;
decline of collectivism in, 202,
205–6; economic changes in, 202,
205–6; as reflection of Israeli
society's values, 198, 201, 214; as
societal elite, 200, 205, 208; see
also Collective values; Individualism; New Jews; Zionism
Kirshner, Susan, 8, 51, 79, 181; on
Aguda attitudes toward women,

47; on political successes, 17, 26; and youth groups, 74–75

KLAF, 14, 30, 31, 34, 44, 47, 53, 60, 62, 76, 152, 271n14; and Arab lesbians, 245–46; contribution to peace movement, 46; and Education Ministry tolerance fair, 35; founding of, 46; generation gap in, 45–46; image of, 44, 46; and *Klaf Chazak*, 154; lecture service of, 61; on mainstream political strategy, 55; and Mizrachiot, 44, 48; and *Open Cards*, 70; and Weizman affair, 14

Klaf Chazak, 133, 152, 154, 194, 250

Klein, Chana, on lesbian split from Aguda, 46–47

Knesset, 7, 17–22, 25; impact of structure on gay rights, 26; and sexual harassment law, 25

Kol ha-Isha, 42

Labor Party, 13, 16, 18, 19, 23, 28, 33, 202, 222, 256; appeals to gay voters, 28–29; and Mizrachim, 49; need for religious parties as coalition partners, 91; and Palestinian citizens of Israel, 217–18; *see also* One Israel

Lachman, Dani, 36

Lapid, Tomi (MK), 175, 257

Lau, Yisrael Meir (Chief Rabbi), 95

Lesbians: development of culture, 156–57, 164; and feminist movement, 44–47; and military service, 132–34; Palestinian, 220, 228, 230–31; religious, 104; youth groups for, 76

Levinson, Jerry, 245; and Jerusalem Open House, 52–53; and youth groups, 74

Leviticus, 86, 104, 111

Levy, Amnon, 97

Levy, Patrick, 37, 39, 270n32; *see also* Israel AIDS Task Force

Levy, Yitzhak (MK), 94, 173

Likud, 13, 16, 23, 25, 64, 91, 271n14; economic populism of, 54; and 1999 elections, 256, 258; Mizrachi support for, 49

Literature, lesbian and gay, 143–44; lesbian literature, 164; positive images of gays, 157; *see also* Culture, gay/lesbian

Lorentz, Dalia, 61, 271n5; *see also* Same-Sex Orientation (Homosexuality and Lesbianism)

Luz, Devora, 79–80, 191; and *Open Cards*, 72

Ma'ariv: gay journalists at, 151; political orientation of, 148; *see also* Media, mainstream

Maga'im, 1, 2, 3, 5, 28–29, 153; coverage of gay Palestinians, 233

Maimonides, 86, 87

Mainstream strategy, 11, 54, 252; ability to address previously taboo issues, 55–56; as viewed by Palestinians, 225, 230

Mainz, Theo, 103, 108; on Israelis' lack of interest in religion, 102

Maisel, Doron (Colonel), 21, 136–39

MARAM (Council of Progressive Rabbis), on religious ceremonies for same-sex couples, 109–10; *see also* Reform Judaism

Marom, Tzvi, 148–49

Marx, Tzvi (Rabbi), 88–90, 96, 99

Media, gay and lesbian, 153–56: coverage of gay Palestinians, 233, 243; as platform for internal community debate, 154

Media, mainstream: concentration in, 148; coverage of lesbian issues, 152; impact of gay/lesbian journalists on gay coverage, 152–53; impact on gay political advances, 145, 277n11; left-wing bias of, 148–49; portrayals of gays, 145–

47, 150–51; youth press coverage, 73–4

Meiri, David, 60, 136

Meiri, Shmuel: on aggressiveness of Israeli media, 149; on AIDS coverage, 39; on gays in IDF, 120

Meretz, 8, 14, 19, 21, 29–33, 56, 98, 218, 253, 256, 257, 259; as source for future gay/lesbian Knesset members, 258; support of Gei'ut, 29

Milo, Roni, 22, 23, 106, 258; on tolerant reputation of Tel Aviv, 22

Mishna, 87, 88

Mishpachti'ut, 179–80

Mitzna, Amram, 50–51

Mizrachi, Sima, 188–90, 192; *see also* Same-sex couples

Mizrachim, 48–50; and Ashkenazim in gay community, 49–50; ethnic revolt of, 32–33, 48–49; and Michal Eden, 30; political attitudes of, 30

Mo'ach Gavra, 102–3, 104

Moledet, 19–20

Mordechai, Yitzhak (MK), 93, 257; and Doron Maisel, 137–39

Moriel, Liora, 8, 51, 79; and *Hot Night*, 47, 156; on lesbian culture, 156–57; on reasons for political successes, 17; role in achieving recognition for same-sex couples, 181; on women in the Aguda, 47

Mosinzon, Ranen: on coverage of gay issues by gay/lesbian reporters, 153; on coverage of lesbians in mainstream media, 152

Music: Carmela, Gross, and Wagner, 169; closetedness of singers, 167; Dana International, 170–75; Eurovision, 172–73; Ice Nine, 167–68; Sharon Ben-Ezer, 169–70; Si Heiman, 168–69; *see also* Culture, gay/lesbian

My Darling Alexandria, 159–60, 243; *see also* Literature, gay/lesbian

Nader, Gil, 71, 101, 106, 248; and *A Different Dictionary*, 166; gay and Israeli identity in work of, 166–67; and transgender issues, 55; on Wigstock riots, 35

Namir, Hadar, 7, 11, 17, 28, 50, 269n24; Aguda community center fund-raising trip, 7; on mainstream strategy, 55; military's impact on gay and lesbian community agenda, 132–33; and Wigstock riots, 34–35

Natanel, Sa'ar, 24, 49, 245; and Wigstock, 34–35

National Religious Party, 19, 70, 92, 94, 100, 173, 259

Nativ Nosaf, 103, 244

Nekuda, 99

Nesher High, 60–66

Netanyahu, Benjamin, 11, 12, 13, 14, 18, 20, 23, 39, 249, 256, 257, 258; and 1999 elections, 255–8; and reaction to Dana International victory, 174

New Israel Fund, 52, 53

New Jews, 102, 198, 200, 201; as cultural ideal, 144; Ilan Sheinfeld's poetry as counterpoint to, 162–63; kibbutzniks as exemplars of, 200; *see also* Collective values; Individualism; Kibbutzim; Zionism

Nissim, Ofer, 106, 171

No'ar 2000, 250

Ochovsky, Gal, 173; gay column in *Ha-Ir*, 147; impact of gay journalists on media coverage, 153; on reserve duty, 117; on same-sex couples, 186–87

One Israel, 118, 137, 255, 256, 257, 259; *see also* Labor Party

Open Cards, 21, 70–73, 79

Orthodykes, 83, 104, 109

Palestinian citizens of Israel, 144;
    attitudes toward gay rights/
    homosexuality, 217, 222, 225,
    231; attitudes of Israeli Jews
    toward, 241–42; discrimination
    against, 216, 227, 280nn3–4; and
    government representation, 217–
    18, 257; identification of with
    Palestinian cause, 217; and
    military government, 217;
    preservation of culture, 219;
    status as Israelis, 218, 246
Palestinians, gay and lesbian: Arabic
    terminology for, 221–22; Arab
    perceptions of gay Israeli attitudes
    toward, 233, 235; attitudes to-
    ward Israelis, 235–36; and family
    honor killings, 228; future pros-
    pects of, 246–47; and gay identity,
    220–21; identification of with Pal-
    estinian cause, 217, 237; Israeli
    gay attitudes toward, 234, 242–
    46; from Jerusalem and Occupied
    Territories, 236–40; marginaliza-
    tion of lesbians, 220, 230; partici-
    pation in gay community, 233–34,
    236–37; same-sex relationships of
    with Israelis, 237–42
Peres, Shimon, 13, 218
Piccolo, 6
Popolitika, 257: and Dana
    International, 174–75; and Yad
    Vashem incident, 8
Porat, Chanan (MK), 19, 100
Pride events, 15, 22–23, 33, 249, 258

Rabin, Yitzhak, 13, 25, 61, 91, 122,
    216, 218, 255; assassination of as
    backdrop to Florentin, 141–43;
    and Doron Maisel, 137, 276n37;
    on IDF policy toward gays, 118;
    and permanent residence for gay
    Palestinian, 238

Radio, gay, 151
Ravitz, Avraham (MK), 94
Rayside, David, 26
Reform Judaism, 82–83; approach to
    homosexuality in Israel, 109–13,
    274n53; and 1998 gay pride, 107
Regev, Uri (Rabbi), 111
Religious parties and approaches to
    homosexuality and gay rights,
    94–100, 251, 259; political power
    of, 90–91, 253–54
Reuveni, Yotam, 143, 157
Rivkin, Dori, 193
Rivlin, Reuven "Rubi" (MK), 25
Rubinstein, Amnon (MK), 198, 199;
    on including same-sex couples in
    civil marriage, 188

Safran, Chana, 45
Same-sex couples: bureaucracy
    recognition of, 181–82, 249;
    children of, 190–96; community
    discussion of, 186–88; issues of,
    188–90; Jewish-Arab, 237–42;
    judicial recognition of, 182–84;
    legislative recognition of, 181; as
    successful political issue, 178, 180
Same-Sex Orientation (Homosex-
    uality and Lesbianism), 25, 69–
    70, 271n14
Sarid, Yossi (MK), 29, 259
Secular: attitudes toward Judaism,
    113, 253–54; fear of religious
    parties, 92–93, 251; gay com-
    munity as part of, 101; portrayals
    of religious, 92–93; religious
    practices of, 91
Segev, Tom, attitudes toward gay
    representation in Knesset, 30, 32
Sexual Harassment Law, 25
Sexual liberation, 179
Shalom, Chaya, 49; and establish-
    ment of KLAF, 46; impact of
    security situation on feminism, 44
Sharoni, Simona, 44

Shas, 24, 25, 96, 99, 259; role in torpedoing benefits for same-sex couples, 96

Sheinfeld, Ilan, 145, 160–64; eroticism in works, 163–64; on mainstream media coverage of gays, 153; relationship between gay, Jewish, and Israeli identity, 162; relationship between Judaism and homosexuality in work, 160–62; religious themes in work, 162

Sheinfeld, Iris, 76

Sheizaf, Menachem, 22–25, 107, 268n12; on gay role in municipal politics, 23; on Israel as gay rights trendsetter, 23; on Netanyahu victory, 23; on 1999 Israeli elections, 257, 259; and pride parade, 33; on religious response to gay rights, 100; on remaining legislative goals, 23; and transgender issues, 56; on Weizman affair, 24

Shoham, Uri (Brigadier-General), 121, 125; on education on gay issues in IDF, 123; on harassment issues, 123, 135; on IDF policy change, 122; on Steiner lawsuit, 139; on U.S. "gays in military" debate, 122

Shulchan Aruch, 87

Sodomy law, repeal of, 17, 252, 270n50

Sofer, Avi, 24, 49; children of, 194; on lack of Israeli attendance at gay and lesbian Jewish conferences, 101–2; on outreach to gay Arabs, 244; on political strategy, 17; on Weizman affair, 15

Somkai-Fink, Amir, 60, 81

Spivak, Dori, 35, 191; and Steiner suit, 139–40

Status Quo: battles over, 90–93; origins of, 90; prospects for, 253–54

Steiner, Adir, 21, 258; lawsuit against

IDF of, for recognition as IDF widower, 136–40, 276n43

Supreme Court: and artificial insemination regulations, 190–91; Danilovitz v. El Al Israel Airlines, 94, 183–84; Open Cards, 70–73; religion cases, 91; and second-parent adoptions, 191

Tagari, Hadas: on origins of yedu'im ba-tzibur, 180; on second-parent adoption, 191

Talmud: on frequency of sexual relations in marriage, 85; on homosexuality, 86–87; on lesbianism, 88

Tat-Tarbut, 98, 144, 239

Television: gay-themed programs on, 150; impact of on social attitudes, 150; news coverage of gays and lesbians, 152

Tehila, 79–80, 191

Television, coverage of gay/lesbian issues, 150–51; gay-themed shows, 150

Temkin, Beni (MK), 8

Tennenbaum, Marc, 28, 269n24

Tomerkin, Yigal, 92

Tzomet, 21, 256

Ultra-Orthodox: view of secular, 93; view of State of Israel, 91, 99; view of Supreme Court, 91

Vilnai, Matan, 27

Vitemberg, Ilan, 59, 136, 197, 211–12; kibbutz life of, 204–7; security clearance investigation of, 125

Waxman, Yossi, 143, 145; see also My Darling Alexandria

Weisberg-Bloch, 7, 80, 81; bureaucracy's recognition of relationship, 181–82; children of, 194–96; comparison of Israel and

U.S. on gay rights, 10; lecture at Nesher High, 61–64

Weishut, Daniel, and study of university students' attitudes toward gays and lesbians, 68

Weizman, Ezer, 24–25, 249, 267–68n3, 278n42; antigay remarks of, 13–15; opinion on Prime Minister Netanyahu, 13; transformation of presidency, 13

Wigstock, 15, 34–36, 156, 249

Women Against Violence, 228, 229, 231

World Congress of Gay, Lesbian, and Bisexual Jewish Organizations, 7, 101; and Yad Vashem incident, 7–8

Yakir, Dan, 71; on mainstream image for court plaintiffs, 36, 184

Yarus-Chakak, Avital, 46, 49, 60, 190; children of, 190–91, 193–94; on demonstrations as tool for community building, 34

Yarus-Chakak, Tal, 190; children of, 190–91, 193–94; on coming out, 60; on mainstream image, 36, 55; on relations with Palestinian feminists, 245–46; on women's roles in IDF, 132

Yediot Achronot: gay/lesbian journalists at, 151–52; political orientation of, 148; see also Media, mainstream

Yedu'im ba-Tzibur, 180–81

Yonai, Yuval: on coming out, 60; on minority struggle, 35; on sodomy law repeal, 56

Yosha, Itzik, 23, 49, 173; on reasons for gay political success, 22

Youth: attitudes on discrimination against gays, 66–67; attitudes toward homosexuality, 66–68, 80, 251; and youth press approach to gay issues, 73–74

Youth groups, 58, 62, 74–77, 250; fears of adult gays about, 75; for gay and lesbian kibbutzniks, 213–14; for gay Arabs, 233–34, 236; for lesbians, 58, 76

Zaks, Yael, 61

Zandberg, Eliezer "Modi" (MK), 256; on gay rights, 21; on left-right political divide, 21

Ze'evi, Rechavam (MK), 20

Zionism, 27, 28, 78, 171, 175, 208, 225; attitudes toward Diaspora, 102; and ethnic politics, 32; and image of Israel, 39; and Israeli culture, 144; and Judaism, 102, 199; and kibbutzim, 198–99; and Mizrachim, 48; and New Jews, 162–63; religious view of gays as proof of corruption of, 99; see also Collective values; Individualism; Kibbutzim; New Jews

Ziv, Amalia, 157, 164; on feminism in Israel, 47–48; on individualism, 54; on Israeli attitudes toward identity politics, 33; on lesbian literature and Zionist ethos, 144; Women Writing Poetry, 169

Zushi Bar, 166

Copyright Acknowledgments

Selections from *Karet* by Ilan Sheinfeld. Copyright © 1997 by Ilan Sheinfeld. Reprinted by permission of Ilan Sheinfeld.

Selections from *Tashlich* by Ilan Sheinfeld. Copyright © 1994 by Ilan Sheinfeld. Reprinted by permission of Ilan Sheinfeld.

Selections from *Zman Elul* by Dov Elbaum. Copyright © 1997 by the Harris/Elon Agency. Reprinted by permission of the Harris/Elon Agency.

Selections from *Alexandriya Yakirati (My Darling Alexandria)* by Yossi Waxman. Copyright © 1998 by Keter Publishing House Jerusalem. Reprinted by permission of Keter Publishing House Jerusalem.

Selections from *Mazon M'lachot* by Noga Eshed. Copyright © 1998 by Sifriat Poalim Publishers. Reprinted by permission of Sifriat Poalim Publishers.

Excerpts from the lyrics of "Ziva" and "Dykes and the Holy War" by Sharon Ben-Ezer. Copyright © 1990 by the Third Ear Music (1991) Ltd. All rights reserved. Used by permission of the Third Ear Music (1991) Ltd.

Excerpts from "Wet and Hot" by Eran Tzur. Copyright © Eran Tzur. Reprinted by permission of Acum, Israel.

Excerpts from "Women Writing Poetry" by Amalia Ziv. Copyright © Amalia Ziv. Reprinted by permission of Acum, Israel.

Excerpts from "Good Morning Iran" by Aviv Gefen. Copyright © Aviv Gefen. Reprinted by permission of Acum, Israel.

Excerpts from "With Him Forever" by Noam Rotem, Koski Ohad, Meiselman Uri, Haddas Roy, Gilead Ron. Copyright © Noam Rotem, Koski Ohad, Meiselman Uri, Haddas Roy, Gilead Ron. Reprinted by permission of Acum, Israel.

Between Men ~ Between Women

Lesbian and Gay Studies
Lillian Faderman and Larry Gross, Editors

Richard D. Mohr, *Gays/Justice: A Study of Ethics, Society, and Law*
Gary David Comstock, *Violence Against Lesbians and Gay Men*
Kath Weston, *Families We Choose: Lesbians, Gays, Kinship*
Lillian Faderman, *Odd Girls and Twilight Lovers: A History of Lesbian Life in Twentieth-Century America*
Judith Roof, *A Lure of Knowledge: Lesbian Sexuality and Theory*
John Clum, *Acting Gay: Male Homosexuality in Modern Drama*
Allen Ellenzweig, *The Homoerotic Photograph: Male Images from Durieu/Delacroix to Mapplethorpe*
Sally Munt, editor, *New Lesbian Criticism: Literary and Cultural Readings*
Timothy F. Murphy and Suzanne Poirier, editors, *Writing AIDS: Gay Literature, Language, and Analysis*
Linda D. Garnets and Douglas C. Kimmel, editors, *Psychological Perspectives on Lesbian and Gay Male Experiences*
Laura Doan, editor, *The Lesbian Postmodern*
Noreen O'Connor and Joanna Ryan, *Wild Desires and Mistaken Identities: Lesbianism and Psychoanalysis*
Alan Sinfield, *The Wilde Century: Effeminacy, Oscar Wilde, and the Queer Moment*
Claudia Card, *Lesbian Choices*
Carter Wilson, *Hidden in the Blood: A Personal Investigation of AIDS in the Yucatán*
Alan Bray, *Homosexuality in Renaissance England*
Joseph Carrier, *De Los Otros: Intimacy and Homosexuality Among Mexican Men*
Joseph Bristow, *Effeminate England: Homoerotic Writing After 1885*

Corinne E. Blackmer and Patricia Juliana Smith, editors, *En Travesti: Women, Gender Subversion, Opera*

Don Paulson with Roger Simpson, *An Evening at The Garden of Allah: A Gay Cabaret in Seattle*

Claudia Schoppmann, *Days of Masquerade: Life Stories of Lesbians During the Third Reich*

Chris Straayer, *Deviant Eyes, Deviant Bodies: Sexual Re-Orientation in Film and Video*

Edward Alwood, *Straight News: Gays, Lesbians, and the News Media*

Thomas Waugh, *Hard to Imagine: Gay Male Eroticism in Photography and Film from Their Beginnings to Stonewall*

Judith Roof, *Come As You Are: Sexuality and Narrative*

Terry Castle, *Noel Coward and Radclyffe Hall: Kindred Spirits*

Kath Weston, *Render Me, Gender Me: Lesbians Talk Sex, Class, Color, Nation, Studmuffins . . .*

Ruth Vanita, *Sappho and the Virgin Mary: Same-Sex Love and the English Literary Imagination*

renée c. hoogland, *Lesbian Configurations*

Beverly Burch, *Other Women: Lesbian Experience and Psychoanalytic Theory of Women*

Jane McIntosh Snyder, *Lesbian Desire in the Lyrics of Sappho*

Rebecca Alpert, *Like Bread on the Seder Plate: Jewish Lesbians and the Transformation of Tradition*

Emma Donoghue, editor, *Poems Between Women: Four Centuries of Love, Romantic Friendship, and Desire*

James T. Sears and Walter L. Williams, editors, *Overcoming Heterosexism and Homophobia: Strategies That Work*

Patricia Juliana Smith, *Lesbian Panic: Homoeroticism in Modern British Women's Fiction*

Dwayne C. Turner, *Risky Sex: Gay Men and HIV Prevention*

Timothy F. Murphy, *Gay Science: The Ethics of Sexual Orientation Research*

Cameron McFarlane, *The Sodomite in Fiction and Satire, 1660–1750*

Lynda Hart, *Between the Body and the Flesh: Performing Sadomasochism*

Byrne R. S. Fone, editor, *The Columbia Anthology of Gay Literature: Readings from Western Antiquity to the Present Day*

Ellen Lewin, *Recognizing Ourselves: Ceremonies of Lesbian and Gay Commitment*

Ruthann Robson, *Sappho Goes to Law School: Fragments in Lesbian Legal Theory*

Jacquelyn Zita, *Body Talk: Philosophical Reflections on Sex and Gender*

Evelyn Blackwood and Saskia Wieringa, *Female Desires: Same-Sex Relations and Transgender Practices Across Cultures*

William L. Leap, ed., *Public Sex/Gay Space*

Larry Gross and James D. Woods, eds., *The Columbia Reader on Lesbians and Gay Men in Media, Society, and Politics*

Marilee Lindemann, *Willa Cather: Queering America*

George E. Haggerty, *Men in Love: Masculinity and Sexuality in the Eighteenth Century*

Andrew Elfenbein, *Romantic Genius: The Prehistory of a Homosexual Role*

Gilbert Herdt and Bruce Koff, *Something to Tell You: The Road Families Travel When a Child Is Gay*